Mental Reality

Representation and Mind
Hilary Putnam and Ned Block, editors

Mental Reality

Galen Strawson

A Bradford Book
The MIT Press
Cambridge, Massachusetts
London, England

This book was set in Sabon by DEKR Corporation and was printed and bound in the United States of America.

First printing, 1994.

Library of Congress Cataloging-in-Publication Data

Strawson, Galen.
  Mental reality / Galen Strawson.
     p.   cm. — (Representation and mind)
  "A Bradford book."
  Includes bibliographical references and index.
  ISBN 0-262-19352-3
  1. Consciousness. 2. Behaviorism (Psychology). 3. Mind and body.
4. Materialism. 5. Philosophy of mind. I. Title. II. Series.
B808.9.S73 1994
128'.2—dc20
                                             93-47905
                                               CIP

To my friend Simon Halliday, 1951–1975

Contents

Preface

Behaviorism is dead. No one still believes that mental concepts can be satisfactorily analysed just in terms of behavior and dispositions to behavior.

Neobehaviorism survives—the view that mental life is linked to behavior in such a way that reference to behavior enters essentially and centrally into any adequate account of the nature of almost all, if not all, mental states and occurrences. This view is very widely accepted.

One of my purposes in this book is to argue that neobehaviorism is false, given the common philosophical understanding of the word 'behavior', and that reference to behavioral phenomena is given the wrong place in most contemporary accounts of mind. This argument can be extended, for the same seems to be true of reference to publicly observable phenomena in general and also, perhaps, of reference to nonmental phenomena.

Such arguments are negative. Insofar as a positive view is put forward in this book, it might be called 'naturalized Cartesianism'. Naturalized Cartesianism couples belief in materialism with respect for the idea that the only distinctively mental phenomena are the phenomena of conscious experience.

In chapter 1, I declare some assumptions and make some comments about what it is to be a realist—a real realist—about conscious experience. In chapter 2, I raise and develop three large questions:

1. *The nonmentality question.* What part does reference to nonmental phenomena play in a satisfactory account of the nature of mental phenomena?

2. *The public-observability question.* What part does reference to publicly observable phenomena play in a satisfactory account of the nature of mental phenomena?

3. *The behavior question.* What part does reference to behavioral phenomena play in a satisfactory account of the nature of mental phenomena?

Most of the rest of the book is my attempt to answer these questions.

Chapters 3, 4, and 5 consider the nonmentality question. Chapters 3 and 4 discuss materialist approaches to the "mind-body" problem. They defend the view that we must be radically ignorant about fundamental aspects of the nature of the physical, if materialism is true, and argue that the espousal of materialism is partly a matter of faith. Chapter 5 then considers some nonmaterialist or idealist approaches. Descartes and Berkeley are discussed at some length because their problems are exemplary and because they are independently interesting. I argue that there are strong but ultimately inconclusive reasons for supposing that the existence of certain sorts of mental phenomenon essentially requires the existence of nonmental phenomena.

The first five chapters assume that we have a reasonably robust and widely shared understanding of the word 'mental' that is well anchored in agreement about paradigm cases. Chapter 6 discards this assumption and raises directly the question of which phenomena are mental phenomena. No firm conclusion is reached. Some recommendations are made. The suggestion that all truly mental phenomena are conscious, experiential phenomena is considered at some length.

This precipitates a discussion of intentionality in chapter 7. I argue that much of the supposed difficulty of the problem of intentionality is illusory. More particularly, I argue that if any deep difficulty arises in giving a "naturalistic" account of the existence of intentionality, it is not really distinct from the difficulty that arises when one tries to give a naturalistic account of the existence of conscious experience. The account of the nature of the mental and of intentionality developed in chapters 6 and 7 constitutes the second main focus of this book.

Chapters 8 and 9 turn back to questions (2) and (3), the public-observability question and the behavior question. Together the two chapters constitute the main attack on neobehaviorism. I consider pain and desire, and hence, more generally, sensations and so-called "propositional attitudes." I argue directly for the view that reference to behavior does not have the place it is commonly thought to have in a correct account of the nature of mental phenomena. Chapter 8 confronts Wittgensteinian arguments for the centrality of reference to behavior, arguments that appeal essentially to facts about language and meaning. Chapter 9 takes on functionalist and other arguments that make no such appeal.

Pursuing the behavior question, chapter 10 reconsiders our use of the word 'behavior'. I argue for a realignment of the notion of behavior that has the consequence that neobehaviorism is after all partly true, and indeed trivially true, although not for the reasons for which it has usually been thought to be true. If the realignment is acceptable, it follows that the answer to the behavior question can be 'A large part', even if the answer to the public-observability question is 'Very little part' or even 'No part'.

Chapter 11 offers a brief summary of the argument and suggests that the correct conclusion for the philosophy of mind to draw from the study of artificial intelligence is the opposite of the most common conclusion.

The book does not form an indissoluble unity so that it must be read as a whole or not at all. Chapter 2 is programmatic in character, and chapters 3 and 4 form a unity, but all the other chapters can be read separately without much difficulty. Major dependencies of one chapter on another are indicated by cross-references.

I conceived this book in 1979, when writing a D.Phil. thesis on free will. At that time I wrote sections 1.4, 1.7, and parts of chapters 5, 6, 8, 9, and 10. The Weather Watchers, who appear in chapter 9, featured in my D.Phil. thesis (1983) and survived in an obscure footnote in the resulting book, *Freedom and Belief* (1986). I wrote a brief first draft of this book in 1986, while at New College, Oxford, but then turned to other work until 1988–1989, when I wrote the first full-length draft and began to use the material in seminars at the University of Oxford. I am grateful to many of those who attended those seminars for their comments, as I am to audiences at the Australian National University, Birkbeck College, Princeton University, Rutgers University, and the universities of Aix-en-

Provence, California at Los Angeles, Hong Kong, Liverpool, Reading, and Sydney.

I wouldn't be surprised to be told that everything here that is both true and of philosophical interest has been said somewhere by somebody else. It is over 350 years since Descartes remarked, "It is impossible for each individual to examine the vast numbers of new books that are published every day" (Descartes 1985, 2:386), and the situation has not improved. Philosophers often have the experience, when reading something recently published, of thinking "I've already said that," and this is unsurprising, for the same thoughts occur independently to different people, and no one can hope to read more than a small part of what is written. People also forget where their ideas come from. Often they wrongly think that they have had a new idea because they have couched it in an idiom or context different from the one in which they first encountered it. Occasionally they are disinclined to acknowledge the source even when they can remember it. I have recorded debts where I am aware of them, and I have recorded debt-free convergences of opinion. No doubt I have debts of which I am not conscious. I hope that the way in which I have put things together will be of use in current philosophical debates about the mind.

I would particularly like to thank Sebastian Gardner, Mark Greenberg, John Heil, Derek Parfit, Paul Snowdon, and P. F. Strawson for their comments on various parts of the text. They have corrected me on some matters and helped me to take others further. I would also like to thank John Searle for sending me, in advance of publication, two draft chapters of his book *The Rediscovery of the Mind* (1992), and George Bealer, Ron Chrisley, Jerry Cohen, Dan Dennett, Jerry Fodor, Brian Garrett, Edward Harcourt, Ward Jones, Martha Klein, Stephen Law, Dan Lloyd, Michael Lockwood, Penelope Mackie, Fred Schueler, Seana Shiffrin, Steve Simpson, Michael Smith, Helen Steward, Charles Taliaferro, and Alan Thwaits for a variety of useful objections and observations. For help of a less philosophical kind, I would like to thank Redmond O'Hanlon, Andrew Rosenheim, Ann Strawson, Emilie Strawson, Anna Vaux, and Teri Mendelsohn of the MIT Press.

Acknowledgment

The passage from the poem *A Martian Sends a Postcard Home*, copyright 1979 by Craig Raine, is reprinted by permission of the Oxford University Press.

Mental Reality

1

Introduction

Philosophy is essentially world-wisdom; its problem is the world.
Schopenhauer (1969, 2:187)

1.1 A Default Position

In this book I assume that there is a physical world and that there remains, after all the complications of science, a fundamental sense in which it is more or less as ordinary people suppose. 'Physical', however, is a natural-kind term (it is the ultimate natural-kind term), and we may be very wrong about the nature of the physical.

I also assume that some variety of monism is true and that there is, in spite of all the variety in the world, some fundamental sense in which there is only one kind of stuff. These two assumptions amount to the assumption of materialism.

Some may doubt that the position adopted in this book is materialist, because of the way in which it will be qualified by agnosticism and by doubts about the notion of monism in chapters 3 and 4. Nevertheless it accepts the familiar idea that human mental goings-on are entirely realized in or by physical goings-on, in some sense of 'realized' that will need to be discussed.

I also assume that the theory of evolution gives a true (if so far incomplete) account of how beings like ourselves came to exist in an already existing physical world and that we must adopt a naturalistic approach to the question of the nature of mind. But some of what follows may be thought to be incompatible with naturalism as ordinarily understood.[1]

In fact, the term 'naturalism' is no more determinate than the terms 'physical' and 'material'. All it really involves is a rejection of anything classified as supernatural relative to a given conception of the natural. But we do not know the limits of the natural. We cannot be sure we know the nature of the natural, any more than we can be sure we know the nature of the physical. Most naturalists think that all naturalists must be materialists. But this is true only if everything natural is physical or material. We can't know that it is true unless we make it true by definition.

Much is uncertain, and must remain so. Nevertheless, the assumptions above constitute the default position, the background against which the following discussion of mind takes place unless the background is itself the subject of discussion.

The argument is articulated by three questions. In their most general form, they are as follows: What is the relation of mental phenomena to nonmental phenomena? What is the relation of mental phenomena to publicly observable phenomena? What is the relation of mental phenomena to behavioral phenomena? But I will be principally concerned with the more specific questions already mentioned in the Preface. What part does reference to nonmental phenomena, publicly observable phenomena, and behavioral phenomena play in a satisfactory account of the (essential) nature of mental phenomena?

1.2 Experience

I want to establish a certain broad use of the word 'experience'. In talking about mental goings-on, I will rarely use the words 'conscious' and 'consciousness'. Instead I will talk of experience: of experience in general, of experiencers, particular experiences, experiential states, experiential episodes, experiential phenomena—human, Martian, dolphin, canine,

---

1. As applied to this planet, the theory of evolution is incomplete without a plausible account of how DNA evolved. It also faces the difficult question of how to give a direct evolutionary explanation of the phenomenon of consciousness or experience. This is as much of a problem for physics as for the theory of evolution.

and so on. I will use the term 'experience' to cover everything that philosophers usually have in mind when they talk of consciousness or conscious experience, taking it that "the stream of consciousness" could equally well be called 'the stream of experience' and that the expression 'conscious experience' is, strictly speaking, pleonastic. All experience is conscious experience, as I use the term.

I will also talk of subexperiential or nonexperiential states and processes in the brain, rather than talking in the standard way of subpersonal states and processes. 'Subexperiential' is preferable to 'subpersonal' because subexperiential states of the kind that interest us can occur in experiencing beings that are not persons. In chapter 6, I raise the question of whether any of the states and processes that philosophers usually have in mind when they consider such subexperiential states and processes are correctly or usefully thought of as mental states or processes.

Experience is necessarily contentful, e.g., sensorily or conceptually contentful. Like many familiar things, it appears extraordinary on reflection, and is very hard to describe in detail. It outruns language in many ways. In chapter 4, I will argue that it is the only thing that makes the mind-body problem a problem. It is part of reality. It is as real as rock. The experience of an experiencing being is everything about what it is like to be that being, experientially speaking, from moment to moment as it lives its life. There is an enormous quantity of experience. Consider the four billion human streams of experience in progress at this moment (assuming that the rest of us are dreamlessly asleep).

It is significant that we may feel a difficulty with the idea of the quantity of experience. This may indicate a bias in our conception of the real. It may be connected with our sense that experiential points of view can't be summed in any clear way. And this may connect with William James's observation that "the breaches between . . . thoughts . . . belonging to different . . . minds . . . are the most absolute breaches in nature" (1950, 1:226; compare Nagel 1986, chaps. 3 and 4). The fact remains that there is an enormous quantity of experience.

1.3 The Character of Experience

When people talk of experience, they often have sensations and perceptions primarily in mind. But thinking a thought or suddenly remembering something or realizing that the interval between the perfect squares increases by 2 is as much of an experience as feeling pain when one has burnt one's finger or seeing a raven flying low over bracken. So I will not speak of thoughts *or* experiences, opposing them in the way that some do. Episodes of conscious thought are experiential episodes. Experience is as much cognitive as sensory. It includes everything a bat or a new born baby can feel, and everything a great mathematician can experience in thinking.

The spectrum of experience ranges from the most purely sensory experiences to the most abstractly cognitive experiences. In between, the sensory and the cognitive are inextricably bound up with each other: virtually all experiences have both sensory and cognitive content in varying and unquantifiable proportions. (Some think that there are no pure cases at the two ends of the spectrum, but it is not clear why there could not be.) There are visual, tactile, auditory, gustatory, and olfactory sensations, as well as kinaesthetic and proprioceptive sensations, including sensations of pain, nausea, orgasm, muscular fatigue, pins and needles, "butterflies," and itchiness. There are emotional feelings, experienced moods, complicated sensory-conceptual experiences associated with love, nervousness, fear, anger, happiness, depression, and so on. There is such a thing as the experience of desire. There is the experience of consciously entertained thought, of reading and understanding, of unplanned fantasy, and of directed imagining.

Perceptual experiences, e.g., visual perceptions, are usually taken as the paradigm of sensory experiences that are also essentially conceptually informed. You look out of a window, and you see an armoured personnel carrier rusting under a tree on the far side of a river. In such a case, you take in a spatially distributed array of color patches, whatever else you do. But the character of your experience is fundamentally determined by your sense of your position relative to other objects, your immediate and automatic judgments of size, three-dimensional shape, and distance, and your equally immediate experience-conditioning deployment of specific concepts, like the concepts of tree and water.

These facts are very familiar and need no special discussion here, although they raise interesting questions of detail. It is widely agreed that one cannot sharply separate out the sensory and conceptual elements in perceptual experience. It is well known that the phenomenology of ordinary perceptual experience is conceptually driven, in the sense that many of the aspects of perceptual experiences that seem immediately given in sensation are given as they are only because, in having perceptual experience, one is automatically deploying certain concepts and is subject to a great number of concept-involving expectations.[2]

All this is well known, but it may be worth reflecting on another case. Consider what it is like, experientially, to hear someone speaking nontechnically in a language that one understands. One understands what is said, and one undoubtedly has an experience. How do the understanding and the experience relate? Most will agree that the experience is complex, and that it is not merely sensory, not just a matter of the sounds. But they will hesitate if it is suggested there is *experience (as) of understanding*.

Nevertheless, I will now argue that there is such a thing as experience (as) of understanding, or "understanding-experience" for short, just as there is such a thing as visual experience. Defense of this view should help to illustrate the intended force and extent of my use of the word 'experience'. It needs separate discussion because it may be thought to be deeply dubious, given the recent history of the subject. Perhaps I should say straight away that I will only be concerned with linguistic understanding, not with experiences like the experience of finally understanding how some machine works or the phenomenology of the *Aha! Erlebnis*.

1.4 Understanding-Experience

Philosophers will ask whether there is really such a thing as understanding-experience, over and above visual experience, auditory experience, and so on. Behind their questioning there may lie a familiar doubt as to whether there is anything going on, experientially, that either is or necessarily accompanies the understanding. This question may be asked: does the difference between Jacques (a monoglot Frenchman) and Jack

2. For a good recent discussion see Dennett 1991b. For simplicity, I am contrasting *sensory* with *conceptual*. If one were to go into more detail, one might do better to contrast *sensory* with *nonsensory* and subdivide *nonsensory* into *conceptual* and *nonconceptual* (see Peacocke 1992).

(a monoglot Englishman), as they listen to the news in French, really consist in the Frenchman's having a different *experience*?

Well, it may be wrong to suppose that there is any set of experiential phenomena that can be picked out as constituting the understanding on the part of Jacques. This is not part of my claim. Nor is there any suggestion that his understanding is any sort of directed activity, for it is no such thing. It is an entirely automatic, involuntary, and seemingly immediate process. The present claim is simply that Jacques's experience when listening to the news is utterly different from Jack's, and that this is so even though there is a sense in which Jacques and Jack have the same aural experience.[3]

It is certainly true that Jacques's experience when listening to the news is very different from Jack's. And the difference between the two can be expressed by saying that Jacques, when exposed to the stream of sound, has what one may perfectly well call 'an experience (as) of understanding' or 'an understanding-experience', while Jack does not. Unlike Jack, Jacques automatically and involuntarily *takes* the sounds *as* signs, and indeed as words and sentences, that he automatically and involuntarily understands as *expressing certain propositions* and as representing reality as constituted in certain ways. As a result, Jacques's *experience* is quite different from Jack's. And the fact that Jacques understands what is said is not only the principal explanation of why this is so, it is also the principal description of the respect in which his experience differs from Jack's.

To talk about understanding-experience is to talk about such simple facts as these. It is not to postulate anything suspect or mysterious in the world, because it is to postulate nothing that is not found in these facts. For a being to have understanding-experience is just for things to be for it, in one central respect, as they can be for us, experientially,

---

3. In one sense, of course, they do not have the same aural experience, because of Jacques's automatic segmenting of the stream of sound into words. But this is unimportant here. Consider another case in which two English speakers hear a coded message in which nothing but whole English words are used to stand for other English words. One of them is intensely familiar with the code, the other does not know it. Here the basic aural experience of the two people may be very similar indeed, although one has an automatic and involuntary understanding-experience that the other does not have.

when we hear utterances that we understand—or think consciously or realize something in silent words. Note that misunderstanding involves understanding-experience as much as genuine understanding does, for understanding-experience is experience *as of* understanding and need not be veridical. (It could be called 'meaning-experience'.)

To talk of understanding-experience, then, is not to commit oneself to the implausible view that there is some single qualitative type of experience that anyone who has understanding-experience must have. It is not to commit oneself to the view that particular qualitative experiences invariably go with understanding particular sentences. Nor is it to commit oneself to the view that understanding-experience involves any kind of inner mental theatre.[4] The point is simply this: there is in the normal case something it is like, experientially, to understand a sentence, spoken or read. You have just done so and are continuing to do so. Your doing so is not nothing, experientially. It is part of your current *course of experience*, part of the content of your conscious life, and it is happening now.

This is obvious, but the mood of much recent philosophy of mind may make it seem obscure and worth stressing. I take it that it is compatible *plumber's bill* with any sense in which Wittgenstein is correct to say that "understanding is not a mental process" and with any sense in which Ryle is correct to say that there need be "nothing going on" when one understands something (Wittgenstein 1953, sec. 154; Ryle 1949; for the insertion of 'plumber's bill' and the point that it makes about understanding-experience by its unexpected occurrence in a philosophy text, see James 1950, 1:262). Certainly understanding is not something one does intentionally. In the normal case, it is something that just happens. There is, to repeat, an automatic and involuntary *taking* of sounds or marks *as* words and sentences that one understands

4. Schopenhauer dealt with this idea in 1819: "While another person is speaking, do we at once translate his speech into pictures of the imagination that instantaneously flash upon us and are arranged, linked, formed, and coloured according to the words that stream forth, and to their grammatical inflexions? What a tumult there would be in our heads while we listened to a speech or read a book! This is not what happens at all. The meaning of the speech is immediately grasped, accurately and clearly apprehended, without as a rule any conceptions of fancy being mixed up with it" (1969, 1:39).

and that represent something's being the case. Understanding-experience is simply such automatic, involuntary, experientially aspected taking of sounds and marks and involves no sort of intentional action. As McDowell remarks, it is just a fact that beings like ourselves can be such that have sounds or marks "impinge on them with content" whether they like it or not (1980, 137). And as William James remarks, "No word in an understood sentence comes to consciousness as a mere noise" (1950, 1:281). This is a fact about experience.

So something is happening to you experientially, here and now, as you read or hear this sentence. Obviously, there is the visual or auditory experience. In the reading case, there is perhaps a rapid and diaphanous process of forming acoustic mental images. But this is not all, for—*barath abalori trafalon*—one can have all this without the experience of understanding. There is something else that happens—*the mass of the moon is just over one percent that of the earth*—a certain complex modification of the quality of one's course of experience, and not just of one's dispositional set. In a word, there is understanding-experience, understanding-experience whose very existence is sometimes doubted, perhaps because it has no obvious experiential character that it can call its own. It has no striking experiential feel in the way in which experience in any of the sensory modalities usually does. But this does not show that there is nothing that can be correctly called 'understanding-experience'. Rather, it shows that in certain contexts of discussion, we may still be inclined to appeal to an excessively restricted notion of what experience is.

Here it should be noted that understanding-experience, as currently understood, has absolutely nothing to do with what Dennett calls the "phenomenology of comprehension" (1991b, 56–59). He means the various possible imagistic or otherwise sensory-experience-like accompaniments of understanding, and his account of these is generally accurate. 'The Eiffel Tower is going to be dismantled.' Some who hear or read this sentence will form a visual image of the Eiffel Tower. Others will not. Such imaging is not a necessary accompaniment of understanding-experience, nor is it a part of understanding-experience. It is an interesting question whether human understanding-experience always involves experiencing (heard, seen, touched, or imagined) sounds or marks taken as meaningful, especially since understanding-experience occurs as much in the case of conscious thought as in the case of reading or hearing others speak.[5]

To return to the main theme: one cannot separate off all the sensory-experiential aspects of hearing people talk and then say that although there is also understanding going on as one hears them talk, that fact ought not to be adverted to in any way in a full account of what is going on experientially. One cannot say that the difference between Jack and Jacques is just that certain specific changes take place in Jacques's dispositional set (e.g., his dispositions to respond in certain ways to certain questions) that do not take place in Jack's. If that were so, there would be little difference between the case imagined and a case in which both listen to the broadcast in a language that neither of them understands, while Jacques's dispositional set is, unknown to him, altered by direct brain tinkering in just the way that it would have been altered had he understood what was being said. Or, to get closer, there would be little difference between the case imagined and a case in which Jacques has been hypnotized in such a way that (a) he explicitly believes he understands nothing, so that he listens to the broadcast with complete incomprehension, and (b) he none the less takes in what is said, so that he can later respond accurately to questions about the matters discussed in the broadcast. To say that these two cases are similar is to leave out something real that is present in the first case and absent in the second, to wit, Jacques's experience of understanding what was said.

Acknowledgment of the reality of understanding-experience is profoundly important in the philosophy of mind (it will be particularly

---

5. See below, p. 12. William James may be starting to bridge the gap between understanding-experience and Dennett's "phenomenology of comprehension" with his talk of "the halo, fringe or scheme in which we feel the words to lie" (1950, 1:260), but the gap is very large. There are many similar ideas in the philosophical literature, although I am not sure how many of them support the point that I wish to make about *understanding*-experience. Searle (1992, 60) remarks that "beliefs . . . are actually experienced as part of our mental life," and I take it that he means conscious thoughts that are occurrent entertainings of the contents of beliefs. Flanagan observes that "not all qualia are sensational. . . . Conscious moods, emotions, beliefs, desires . . . have distinct qualitative character" (1992, 64). There is a striking discussion of some aspects of the experience of thought in Jackendoff 1987 (see, e.g., chap. 15). See also James 1950, 1:245–246, Peirce 1935, sec. 223 (quoted by Flanagan 1992, 64), Ayers 1991, vol. 1, chap. 31, and Murdoch 1992, chaps. 8 and 9.

important to the discussion of intentionality in chapter 7). It needs to be dwelt on, but I cannot think of any other way to bring the point home. It seems simultaneously obvious and elusive. Perhaps it helps to think of watching a film and of how what the actors say is part of one's overall experience, and to compare this with watching an undubbed film in an unknown language.

Once the general point is granted, it may be added that the claim that there is something that can correctly be called 'understanding experience' is compatible with the view that talk of understanding-experience may not be appropriate in all cases in which it is correct to say that someone has understood something.

The abstractness and colorlessness of philosophical discourse may incline one to think that it does not provide a very good example when one is trying to convey a properly strong sense of the reality of understanding-experience. This is not so, in fact. The understanding of philosophical discourse must be as good an example of understanding-experience as the understanding of any other kind. To think that it may not be is to misunderstand the nature of understanding-experience. There is, after all, and as already remarked, something it is like for you to read and understand these words. It is part of the course of your experience. Nevertheless, philosophy may slip down one's intellectual throat a little too insensibly for one to be convinced, when listening to it or reading it, that there is such a thing as understanding-experience. Perhaps it really does seem that there is in this case a kind of direct absorption of content, of a sort that constitutes understanding, without anything that could be called 'understanding-experience'. I have suggested that this is not really so. Such a view presupposes a naive and unduly restricted conception of the nature, reality, and extent of experience. To try to convince you, in the wake of Ryle and Wittgenstein, of the reality of understanding-experience, let me quote part of the poem *A Martian Sends a Postcard Home* (Raine 1979).

Caxtons are mechanical birds with many wings
and some are treasured for their markings—

they cause the eyes to melt
or the body to shriek without pain.

I have never seen one fly, but
sometimes they perch on the hand.

Mist is when the sky is tired of flight
and rests its soft machine on ground:

then the world is dim and bookish
like engravings under tissue paper.

Rain is when the earth is television.
It has the property of making colours darker. . . .

In homes, a haunted apparatus sleeps,
that snores when you pick it up.

If the ghost cries, they carry it
to their lips and soothe it to sleep

with sounds. And yet, they wake it up
deliberately, by tickling with a finger.

This poem is full of complicated metaphors. It is useful as an example because failure to understand all the images on a first reading presupposes a prior understanding of the standard meaning of the words, so that there are two levels or waves of understanding-experience. In this case, puzzlement or not understanding is itself a form of understanding-experience.

The main purpose of this section is to illustrate the complexity and range of our experience by considering the relatively little discussed example of understanding-experience. I have repeated and varied the point because it may be thought particularly suspect. And yet the facts to which it adverts are familiar facts of common life.

Some may still be worried by the elusiveness of understanding-experience. They may be prepared to concede that there is something that may reasonably be called 'understanding-experience' but be struck by the fact that one can't really do anything much with the idea, theoretically. And they may feel that being able to do something with the idea theoretically is a necessary part of genuinely understanding it, philosophically. They may even think that being able to do something with it theoretically is a necessary condition of accepting it as real.

There is another pragmatic difficulty with achieving a satisfactory grip on the notion of understanding-experience. Suppose that one hears it put forward and discussed, and concludes that there is indeed something that may reasonably be called 'understanding-experience'. One may still remain uncertain as to whether one really knows what it is. This may now be because one is too close to what one is trying to think about, so that it is like looking at an elephant from three inches away.

I don't think either of these problems is serious. One doesn't have to do anything much theoretically with the notion of understanding-experience. Nor does one have to try to get an impossibly detached perspective on it. What philosophy requires of one is simply that one should acknowledge its reality and bear it in mind when trying to form an adequate general conception of the nature of experience. One needs to have such a conception to stay balanced in the philosophy of mind. One needs to remember that experience is a vast part of mental reality, even if mental reality also has nonexperiential parts or aspects.

In discussing understanding-experience, I have focused on reading and hearing others speak. It should now be added that the basic phenomenon also occurs when one thinks consciously. In this case too, apprehension of conceptual content occurs and is part of the course and content of one's experience, part of what has to be detailed in attempting to record one's experience as fully as possible. (It is no good just recording the subvocalized words, as becomes evident when one considers the record of the course of experience of a monoglot speaker of a language one does not know.) This may be clearer to insomniacs, who spend long hours thinking in the dark, than to instant sleepers. It is obvious to nonphilosophers and obscured by much philosophy. It may be an elusive fact, hard to grip, but it is extremely important. In chapters 6 and 7, I will suggest (it is an old thought) that there is a solid and unbudgeable sense in which meaning only really lives—exists—in this experience, however much the experience evades description. One has to take account of this in the philosophy of mind. If this is meaning-psychologism, then we badly need a certain amount of meaning-psychologism.

The mass of the moon is just over one percent that of the earth, but I am pessimistic about being correctly understood by philosophers. Not that the point is not straightforward. It is straightforward, but it is also hard to pin down. My central claim is that the apprehension and understanding of cognitive content, considered just as such and independently of any accompaniments in any of the sensory-modality-based modes of imagination or mental representation, is part of experience, part of the flesh or content of experience, and hence, trivially, part of the qualitative character of experience.

Discussing music in *Culture and Value*, Wittgenstein writes as follows:

Should I say that understanding is simply a specific experience that cannot be analysed any further? Well, that would be tolerable as long as it were not supposed to mean: it is a specific *experiential content*. For in point of fact *these* words make us think of distinctions like those between seeing, hearing, and smelling. (1980, 70)

This raises a number of problems of interpretation that I will not consider. It is useful to quote it here, because the present point is precisely that we need to allow that a particular case of understanding-experience can involve a specific cognitive experiential content while overcoming the tendency of the words 'specific experiential content' to make us think only of distinctions like those found in sensory experience.

I will conclude these introductory sections as follows. In section 1.5, I will briefly note some examples of things that many think of as mental phenomena although they are not experiential phenomena. In section 1.6, I will defend the legitimacy of the notion of purely experiential content. In section 1.7, I will offer a description of four seconds of mental reality.

1.5   A Note about Dispositional Mental States

At some point it will be necessary to face the question of exactly which phenomena are correctly—or usefully—thought of as mental phenomena. There are, for example, many subexperiential processes in the brain, and although many of these subexperiential processes are not plausibly thought of as mental processes (e.g., the circulation of blood), others are more plausible candidates (e.g., the "computational" processes discerned by certain theories of vision). I will try to say something about this difficult question in chapter 6. Until then I will rely on our commonsense view of the matter and take things like sensations, perceptions, emotions, consciously entertained thoughts, imaginings, rememberings, beliefs, desires, hopes, fears, and so on, as paradigm examples of mental phenomena.[6]

---

6. In this book I will use the word 'desire' in the standard way to refer principally to dispositional mental states, although it is more natural to use it to talk of occurrent mental episodes and to speak of preferences, likes and dislikes, attitudes of favor and disfavor, and so on, when discussing the dispositional aspects of desire.

Clearly, these mental phenomena divide into two main types. There are, on the one hand, *occurrent, experiential* mental phenomena, like sensations and conscious entertainings of thoughts, and on the other hand there are *dispositional, nonexperiential* mental phenomena, like beliefs and pro-attitudes. Consider Louis, a representative human being. He may be in a dreamless sleep at time *t*, and possess no experiential properties at all, at *t*, while possessing hundreds of thousands of nonexperiential, dispositional mental properties, such as the property of believing that life is extraordinary, or of being able to interpret chest X rays, or of preferring Busoni to Beethoven, or of being uneasy in the presence of horses.

Later on I will consider the claim that the "mental realm," properly understood, consists of nothing more than experiences. On this view, experiential phenomena are the only true mental phenomena: where there is nothing going on in the way of occurrent, conscious mental phenomena, nothing mental is going on. Mental *predicates* may be true of Louis as he sleeps dreamlessly on, but there are no mental *phenomena* in the part of reality consisting of Louis. For the moment, however, I will accept the ordinary view that there are both occurrent, experiential mental phenomena and dispositional, nonexperiential mental phenomena. It is a further question whether there are occurrent nonexperiential mental phenomena.[7]

1.6 Purely Experiential Content

Louis is a representative human being. He has many beliefs, including the belief that Emily Dickinson was a genius. At present he has a pain in his ankle and is listening to Schönberg's *Verklärte Nacht* in the orchestral version.

7. The claim that all truly mental phenomena are experiential phenomena is fully compatible with the view that we cannot really make sense of the idea that Louis is capable of having cognitively complex experiences without supposing that all sorts of nonexperiential, dispositional predicates are also true of him. Searle expresses this familiar view vividly, although not unproblematically, with his talk of the "Network" and the "Background" (1983, chap. 5; see also Stroud 1991, Searle 1991, and Searle's reformulation in 1992, chap. 8).

According to the default position, human beings are roughly as we think they are. So Louis [1] has a physical body, [2] inhabits a real physical world that is more or less as he thinks it is, and [3] is located in it more or less as he thinks he is. But he also has a number of experiential doubles. There is the experiential double who is in fact not in the default position, as he believes, but is a "brain in a vat." Vat Louis's course of experience is, ex hypothesi, qualitatively indistinguishable from Louis's; it is indistinguishable "from the inside," as it were. But although (1) is true of him in a sense (vat Louis is a brain), (3) is false, and (2) may be false (some would say it is definitely false).

Then there is the experiential double who is a Berkeleyan mind (if such a thing is possible). His course of experience is again qualitatively indistinguishable from Louis's, but in his case (1), (2), and (3) are all false. To these we may add Louis's "twin" on Perfect-Twin Earth, a planet qualitatively identical to Earth on the other side of the universe. Properties (1), (2), and (3) are true of Louis's twin, and his course of experience is also qualitatively indistinguishable from Louis's, from the inside. The theoretical point of these variations is very familiar: there is a crucial sense in which all these people have exactly the *same mental life*, the same course of experience.[8]

Without qualification, this claim is not true. If I look at the George Washington Bridge or think about it or form a belief about it, one has to mention the bridge in giving an account of the content of my experience or thought or belief, and one mentions a quite different bridge in giving an account of the thoughts and experiences of my twin on Perfect Twin Earth. He and I do not experience or think about the same thing. So our mental lives are different. Similarly, even if vat Louis and Berkeleyan Louis have mental lives that are qualitatively speaking

---

8. Perfect Twin Earth is not classical Twin Earth (Putnam 1975). Note that Perfect Twin Earth actually exists on just two assumptions: that the Big Bang was symmetrical and that determinism is true. It seems that there can be no interchange between the two halves of the universe in this case. They are separated by a virtual mirror. Any spaceship trying to cross the axis of symmetry will crash into an identical spaceship. If they try to maneuver past each other, they will mimic the behavior of a fly trying to fly through a mirror. (Perhaps the Big Bang had more than one axis of symmetry, and there are several Perfect Twin Earths.)

exactly like Louis's, they cannot have pains in their ankles if they haven't got ankles. And they cannot have beliefs about Emily Dickinson if she does not exist in the universe they inhabit. Nor can they have beliefs about Emily Dickinson if they have never been in any sort of epistemic contact with her; and we may suppose that they have not been.

All this is certainly so. But it is no less certain that there is a sense in which ordinary Louis, vat Louis, Berkeleyan Louis, and Perfect-Twin-Earth Louis all have exactly the same course of experience. The point can be made by observing that if you knew you were one of the four Louises, you could never know which one you were on the basis of your experience. (There is also 'Instant Louis', a theoretically interesting person who has just come into existence as part of Instant Earth, itself the result of a sudden and entirely fortuitous coming together of atoms.) So too there is a clear restricted sense of the expression 'the content of experience' in which they can all be said to have experience with the same content. Certainly it is not our ordinary or everyday notion of content, and its importance and even its intelligibility has been doubted (Pettit and McDowell 1986, Burge 1989). But it is quite clear what it amounts to, and it is, for certain purposes, a valuable theoretical notion. One could call it 'purely experiential content'. My purpose here is just to introduce it and note its legitimacy.

This naturally leads to a further notion of theoretical interest, which may be expounded as follows: [1] If we set out to consider the nature of actual experience in all its aspects, we consider not only those of its causes that need to be mentioned in a full account of its content (e.g., the George Washington Bridge) but also any other causes it may have (light waves and so on), as well as its nonexperiential substantial ground or realization, if any (the brain, according to materialists). [2] In moving to the notion of purely experiential content, as above, we take one step away from the project of giving an all-embracing account of the nature of experience, for we endorse a conception of the content of experience that no longer involves necessary reference to certain of the causes of experience (like the George Washington Bridge). [3] But the notion of purely experiential content requires that we now take a further step away from the all-embracing project and drop all considerations relating to the substantial or "realizing ground" of experience as well. One good reason for doing this is that while we know for sure that experience exists, we cannot know for sure what kind of nonexperiential substantial ground or realization it has. Thus we seem unable to rule out something like Berkeley's story, for example, obscure though it may be.

It seems, then, that one can detach experience considered just as such from all questions about its substantial ground or realization. Indeed, one can detach it from *everything* that is supposed [a] to be necessary for its existence and [b] to have some nonexperiential aspect or character.[9] One is then left with something aptly named 'purely experiential content'. Purely experiential content is just a matter of "what it is like" for a subject of experience, of (experiential) qualitative character—as much in the case of understanding-experience as in the case of purely sensory experience. Everything else has been stripped away.

It is true that most of us believe that experience is in fact realized in or by the brain, i.e., in something which (we take it) essentially has nonexperiential properties. And it is true that most of us believe that our experience could not possibly have the character it does have unless many nonexperiential processes occurred in our brains. Indeed, it is arguable that the existence of many experiential phenomena *necessarily* involves the existence of nonexperiential phenomena (see section 5.12). May be. None of this matters here. The present point is that even if all these things are true, it is *still* legitimate to consider experience—the stream of experience—just as such, so far as we can. It is legitimate and important to consider experience and its content quite independently of any actual or possible nonexperiential causes and/or nonexperiential substantial realization that it may have. It is important to take full account of its reality, so considered. There are many things that can be said about it, so considered. Thus for any given individual, there are real differences, as real as any of the other differences in nature, between

9. Descartes was quite right, insofar as he argued for this. He went wrong only insofar as he believed that he could prove that experience (or "thinking," in the wide Cartesian sense) might possibly have no nonexperiential ground at all, i.e., that there might possibly be experience (thinking) while there was nothing that fulfilled conditions (a) and (b). Descartes's position is not as simple as is sometimes supposed, however, for he takes it that only pure rational thought (and also, perhaps, a kind of intellectual joy) can normally go on in a disembodied mind; sensations, imaginings, rememberings, and emotions all depend for their normal occurrence on physical goings-on in a brain, even if a *malin génie* can induce apparent sensations, etc., in a disembodied mind.

smell experiences and touch experiences, or between experiences of red and experiences of green. There is an equally real difference between the experience of thinking that squares can't be circles and the experience of thinking that sadness is a complex phenomenon. We can express the fact that this is so without making reference to any nonexperiential causes of such experiences or to the nonexperiential realizing grounds (if any) of such experiences and, indeed, without having any certain knowledge of what these causes and grounds are. In *Consciousness Explained* (1991b), Dennett raises a number of difficulties for the naive-realist view that there is always a determinate fact of the matter about what experience one is having at any given moment. But none of his cases and arguments count in any way against the point just made. It is an old point, but it may still need some defense today.

1.7 An Account of Four Seconds of Thought

I turned a page in a psychology textbook and saw a black and white photograph of a crowd of people crushed against a wall in a soccer stadium. Too fast for subvocalized words my mind flashed with [1] the thought 'I'm glad it wasn't me'. For a moment this thought was completely self-concerned. At the same time, [2] a grasp of the experience of the trapped people became present, which produced [3] a strong feeling of sympathy. Concurrently, there was [4] an impulse of contrition about the occurrence of (1). This blurred with (3) and was simultaneously genuine and apotropaic.

Almost immediately (3) and (4) were jumped on, and [5] accused of insincerity—of being less than immediately spontaneous and therefore under suspicion of having been dutifully produced in the wake of (1). Again almost immediately—this was a familiar routine—there was [6] the thought that (3) and (4) were not really insincere at all and that (1) occurred in thought in spite of (3), the more natural response.

During this process there had also come to be present [7] the idea that I somehow make myself have (or: some agency in me makes me have) thoughts like (1) as a kind of regulatory dare to myself, and in order to keep alert in me a suspicion of myself that I think I ought to have—a suspicion of those of my thoughts that look like naturally good thoughts. And then, immediately after (1) to (7), there was [8] a rapid higher-order thought to the effect that the whole previous process of thought involved impulses of automatic, involuntary superstition. There was superstition not only in (4), insofar as it was an apotropaic reflex, but also in (1), because (1) wasn't just the "fat relentless ego's" natural self-expression (Murdoch 1970, 52). It was also (although it took place in an atheist) [9] a God-daring or Nemesis-daring thought-impulse. That was its main source, even if the fat ego and the business recorded in (7) were also active. Moreover (1) was partly driven by the impulse 'Let me see if I can't think such a thought'. (Children may be particularly subject to this sort of thing.)

Now (4) was partly superstitious, because it was an apology before conscience, superego, or God, as if some placation were needed to avert possible retribution. And (5) jumped on (4) immediately, but it too was classified, in the complex (8)-thought, as a further attempt at superstitious placation insofar as it was an attempt to achieve genuine sincerity by confessing to an earlier insincerity. The content of the impulse behind (5) was seen to be roughly [10] 'I have human faults, but as long as I try to be truthful, I cannot ultimately be condemned.' Like everything else recorded here, the thought that (10) underlay (5) was in some sense present to consciousness.

Also, (8) jostled or ran concurrently with a further routine thought: [11] the thought that (5) was a step in a standard regress, in which each stage condemns its predecessor for insincerity and claims to be the terminus of true sincerity. The regress ran on for a couple of stages through (5) and (6), but after that the mind couldn't be bothered, familiar as it was with the fact that it is difficult to keep track in such disputatious regresses, partly because they confuse and become part of the thing being disputed and can never be resoundingly stopped. As the regress started and died, [12] I was aware of the indefatigable logic driving the process by which every attempt to think 'This thought, at least and at last, is truly sincere' is already suspect simply by reason of its explicit reference to the notion of sincerity.

The (12)-awareness, familiar from many past occasions, didn't occur spelled out in thought. Nevertheless, its content was in some way genuinely and fully apprehended by me. It flashed on the mind as a familiar—wearisome—schema. And with it came its usual accompaniment, itself a mere schema too fast for words, whose content, to spell it out a bit, was [13] that although this automatic activity is indeed wearisome, experience shows that the realization that this is so is no remedy and does not stop its happening. But there was also, as always, a little accompanying shape of hope shadowing the schema, a hope [14] that the ability to be completely aware of the set pattern of what was going on might provide a way out of it. But schema (13) had already encompassed its by-product, the hope-shape, and [15] it had already reckoned it up and ruled it out.

It is worth noticing that (1) was not just apprehended as a content that occurred. It was also thought of as some sort of doing on the part of some impish or morally anxious agency of the mind. Also alive in the mind was the issue of whether (1) was intentionally provocative (see (9)) or whether it was some sort of involuntary reflex—as when someone laughs in a way that seems unkind but is in fact just the product of nervousness. Also, (1) pulled in a fleeting awareness of the immediate surroundings and a new appreciation of their safety: not the soccer stadium, but bookshelves, armchair, carpet, a puddle of light on floorboards. This awareness was also part of the content of the four seconds of thought. And the whole sequence occurred in a certain moral mood. Such moods set a general context for thought and are themselves part of the overall character, and hence content, of experience. In another context I might have had little moral or emotional reaction to the picture, or I might have reacted to the same picture with distress uncomplicated by self-suspicion.

This, then, was some of the content of about four seconds of thought. Four seconds may seem to be too short a time, but it may have been less than four seconds. The speed may be partly explained by the fact that this general course of thought was well worn. The speed is, in any case, of little importance. It is only part of what may interest us in this illustration of one aspect of the nature of mental reality.

This kind of thing happens to me less now (is this neural or moral degeneration?), but I suspect that experiences like this are quite common, especially among the young. Seeing a man with terrible acne at Paddington Station, I had a strong desire to take over his acne so that he could experience normal-faced anonymity in the crowd. This immediately triggered the process of self-suspicion, the regress of doubting the sincerity of the impulse, doubting the doubt, doubting the doubting of the doubt, this running on to the fourth or fifth stage. Concurrently there came the thought that it was easy for me to have this desire, since I knew it wasn't really possible, and on the other side, the thought that there was no obvious reason why I shouldn't be just as likely to have spontaneous admirable thoughts as spontaneous egotistical ones, given human nature. Even as it occurred, this triggered the thought that there might be a special and surreptitious form of moral self-indulgence or spiritual pride in automatic self-denigration, and this, in turn, the thought that the last thought might itself be too easy.

Spelling out this content, it seems clear to me that I am doing just that: writing out content that was present to mind, not elaborating on it or adding to it. If this is some sort of delusion, then the existence of the delusion is itself an interesting phenomenon. But conversation often provides examples of the presence to mind of lightning, compacted content. As the other person is talking, there is a small, silent, pointlike explosion, and one knows one's answer is there—although it may take some time to speak it out, although the words and syntax in which one does so are not already fixed in the explosion but are to a considerable extent chosen as one goes along, and although people characteristically expand on their initial thought in the act of vocalization. (James [1950, 1:253] presumably has a more general phenomenon in mind when he estimates that "a good third of our psychic life consists in . . . rapid premonitory perspective views of schemes of thought not yet articulate".)

This, then, illustrates one of the ways in which experience, and hence mental reality, can be complex. I think it is useful to be reminded of this sort of thing when one does philosophy of mind.[10]

---

10. Rereading this passage several years after having written it, I am struck by how it confirms Dennett's (1991b) suggestions about the nature of the processes that underlie thought and speech.

2
Three Questions

2.1 Introduction

This chapter is a speculative and somewhat abstract preamble to the main work of the book. It offers some general reflections on the three large questions mentioned in the preface. It contains a number of promissory notes and tries to address philosophers working on very different fronts—both those who think that philosophy of mind is directly continuous with science and those who think that questions about the coherence of idealism are important in an analysis of the nature of mind. I think that both groups are right, and so this chapter will probably satisfy no one.

2.2 The Mental and the Nonmental

Question 1: is reference to *nonmental* phenomena central and indispensable in a satisfactory account of the nature of mental phenomena? This question, the nonmentality question, is fundamental for the philosophy of mind, and it seems plausible that one cannot hope to answer it decisively unless one can first draw a clear line between the mental and the nonmental.

This may be doubted. It may be argued that one does not need to draw a clear line between the mental and the nonmental, because it is a priori that the nonmental cannot have any essential part to play in an adequate account of the nature of the mental. Here is such an argument. [1] Everything is what it is and not another thing, as Bishop Butler said. [2] If two things are defined complementarily, as x and non-x, then non-x cannot, by definition, be any part of the essential nature of x, and hence cannot be part of what has to be mentioned in a full account of *x* considered in itself and in its essential nature. (Counterexamples of the hill/valley type may be offered, but few suppose that the mental/nonmental distinction is of this kind.) Conclusion: reference to the nonmental cannot have any essential part to play in an adequate account of the mental.

Another argument proceeds in the opposite direction. It claims that one does not need to draw a clear line between the mental and the nonmental in order to show a priori that the nonmental must have some essential role to play in any fully adequate account of the nature of the mental as we know it. According to this argument, one cannot even make sense of the idea that things like memories and thoughts exist without supposing that something nonmental exists. I will consider such an argument in section 5.12.

A third argument claims that a gray area does not vitiate a distinction. One can state a valid distinction between *x* and non-*x*, and provide clear cases on both sides, without being able to draw a sharp line that allows one to classify every relevant case as *x* or non-*x*. (The analytic/synthetic distinction is perhaps an example of this.)

Such arguments are interesting, but I will say no more about them here. Whatever their force, it would undoubtedly be useful to be able to draw a clear line between the mental and the nonmental when doing philosophy of mind.

It might seem that this should be an easy thing to do, but it isn't. There is massive disagreement about where the line goes, and it isn't only a matter of classical metaphysical disagreement between idealists, dualists, and materialists. There is radical disagreement even among those who think of themselves as materialists. And even when philosophers fully agree about where the line should be drawn, they may still violently disagree about the answer to the question of what part reference to nonmental phenomena should play in a satisfactory account of the nature of mental phenomena.

So there are many demarcation problems. I will consider some of them in chapter 6. In the meantime, I will continue to rely on standard intuitions about mental and nonmental phenomena and about the differences between them and try to raise up some more philosophical dust. As in chapter 1, I will take sensations, thoughts, emotions, beliefs, and desires to be paradigms of mental phenomena, while saluting those who think that some or most of them do not exist.

"Instrumentalists" or "antirealists" may claim that the question about the line between the mental and the nonmental is not really fundamental in the way that it seems. They may say that there aren't any ultimate facts of the matter about what is mental and what is not: it is just that sometimes it is natural or convenient or practically indispensable for us to think of a being in a certain way, as having properties we are inclined to call 'mental' properties, and sometimes it is neither natural nor convenient nor practically indispensable, and that's that (see Dennett 1978c, 1987).

Those who say this do not take the reality of experience seriously enough, however. The reality and mentality of experience do not depend on our inclinations, our convenience, or our needs. For a long time instrumentalists thought too much about propositional attitudes and other dispositional mental states or characteristics. They paid too little attention to the phenomena of experience and somehow deluded themselves into thinking that instrumentalism could provide a general theory of the mental.

So much, for the moment, for the first question. After discussing the second and third questions I will return to the first question and consider five arguments for the view that reference to the nonmental does enter centrally into a satisfactory account of the essential nature of the mental.

2.3 The Mental and the Publicly Observable

Question 2: is reference to *publicly observable* phenomena central and indispensable in a satisfactory account of the nature of mental phenomena? This question, the public-observability question, has come to seem fundamental in the twentieth century. I will consider it generally in this chapter and discuss some details later.

Some think that it is the same question as the first question about nonmental phenomena, because the class of nonmental phenomena is identical with the class of publicly observable phenomena. But this is not obvious. It is not obvious [1] that *nonmental* entails *publicly observable*, or [2] that *publicly observable* entails *nonmental*. As for (1), it seems that there could be nonmental phenomena that were not even potentially publicly observable, at least by us, given our make-up and limitations. The word 'observable' raises the question 'Observable by whom?' and this question does not seem to have a satisfactory nontrivial answer (compare chapter 9, note 2, and chapter 10, p. 307).

As for (2), there are philosophers, including Wittgensteinians, who want to say that some publicly observable phenomena are mental phenomena. They agree that reference to publicly observable phenomena (and in particular, behavioral phenomena) plays a large part in a satisfactory account of the mental. But they go on to say that what this shows is that some of the (behavioral) phenomena in question—which it may at first seem natural to think of as entirely nonmental—are themselves mental phenomena, part of what 'the mental' consists of. In support of their view, they argue that observable human behavior is essentially informed by desire, belief, emotion, and so on, in such a way that it is appropriate to say that the behavior is itself a mental phenomenon, part of what the mental consists of. (This is one of the demarcation disputes alluded to in section 2.2.)

Others may say the same about the physical brain processes that are presumed to "realize" mental states or occurrences. They may say that these physical goings-on cannot be thought of simply as nonmental and that even when they are considered as publicly observable goings-on, they just are mental goings-on. (See chapter 3.)

So it is not clear that *nonmental* entails *publicly observable* or that *publicly observable* entails *nonmental*. But those who question these entailments are likely to agree that being publicly observable entails having nonmental features or aspects, at least. Even if they insist that the nonmentality question is not the same question as the public-observability question, they are likely to concede that they are closely related, and that if you claim that reference to publicly observable phenomena plays a large part in any satisfactory account of mental phenomena, you must say the same about nonmental phenomena.

This may be offered as a necessary truth. It seems, however, that we can imagine a race of beings who are "mentally transparent" to each other in such a way that their conscious, occurrent mental goings-on are publicly observable—directly experienceable by others. They may pick up each other's thoughts by adjusting their mental wavelengths rather in the way we pick up radio stations by twiddling a knob. They may even be mentally transparent to each other in such a way that their beliefs, preferences, hopes, and so on, are publicly inspectable. They may have no conception of the mechanism that makes this possible and no reason to think that there is anything nonmental involved in the process. (It is a further question whether we can make sense of the idea that there might be such thought transmission without supposing that certain nonmental processes exist. The answer depends on whether some form of mentalistic idealism is coherent—an issue discussed in chapter 5.)

This may be thought to be too fanciful. And it may be said that even if this kind of mental transparency is a real possibility, there is still a necessary connection between the mental and the publicly observable nonmental, one that is mediated by two further connections. The first links mental phenomena logically or conceptually to behavioral phenomena, and the second links behavioral phenomena logically or conceptually to nonmental, publicly observable phenomena.

Both these assertions of necessary connection may be questioned, however, and if either fails, they can't jointly secure the link between the mental and the publicly observable nonmental. The first is one of the main targets of chapters 8 and 9. The second is rejected in chapter 10.

2.4 The Mental and the Behavioral

This brings me to question 3. Is reference to *behavior* central and indispensable in a satisfactory account of the essential nature of the mental? According to the current orthodox view, the answer to this third question, the behavior question, is 'Yes'. I will argue that this is wrong.

I think that there are a number of reasons why we now find this hard to see. One of them is simply that at certain points, in philosophy as in everyday life, we think too much about ourselves and not enough about other possible species. Another, opposing reason is that at certain points we think too much about nonhuman animals and about the evidential grounds we have for attributing mental states to them, and not enough about ourselves. When philosophers do the first thing, they tend to underestimate the possible forms of mental life—of experience. When they do the second thing, the consequences can be even more curious: concentration on the study of nonhuman animals was perhaps one of the main motivations for behaviorism. (The imprecision of the data of introspection was another.) But who among the wise could have predicted the extension of behaviorism from the case of nonhuman animals to the human case, accompanied by its transubstantiation from a methodological thesis about scientifically admissible evidence for the existence of mental phenomena into a metaphysical thesis about the nature of mental phenomena? In chapter 8, I will consider the Wittgensteinian version of this transmutation, which is routed through considerations about language and meaning. (It also has Quinean and Davidsonian versions.)

What is the relation between the third question and the first two? Many suppose that it is a very simple one, for they take it that all behavior (third question) is both publicly observable (second question) and nonmental (first question). Even if doubts are raised about the status of behavior as intrinsically nonmental (as in section 2.3), it is standardly assumed that all behavior is publicly observable.

Against this it may be argued that much behavior is not publicly observable. But those who hold the standard view about the relation between the mental and the behavioral can grant this without altering their main claim. They can grant that not all behavior is publicly observable, while continuing to insist that reference to behavior that *is* publicly observable is essential in a satisfactory account of the nature of sensations, thoughts, emotions, beliefs, desires, and so on.

For most of this book I will respect standard usage and take it for granted that when one is talking about behavior, one is thereby talking about publicly observable behavior. I will assume this in chapter 9, for example, where I will argue that a being may have a complex mental life without behaving in any way and without even being disposed to behave in any way. Then, in chapter 10, I will argue that we need to endorse a wider conception of behavior, according to which not all behavior is publicly observable behavior. Both chapters will question the view that reference to publicly observable behavior is indispensable and central in a satisfactory account of the essential nature of mind.

My three main questions keep raising a fourth: what are the relations between the nonmental (NM), the publicly observable (PO), and the behavioral (B)? There are six possible entailments, of which two are obviously false: [PO → B] and [NM → B]. We have also seen reason to doubt three of the remaining four: [NM → PO], [PO → NM], and [B → NM], And the last one, [B → PO], will, as remarked, be challenged in chapter 10.

2.5 Neobehaviorism and Reductionism

The idea that reference to behavior has only a small part to play in a correct account of the essential nature of mental states and occurrences is hardly new. The history of philosophy is full of conceptions of the mental that give no essential role to reference to behavior. Here, however, I want to consider the prospects of such a conception while attempting to take adequate account of the insights of the twentieth century.

I will call the view I wish to question 'neo-behaviorism'. The name is not ideal, but it will do. Neobehaviorism holds that mental life is linked to behavior in such a way that reference to behavior, or at least to dispositions to behavior, enters essentially—constitutively and centrally—into any adequate account of the fundamental nature of almost all, if not all, mental states and occurrences, like emotions, sensations, thoughts, beliefs, and desires. Many philosophers today would wish to endorse some version of the neobehaviorist view that one of "the *essential* or *defining* feature[s] of *any* type of mental state is the set of causal relations it bears to . . . bodily behavior" (Churchland 1984, 36; my emphasis).[1] Others would lay less stress on causal relations but would agree with Wittgenstein that "psychological concepts are not logically independent of behavioural concepts" (Hacker 1972, 305).

In fact, the first of these quotations is from Paul Churchland's definition of functionalism. But the functionalist idea that one can capture the whole nature of certain (or all) types of mental state or occurrence by giving an account of their typical or characteristic causes and effects is still extremely influential in contemporary philosophy of mind, and I do not know of any version of functionalism that is not neobehavior- ist in its assumption that types of mental state and occurrence are essen-

---

1. Although reference to typical *causes* of mental states and occurrences is usually thought to be as important as reference to typical publicly observable behavioral *effects* of mental states and occurrences, I will say little about this for the time being.

tially (if only partly) defined by their causal relations to types of bodily behavior.[2]

This raises the question of whether neobehaviorism is an essential part of functionalism. I do not think it is, and I will try to get them apart, preserving the truth in functionalism while arguing that neobehaviorism is false.[3]

More specifically, I will argue that neobehaviorism is incorrect insofar as it incorporates or entails anything like the following conditional claim:

If a being has sensations, thoughts, emotions, beliefs, desires, and such like, then it must behave in certain ways, or at least be *disposed* to behave in certain ways; even if it never actually behaves in any way at all.

It is the claim about dispositions to behave in certain ways that is important, if only because a completely paralysed being can have beliefs, sensations, and so on. Many are inclined to think that this claim about dispositions is a conceptual truth, or at least a truth about the essential nature of mental phenomena like beliefs and sensations. It may be, however, that we radically overestimate the tightness of the connections between mind and behavior as ordinarily understood.

Obviously, neobehaviorism is not outright (philosophical) behaviorism. It is not the truly extraordinary view that the whole story about what it is for a being to be in a certain mental state, or to be the locus of a certain mental occurrence, is just that it is behaving in certain ways or is disposed to behave in certain ways. It is not the view that statements about mental states and occurrences can be *reduced* to statements about behavior, so that the whole meaning or ontological

2. This is a rough statement of the functionalist thesis, for three reasons: First, it is the tokens or individual instances of the types that actually have causes and effects. Second, this way of putting it has to be further adjusted to take account of the fact that mental states are not things in us but rather states that things, e.g., we, are in. Third, the idea that states are causes needs a certain amount of explanation.

3. See Section 9.4. The objection to functionalism that some have had since the beginning—that it could never work as a full account of the nature of sensations and experience in general, even if it could work as an account of the nature of propositional attitudes—has recently gained wider acceptance. It has come to seem better to say that one can (at most) give a functional *characterization* of certain types of mental state, rather than a functional *definition* of (all of) them.

import of statements about mental states and occurrences can be fully captured by statements about behavior.[4] Neobehaviorism is the much more moderate view that although statements about mental states and occurrences cannot be reduced to (that is, replaced without loss of semantic or ontological import by) statements about behavior, nevertheless reference to behavior enters essentially and centrally into any adequate account of what it is for a being to be in a mental state or to be the locus of a certain mental occurrence.

Behavioristic reductionism has gone out of fashion because it is plainly false. (This does not usually prevent a view from coming into fashion.) It is obvious that to be looking at the sea is to be having certain complex visual experiences whose nature cannot be captured by any number of statements about behavior or dispositions to behavior. It is obvious that depression in human beings standardly involves feelings that cannot be captured by statements about behavior or about dispositions to behavior. At the same time, of course, to be depressed is ipso facto to be disposed to act or behave in certain ways (at least in the case of human beings). And to be clearly perceiving a velociraptor is ipso facto to be disposed to respond in the affirmative to the question 'Is there a velociraptor around here?', if one knows what velociraptors are and are called and wishes to speak truthfully, and to be disposed to act warily if one does not wish to be eaten, and so on. There are indefinitely many such facts about dispositions to behavior, and as they pile up, it can easily come to seem that reference to dispositions to behavior will indeed enter essentially and centrally into any adequate account of what it is to be in a mental state, even if it enters in only as one element among others.

Putting specifically behavioristic reductionism aside, one can ask whether any other sort of full reduction of the mental to the nonmental might be possible. I think many neobehaviorists—many of whom are functionalists of some sort, partial or total—do still hope that their final account of the mental will somehow be given in nonmental terms, and that an unqualified 'Yes' will be given in answer to the nonmentality question, the first of the three large questions raised in this chapter. (On

4. There are many varieties of reductionism, but the differences between them do not matter much at present. See chapter 3, note 4.

this view, reference to the nonmental is not only essential in an account of the nature of the mental, it is the only thing that is essential.) Many are committed to the general project of *naturalism* in the philosophy of mind and think that naturalism depends on the possibility of such elimination of mental terms—an understandable though disputable thought. Many also think that the general project of *materialism* depends on the possibility of such elimination—another understandable but disputable thought.[5]

Here is one fast argument for the claim that some such elimination or reduction is necessary if we are to give a satisfactory philosophical account of the nature of the mental: [1] Any satisfactory account of any notion must be noncircular. [2] It follows immediately that any satisfactory general theoretical account of the notion of the mental must be given in nonmental terms.

A sufficient reply to this, perhaps, is that no one thinks of giving an argument like this in the case of the notion of the physical, although reductions of the physical to the mental have in fact been attempted as often as reductions of the mental to the physical (or at least to the nonmental). Unlike the notion of the mental, the notion of the physical is usually accepted as an untroublesome terminus for thought. It is accepted as a notion that cannot be satisfactorily analysed further in any noncircular, and therefore nonphysical, terms.

It is not entirely clear what can justify this difference in attitude toward the notions of the mental and the physical, since there is no reason to think that the notion of the physical is less problematic than

5. For the disputability, see chapters 3 and 4. Fodor (1981, 10) and Churchland (1984, 36) are among those who suppose that functionalism is not a reductive theory (Churchland, however, may be claiming only that reductive definitions of *individual* types of mental state are unavailable). But Block reckons that "functionalism in most of its forms . . . is a version of [the reductionist view that] mental terms . . . can be defined in nonmental terms" (1978, 263). He quotes Shoemaker's claim that "on one construal of it, functionalism in the philosophy of mind is the doctrine that mental, or psychological, terms are in principle eliminable in a certain way" (Shoemaker, 1975, 306–307), and he notes how "in Lewis's version of functionalism, mental-state terms are defined by means of a modification of Ramsey's method in a way that eliminates essential use of mental terminology from the definitions." Since then, however, it has come to be fairly widely conceded that no reductive account of the nature of sensory-experience properties can be given (see, e.g., Block 1986).

the notion of the mental. Indeed, the repeated failure of mental-to-physical reductionist programs in the philosophy of mind suggests that neither notion is less problematic than the other. Some philosophers go further, arguing that there is a crucial sense in which the mental is *better* understood than the physical and that the prospects for physical-to-mental reduction are better than for mental-to-physical reduction (see Foster 1981, 294).

Here are mysteries. There is, however, little need to discuss reductionism when one's target is neobehaviorism. It is true that most reductionists are neobehaviorists, but so are most nonreductionists (who hold that no account of the mental in entirely nonmental or nonintentional terms is possible). Most nonreductionists still think that reference to behavior enters essentially and across the board into any adequate general account of the fundamental nature of the mental. So the view I want to challenge is common to nearly all contemporary reductionists and nonreductionists.

2.6 Naturalism in the Philosophy of Mind

Neobehaviorism claims that reference to behavior enters essentially and centrally into any adequate account of what it is to be in a (or any) mental state. One way to question it is to try to produce a clear description of a case in which certain beings have sensations, thoughts, emotions, beliefs, desires, and so on, but never "behave" in any way, and are not even disposed to "behave" in any way. (There are quotation marks round this use of the verb 'behave' because it is worth recalling at least once that it is extremely unnatural in ordinary English.) Part of my main argument will consist in an attempt to give such a description: a description of the Weather Watchers.

Some may doubt whether any such argument by description can really have the force to establish anything that a neobehaviorist must deny. I will consider this doubt in chapter 9. Here it is worth saying that I do not intend there to be anything antinaturalistic in the present approach.

This may seem implausible. It may look as if the present approach is bound to be incompatible with a naturalistic account of the mental. But the appearance of incompatibility may arise because current views about how a naturalistic account of the mental should go are too narrow.

The main error may be an old one: a confusion of genetic questions with analytic questions. At the simplest level, it may be said that belief and desire have always evolved to control behavior, and that one can argue from this fact to the conclusion that it is some sort of necessary truth that belief and desire always involve dispositions to behavior. The facts of evolution and history do not make this a necessary truth, however. One can acknowledge the intimate connection that exists between mental phenomena and behavioral phenomena on earth while insisting on the respects in which mental notions are independent of behavioral notions (or the respects in which mental phenomena are ontologically independent of behavioral phenomena). A properly naturalistic approach to the study of mind and behavior does not foreclose on the question of whether their intimacy of connection is conceptual, constitutive, causal, or contingent. It may be that mental notions are definitionally independent of behavioral notions in a way that is obscured by the whole family of currently dominant approaches to the question of the nature of mind. The members of this family, whether functionalist or Wittgensteinian in their primary affiliation, are all descendants of behaviorism. They are all neobehaviorist, even though they are not behaviorist.

2.7 Conclusion: The Three Questions

The questions raised in this chapter are difficult, but simple to state. Is reference to [1] nonmental phenomena, [2] publicly observable phenomena, and [3] behavioral phenomena central or indispensable in a satisfactory general philosophical account of the essential nature of mind?

I think that the answer to (3), the behavior question, is 'No', given the ordinary understanding of 'behavior'. I will consider some Wittgensteinian objections in chapter 8 and some other (functionalist and conceptual) objections in chapter 9. In chapter 10, I will suggest that it might be best to modify our common understanding of the word 'behavior' and give a rather different answer to the question.

I think that the answer to (2), the public-observability question, is also 'No' as far as many mental phenomena are concerned. It is, no doubt, a natural fact that many mental phenomena have publicly observable causes and effects, but it is not part of their essence, considered general type by general type (i.e., as beliefs, desires, sensations, thoughts, and so on). I will argue that this is so even if mental phenomena must have publicly observable causes and effects in order for a (public) language for mental phenomena to evolve. And I will argue that it is so even if many beliefs, desires, sensations, and thoughts have content that is essentially *about*, or *of*, publicly observable phenomena.[6]

Mind on earth is no doubt a product of biological evolution, but the general philosophical answer to (1), the nonmentality question, presumably depends partly on whether idealism is coherent. If idealism is a genuine metaphysical possibility, then it is arguable that reference to nonmental phenomena may have no necessary role to play in an adequate account of the essential nature of the mental.[7] At the very least, we may be able to reach the conclusion, call it (C), that reference to nonmental phenomena does not have anything like the role it is ordinarily thought to have.

6. Here is a relatively complicated objection. [1] Many complex mental states or occurrences (e.g., thoughts, beliefs, desires, etc.) are not possible without language. [2] Language cannot evolve in a group of creatures without there being a common, publicly observable realm for them to (learn to) talk about. [3] Reference to the publicly observable is therefore necessary in a satisfactory account of the nature of certain types of complex mental state or occurrence, just because it is necessary in a satisfactory account of the evolution of the language that makes them possible.

Three points in reply. First, this argument does give reference to the publicly observable a place in an account of part of the mental, but it does so only indirectly, and it does not give it the place it is usually supposed to have. Second, it is arguable that grasp of language, or at least possession of a capacity for thought that appears to involve something very like language, could possibly be fully innate and possessed by solitary individuals. In this case, a correct account of the conditions of its existence would not require reference to publicly observable circumstances of learning of the sort envisaged in (2) above. (Wittgenstein considered this idea; see chapter 8, note 4). Third, it is simply not clear why it should be thought to be true that there cannot be (complicated) thought without language, though the word 'language' may be used very loosely to mean any symbolic system of representation that may be employed in thought.

7. The 'may' is prompted by at least two things. First, some varieties of idealism appear to postulate nonphysical but nonmental existents, and those that do not do this may be dubiously coherent, for reasons discussed in chapter 5. Second, it is arguable that even absolute mentalists will have to reproduce something like the distinction between the mental and the nonmental in their account of the nature of things, and the consequences of this fact are not entirely clear.

I will address the question of whether idealism is coherent in chapter 5. Many, however, will think it to be of little interest. They will be more interested in an argument that attempts to show that (C) is true even if materialism is assumed to be true; and this will be my main concern. Others, no doubt, will want to endorse positivist reasons for thinking that questions about the coherence of idealism are illegitimate in some way. They too will be more interested by an attempt to establish (C) that does not appeal to the possible coherence of idealism, and this seems reasonable enough. It is worth adding, however, that those who take this line about idealism should remember that materialism is no better off than idealism, from the positivist point of view, as an over-arching metaphysical hypothesis about the ultimate nature of reality.

In conclusion, here are five partly overlapping arguments for the claim that reference to the nonmental is indeed essential and central in a satisfactory account of the general nature of the mental, and that the answer to the nonmentality question must after all be 'Yes'. I will examine most of them in more detail later on.

First, the argument from behavior. According to this argument, reference to the nonmental enters essentially into a satisfactory account of the nature of the mental because reference to behavior does, and behavior is itself essentially nonmental in character (either wholly or at least in part). I have already mentioned this argument and will criticize it in chapters 8 and 9.

Second, the argument from the nature of concept-structured thought. According to this argument, one cannot make sense of the idea that a being lacking nonmental attributes could have complex concept-structured thoughts. This argument is one of a family of arguments that are well worth considering, and I will do so in section 5.12.

Third, the argument from the "realizing ground" of the mental. Here the claim is that the mental has *in fact* a nonmental and indeed physical realizing ground and that one obviously cannot give a satisfactory account of the general nature of the mental, even when one claims to be considering it "just as such," without referring to its realizing ground.

I have already noted reasons for doubting this claim in chapter 1 (pp. 16–18), and I will propose others below. Obviously, this suggestion raises the question of whether one can prove that the mental has a nonmental realizing ground. It does not seem to follow from the concept of the mental that it must do so (though see chapter 5). It may be added that functionalism is a well-known example of a theory that entirely rejects the idea that any reference to facts about realizing grounds should feature in an account of the essential nature of the mental.

All in all, this third argument looks ill conceived. One could summarize the objection to it by saying that even if materialism is true, it does not follow that reference to the nonmental is central or indispensable in a satisfactory account of the essential nature of the mental.

Fourth, the argument from (the specification of mental) content. According to this argument, many beliefs, thoughts, perceptions, etc., are about or of nonmental things, like the South Kurile Islands or C_{60}. Clearly, one cannot specify their content without reference to nonmental things; so one cannot give a satisfactory account of the nature of thought, belief, and perception in general without reference to nonmental things.

If anything like Berkeleyan idealism is coherent, however, it seems that perceptions, thoughts, and beliefs may have the character of being of or about nonmental things without really being of or about nonmental things. Insofar as we cannot prove that this is not the case, the fourth argument fails.

More moderately: let us grant that there are beliefs and thoughts (etc.) about irreducibly nonmental things. It seems nevertheless that there may be beliefs and thoughts (etc.) that are only about mental things. And if there are such beliefs or thoughts, then they will not lack anything essential, so far as their status as beliefs or thoughts is concerned, in being only about mental things. In which case, it seems that reference to nonmental things is not indispensable in a satisfactory account of the *general or essential nature* of beliefs, thoughts, and so on, even if nearly all beliefs and thoughts are in fact of such a kind that one cannot give an adequate account of their content without reference to nonmental things. Beliefs and thoughts about nonmental things will form a major subclass of beliefs and thoughts, but the property of being about something nonmental will not be an essential property of any fundamental category of mental state or occurrence (like belief, hope, desire, thought, etc.).

This reply may be rejected on the grounds that materialism is true, and that if materialism is true, then all thoughts about mental things are ipso facto thoughts about nonmental things (or things with nonmental features or aspects, at least). But this conditional, strictly speaking, is false: materialism claims only that everything is physical, and hence that everything mental is physical, not that everything mental is therefore at least partly nonmental. The conditional could be repaired by the stipulation that materialism involves the further claim that anything physical must have nonmental features or aspects. But the possibility that there might be mental things that had no nonmental aspect, and that could be thought about would still remain, since materialism cannot be proved to be true. In general, and as already observed, it seems that appeal to the de facto truth of materialism simply does not provide the right kind of ground for arguing that reference to the nonmental is necessary in an adequate account of the essential nature of the mental.

Still under the heading of the argument from content, it may next be said that one cannot give an adequate account of *intentionality* without considering cases in which thoughts (etc.) are about nonmental things. But there is no good reason to suppose that this is so. Thoughts can be about mental things, e.g., other thoughts, just as they can be about nonmental things, and in just the same sense of 'about'. So even if the intentionality or aboutness of thoughts is a phenomenon that must be discussed in an adequate account of the nature of the mental, it does not follow that reference to the nonmental is essential or central to such an account.

It may be said that thoughts can indeed be about mental states and occurrences—about desires and other thoughts, including thoughts that are themselves about other thoughts—but that at the end of any such chain of thoughts about thoughts or desires (etc.) there must be a mental state or occurrence with nonmental content. This is not obvious, however. For, first, a thought can be about a desire for a certain experience of merely mental well-being. Second, once again, if idealism is coherent, then the correct account of the content of mental states and occurrences that appear to have nonmental content will not in fact make reference to nonmental phenomena. (Positivistic phenomenalists, who attempted to shun all metaphysics, were close to idealists on this point. Like the outright idealists, they held that the correct account of the content of mental states and occurrences that appear to have nonmental content, e.g., thoughts about tables and chairs, did not in fact make reference to nonmental phenomena as ordinarily conceived of. Statements about tables and chairs reduced without residue to statements about mental contents or "sense-data.")

The argument from content may still be pressed. Some argue that concepts like the concept *square* are concepts of essentially nonmental things, namely, "objective" properties that are real existents and that "exist . . . independently of minds" (McGinn 1989a, 41). Clearly, if one holds this "weak externalist" view, one is likely to think that reference to the nonmental gets essentially into the specification of the content of almost all thought, even on a Berkeleyan view according to which there is no physical world as we ordinarily conceive of it. Berkeleyans may reply, however, that squareness and space itself are purely mental constructs in their universe, and are to that extent purely mental in character.

This reply may not convince those who endorse weak externalism. But even if it is not found convincing—even if concepts like the concept *square* are held to be aspects of nonmental reality that have to be mentioned in specifying the content of much thought—it remains true, in this version of the argument from content, that reference to the nonmental is not gaining a place in an account of the essential nature of the mental in anything like the way in which it is ordinarily supposed to (e.g., via the necessity of reference to behavior, as in the first argument). I will return to this question in chapter 7.

A fifth and final reason for thinking that reference to the nonmental must feature centrally in an adequate account of the essential nature of the mental has already been mentioned. It takes the form of an argument from the natural history of the mental: Mind has in fact always come into existence (via a process of evolution) in order to govern behavior in a nonmental world. This is the purpose of mind i.e., the reason why it exists. If a thing has a purpose in this sense, then understanding its essential nature necessarily involves understanding its purpose. In the particular case of mind, explaining its purpose necessarily involves reference to nonmental things.

In reply, first, if idealism is coherent, then, once again, mind can exist in the absence of nonmental things, and the argument fails. Second, leaving aside the question of idealism, there is a sense in which it is true that part of knowing what a thing is is knowing how it is that it exists, and what it is for, if it is for anything; but there is equally a sense in which it is not true. If I know nothing about tables and come across a wooden one, there is a sense in which I can know exactly what it is, and how it is, considered as a physical object, without knowing that it was made for a purpose. An identical object could have come into existence by chance or could have been made just for fun, and I could know exactly what it was, and how it was, considered as a physical object, without knowing about tables.

We do not have to know how gold came to be (as a result of nuclear fusion inside stars) to know what its essential nature is, qua gold. Similarly, we do not have to know how conscious thought or sensation or desire came to be to know what its essential nature is, qua conscious thought or sensation or desire. Gold could possibly have come to exist in a different way from the way in which it actually came to exist and still be what it is. So too conscious thoughts, sensations, and desires could possibly have come to exist in a different way from the way in which they actually came to exist and still be what they are.

To give a satisfactory account of the essential nature of things like conscious thought, sensation, and desire, then, we do not have to know that they evolved, still less that they evolved because they had a certain function: that of helping their possessors to negotiate a nonmental world. They are what they are, however they came to be. (Here I am in conflict with Millikan 1984, 1993.) And if a being *B*, qualitatively identical to a human being, were to come into existence by chance, we could not plausibly say that its apparent conscious thoughts, sensations, and desires were really no such things at all, simply because they had the wrong origins and were not the product of a process of evolution. Some philosophers have been tempted by such a claim, but no sensible naturalism could possibly require one to make it (compare Papineau 1987, 72–75). The case of sensation is plainest. Suppose the sensation of pain first came into existence as the result of random mutation. Did it fail to be painful until it proved to have survival value? No. Suppose that random mutation gave rise to a trait that had the consequence that occurrences highly beneficial to the organism caused sensations of pain and that this trait soon died out. Did these sensations fail to be painful? No.

We can say that *B* is not really a human being, not really a member of the species *Homo sapiens sapiens,* and we can say this because *B* has the wrong causal ancestry, and even if *B* can interbreed with human beings. We can say that something not made as a table or a knife is not really a table or a knife because it was not made as one, or that a drink qualitatively identical to Laphroaig is not Laphroaig, or even whisky, because it was not made in Scotland, or on the isle of Islay. But we can't, I submit, plausibly take the same line about *B*'s apparent mentality. Suppose that what it is like for *B*, experientially speaking, is exactly the same as what it would be like for you if you were walking on Weymouth Sands with a headache, hoping for the sun to break through, and wondering whether every even number is the sum of two prime numbers. To invoke *B*'s origins in order to reach the conclusion that *B* *really* has no conscious thoughts, sensations, or desires in this case would be like saying that the hemoglobin in *B* is not really hemoglobin, because it has not got the right causal history—thereby committing oneself to the view that it is logically impossible to synthesize hemoglobin.

Some philosophers seem committed by their conception of naturalism to granting that *B* has real hemoglobin while denying that *B* has real thought or desire. But this difference of attitude may indicate a failure to be thoroughgoing in one's naturalistic materialism, rather than constituting a necessary part of it. It may be a new manifestation of the old tendency to treat the mental as somehow metaphysically special. It may involve a failure to think through the consequences of the materialist view that conscious mental phenomena are just one more variety of physical phenomenon and must therefore be potentially reduplicable by a chance collocation of atoms, like all the other physical properties of human beings.[8]

Even if one is determined to withhold terms like 'desire', 'sensation', and 'thought' in this case and substitute other neutral terms like '*X*', '*Y*', one still has a problem. One still has a variety of real phenomena

8. Obviously, conscious mental phenomena are reduplicable only when considered at the purely experiential level of description (see chapter 1, section 6). *B*'s apparent thought that Hillary Rodham Clinton is president of the United States is not in fact about Mrs. Clinton, even if it is just like your thought, experientially speaking.

whose claim to be called 'mental' is powerful, even if they are not desires or sensations but only Xs and Ys; phenomena whose connection with the nonmental cannot be established by an appeal to evolution in the way that the fifth argument proposes.[9]

I conclude, somewhat rapidly, that this "naturalistic" argument for the centrality of reference to the nonmental in an adequate account of the mental does not succeed and that the possibility that the answer to the three questions may be 'No' has not yet been ruled out.

Overall, I am less concerned with the first question than with the second or third, but in the next three chapters I will say something about materialism and idealism in order to provide more materials for thinking about the first question.

9. A final protest: Reference to the nonmental is essential in the case of certain sensations, at least, because they involve, by definition, a physical (nonmental) sense organ and an external physical cause. Reply: We cannot prove the reality of the physical world just by pointing to the existence of those occurrences we call 'sensations'. So long as we have failed to prove that Berkeleyan idealism is metaphysically impossible, we have to acknowledge the possibility that mental occurrences of the sort we call 'sensations' may be able to exist, with all their familiar characteristics, without any physical thing existing.

3

Agnostic Materialism, Part 1

3.1 Introduction

Belief in the truth of materialism is a matter of faith and needs to be tempered by agnosticism. This is particularly apparent when it comes to the "mind-body" problem.

In arguing for this view, I will start with a fairly general discussion of monism. I think that reflection on some traditional metaphysical options can give us a better understanding of what we are doing when we declare ourselves to be, say, materialists.

The dispute between dualists and monists has long been central to the mind-body problem, but I will ignore it and stick to monist theories. Classical dualism faces well-known problems, and there seems to be no reason to think that monism, in one form or another, cannot deliver everything that dualists have traditionally wanted. (Immortality of the soul can be provided for by monist hypotheses that are no more extravagant than standard dualist hypotheses.) This said, it is worth adding that some dualists may recognize something close to their own position in at least one of the monist positions described below.

In fact, there are considerable unclarities in the notion of monism. These deserve a mention. Monists hold that there is, in spite of all the variety in the world, some fundamental sense in which there is only one basic kind of stuff. But questions about how many kinds of stuff or thing there are are answerable only relative to a particular point of view or interest. The following question duly arises. What point of view is so privileged that it allows one to say that it is some sort of absolute metaphysical fact that there is only one kind of thing or stuff in reality? Materialists call themselves monists, for they think that all things are of one kind: the physical. But many of them also believe that there is more than one kind of *elementary* particle. And to believe this is arguably to believe that there isn't after all any fundamental single stuff out of which all these elementary particles are constituted, insofar as they are themselves, in their diversity, the ultimate constituents of reality. That is, it is arguably to believe that there is kind plurality or stuff plurality right at the bottom of things.

To this it may first be replied that the elementary particles are nevertheless all *physical*, and in that sense of one kind. But to say that they can be classed together as single-substanced in this way is just a verbal decision and question-begging until it is backed by a positive theoretical account of why it is correct to say that they are all ultimately (constituted) of one kind (of substance). To claim that their causal interaction sufficiently proves them to be of the same substance is to beg the question in another way, for classical substance dualists simply deny that causal interaction entails being of the same substance.

It may be replied that all the elementary particles *are* in some sense different forms of the same stuff—energy, say. Or it may be said that the so-called elementary particles are not strictly speaking elementary and are in fact all constituted by just one kind of thing: superstrings or twistors. And probably something can be made of these suggestions. I will not pursue them any further, however. Prefaced by the above doubts, the usual notion of monism will serve well enough for present purposes.

My problem is the old problem, and I will initially state it in the standard terminology (later I will argue that materialists must abandon this terminology): What is the relation between mental phenomena and physical phenomena? More restrictedly, what is the relation between the phenomena of conscious experience and physical phenomena? In other words, what is the relation between *experience* and *matter*? What is the relation between the reality of experience as we have it from moment to moment and physical reality as we take ourselves to know it in everyday life and in science?

This question about experience is the difficult question. I think that it is really all there is to the mind-body problem: nothing else that we are inclined to think of as mental raises any really deep philosophical difficulty, so far as the general mind-body problem is concerned.

I will defend this view in section 4.4 and again, indirectly, in section 6.6 and chapter 7. Meanwhile, I will use the words 'mental' and 'experiential' almost interchangeably; not because they mean the same but because experiential phenomena are the only ones that cause real difficulties when it comes to the mind-body problem, even if there are also many nonexperiential mental phenomena. Much recent discussion has focused on desires, beliefs, and other dispositional "propositional attitudes," which are not intrinsically experience involving, even if it is true that they can be correctly attributed only to beings that are capable of experience. This may be partly because such propositional-attitude phenomena appear to be relatively easy to deal with in a standard materialist framework, when compared with experiential phenomena. All the more reason, then, to concentrate on the latter.

Now for a terminological preliminary, prepared for in chapter 1 but worth repeating. Most philosophers are materialists who suppose that experiences have nonconscious or nonexperiential aspects as well as conscious or experiential aspects. They may very well be right, and I will reserve the plural-accepting, count-noun use of 'experience' for talking of experiences as things—events—that may have nonexperiential properties as well as experiential properties. By contrast, I will reserve the adjective 'experiential', and the noun 'experience' considered as a mass term that has no plural, for talking about the character that experiences have just insofar as they involve conscious experience. I will take these words to refer only to the "what-it's-like-ness" characteristics of experience considered in all their variety. No one sensible denies that this what-it's-like-ness exists. Here I am co-opting two words to refer to it in a general way. What am I talking about? I can adequately secure the reference by saying that you know what it is like from your own case, as you look about you, burn your finger, etc. (a theoretical defense of this move is given on pp. 243–247 below).

When I speak of 'experience' or 'experiential phenomena', then, I am not concerned with any properties that particular experiences may have insofar as they are, as events, describable in terms that do not advert to their conscious or phenomenal or experiential character—e.g., the terms of physics or computational science. Nor am I concerned with any *relational* properties that experiences may have insofar as they are caused by one object rather than another. I am concerned only with the overall qualitative or experiential character of experience: with everything about one's experience that could possibly be just the same if one were not located in a physical world as one thinks, but were rather a Berkeleyan mind or a "brain in a vat" or something even stranger. In the present terms, experience is *just* a matter of what-it's-like-ness—of the overall, indescribably complex experiential character that experiences have for those who have them as they have them. Experience is a matter of everything that life is like for those who live it as they live it—dogs or bats or human beings. Experiential phenomena are those phenomena that are entirely constituted by experiences' having the experiential character they have for those who have them as they have them. It is important to bear this in mind, and I will recall it at various points.

3.2 Monism

I have assumed that a satisfactory account of the relation between experience and matter must be monist. So what are the possible positions for monists?

If one stands back far enough, there are four. Monists assert that there is a fundamental sense in which all things are of the same single type, in spite of all the variety in the world. Compatible with this, they may hold any of the following positions:

[1] There is a fundamental sense in which reality is only physical.

[2] There is a fundamental sense in which reality is only mental.

[3] There is a fundamental sense in which reality is neither mental nor physical, as we understand these terms.

[4] Reality is, in its essential single-substanced nature, both mental and physical, both experiential and physical.

Given the structure of this fourfold division the thought behind (4) must be that single-substanced reality is both experiential and physical in such a way that neither (1) nor (2) can be true.

Each of the positions may be given a name: (1) is *materialism*, (2) is *idealism*, and (3) may be called *neutral monism*, although this use of the name may not exactly coincide with its historical use.

Position (4) is less familiar. I will call it *mental and physical monism*, or M&P monism for short, and initially define it quite weakly as follows: According to M&P monism, reality is both mental (experiential) and physical while being substantially single in some way W we cannot yet claim to understand, though we take it to be true by definition that W is a way of being substantially single that does not involve any sort of *asymmetry* between the status of claims that reality is physical in character and claims that reality is mental or experiential in character. The no-asymmetry claim makes (4) incompatible with (1) or (2), given the traditional terms of debate.

Mindful of the positivist impulse to say that debate about differences between the four positions is vacuous, I will suggest that one can espouse (1) without slighting the claims of the mental or experiential in any way. In this I agree with many other materialists, who want to say that in some sense there are only physical phenomena but who also want to grant the undeniable and say that experiential phenomena, as characterized at the end of section 3.1, are fully real.

It is easy to see what this requires one to go on to say, if one is a materialist. It requires one to say that experiential phenomena just are physical phenomena. But if they are, then it seems that we must be ignorant of the nature of the physical in some fundamental way, for experiential phenomena (remember the characterization in section 3.1) just do not show up in what we think of as our best account of the nature of the physical: physics (or physics plus the sciences that we take to be reducible to physics).[1] There is truth in Nagel's remark that "physicalism [or materialism] is a position we cannot understand because we do not at present have any conception of how it might be true" (1979, 176). If we are not seriously ignorant of the nature of the physical, then it looks as if dualism is, after all, the most plausible option when it comes to the mind-body problem. Or so I will suggest.

---

1. I take it that this includes chemistry, biology, geography, and so on. The reducibility claim I have in mind is *not* the (highly dubious) claim that the properties alluded to in the laws or lawlike generalizations of these special sciences have neatly or even finitely specifiable counterparts in physical theory. It is rather that if we look at the details of any process that is naturally identified as a distinctively biological or chemical (etc.) process, we will be able, step by step, to give an account in terms of physical theory of why what happens happens as it does.

3.3 The Linguistic Argument

There are at least three objections to the fourfold classification given in section 3.2. First, there is the positivist inclination to say that the classification, with its apparent differentiation of metaphysically distinct but empirically indistinguishable possibilities, is vacuous, like all metaphysics. I have some sympathy for this inclination, but I think that it is excessive—undecidability does not entail vacuity—and that we are in any case condemned to metaphysics (see section 3.10). It is particularly important for materialists to realize that they cannot adopt a fully fledged positivist position while continuing to call themselves materialists. For to be a materialist is to go beyond the empirically available evidence and into metaphysics.

I will say more about this when discussing the second objection, according to which facts about language make all monists M&P monists, whether they are prepared to admit it or not. The third objection considers the fact that many contemporary materialists wish to count themselves as occupying some version of position (4), although they have been classified as occupying position (1), and concludes that the distinction between (4) and (1) is dubious. I will return to the third objection in section 3.4 after discussing the second objection.

The second objection goes as follows.

a. As we currently have them, the terms 'mental' and 'physical' undoubtedly have a correct application to phenomena that we encounter in everyday life. For they undoubtedly have a correct use as applied to such phenomena, and it follows immediately that they have a correct application to—that they really mean or denote—phenomena that we encounter in everyday life.

b. Insofar as they have a correct application to things that we encounter in everyday life, the terms 'mental' and 'physical' are natural-kind terms or are at least importantly similar to natural-kind terms in their semantic (and in particular referential) behavior.

c. Hence reality is *certainly* both mental and physical in its essential nature. For 'mental' and 'physical' *just mean* the phenomena encountered in everyday life (thoughts, sensations, rocks, radishes) to which the terms 'mental' and 'physical' are correctly applied by those who have mastered their use, *whatever* hidden nature these things may have and however little we know about them. Hence position (4) must be correct. M&P monism must be true if monism is true.[2]

Metaphysics is not so easy. Premisses (a) and (b) may both be questioned. But another way to try to reply to this argument in favor of (4) is to suggest that even if we grant its general drift, it still leaves room for us to distinguish positions of types (1), (2), and (3) within its compass.

Thus neutral monists, defenders of position (3), may argue as follows: The terms 'mental' and 'physical' can be allowed to have referential force that is somehow similar to the referential force of natural-kind

2. This is a version of an old antirealist line of argument, and is reminiscent of the "paradigm-case argument". Those who accept that 'physical' is a natural-kind term may doubt that 'mental' or 'experiential' is, on the ground that it covers a diffuse variety of things, or on the ground that mental or experiential phenomena can be physically realized or substantially realized in various different ways, and therefore cannot be supposed to have a single "essential nature". If, however, we hold [1] that the experiential is physically realized, or at least realized in or by something nonexperiential, and also grant [2] that if (1) is true, then the experiential may possibly be *variably* realized, what follows is not that experience doesn't have an essential nature, but only that its essential nature is not a function of what realizes it. Consider the analogy of pain, and let 'P' be the supposed essence-defining property of pain (thus pain has P in every possible world, and nothing can possibly be pain which does not have P). It follows from the fact that pain may be physically realized in an indefinite variety of ways that P cannot be any particular physical-realization property (I ignore the theoretical possibility that each mental kind is in fact correlated with a single physical kind that is not detectable as such, given current physical theory; compare Heil 1992, 133–134). It does not follow that pain has no essence. That is, it does not follow that there is no feature that all pain occurrences have in common in every possible world and that, so to say, makes them pain. I take it that what they all have essentially in common, in spite of their possible differences in respect of physical realization and their possible differences in respect of qualitative character, is simply their property of being experienced as unpleasant by those who have them as they have them. (Masochists constitute no objection to this view.) Similarly, what all cases of experience have in common—their essential characteristic—is just their "something-it-is-like-ness" for those who have them.
   In fact, the present argument does not need to show that 'mental' or 'experiential' is any sort of natural-kind term. Dualists or idealists may perhaps say that there are just the same sorts of reason for saying this about 'mental' as there appear to be for saying it about 'physical'. But all the present argument needs is the claim that the semantic behavior of the term 'mental' or 'experiential' may be importantly similar to that of a natural-kind term, or even a proper name.

terms. But they also have definite *descriptive* force, and this being so, it seems intelligible to suppose that they could go dramatically wrong; to such an extent that the best thing to say about the nature of reality might be that it is not really either mental or physical, *as we conceive of these things* (God, as it were, might not think much of these descriptive categories). This is apparently Kant's position in the *Critique of Pure Reason*, where he writes, "Neither the transcendental object which underlies outer [physical] appearances, nor that which underlies inner intuition [or mental appearances], is in itself either matter or a thinking being." It is rather "a ground (to us unknown) of the appearances which supply to us the empirical concept of the former as well as of the latter mode of existence" (Kant 1933, A380; see also A358–A359).

There are many difficulties here. But perhaps one can give sense to the idea that our terms 'mental' and 'physical' are deeply inadequate, as descriptions of reality, by means of an analogy. Imagine a physical creature that has a pattern of electrical impulses transmitted to its brain with the result that it has color experience and nothing else. It has no conception of electrical impulse or of physical objects. From our point of view, it simply does not have the resources to attain any kind of adequate conception of the nature of the reality with which it has to do. And perhaps there is a point of view from which our conceptions look similarly inadequate. We cannot know that this is not the case. It is a constant lesson of contemporary science that things are almost unimaginably strange, relative to our ordinary view of them. And for all those things that are almost unimaginably strange but of which we take ourselves to have some inkling by means of various sorts of theoretical construction, there are, no doubt, other things that are entirely unimaginable by us. The mysteriousness, for us, of the relation between the experiential and the physical-as-discerned-by-physics is itself an example and a sign of how much is at present, and perhaps for ever, beyond us.

As a defense of neutral monism, this is at best only partially convincing. For the neutral-monist claim (at least as presented here) is much easier to make sense of in the case of 'physical' than in the case of 'mental'. At some future stage of evolution, we might conceivably come to think that there was not much to choose between twentieth-century physics and tenth-century folklore. But it seems that we cannot be as wrong about the mental, and in particular the experiential, as we can be about the physical. No account of reality can be correct if, for example, it denies that experience of pain is really (or ultimately) real, or holds that there may be some sense in which we are *entirely* wrong about the real nature of pains we undergo even as we undergo them. For their real nature unquestionably includes their experiential character, whatever else it may include. And as regards their experiential character, how they seem is how they are. There is no room for error of the sort envisaged.

Philosophers may conceivably propose a radically new theory of what pain really is, and say that relative to this theory, our experience of pain can correctly be characterized as illusion or mere seeming. The reply is immediate, however: *whatever* the proposal, the seeming is itself and ineliminably a real thing, and whatever the nature of the universe, it is what we denote when we use the word 'pain'. (I reject Wittgensteinian objections to this claim in chapter 8.) There is simply no room for total error, for the seeming is unquestionably real, and the seeming just is the reality in question.

Philosophy is so good at breeding doubt that one may need to do an exercise: to look around one, experience what one experiences, and ask oneself 'Could this experience just not exist? Could I be completely wrong about this? Could there be no experience or consciousness at all? Could there really be nothing it is like to be me, experientially speaking, at this moment?' The answer 'No' comes quickly and correctly, as it came to Descartes. What is it to suppose that one might be completely wrong? It is to suppose that although it *seems* to one that there is experience—for this cannot be denied—there really isn't any experience. But this is an immediate reductio ad absurdum. For this seeming is already experience.

It has been suggested that experience might not really be a matter of qualitative character or phenomenology at all, that it might somehow be wholly the product of some cognitive faculty, the "judgment module" or "semantic intent module," and that we might to that extent be entirely deluded about its nature. Thinking along some such lines, Dennett has suggested that "there is no such thing [as] . . . phenomenology." "*There seems to be phenomenology*," he concedes, "but it does *not* follow from this undeniable, universally attested fact that *there really is* phenomenology" (1991b, 365–366; compare Rey 1993). It is very unclear what Dennett means by 'phenomenology', but this move fails immediately if it is taken as an objection to the present claim that we can be certain both that there is experience and that we cannot be radically in error about its nature. It fails for the simple reason already given: for there to seem to be rich phenomenology or experience *just is* for there to be such phenomenology or experience. To say that its apparently sensory aspects (say) are in some sense illusory because they are not the product of sensory mechanisms in the way we suppose, but are somehow generated by our processes of judgment, is just to put forward a surprising hypothesis about part of the *mechanism* of this rich seeming that we call experience or consciousness. It is in no way to put in question its existence or reality. *Whatever* the process by which the seeming arises, the end result of the process is, as even Dennett agrees, at least this: that it *seems* as if one is having phenomenally rich experience of Beethoven's fifteenth quartet or of Hong Kong lit up for Christmas. And if there is this seeming, then, once again, there just is phenomenology or experience. (See Strawson 1992. The attack of italics is prompted by the realization that however one puts the point, there will always be ingenious ways of misreading it.)

The point is quite general. Philosophical theories that attribute radical error to us depend on the idea that we are very wrong about how things are, given our experience. But then there must at least be experience. If there is illusion, the occurrence of illusion must itself be real and involve experience. Let us suppose that we are wrong about the nature of the mental in many ways. The fact remains that we can be sure that our existing general concept of conscious experience is, as it stands, correctly applicable to reality.

Once again, however wrong we may be about the mechanisms that underlie conscious experience, we are not wrong about the existence or general nature of conscious experience considered just as an experiential phenomenon in the sense of section 3.1. It seems that some philosophers want to say that sensations are really just judgments. Let them, so long as they grant that the class of judgments or judgings, considered as episodes of our lives, can contain all the experiential differences that ordinary people find between thinking about entailment, mourning a child's death, burning one's finger, and descending the water chute on Splash Mountain. Let them say that sensations are really just judgments, so long as they are prepared to grant that the ordinary view makes no error about the qualitative or experiential or lived differences between the four things mentioned in the last sentence. Writing after a very painful ear infection and after having had to hold my daughter down in a hospital casualty department while she underwent incompetent treatment, I find the suggestion that common sense makes any error about the qualitative or experiential or lived nature of pain inexplicable except as an extreme case of theory-driven Procrusteanism. If there is any sense in which these philosophers are rejecting the ordinary view of the nature of the experience of things like pain, their view seems intellectually and morally surd. If there is no sense in which they are rejecting it, they have not made themselves clear. As it stands, their view seems to be one of the most amazing manifestations of human irrationality on record. (It is much less irrational to postulate the existence of a divine being whom we cannot perceive than to deny the truth of the commonsense view of experience. Note that scepticism about other minds involves no such denial. It merely points out that one can't know for certain that other people have experience.) The British empiricists were mocked for treating thinking as a species of (inner) sensation. The new fashion for treating sensation as a species of thinking is hardly more plausible.

Neutral monists got into trouble with the linguistic argument because of their indefensible claim that experience itself might be mere appearance, not really real at all. Perhaps materialists and idealists can do better, while continuing to make their distinctive and opposing claims. Thus materialists can agree that our mental terms, as well as our physical terms, have some sort of genuine referential force, while insisting that the truth about the essential nature of the (real) things we talk about, when we talk in mental terms, is precisely that they are *really* just physical. And idealists can agree that our physical terms, as well as our mental terms, have some sort of genuine referential force, while insisting that the truth about the essential nature of the things we talk about, when we talk in physical terms, is precisely that they are *really* just mental. Both sides can make the same sorts of move as the neutral monists, differing from them only in claiming that one of the two disputed concepts is, in virtue of its descriptive force, essentially accurate in representing the nature of reality in a way in which the other is not.

Here again, however, it looks as if the idealists have the advantage. For, very briefly, idealists seem readily intelligible (if strange) when they say that physical phenomena do not really exist at all and that all that really exist, so far as apparently physical phenomena are concerned, are certain mental phenomena, i.e., experiences that appear to be of a physical world. To this extent, idealists can take our ordinary view of what the physical is—something entirely mind-independent in nature—to involve some sort of total illusion. If materialists equate 'really just physical' with 'nonmental' or 'nonexperiential', they cannot make the same move. They cannot take our view of the mental or experiential to involve some sort of total illusion. They cannot hope to treat experience itself as some sort of total illusion, for illusion presupposes—it is a form of—experience.

Anyone who doubts this has to face the fact that if experience is indeed a total illusion, then we are (right now) totally experienceless creatures. This is not believable. As remarked, there is truth in the old view that we can know for certain that we have experience that appears to us to have a certain character, whatever else we can or cannot know; and there is truth in the old view that we can be certain that we have experience in a way in which we cannot be certain that there is mind-independent or nonexperiential reality. If one is determined to be a monist, then it is arguable that idealism is the easiest or smoothest option; which is not to say it is the most plausible.

So much for the linguistic argument. It cannot hope to settle the question in favor of M&P monism. It cannot, for example, establish the incoherence of the idealist hypothesis that the business of our having experiences, including experiences that we take to be experiences of a physical world, involves nothing remotely like anything postulated in our current theory of physics.

It is also in danger of being too powerful. Suppose that all sides agree with the basic realist view that it is reasonable, when thinking generally about the nature of things, to suppose that there exists something that is other than oneself and that affects one (whatever one is oneself) and that is the cause of those of one's experiences that appear to be experiences of a physical world. Proponents of the linguistic argument may then say that this something is correctly called 'physical', *whatever it is*. But then Berkeley's God is a physical thing, and nobody is really disagreeing with anybody else (as some positivists have always insisted). On this view, 'physical' becomes like a mere proper name with no descriptive force at all, and no one need disagree with the linguistic argument, because it amounts to little more than the claim that we use the word 'physical', and use it in the way we use it.

Some may think that the linguistic argument is a sideshow, but it raises important issues. It casts doubt on the coherence of the metaphysical speculations that come so naturally to us ("hard-nosed" materialists or "identity theorists" are up to their ears in metaphysics). Equally important, it dramatizes the fact that there is a strong tension between a descriptively committed use of the term 'physical' and a less descriptively committed, natural-kind-term-like (or, at the limit, proper-name-like) use. The tension is a source of potentially bewildering indeterminacy: it is right that we should be ready to admit the incompleteness of our understanding of the nature of the physical and still feel able to go on talking of the physical—of the physical-whatever-exactly-its-nature. And yet we would presumably go too far if we began to treat 'the physical' as a mere proper name, so that we were *indefeasibly* correct in asserting the existence of the physical, since the word now meant 'whatever it is that gives rise to the experiences that we think of as experiences of physical phenomena'. (See Putnam 1981; compare Crane and Mellor 1990, Pettit 1993.)

3.4 Materialism and M&P Monism

According to the third objection to the fourfold classification of positions, the distinction between (1) and (4)—between materialism and M&P monism—is dubious, for the former can swallow the latter. This is because sane materialists, being sane, are determined to make adequate room for the fact that the experiential is real—as real as the nonexperiential physical, as apprehended by physics. Faced with the vivid facts of experience, sane materialists are obliged to be as realist in their attitude to the experiential as M&P monists. And such realism is probably standard among materialists, although not universal. It is typically endorsed by the majority, who call themselves 'nonreductive identity theorists' or 'nonreductive monists'. (They have this name, very briefly, because they endorse the *irreducibility thesis*: the thesis that although mental goings-on are identical with physical goings-on, statements attributing mental properties cannot be reduced to—cannot in any sense be equivalent to—statements containing only the nonmental terms of physics.)

The question therefore arises, Are (standard, nonreductive) materialism and M&P monism really the same thing? Can't standard nonreductive materialism count as a version of M&P monism? I will begin by arguing that it cannot, and I will continue to concentrate on the experiential rather than on the mental in general, on the grounds that the experiential is the only part of the mental that causes any real difficulty so far as the mind-body problem is concerned.

'Materialism' is a capacious term, and I will later argue that some forms of materialism can be counted as forms of M&P monism. It seems nevertheless that no standard materialists can claim that they are really M&P monists, given the definition of M&P monism at the end of section 3.2. This is because standard materialists are committed to the *asymmetry thesis*. That is, they are committed to the idea that there is a crucial asymmetry in the status of mental and physical phenomena given which it is correct to say:

[1] that the mental is based in, or realized by, or otherwise dependent on, the physical,

and incorrect to say either

[2] that the physical is based in, or realized by, or otherwise dependent on, the mental

or

[3] that they coexist in such a way that neither can be said to be based in, or realized by, or in any way asymmetrically dependent on, the other.

(Idealists may reverse 'physical' and 'mental' in the last sentence, or say something to the same general effect.)

The issue of asymmetry splits the four positions into two groups. Positions (1) and (2), materialism and idealism, are asymmetry theories.

Indeed (and unsurprisingly) both tend toward the strong asymmetry of *reductionism*, which I will consider in sections 3.5 and 3.7.

Positions (3) and (4), by contrast—M&P monism and neutral monism—are *equal-status* theories. They grant equal status to the mental and the physical, albeit in different ways, since one says that reality is ultimately and irreducibly both mental and physical, and the other says that it is neither.

This equal-status/asymmetry difference may look like a clear difference between the M&P-monist position and standard materialist monist positions. However, things are not so clear. Consider materialists who say, 'Experiences are fully real, and they are physical phenomena in every respect. That is, even their having the phenomenal or experiential character they do just is a physical phenomenon.' These materialists appear to endorse the claim that was supposed to define M&P monism in section 3.2: the claim that reality is both experiential and physical, while being substantially single in some way we cannot at present understand, although we may take it that there is no asymmetry between the status of claims that reality is physical in character and the status of claims that reality is experiential in character.

Furthermore, materialists who say this kind of thing are not eccentric. On the contrary. All serious materialists must say this, for they must admit the reality of experience (it is still, after many centuries of philosophy, the thing of which we can be most certain), and they hold that reality is purely physical, and the rest follows immediately: natural reality (nature) is entirely physical; all natural properties of physical things are entirely physical properties; all experiential properties of physical things are natural properties; hence all experiential properties are themselves entirely physical properties. To put this in terms of phenomena rather than in terms of properties: all natural phenomena are wholly physical phenomena; experiential phenomena are wholly natural phenomena; hence experiential phenomena are wholly physical phenomena.

Serious materialists, then, must hold that experiences (mental phenomena in general) are physical phenomena in *every* respect, and hence even in respect of their having the experiential character they have; and thus not just in respect of their having the character they appear to have to physics and neurophysiology as they inspect the brain. So they cannot talk of the physical *as opposed to* the mental or experiential at all. If they do talk like this—and they do all the time—they can only really mean to talk of the nonexperiential physical as opposed to the experiential physical (or the nonmental physical as opposed to the mental physical). When it comes to the mind-body problem, the distinction that concerns them cannot be a distinction between the mental and the physical, because any distinction must be drawn entirely *within* the realm of the physical, on their view. If one is a materialist, to say that there is a fundamental distinction between mental or experiential phenomena and physical phenomena is like saying that there is a fundamental distinction between cows and animals—that on the one hand there are cows and on the other hand there are animals.

Certainly the mental/physical distinction seems very natural. Materialist books and articles about the mind-body problem speed along in the standard idiom. But the question always arises: what exactly are they saying, given their materialist premise? What they tend to mean is that there is a problem about the relation between the experiential or mental, on the one hand, and the physical *as conceived of by current physics*, on the other hand. And, of course, there is. This is the whole problem, and it is the old problem.[3] But to be a materialist is to believe that the experiential is as much of a physical phenomenon as electric charge. It is to hold that there is no more ontological difficulty in the idea that physical things can have the wholly physical property of having experience, as well as the physical properties currently discerned by physics, than there is in the idea that physical things can have mass as well as extension.

Now let me try to block a misunderstanding, by recalling the ruling about the words 'experience' (in the noncount-noun use) and 'experiential' in section 3.1. When I say that the experiential *just is* physical, or that experiential properties *just are* physical properties, I don't mean to be saying anything like what I think some materialists have meant by saying such things as that 'Experience is really just neurons firing'. I don't mean to be saying that all that is really going on is what can be

3. Perhaps it only came to seem acute in the sixteenth and seventeenth centuries, when the evolution of a scientific conception of the physical as nothing more than particles in motion made it unclear how experiential phenomena could be physical.

discerned and accounted for by current physics, or what could be discerned and accounted for by any nonrevolutionary or conceptually conservative extension of current physics. Such a view is obviously false (it amounts to some kind of radical eliminativism). It follows from the ruling in section 3.1 that to say that the experiential just is physical is not to say anything like this. For, given section 3.1, 'the experiential' here refers *only* to that part of reality which consists of: the (indisputably real) phenomenon of experiences' having the qualitative, experiential character they do for those who have them as they have them. It is this—the experiential as such, the portion of reality we have to do with when we consider experiences specifically and solely in respect of the experiential character they have for those who have them as they have them—that *just is* physical. It is your experience considered solely in respect of the experiential character it has for you right now that just is physical, and that must, specifically in respect of its complex experiential character, be as comprehensively accounted for by any hypothetical complete physics as the motions of billiard balls; if materialism is true.

3.5   A Comment on Reduction

This point has consequences for the question of reduction, and I will now and in section 3.7 comment briefly on this.

Reductionism has many varieties—one may, for example, distinguish between semantic and ontological reductionism—but I wish to say as little about this as possible, because I do not think it matters much for present purposes.[4] I will treat reduction as a relation between properties

4. Generally, the issue of reduction arises when it is suspected that what seems to be talk about two sorts of thing is really talk in two different vocabularies about only one sort of thing. Semantic reductionism is explicitly stated as a thesis about language, and says that the content of sentences in a certain (e.g., mentalistic) vocabulary can be expressed without loss in another (e.g., physical-science) vocabulary. Such semantic reductionism may be distinguished from ontological reductionism, and it seems that one can endorse the latter without endorsing the former, but I think there is a key sense in which they ultimately come down to the same thing. Roughly, faced with the two vocabularies, both versions of reductionism claim that the aspects of reality apparently talked about by means of the first vocabulary are not really ontologically distinct from the aspects of reality talked about by means of the second vocabulary.

rather than sentences or statements (the talk of properties can always be converted into talk of sentences or statements). I will suppose the fundamental entailment of 'x is reducible to y' to be 'x is (fully) theoretically explicable by reference to y' and take the notion of explanation for granted until section 4.3. (Here it may help to note that a strong and well-confirmed correlation statement of the form 'x occurs when and only when y occurs' is no sort of explanation.) To keep things simple, I will restrict my attention to basic, sensory experiential properties like the property of having color experience or sound experience.

One reason for doing this is as follows. Some materialists feel that experiential phenomena like the phenomenon of someone's consciously wondering whether Goldbach's Conjecture is true are patently irreducible to the terms of physics (although they are wholly physical phenomena), because their explication necessarily involves reference to linguistic conventions, and so on. It is quite unclear that they can take this position if they accept the asymmetry thesis (p. 56), but I will leave the questions raised by such phenomena until chapter 7, because the point I wish to make can be made by reference to more basic, sensory experiential properties like having color experience.

If one is a materialist and a real realist about experiential properties, then one holds that experiential properties like the property of having color experience just are physical properties, as remarked in the last section. For they are real, natural properties of natural living things, and all such properties are physical. As a materialist, then, it seems that one faces a choice. Either experiential properties, being natural physical properties, are reducible to other natural physical properties, in something like the way we take physical properties like liquidity or acidity to be, or they are not. But if they are not so reducible, then at least some of them must themselves be fundamental physical properties, like electric charge, not reducible to (or theoretically explicable in terms of) any other physical properties. There is no other plausible option, so long as one is a materialist and a (real) realist about experiential properties. It seems, then, that nonreductive materialist monists must hold at least some experiential properties to be fundamental physical properties, like electric charge, even if some experiential properties are reducible to others. They must hold this if they are real materialists.

Some will think this very alarming. And it is perhaps not surprising that many philosophers who think of themselves as materialists are not really realists about many mental properties. In particular, they tend not to be realists about dispositional propositional-attitude properties like believing that grass is green or liking olives. They see our talk of likes, beliefs, and so on, as placing some kind of useful explanatory grid over people and their behavior, and they hold that this grid does not really pick out or accurately describe the (ultimately) real properties of the things over which it is so successfully and irresistibly cast (for a good account of this, see Dennett 1991a).

I will say more about this view in sections 4.6 and 6.6. At present it is unimportant; one could even grant that it is wholly true. For here the primary concern is with occurrent experiential properties. These are the difficult properties when it comes to the mind-body problem, and they cannot possibly be thought to admit of any antirealist or irrealist treatment of the sort sometimes applied to dispositional propositional-attitude properties. So serious materialists do face the choice described two paragraphs back. By definition, they hold that the experiential (or phenomenal or what-it's-like-ness) properties of experiences are entirely physical properties (they are natural properties, and all natural properties are physical properties). So either these experiential physical properties are reducible to other, nonexperiential physical properties, and do not feature as fundamental in an optimal physics; or they are not reducible to nonexperiential physical properties, and at least some of them feature as fundamental in an optimal physics. There is no other possibility. Materialists who cannot accept the idea that experiential properties might be fundamental physical properties must suppose that their appearance of constitutive irreducibility to the terms of physics is an illusion, an artifact of the limits on human understanding and human physics.

To be a nonreductive materialist monist, then, is either to hold that reduction of experiential to nonexperiential properties is in principle possible, and that the appearance of irreducibility merely shows that human physics is fundamentally incomplete; or to hold that such reduction is in principle impossible. But to hold this second thing, as a materialist who is also a real realist about experiential properties, is simply to hold that experiential properties are—that experientiality is—among the fundamental properties that must be adverted to in a completed or optimal physics. Some have been lulled into thinking that there is a comfortable and strictly materialist middle position that combines rejection of the idea that any experiential properties are fundamental physical properties with endorsement of the idea that they are in principle irreducible to nonexperiential properties. To see that this won't do, one has to register fully the point that to be a materialist is to grant that these experiential properties are wholly physical properties.

3.6   The Impossibility of an "Objective Phenomenology"[5]

In theory a *panpsychist* version of materialism could handle the idea that experiential properties might be fundamental physical properties. I will say something about this in section 3.9. There is, however, a deep (insoluble) problem about the idea that adequate terms for experiential properties could ever come to feature in an optimal physics. The problem is simply that experiential phenomena outrun the resources of human language in a way that makes a human science of experiential phenomena look impossible.

The point can be made as follows: there is an experiential fact of the matter about what it is like for me, in respect of color experience and sound experience, when I look at and hear a red piano. So too there is an experiential fact of the matter about what it is like for you, in respect of color experience and sound experience, when you look at and hear the same piano. But even if you and I are fully similar in agreeing that we experience red and legato arpeggios in E-flat major, so that we count as fully similar (identical) so far as our best language for experiential phenomena goes, still we cannot know that we are similar (identical) in respect of our experiential properties. Our ordinary terms for experiential properties predicable of people ('sees green', 'feels a sharp pain in the head', 'smells cloves') can never be guaranteed to pick out objectively similar experiential properties when applied to different people. (I will ignore the point that they can't even be known to pick out objectively similar experiential properties when applied to the same person at different times.) What it is like for *A*, experientially speaking, when *A* has the property of smelling cloves, may well not be the same as what

5. This phrase is taken from Nagel 1979 but used in a rather different way.

it is like for *B*, experientially speaking, when *B* has the same property. Given that we will never be able to find out whether it is or is not the same, it seems clear that we will never be able to evolve a publicly and interpersonally applicable vocabulary for discriminating experiential phenomena that we can know to cut along the real (objective) lines of difference among experiential phenomena in such a way as to be capable in principle of being integrated with the existing objective-difference-discriminating terms of physics (see Jackson 1982). Even if we appealed to the "supervenience thesis" (see Kim 1982, 1984) to underwrite a judgment of true experiential sameness in the case in which *A* and *B* were demonstrably neurally identical, this would not provide a route to such a vocabulary.

Let me rephrase. It is an objective fact that there is something it is like for me to hear and see the piano. It is an objective fact that there is something it is like for you too, and for these identical twins standing beside us. And we may all fully agree in language about what it is like. But this doesn't prove that we are identical, experientially speaking. There remains a real and unanswerable question about whether the experience is the same or different for any two of us. We can never hope to establish directly that *A* and *B* are identical with respect to these sorts of experiential property, in the way that we can hope to be able to establish that they are identical with respect to some property discerned by current physics. There is nonetheless a fact of the matter. Just as there is a fact of the matter about whether the color experience of the piano is the same or different for the twins (a case that seems much easier to understand and accept), so too there is a fact of the matter about whether it is the same or different for any other two people.

Some find that this suggestion induces a kind of philosophical vertigo. They have a sense that the experiential contents of two subjective points of view are radically incommensurable—to such an extent that asking about sameness or difference doesn't really make sense. At the same time, common sense is clear on the point that experience of colors, sounds, smells, injections, and so on, is probably very much the same for others as it is for oneself; and the idea that there is a fact of the matter about whether color experience is the same or different for two different people is a necessary part of realism about the experiential. After all, there really is something my color experience is like for me, considered just as color experience, and there really is something your color experience is like for you, considered just as color experience. There is, therefore, a real question about sameness or difference, even if our awareness of its radical unanswerability makes the question seem bizarre.

Let me add a slightly more technical remark. My claim is not that nonexperiential or N properties cannot in fact be paired with experiential or E properties in correlation statements of the form '$[N_1 \to E_1]$'. It consists of two main points. [1] Even if we attempted to put forward correlation statements of the form '$[N_1 \to E_1]$', we could never hope to verify such statements across a human population by checking independently on E_1 and N_1 and thereby establishing the correlations, because we could never check independently on E_1. If we somehow knew some of the correlation statements to hold true in the case of a single individual, we could perhaps take their general truth to be guaranteed by the truth of the supervenience thesis, but it is unclear whether even this would be acceptable, given the extent of our ignorance of the nature of the physical. Further, even if some statement of the form '$[N_1 \to E_1]$' were somehow known to be true, the only people who could know for sure what 'E_1' referred to would be those who had been shown to have N_1 and had been told which of their experiences was specially correlated with, or realized by, N_1 ('It's whatever visual experience you are having . . . wait . . . now').

[2] We could never make a start on testing interpersonally applicable correlation statements of the form '$[E_1 \to N_1]$', because we could never be sure that we had distinguished the same experiential property in the case of two different people, even if they fully agreed in language about what experiences they were having. It is plausible that '$[E_1 \to N_1]$' correlation statements would have to be of the form '$[E_1 \to N_1 \vee N_2 \vee N_3 \vee \ldots]$': they would have to be disjunctive and open-ended on the right-hand side, because of the possible "variable physical realization" of any experiential property. The present point, however, is that even if one could identify exactly which nonexperiential neural goings-on were involved in the occurrence of a particular type of experience in one's own case, and at a given time, one could never fill out the disjunctive right-hand side of the correlation statement by including other people,

because one could never know that one was really dealing with the same type of experience in their case. End of the mildly technical remark.

The general difficulty raised in this section is important, but I will not pursue it. I mention it only to put it explicitly to one side. In this way I hope to make it clear that I am concerned with a problem for materialists that arises even on the assumption that this difficulty can be entirely solved. That is, the problem would be undiminished even if we came to possess a magic psychoscope that permitted an objective, interpersonally applicable classification of types of experience, allowing us to say that I am having color experience of type 1681 on the Objective Color Experience Scale when looking at the red piano, whereas you are having color experience of type 873; and thus allowing us to test the inverted color-spectrum hypothesis. The point is simple. Even if we had this magical machine and somehow knew that it worked and could establish an Objective Color Experience Scale, the mind-body problem would be undiminished. For, so long as we still possessed only the resources of current science, we would still have no account of how experience is possible, given everything we know of the physical.

It is possible to establish a list of names for distinct types of color experience without the impossible machine. One can do it by reference to a particular individual A, a set of times t_1-t_n, and a set of lighting conditions L. One may take a color-swatch book and rule that color experience of type 1 is color experience of the type that A has when looking at page 1 at t_1 in L, color experience of type 2 is color experience of the type that A has when looking at page 2 at t_2 in L, and so on. Here one can give names to real, objectively distinct types of color experience. The trouble with setting up this list of names is that it is theoretically useless. One cannot apply it to others; one does not even know what types of color experience are picked out by these terms (only A does). It is worth adding that one cannot escape from the problem by stressing the various sorts of indeterminacy affecting ascriptions of experiential content that are discussed by Dennett in his book *Consciousness Explained* (1991b). For these indeterminacies only make the problem worse.

So much for the impossibility of an objective phenomenology. I have suggested that even if it were not impossible, the mind-body problem would be untouched, and I will take this idea further in chapter 4. But let me first return to the issue of asymmetry.

3.7   Asymmetry and Reduction

Suppose that serious materialists grant what they must: that the experiential is just physical and is as real as any other part of the physical. Does this leave them with no room for any sort of asymmetry claim? That would be surprising. The idea that materialism involves some sort of asymmetry claim is extremely influential. And one reason why it seems so attractive is this: we find it natural to suppose that wherever and whenever there is experiential reality there is nonexperiential reality, but that the converse of this is not true—there can, we think, be nonexperiential reality without experience.[6] And this immediately makes it seem that experiential reality must *depend* on nonexperiential reality in some way.

So the natural materialist position seems to involve an asymmetry claim, and to be as follows: Experiential physical reality exists, and it is, of course, as real as nonexperiential physical reality, for there are no degrees of reality (*pace* Descartes), and so there can be no asymmetry in the reality status of experiential reality and nonexperiential reality. And yet there is an asymmetrical relation of dependence of experiential reality on nonexperiential reality. Or rather—a more complicated statement of the point seems worth while—there is an asymmetrical relation of existential dependence of experiential features of physical reality on features of physical reality that are taken account of in a physics that, like our current physics, contains predicates only for nonexperiential features of physical reality.

According to this view, then, some things have experiential physical properties, all things that have experiential physical properties also have nonexperiential physical properties, and they have the particular experiential physical properties they have in virtue of having certain of the

6. Stones, water, air, etc. We also believe that there was once no experiential reality on earth but plenty of nonexperiential reality, and that experiential reality came to exist as life evolved.

nonexperiential physical properties they have—whatever exactly 'in virtue of' means.[7]

This is a version of the asymmetry thesis given on p. 56, which may now be restated in terms of the distinction between the experiential and the nonexperiential rather than the distinction between the mental and the physical. It says [1] that the experiential is based in, or realized by, or otherwise dependent on, the nonexperiential, and that it is false to say either [2] that the nonexperiential is based in, or realized by, or otherwise dependent on, the experiential or [3] that they co-exist in such a way that neither can be said to be based in, or realized by, or in any way asymmetrically dependent on, the other. (It is arguable that the use of the idiom 'in virtue of' makes this a relatively strong version of the general dependency thesis, which is not forced on one merely by acceptance of the view that wherever there is experiential reality, there is nonexperiential reality but not conversely. See the last paragraph of this section.)

The asymmetry thesis can sound very plausible. But it is important to be clear about what it amounts to, if one is both a materialist and a realist (as one must be) about experiential properties. I suggest, to return to the theme of section 3.5, that it must in the end amount to the claim that experiential physical properties, like the property of having color experience, resemble nonexperiential physical properties, like liquidity,

---

7. In fact, there is no need to say that a being *B*'s experiential properties depend only on its own nonexperiential properties and do not also depend on certain of the wider world's nonexperiential properties. Nor is there any need to restrict attention to *B*'s nonrelational nonexperiential properties. I do these things here to bypass currently unimportant complications. It is natural to restrict attention to *B*'s own nonexperiential (and nonrelational) properties when one is considering *B*'s experiential properties only in respect of their narrow or purely experiential content, and I am at present concerned with the asymmetry thesis only as applied to phenomena discernible at the purely experiential level of description, the level at which I and my Twin Earth twin and vat-twin can be said to have identical experience (see section 1.6). One reason why these phenomena are all that need concern us at present is that the mind-body problem already arises in all its glory for a being whose experiences have no content relating to an external world. It arises in all its fullness for a being that suddenly comes into existence by chance and lies in a sealed room with its sense organs inoperative, while having experiences just like yours or mine on account of the internal activity of its brain.

in one crucial respect, *however much they may also differ from them*: they resemble such properties in being physical properties possessed by things in virtue of their possession of other physical properties that we naturally think of as more fundamental physical properties. The reason why it seems that this is all the asymmetry claim can really amount to is that it seems that this is really the only relevant sort of asymmetrical dependency that one natural physical property can be said to have on another, within the materialist scheme of things.

This conclusion about what the asymmetry thesis amounts to appears to have a striking consequence. It appears to have the consequence—which some will think clearly false—that if one accepts the asymmetry thesis, one must reject the irreducibility thesis (p. 56). and vice versa: given the asymmetry thesis, and materialism, it seems that experiential physical properties must be reducible to nonexperiential physical properties in a way that is ultimately similar to the way in which the property of liquidity is held to be reducible to van de Waals molecular-interaction properties, however great the difference between the two cases may also be. (The case of liquidity is not chosen because it is comfortable or tractable as an analogy. It isn't. There is no comfortable analogy, and that is part of the point.)

This reduction is very hard—impossible—to imagine. If one thinks of reduction in a standard way as semantic or ontological reduction (see n. 4), then it looks as if it amounts to the claim that when you have said all there is to say about a segment of the world (say a person) in nonexperiential terms, there is a fundamental sense in which you have described everything there is to describe. So although there may perhaps be other natural, perspicuous, and theoretically interesting ways of putting things, they will not advert to facts, or aspects of facts, other than those already detailed in nonexperiential terms. But this claim cannot possibly be true, for in deploying only nonexperiential terms, you will not have described the person's experience considered just as such. The problem is not diminished if one thinks of reduction in the way proposed in section 3.5, and takes the fundamental entailment of '*x* is reducible to *y*' to be '*x* is (fully) theoretically explicable by reference to *y*'. For how can the nature and existence of an experiential property be thought to be (fully) explained by reference to essentially nonexperiential properties?

So it is easy to sympathize with nonreductive monists who think the irreducibility thesis is just obviously true. But it is arguable that they will have to abandon the standard asymmetry thesis. They will either have to abandon the asymmetry thesis or treat the irreducibility thesis as a rather banal thesis about the limitations on human understanding. That is, they will have to grant that there is no irreducible irreducibility, that experiential properties are reducible to nonexperiential properties in some possible optimal physics, and that the appearance of irreducibility is just an illusion generated by human ignorance. This seems profoundly implausible, given the nature of the case. (The attractions of neutral monism seem more apparent than ever.)

Some may talk of levels of description, and of how facts registered at one level of description (e.g., the sociological level) may depend on facts registered at another (e.g., the level of physics) while being clearly irreducible to them. But even if this case of irreducibility were granted, it would not provide a good analogy for the present case, because all sorts of convention-involving properties—properties that depend for their existence on human conventions—are ascribed at the sociological level, and there is no parallel for this alleged source of in-principle irreducibility in the case of basic, non-convention-involving, sensory experiential properties like color experience or sound experience.

Once again, then, if experiential phenomena (like color experiences) really are somehow (wholly) dependent on nonexperiential phenomena, then naturalistic materialist realism about them necessarily implies that there is a correct way of describing things (a level of description) that allows one to relate color experience, considered just as such, to the nonexperiential phenomena on which it is supposed to depend in such a way that the dependence is as intelligible as the dependence of the liquidity of water on the interaction properties of individual molecules. The alternative, after all, is that this total dependence is not intelligible or explicable in any possible physics, not intelligible or explicable even to God, as it were (see McGinn, 1989b).

It may be objected that I am simply assuming that if there is a single, unified, nonmiraculous physical reality, there must be some possible valid unified theoretical account of it. It may also be objected that this use of the notions of intelligibility and explicability is dubious. Both these objections deserve a response, which I will give in section 4.3.

For the moment, the question that must be faced by nonreductive monists who are unconvinced by the present discussion, but who are genuine realists about the experiential, is 'How is it possible for there to be asymmetrical dependence without reducibility in some possible or optimal physics?' I feel I will have got somewhere if I have managed to revive anyone's sense that a positive answer to this question is very hard, if not impossible. There can't be [1] wholly physical properties that are [2] wholly dependent on other physical properties and [3] wholly irreducible to them, or wholly inexplicable by reference to them, in any possible valid physics. As far as I can see, many nonreductive monists want to accept (2) and (3), in the case of experiential properties, although they are also committed to the view that experiential properties satisfy (1), if they are genuine materialists.

Two (connected) points in conclusion. First, I have concentrated on (occurrent) experience when discussing reduction, although many who call themselves nonreductive monists are convinced of the impossibility of reduction primarily by the case of dispositional mental phenomena like desires and beliefs. I have ignored such dispositional phenomena because I do not think they pose any difficulty when it comes to the mind-body problem, any more than the phenomenon of intentionality does. I will discuss this point briefly in section 4.4 and then at more length in section 6.6 and chapter 7. For the moment it can be put by saying that there is a crucial sense of 'mental reality' that allows one to say that such dispositional mental phenomena are not really part of mental reality; or it can be put by saying that insofar as they are part of mental reality, reduction is easy in their case.

Second, in talking of reduction, I have concentrated on basic sensory experiential phenomena like color experience. According to the definition of 'experience' in section 1.2, however, conscious entertainings of thoughts are also counted as experiential phenomena, and it may be thought that the difficulty of making the existential dependency of experiential phenomena on nonexperiential phenomena intelligible will be far greater in the case of propositionally contentful thought experience than in the case of sensory experience. On this view, showing the occurrence of the experience of thinking 'Every even number greater than 2 is the sum of two prime numbers' to be intelligibly related to the nonexperiential brain phenomena on which it supposedly depends will be fundamentally more difficult than showing the result of looking unreflectively at an Abstract Expressionist painting to be so related. My conviction is that this is a mistake: if there is a difficulty, it is at most a difference of degree, not of kind. It is, certainly, true that one cannot have thoughts about prime numbers unless certain special complex structures exist in one's brain that need not exist when one has color experience. The fact remains that both experiences, considered just as experiences, are ultimately just that—*experiences*—episodes whose whole nature, considered specifically in its experiential aspect (in the sense of section 3.1), consists in the fact that they have, for the experiencer, a certain highly complex *qualitative* character or what-it's-likeness (which may be as much cognitive as sensory).

I think this point is of great importance. Attempts to give a naturalistic account of the mental are beguiled by the idea that mental states have propositional content in some way that transcends both their experiential content, on the one hand, and features of the brain as discerned by physics and neurophysiology, on the other hand. It seems to me that this idea is incorrect, and that it causes a great deal of unnecessary grief. I will return to it in section 6.6 and chapter 7. For the moment, if someone wishes to insist that the case of conscious thought is fundamentally different from the case of sensory experience insofar as it involves language, conventional properties, and so on, I am content to be skeptical, and to restrict my insistence on the incompatibility of asymmetry with irreducibility to the sensory case for present purposes.

It may finally be protested that I have failed to consider an "emergentist" suggestion about how to combine asymmetry and irreducibility within the materialist framework. Some may hold that the asymmetry thesis is compatible with the view that there is an essentially *indirect* dependency relation between the experiential and the nonexperiential. On this view, experiential physical properties simply cannot be instantiated, at a given time and place, unless nonexperiential physical properties are also instantiated, while the converse is not true. But this is not because the experiential physical properties depend on the nonexperiential physical properties in a way that implies that (statements about) the former are in principle reducible to (statements about) the latter in some possible, optimal physics. It is because although the former do not directly depend on the latter, they somehow just need the presence or company of the latter. Some of those who talk of experiential properties as "emergent" nonexperiential properties may feel that this represents their position accurately, although it seems to turn the relation between the experiential and the nonexperiential into a guaranteed mystery, where before it was merely a mystery.

3.8 Equal-Status Monism

No doubt there are other ways of attempting to reconcile the asymmetry thesis and the irreducibility thesis. I will consider the question no further. Instead I will return to the fact that many are strongly attracted to the asymmetry thesis; they are (for example) strongly committed to the belief that wherever and whenever there is experiential reality there is nonexperiential reality, while the converse of this is not true.

This being so, it is worth completing a movement begun in section 3.4, by pointing out that we can indeed adopt a view that appears to fulfill the defining conditions of both equal-status M&P monism (section 3.2) and standard asymmetrical materialist monism. (There may seem to be something rather grim about all these metaphysical distinctions, but perhaps they are good exercise. Those who have had enough could skip to section 3.10.) According to this view, the experiential and the nonexperiential (the mental and the nonmental) are each as really real as each other (to this extent they have equal status), and yet it is still true to say that the former depends on the latter in some way (to this extent there is asymmetry).

This, I suppose, is a common materialist view. But M&P monism ought not to be so easily swallowed by asymmetrical materialist monism, given the idea that lies behind it. To prevent the swallowing, the equal-status aspect of its definition needs to be slightly augmented, and I will now do this.

First, though, its name needs changing, on account of the unsatisfactoriness of the mental/physical distinction (p. 58). It could be called 'equal-status mental and nonmental monism', or, better, 'equal-status experiential and nonexperiential monism', but I will just call it 'positive equal-status monism' for short, or 'equal-status monism' for shorter. (It is *positive* equal-status monism because it says that reality is both experiential and nonexperiential, as opposed to *negative* equal-status monism or neutral monism, which says that reality is, ultimately, neither mental nor physical.)

Equal-status monism, then, like its predecessor, involves the following thesis:

Thesis 1 Reality is irreducibly both experiential and nonexperiential (both mental and nonmental), while being substantially single in some way *W* that we do not fully understand, although we take it that *W* is a way of being substantially single that does not involve any sort of *asymmetry* between the status of claims that reality has nonexperiential (nonmental) aspects and claims that reality has experiential (mental) aspects.

But I have argued that there is a sense in which standard materialist monism can accept thesis 1. So what now distinguishes equal-status monism is that it also involves the following thesis:

Thesis 2 It is not correct to say [1] that the experiential is based in or realized by or otherwise dependent on the nonexperiential, or [2] vice versa. The truth is rather [3] that the experiential and nonexperiential coexist in such a way that neither can be said to be based in or realized by or in any way asymmetrically dependent on the other; or if there is any sense in which one can reasonably be said to be dependent on the other, then this sense applies equally both ways.

Thesis 2 directly rejects the central claim of standard asymmetrical materialist monism. But it is still compatible with materialism as such. To get an explicitly materialist form of equal-status monism one simply has to add in the words 'properties of the physical' in thesis 2, part (3), to get 'The truth is that the experiential and nonexperiential properties of the physical coexist in such a way that neither can be said to be based in, or realized by, or in any way asymmetrically dependent on, the other, etc.'[8]

This is *equal-status* materialist monism. It is, perhaps, the view that many nonreductive monists should hold. It is the view they should

8. Note that some substance dualists might feel they could endorse both theses simply by replacing 'substantially single' in thesis 1 with some such expression as 'unified' or 'causally unified'.

hold if they believe in the in-principle irreducibility of the mental or experiential to the nonexperiential, and do not think that the appearance of irreducibility is at bottom just an effect of human limitation. I will restate the view although it is clear enough. [1] All reality is physical (the basic materialist premise). [2] There are experiential and nonexperiential phenomena (unavoidable realism about the experiential, *plus* the assumption [!] that there is more to physical reality than experiential reality). [3] Among physical phenomena, experiential physical phenomena do not depend on nonexperiential physical phenomena (recall again the definition of 'experiential phenomena' in section 3.1), or do not depend on them in any way in which nonexperiential phenomena do not also depend on experiential phenomena.

Standard *asymmetrical* materialist monism rejects (3). It positively asserts the dependency of the mental or experiential on the nonmental or nonexperiential, rather than positively denying it. It suggests that our knowledge of co-occurrence relations between brain events and experiential or mental events, and of the effects of damage to the brain, strongly supports asymmetrical materialism, as opposed to equal-status monism. It points out that when a presumably nonexperiential phenomenon like the intrusion of a bullet affects part of X's brain and destroys certain of X's experiential capacities and properties, we take it that it does so *because* it has certain consequences for the nonexperiential properties of X's brain. When alcohol and cocaine do what they do, they do it because they have certain consequences for the nonexperiential properties of one's brain. PET, MRI, and MEG (positron emission tomography, magnetic resonance imaging, and magnetoencephalography) also appear to weigh in heavily on the side of asymmetrical materialism.

Overall, asymmetrical materialist monism seems to be extremely strongly supported. But the mind-body problem is too difficult for us to suppose that these considerations are conclusive. This may seem like a weak response, but it is perhaps a measure of the difficulty of the mind-body problem that it appears appropriate. Both equal-status monism and asymmetrical monism come up against our deep ignorance of the nature of the relation between the experiential and the nonexperiential, and of what dependency relations might possibly be like, and although the difference between the two positions seems well enough defined, it is not clear that we really know what it amounts to. Insofar as we are committed to naturalistic no-miracles materialism, we seem obliged to hold that the appearance of radical disconnection between experiential properties and nonexperiential properties is a kind of illusion, an accident of our sensory-intellectual constitution. But it won't go away, and it constitutes a vivid proof of the limitations on our understanding of reality.

The point can be put as follows. Experiential phenomena and nonexperiential phenomena constitute two realms of systematic difference that seem radically disparate in their intrinsic character, in spite of all the co-occurrence correlations that we may be able to establish between their respective elements. A rough analogy for this radical disparateness is provided by the disparateness of the realm of color differences and the realm of smell differences. If, however, we had been differently constructed, we might have been able to see how the two realms of difference relate; and in this second case an analogy is provided by the way we take our visual and tactile perceptions to interrelate as sources of information about shape. Considered merely in their qualitative character, and hence entirely independently of any construction we put on them, visual experiences are utterly unlike tactile experiences. And yet we soon come to think of them as two ways of experiencing the same thing: shape.

Combining the two analogies, we may say that the experiential and the nonexperiential appear as disparate as color and smell. And yet we can imagine that we might have found them as profoundly intelligibly related as visual shape perception and tactile shape perception. And we can suppose that there must be some possible perspective from which they appear so related (see section 4.3 below).

3.9 Panpsychism

It may be suggested that equal-status monism forces us into a form of *panpsychism*. Is this so? I think the matter is worth considering briefly, first, because the problem of the relation between the experiential and the nonexperiential is so difficult that panpsychism deserves to be taken seriously, and second, because whether or not panpsychism is a serious candidate, it is instructive to see how the metaphysical possibilities proliferate. (This section is rather dense and can be omitted.)

Consider the version of panpsychism that holds that there is a material universe, and that a fundamental and universal (and not at all understood) property of all matter, from the smallest portion up, is that it is *experience-realizing* or *experience-involving*. Put into the more circumspect terms mentioned above, this becomes the thesis that there is such a thing as nonexperiential reality, and yet it is a fundamental feature of this reality that every portion of it is experience-realizing or experience-involving. Just for the purposes of exposition, I will endow these two terms with different implications, so that they give rise to two different versions of panpsychism.[9]

The panpsychist claim that all matter is experience-*realizing* preserves the asymmetry thesis. It preserves the idea that there is some fundamental asymmetry in the status of experiential reality and nonexperiential reality given which it is correct to say that experience is based in or realized by or otherwise dependent on nonexperiential reality, and incorrect to say either that nonexperiential reality is based in or realized by or otherwise dependent on experience, or that they coexist in such a way that neither can be said to be based in or realized by or otherwise dependent on the other. This version of panpsychism seems coherent enough, and can be classified with standard asymmetrical materialism. It differs from the ordinary view just in holding not only that some arrangements of nonexperiential reality realize experience but that all do. It lacks one motivation for an asymmetry of attitude noted above, but it is nonetheless an asymmetry theory.[10]

9. There are also idealist versions of panpsychism, but I will not consider them. It may also be said that panpsychism is, strictly speaking, the view that everything that exists is or has a soul. But I define it in terms of experience, as in the text.

10. It lacks the motivation that derives from the intuition that wherever there is experience or a capacity for experience, there is matter, while the converse is not true; for it asserts the converse as well. Note that it does not have to suppose that all matter is always actually experience-realizing at every moment. It may make the weaker claim that all matter is always *capable* of realizing experience (capable of realizing experience with its present arrangement, and not just because it could be rearranged into a brain). This panpsychism can allow that "matter thinks not always" (to adapt Hobbes's objection to Descartes), and that if a human being can be in an experienceless sleep, so can a stone or an atom.

To claim that all matter is experience-*involving*, by contrast, is to reject the asymmetry thesis. I will take it that it is to adopt *equal status panpsychism*, according to which experiential reality and nonexperiential reality do precisely exist in such a way that neither can be said to be based in or realized by or in any way asymmetrically dependent on the other. This version of panpsychism is a version of equal-status monism and can also be counted as a form of materialism.

What about the other way round? Is equal-status monism, as defined in section 3.8, necessarily a form of panpsychism? This is the question I began with, and it seems that the answer is 'No'. Equal-status monism need not be panpsychist, for it doesn't have to hold that all nonexperiential reality is intrinsically experience-involving. Equal-status monists can hold that some parts of matter are experience-involving and others are not. This does not immediately commit them to any form of the asymmetry thesis. They could even suggest that many particles come in two types, hitherto indistinguishable by physics, some of which are experience-involving and some of which are not. This need not be thought to push them into a kind of dualism.

It is less clear that equal-status monists can claim that some *arrangements* of matter are experience-involving, while others are not. For this sort of claim makes an asymmetrical-dependency thesis look very plausible. "Dual-aspect" theorists may consider themselves to be equal-status monists, but it is not clear that they can plausibly claim that experiential properties are to be found only in some cases—e.g., only when nonexperiential properties of the sort instantiated by things like brains are also found—while denying any sort of dependency of the experiential on the nonexperiential. If they are really equal-status monists, there is pressure on them to be panpsychists (compare Nagel 1986, 49).

To summarize, [1] panpsychism can be a form of equal-status monism. To suggest that all reality is experience-involving is to suggest that being experience-involving is a fundamental property of existing things on a par with extension, rest mass, or electric charge. [2] Panpsychism is not necessarily a form of equal-status monism: it may also be a form of asymmetrical materialist monism. [3] Equal-status monism is not necessarily a form of panpsychism, although they can go naturally together. In sum, the two positions can be combined, but neither implies the other.

3.10   The Inescapability of Metaphysics

Where does this leave us? Alarmed, perhaps, by the uncontrollable fertility of metaphysics, but with two potentially useful things: an apparently surviving distinction between the asymmetrical and equal-status versions of monism and also, perhaps, a better feeling for our ignorance. The fertility of metaphysics may be fruitless, but it may be useful to have a reasonably well-developed sense of this fact, for one may be favoring a particular metaphysical option, implicitly or explicitly, without really possessing any good grounds for preferring it to the other possibilities with which it is in competition in the rich regions of metaphysical space. I think this is a danger for contemporary materialists.

That is to put it mildly. To put it less mildly: one cannot get out of metaphysics. As soon as one admits that something exists—and one must do that—one has to admit that it has some nature or other. For to be is to be somehow or other. And as soon as one admits that it has some nature or other, either one has to hold that one knows what its nature is—in which case one endorses a particular metaphysical claim about the nature of reality—or one has to admit that one might be wrong about its nature, at least in the sense that one might have an *incomplete* picture of its nature—in which case one admits that there are various metaphysical possibilities, even if one can never know for sure which is correct.

The great flight from metaphysics culminated in verificationist positivism. But verificationist positivists do not escape from metaphysics. For even they grant that there are sense data. And if they go on to say that sense data are all that exist, they adopt a patently metaphysical position—one of the most amazing on record. They may instead say that sense data are all that we can know to exist, and admit that it is, after all, not actually meaningless or incoherent to suppose that other things may exist, things of which we have no conception, things, perhaps, of which we can have no conception. But if they admit this, they must be prepared to grant that in the case of sense data too, there may possibly be more to them than we know, or can know. Either sense data are mere contents with no hidden nature—and this is a form of radical metaphysical idealism[11]— or they are not mere contents with no hidden nature and there is something more to them, in which case some other unknown and perhaps unknowable metaphysical possibility is realized. Either way one is metaphysically committed. And yet the illusion persists—the illusion that one can be free of metaphysics. Today the most common form of the delusion is to think that one can be a tough metaphysics-eschewing positivist and also a hard-nosed materialist. Quine never made this mistake: he talked cheerfully of the "myth of physical objects, . . . posits comparable, epistemologically, to the gods of Homer" (Quine 1961, 44).

11. On this view, we think of ourselves as, somehow, mere assemblages of sense data with no hidden nature—more wild metaphysics.

4
Agnostic Materialism, Part 2

4.1 Ignorance

Serious materialists have to be outright realists about experience (as defined in section 3.1). So they are obliged to hold that experiential phenomena just are physical phenomena, although current physics cannot account for them. As an acting materialist, I go along with this and assume that experiential phenomena are realized in the brain (to stick to the human case). But this assumption doesn't solve any problems for materialists. Instead, it obliges them to admit ignorance of the nature of the physical—to admit that they don't have a fully adequate idea of what the physical is or of what sort of thing the brain is. The brain is a physical thing—this is a commitment of materialism. But it is no part of this commitment that we should slide into supposing that the expression 'the brain' somehow refers especially to the brain-as-revealed-by-current-physics (or by any future nonrevolutionized version of physics). 'The brain' refers to the brain as a whole, the brain in its total physical existence and activity. And this physical existence and activity, as all serious materialists must agree, is as much revealed by, and constituted by, experiential phenomena as by all the nonexperiential phenomena discerned by physics.

In talking of our ignorance, I have one well-known thing primarily in mind: when we consider the brain as current physics and neurophysiology presents it to us, we are obliged to admit that we do not know how experience—experiential what-it's-like-ness—is or even could be realized in the brain. This is why any serious statement of materialism needs to acknowledge that our current physical-science conception of the physical is radically incomplete. The physical-science (and neurophysiological) story of my brain is in many respects rich and detailed, but it fails to provide any account of how something undeniably real is even so much as possible: it just leaves out the phenomenal or experiential character of my experience. If I am watching a tree roaring in the wind, there is a remarkable electrochemical, computational story of what is happening to me that involves photons and retinas and rods and cones. But this story leaves out the experiential properties of my experience. It fails to explain even how they are possible.

This claim is familiar. I repeat it in order to consider two objections. The first and more important challenges this use of the notion of explanation. The second accepts this use and denies that there is such a total failure of explanation. I will take them in reverse order.

4.2 Sensory Spaces

The second objection is that work in neurophysiology does in fact give us some information on, or explanation of, how experience may be realized in the brain as conceived of, or represented by, current physics and neurophysiology. And there is at least one sense in which this is true, although there is also a fundamental sense in which it is false.

One sense in which it is true is this: Neurophysiologists identify areas of the brain that they take to be crucially implicated in particular sorts of experience (such as color experience or sound experience). It seems that we can give plausible explanations of how we are able to make the *range* of color or sound discriminations that we do, by reference to features of the structure of these areas of the brain. We may be able to explain how a dog is able to discriminate such an astonishing range of smells by reference to a structure of neural connections, using only what physics tells us about the physical.[1]

---

1. For a speculative discussion of such mechanisms and of sensory "state spaces," see Churchland 1986. See also Lockwood 1989, chap. 7, and Edelman 1992, chap. 3. Churchland's discussion might be seen as a first step toward Nagel's "objective phenomenology" (section 3.6)—an account of the nature of experiential states designed to render them more amenable to integration with physics. It would, however, be very much a first step (and it is not clear what the second step could be), because it would merely study what one might call the *abstract morphology* of sensory modalities, like hearing and smell, in giving an

More generally, a tide of evidence is rising to support the view that there is a sense in which "mind is mindless," in the sense that even its highest achievements may be the result of many simple and individually philosophically unproblematic processes acting in concert without any central coordinating control (see Dennett 1991b, Edelman 1992; the idea is anticipated in Kant 1933, A352–A353).

All this is important. We can study in depth, and in nonexperiential terms, physical mechanisms and structures that are undoubtedly intimately involved in the occurrence of experience. But whatever we may reasonably claim to be able to explain, there is something we entirely fail to explain. For so far, such neurophysiological and physical-science explanations tell us nothing about how experience (what-it's-like-ness in general) is possible. To explain how a creature is capable of making a great range of discriminations, given the particular structure of parts of its brain, is not to explain how experience is possible. An experienceless machine can be designed to make a great range of discriminations, responding differentially to different wavelengths of light and displaying color words on a monitor. Discriminatory *range* is, in any case, unimportant. A creature capable of experiencing only one shade of red and one shade of blue raises the problem of experience in its entirety. A worm raises it, if worms can feel (Darwin had a very high opinion of worms). Whatever the level of detail and complexity attained by explanations of the sort just described, there remains a fundamental sense in which we are in the dark about how experience is possible, given the nature and structure of physical states as described by current physics and neurophysiology.[2] All we can do at present is to say 'That's just

---

account of how certain complex physical structures are implicated in our capacity to make the range of sensory discriminations that we can make within a given sensory modality. It would say nothing at all about the intrinsic phenomenal character of the particular experiences delivered by the sensory modalities, but only something about their relational or positional properties in the sensory "space" in question.

2. One of the problems we encounter is an aspect of the "grain" problem (Sellars 1965): how is it that different parts of the brain, apparently so similar in their basic constituents, can be the seats of such utterly different things as sound experience, taste experience, and visual experience? For a recent statement, see Lockwood 1993, 275–277.

how things are'. And while this response is sometimes inevitable in science, for explanations come to an end, it can seem untroublesome in some cases but not in others. When we are told that the charge on the electron is 1.602192×10^{-19} coulombs, we may say 'That's how it is' and rest easy (though not all physicists do). But when we are told that goings-on in the brain, as described by physics, are the basis of, or realize, or are, experiential goings-on, 'That's just how things are' does not seem to be an adequate response in the way that it can seem adequate when we consider fundamental physical constants like Planck's constant, or features of the universe that are the result of "symmetry-breaking." It is not a response that we can make as serious materialists, in an attempt to deny the charge that our physics is radically incomplete in some way.

4.3   Experience, Explanation, and Theoretical Integration

This last point connects with the first objection, which can take many forms. I will consider it at some length, for it is likely to be thought powerful. In one form, it goes like this: Science is not really (or ultimately) concerned with explanation at all. It is true that we cannot really explain (or understand) the relation between experiential phenomena and nonexperiential phenomena. But there is no special failure here, because we cannot really explain (or understand) the relations between nonexperiential phenomena either.

The objection concedes that we use the idiom of explanation. We use the word 'because'. We say that *A* happened *because B* happened. We say that the reason why the first billiard ball moved off in direction *d* at velocity *v* is that it was struck by the second billiard ball in the particular way that it was. And if we are questioned, we may talk of impact and energy transfer, momentum, force, and mass. But we may be pressed further, and if we are, we will eventually come to the end of our explanatory resources. And when we are asked why the facts appealed to in our final explanation are as they are, we will not be able to say anything but 'This is (just) how things are'.

This is obvious enough, and it leads straight to the starting point of the objection, which continues as follows: Since explanation must come to an end, nothing in science is ever truly or ultimately explained. It is true that there are scientific explanations that seem completely satisfying, given what they take for granted. But it is also true that the question 'Why?' can always be raised about what they take for granted, and that in the end one will be unable to give any further answer.[3] It follows that all science really delivers, in the end, are statements of correlation, causal or otherwise, e.g., statements of the form 'When events of type *A* occur, events of type *B* occur', statements to the effect that this is just how things are. What is more, we may eventually be just as successful in the attempt to formulate well-confirmed statements of correlation that link experiential predicates to nonexperiential predicates as we have been in the attempt to formulate well-confirmed statements of correlation that link nonexperiential physics predicates to each other. If so, there will be no special failure of physics, or of explanation, when it comes to giving an account of the experiential and its place in nature. There will be no need to suppose any special inadequacy in this area. So far as causal correlations are concerned, as opposed to correlations that might obtain because of some hidden identity, it is an old point, powerfully stated by Hume in his discussion of the mind-body problem (1978, 247–248), that causal connection is no more "intrinsically intelligible" when it holds between two nonexperiential phenomena than when it holds between an experiential phenomenon and a nonexperiential phenomenon. So runs the objection.

There are various problems with the idea that we could produce well-confirmed exceptionless statements of correlation linking experiential

---

3. Explanations of action in terms of reasons may be thought to offer a paradigm of explanation where we are not just left with something unexplained. Why did Georgia turn on the light? Because it was dark, and she believed it was dark, and she wanted to see across the room and believed that turning on the light would make this possible and also that it was the best or only way available to her, and she had no reason not to turn on the light, etc. Of course, one can go on to ask why she wanted to see across the room. But to ask 'Why should it be the case that someone who wants to see across the room turns on the light, even given everything else stated in the explanation?' is simply to show that one has failed to understand what has been said. To say 'That's just the way things are'—'That's just the way things are with desires, beliefs, and actions'—is not, in this case, to admit that these connections are ultimately a matter of brute, unintelligible correlation.

predicates and nonexperiential predicates, but they are not important at present (they were briefly discussed in section 3.6). For even when it is allowed that we can produce them the essential claim remains: mere correlations cannot provide any sort of explanation or understanding of the existence of experience or what-it's-like-ness or "qualia" in physical-science terms.

But what exactly does this claim come to? It has already been granted that explanation comes to an end. It has been granted that when we are pressed, in science, we end up with statements about how things are (and are correlated) that offer no (ultimate) explanation of why they are that way. And it has been granted that for us to feel that we have been given a scientific explanation when someone says '*A* happened because of *B*', as opposed to a statement of essentially unexplained correlation that uses the idiom 'because', is really just a matter of what we happen to find theoretically satisfying, given other things that we already accept. So what does this claim that we lack any explanation of the occurrence of experience amount to?

The first point is this. The weak-looking notion of what we find theoretically satisfying is not unimportant. Even if explanations come to an end, there are many explanations that we do find theoretically satisfying in science, and this satisfaction is one of the things we aim at in scientific enquiry. It is, as Quine remarks, the goal of *understanding*, of what we take to be understanding, of what satisfies us as constituting understanding (Quine 1990, 2). It is something we feel we manage to achieve in many areas of physics, and something that we find we have utterly failed to achieve in the case of the relations between experiential phenomena and nonexperiential phenomena, and will still have failed to achieve even if we manage to come up with promising statements of correlation.

This is why it seems reasonable to say that we should—as materialists who think that experiential phenomena, like nonexperiential phenomena, are entirely physical phenomena—suppose ourselves to be ignorant of the nature of the physical in a specific way that will remain undiminished until we have achieved something like the sort of theoretical satisfaction, in our account of the relation between experiential and nonexperiential phenomena, that we are familiar with in other areas of science; the sort of theoretical satisfaction that regularly leads us to say that we can really explain or understand why things behave in the way they do, or are related in the way that they are, or co-occur in the way that they do. Obviously, the experience of theoretical satisfaction is not self-validating and can be unwarranted, and it always presupposes a background of things taken for granted. But this is compatible with the view that it is sometimes justified, and with the fact that it appears attainable in some areas of science and utterly unattainable (at present) when it comes to the question of the relation between experiential and nonexperiential phenomena (recall the definition of 'experience' and 'experiential phenomena' on p. 45).

Next objection. One cannot infer ignorance of the nature of the physical from the unavailability of any sort of theoretically satisfying account of why or how some feature of it is as it is, relative to the rest of physics. For we can give no such account of, e.g., certain fundamental physical constants, but we are not therefore necessarily ignorant of what they are, or of the nature of the physical.

This is true. As remarked at the end of the last section, we may be untroubled by the 'This is just how things are' status of Planck's constant, relative to the rest of physics. Planck's constant fits smoothly into our theory of the physical in spite of having this status. But the same cannot be said of experiential phenomena when considered relative to the nonexperiential features of the brain as described by physics. Serious materialists—and physicists committed to the advance of their subject—cannot so easily pass over our dramatic lack of theoretical understanding of how experiential phenomena relate to nonexperiential phenomena in the brain, by saying nothing more than 'Well, that's just how things are'. They might decide to say this, but their doing so would not change the fact that experiential phenomena simply do not fit into our existing theory of the physical. That is why they raise a problem that does not exist in the case of things like Planck's constant or the products of symmetry breaking. And that is why it seems reasonable to talk of ignorance and incompleteness when confronted with them.

It may next be objected that quantum mechanics, often called the most successful theory in the history of science, notoriously fails to provide us with the feeling that we can really explain or understand why things happen as they do at the quantum level (e.g., why light behaves as it does in the two-slit experiment). Why, then, should one criticize a theory that successfully correlates types of experiential phenomena with types of nonexperiential phenomena for failing to deliver any real understanding of the relation of the phenomena in question? It seems that it is not in general true that a satisfactory scientific theory must supply one with a sense of understanding the phenomena it deals with. A theory may be theoretically satisfactory—beautiful and powerful—without supplying a sense of understanding. Perhaps it is not generally true that lack of understanding indicates ignorance of the nature of the phenomena in question.

In response, let me try to put the difficulty differently. There is felt to be a certain sort of strong *theoretical integratedness* or *homogeneity* (or at least nonheterogeneity) among many of the existing predicates of physics (and among those predicates and the predicates of other sciences that are held, with good reason, to be reducible to physics, in the sense of chapter 3, note 1). These predicates recognizably form part of the same family, the same overall system of description. The problem is that experiential predicates do not fit into this family or system of description. And we have no idea, at present, of how they might be integrated. This is the problem of experience: all experiential phenomena are physical phenomena, but we cannot fit them into the account of the physical delivered by physics. We know that they are actual, but we do not understand how they are possible or why they occur as they do, given all that we know about the physical as described by physics. We do not understand why they occur as they do in the way that we feel we understand why many other physical phenomena occur as they do, given the account of the physical delivered by physics.

We can hope to be able to relate the *range* features or "abstract morphology" (note 1) of the experiential phenomena of a given sense modality to aspects of brain structure, and we can correlate variations in *intensity* of experiential phenomena with variations in intensity of nonexperiential phenomena. It is the basic qualitative modalities of sense experience considered just as such that seem completely resistant to genuine theoretical integration with physics, and continue to seem so even after we have made such unverifiable and implausible simplifying assumptions as the assumption that all those who have normal verbal color-discrimination abilities have them on the basis of exactly the same qualitative experience—so that the predicate 'experience of pillar-box red', say, has a unique determinate reference. Such theoretical integration would require more than the formulation of statements of correlation linking experiential predicates (e.g., 'the experience of pillar-box red', 'the experience of middle C played on a flute') and nonexperiential predicates, exceptionless or not. It would require a kind of theoretical homogenization that seems at present unimaginable.

It is on these grounds, I suggest, that we must admit fundamental ignorance of the nature of the physical. We have an atomic physics, and all parts of physics integrate with each other, but we don't have a qualitative-character-of-experience physics at all. We don't have a physics of phenomenology, let alone one that integrates with the rest of physics. The view that this must indicate ignorance, and that it must be possible in principle to achieve some deep theoretical homogenization of experiential terms and nonexperiential terms, is, on the present view, a necessary concomitant of the idea that materialism is true and that there is indeed a single, unified physical reality.

This returns us to a question raised in section 3.7. The move is from the claim that there is a single unified physical reality to the claim that there must be a single, unified or homogeneous theoretical description of that reality, whether or not it is attainable by us. (Note that dualists can endorse the move described in the last sentence, after removing the word 'physical'.) If anyone says 'That's just an assumption', so be it. It is an assumption that I make. If a thing is a natural phenomenon, there must be a perspective from which it does not appear mysterious, relative to the rest of what is known about the natural, for it is not mysterious in fact, relative to the rest of the natural. There must be a perspective that integrates an account of this natural phenomenon into an account of the rest of the natural. This is what we lack in the case of the experiential. And perhaps we experience and conceptualize the nonexperiential physical in such a way that the existence of the experiential physical will always appear mysterious or inexplicable, relative to our conception of the rest of the physical (see Jackson 1982, McGinn 1989b). If so, our understanding of the nature of the physical will always seem incomplete in a certain respect: with respect to the relation between the experiential physical and the nonexperiential physical.

Objection: Our physics is necessarily a human physics. It is an account of reality that is necessarily conditioned by the particular perspective on reality that we have as members of a species with a particular kind of sensory-intellectual equipment; so we cannot suppose that we could ever reach the Truth of the matter or think of our physics as giving the complete story.

Reply: This is true, but it does not mean that we cannot identify specific areas in which our current physics appears dramatically lacking or incomplete, even on its own terms—e.g., on account of its failure to provide any satisfactory theoretical integration of two sorts of phenomenon that appear to us as indubitably real. True, our physics is a human physics, but there are aspects of the physical of which we nevertheless feel we have a genuine understanding. And it is relative to this standard of understanding, not some impossible Godlike standard, that it is true to say that if materialism is correct, then there is something fundamental we have not grasped about the physical, and will not have grasped until we have achieved some sort of (valid) theoretical integration of experiential terms and nonexperiential terms. There seems to be an insuperable difficulty about doing this in detail (the "objective phenomenology" problem, noted in section 3.6). But we might still hope to make some more general progress, by revolutionizing physics in such a way as to begin to see how experience in general is possible on the terms of physics.[4]

4. McGinn (1991) has argued that we cannot hope to make progress on the problem in any general way without making at least equal progress on the problem of how to solve it in detail in particular cases.

Cussins (1990, sec. 2) defines a use of 'Intelligible' according to which the relation between two levels of description may be Intelligible to one even if one has not achieved any detailed, theoretically satisfying integration of the terms of the two levels. The relation between them may be said to be Intelligible to one just so long as one has the practical ability to tell, on being presented with a description of something at the "lower" (say nonexperiential) level of description, how it would be described at the "higher" (say experiential) level of description. This seems a promising idea. However, such a practical ability might be based merely on uncomprehending rote knowledge of statements of correlation, in which case the relation between the two levels would not be intelligible to one. Further, even if one's ability were not based on rote knowledge and involved the ability to judge new cases, it might not involve the relation's being intelligible to one in the natural sense of the word, for one may have a practical ability and have no real idea of how one does what one does, or of why what one does works.

It may again be objected that the mysteries of quantum mechanics lie at the bottom of all physics, and that there are terminological-heterogeneity problems within quantum mechanics that are as acute as the terminological-heterogeneity problems raised by experiential and nonexperiential terms. This can be doubted, for things can seem inexplicable, in the way that they do in quantum mechanics, without there being any perceived problem of radical heterogeneity of terms. But it can also be granted. For if it were true, it would merely show something that few would deny—that we are in various ways ignorant of the nature of quantum reality. It would not undermine the suggestion that our inability to achieve a deep theoretical integration of experiential and nonexperiential terms shows (if materialism is true) that our current conception of the nature of the physical is dramatically incomplete on its own terms. Explanation and understanding must stop somewhere. But it does not follow from this that satisfaction of the demand for terminological homogeneity is impossible. For a science could very well reach a stage at which there were things that prompted us to say that we could not understand or explain why they were as they were (we would say of them 'That's just how things are') but at which we nevertheless felt that all the terms of the science were fundamentally theoretically homogeneous with each other, recognizably part of the same overall system of theoretical description.

Faced with the theoretical chasm between experiential predicates and the nonexperiential predicates of current physics, some have tried to avoid the problem by suggesting that we abandon or downgrade one or the other set of terms. They have become absolute idealists or reductive physicalists. But most of us believe that we have to grant both sets of terms equal status in our attempt to describe what is real. We certainly cannot do without the experiential terms, whatever their imprecision, so idealism is the only real option for those who wish to abandon one set of terms completely. Assuming that materialism is true, one wonders how physicists can suppose that they are on the verge of a grand unified Theory of Everything when they have absolutely no account of how experiential physical phenomena are possible. This looks like the greatest unsolved problem of physics. It looks like the greatest unsolved problem of science. It is true, once again, that understanding is always understanding relative to something taken as given. The present claim is just that physics will have a huge hole in it, given its own internal standards of explanation and understanding, so long as it does not provide a framework within which experiential and nonexperiential terms can be brought into some sort of genuine theoretical intercourse. (Here dualists can replace 'physics' with 'our account of reality'.)

It may be pointed out that facts about what satisfy us as explanations are sociological facts, and that human beings may at some future time find statements correlating nonexperiential descriptions of brain events with descriptions of experiential events as theoretically satisfying as statements correlating billiard-ball impacts with billiard-ball movements. In reply: the present position on explanation and understanding allows this as a possibility. The fact remains that there is a difference between being very familiar with a fact and finding it theoretically unproblematic. Familiarity does not necessarily lead to a sense that something is theoretically unproblematic. Even if we became very familiar with the fact that nonexperiential brain events of type X are reliably correlated with experiential events of type Y, this could not lead us to think of the relation between them as theoretically unproblematic in the billiard-ball way, so long as we continued to operate with our current physics or some nonrevolutionary extension of it. It may be denied that what billiard balls do is theoretically unproblematic, and it is true, once again, that what they do seems theoretically unproblematic only relative to things we take for granted. But at this point I am content for my claim to be classified as sociological in character.

It may finally be said that the claim about the intractability of the problem of experience or consciousness is exactly like the claim that used to be made about the "mystery" of life: just as life ceased to seem problematic within the frame of physics, so too will experience. Reply: one should never underestimate the "silent permeative genius of science" (Pattison 1988, 154). But one shouldn't overestimate it either. A revolution is still needed, that's my prediction. Dennett (1991b) has suggested that those who insist on our failure of understanding want there to be an irreducible mystery. But most are materialists who would give a great deal for a convincing naturalistic theory of experience, one that would explain how experience is possible, given the rest of what we know about the physical. Most of those who insist on the acuity of the problem are merely concerned to keep it clearly in view, in the face of all those who are trying to sideline it or deny its existence.

4.4 The Hard Part of the Mind-Body Problem

I will now defend the claim (made in section 3.1) that the existence of experience is the only hard part of the mind-body problem for materialists. I think the point is simple, but I will return to it in chapters 6 and 7.

Many actual and possible beings do not, we assume, have any experience, although they can behave just as if they were both intelligent and capable of sensation. That is, they can behave just as if they had certain properties and abilities of a sort that we naturally think of as mental properties and abilities, when we think of them as possessed by ourselves and other animals. The present claim is that none of these apparently mental abilities and properties pose any problem, so far as the mind-body problem is concerned.

Take the apparently cognitive properties. Consider the ability to play chess or to do sums or to diagnose illnesses on the basis of data. Suppose that the existence of physical beings that possess these properties is said to pose a special problem within the philosophy of mind. One may reply that the existence of physical beings that possess these properties is no more problematic, within the philosophy of mind, and speaking from a materialist point of view, than the existence of experienceless chess computers or pocket calculators or computerized medical expert systems. That is, it is not problematic at all, for the existence of such experienceless devices is not problematic at all, within materialist philosophy of mind. Such devices make it plain that entities can possess apparently cognitive properties and abilities even if they only possess properties that are familiarly accounted for by current physics. What is more, we can see and say exactly how these devices do what they do, in the terms of current physics.

There are, of course, deep problems in physics and the philosophy of physics: Causal processes go on in these devices, and causation is itself a philosophical problem. These devices exist in time, and time again is philosophically problematic. That's why the present claim is specifically that these devices are not philosophically problematic within the restricted area of the philosophy of mind.

The further claim is this: to the extent that the philosophy of mind has no special problem about how entities with only properties recognized by current physics can possess apparently mental properties and abilities of this sort, it has no special problem about how *we* can possess such properties and abilities, given only our possession of all those properties that current physics recognizes us to possess. This general claim is reasonable even if the physical basis of our possession of such abilities is very different from the physical basis of existing machines' possession of these abilities. (The fact that it is we who program the machines to do what they do is irrelevant to the argument—a point that will be made shortly.)

Now consider the apparently sensory abilities. Suppose that the very existence of physical beings that can detect and discriminate differences in their environment is said to pose a special problem within the philosophy of mind. The reply is that their existence is no more problematic, within materialist philosophy of mind, than the existence of experienceless machines that can detect differences of shape or temperature, or differences that we register as color or sound differences. And this is again to say that it is not problematic at all. We can give detailed physical-science explanations of how such discriminatory abilities are or can be realized in or by physical entities that we assume to be experienceless. We can have a full understanding, on the terms of our current conception of the physical, of how it is possible for these abilities to be physically realized. We can build machines that possess them. But we can do nothing like this for experience. Our detailed understanding of how a huge range of (quasi-)cognitive and (quasi-)sensory abilities may be physically based leaves us in the dark on the question of how experience is possible in a physical world—given our assumption (for that is what it is) that our grasp of the nature of the physical is founded primarily in the account of the physical provided by physics rather than in our direct awareness of that equally physical phenomenon, experience.[5]

5. Lockwood (1989, chap. 9) makes the radical and arguably Russellian suggestion that our grasp of the intrinsic nature of the physical might be better thought of as primarily founded in, or better served by, our direct awareness of experience.

One might put the point by saying that even if we could make a machine that had experience, and even if we could know (per impossibile) that we had done so, we still would not be able to give any explanation, in physics terms, of how it was possible that it had experience—so long as we were operating within the confines of our current physics-based conception of the physical. Nor does current physics seem to have any obvious promising gaps or valences, where conceptual extensions could possibly bring in radically new predicates of a sort that might help us begin to see how the physical as described by physics could be the basis of, or involve, or be, experience. Quantum enthusiasts may doubt this, but the strangenesses of quantum mechanics have no obvious affinity with, or potential for explaining, the existence of experience.

One may well wish to define 'mind' and 'mental' very widely indeed when starting from the materialist premise. One may wish to count many nonexperiential phenomena as mental phenomena (e.g., behavioral phenomena—see section 2.2 above—or brain-based computational activities of the sort postulated in the Marr-Nishihara theory of vision—see chapter 6 below). But the problem of how experience is possible remains at the heart of the difficulty created by the existence of mind. It is the heart of the difficulty; the rest is easy. All the other things people want to classify as mental pose no more of a philosophical or scientific problem than the existence of experienceless chess computers, or experienceless color-classification devices that detect light wavelengths, or experienceless robotic devices that pursue goals on the basis of information, being programmed, say, to collect up blue cubes in an environment of geometrical shapes and to plug themselves into a power source when their power supply is low. Purely instrumentally speaking, experienceless beings can simulate a vast range of abilities and properties that we naturally think of as characteristically mental abilities and properties. The present point (to repeat it) is simply that we can take them apart and see—understand—how they do it, given current physics and computational science. It is this that we cannot do with experiential properties.

It may be objected that the devices in question have "derived" intentionality, derived from their creators (e.g., ourselves), who have "original" intentionality, and that they are therefore not good examples of cases in which we find it unproblematic that physical things as understood by physics should have apparently mental properties; since in considering them, we are forced to refer to their designers, who themselves raise the whole problem of how physical things as understood by physics can have mental properties. This objection completely misunderstands the point, however. The fact that the devices are designed is irrelevant. They could conceivably occur randomly and undesigned in an environment. (They could be devices that we find we can use to play chess or calculate income tax, by imposing a certain interpretation on their input-output behavior.) The point they serve to make—whether they are designed or occur randomly—is simply this: whatever they do, whatever we treat them as doing, we can examine their microstructure and see how they do what they do, given the existing terms of physics and standard criteria of what counts as explanation. This is what we cannot do in the case of experiential mental properties.

These, then, are my reasons for taking the mind-body problem to be nothing but the experience-matter problem or, more accurately, and speaking within the materialist framework, to be nothing but the problem of the relation between the experiential physical and the non-experiential physical. The things we think of as higher intellectual achievements are just not a philosophical problem, except insofar as they involve a capacity for experience. Abilities to discriminate environmental features are just not a philosophical problem, except insofar as they involve a capacity for experience. Experience is the problem. In section 6.6, I give further reasons for thinking that propositional attitudes cause no difficulty when it comes to the mind-body problem. In chapter 7, I argue that intentionality does not raise a problem distinct from the problem raised by experience.

4.5 Neutral Monism and Agnostic Monism

I have suggested that materialists must confess their ignorance and their faith. I will now consider the suggestion that they might do better to describe themselves not as materialists but rather as *neutral monists* or *agnostic monists*.

'Neutral monism' is a name that carries a number of historical associations. I take it to be the view that although the universe is indeed composed of one fundamental kind of stuff, this stuff is neither mental nor physical. Or rather, it is neither mental nor physical as we currently understand these terms. Attributing neutral monism to William James, Russell describes it as the doctrine "according to which the material out of which the world is constructed is neither mind nor matter, but something anterior to both."[6]

This makes it easy to see why Kant may also be said to take up a neutral monist position when he claims that what "underlies outer appearances" and "inner intuition" is not "in itself either matter or a thinking being"; rather, it is "a ground (to us unknown) of the appearances which supply to us the empirical concept of the former as well as of the latter mode of existence" (Kant 1933, A380).

One might expand this as follows. We, considered as a part of ("noumenal") reality, are somehow affected by something other than ourselves, which is also a part of (noumenal) reality. One upshot or aspect of this transaction is our deployment of concepts of the mental and the physical. But these concepts of the mental and the physical are not in fact correctly applied to reality considered in its ultimate (noumenal) nature. They are not in fact correctly applied either to ourselves (as we are in ourselves) or to what is not ourselves (as it is in itself).[7]

It has also been suggested that neutral monism is a descendant of the *Identitätsphilosophie* propounded by Schelling and Hegel (and originating with Spinoza). This theory is said to assert the absolute identity of mind and matter, holding [1] "that mind and body are only modes of the same substance," and [2] that "it is this substance to which they are both reducible, not one to the other."[8]

6. Russell 1945, 813. 'Anterior' is obviously unclear. Russell notes an apparently idealist strain in James's neutral monism (as expounded in, e.g., James 1912), and when he adopts it as a name for his own view, he seems to mean something very peculiar (and phenomenalistic) by it.

7. Although Kant endorses the neutralist claim that ultimate reality is neither mental nor physical as we ordinarily understand these terms, he does not actually commit himself to the monist claim that it involves a single kind of substance.

8. Hall 1967, 363. Note the denial of the asymmetry thesis in (2). Note also that (1) is arguably closer to *positive* equal-status monism (section 3.8) than to neutral monism or *negative* equal-status monism. It is the reducibility claim in (2) that seems to turn the position into a version of neutral monism, but it is unclear how the reducibility claim interacts with the language of modes and substance, and

Should anyone ask why philosophers should be attracted to neutral monism, the answer seems clear. It provides a complete if merely promissory solution to the mind-body problem. According to neutral monism, there is no problem about the relation between experiential and nonexperiential phenomena, for they are mere appearances of a single and single-natured substance whose nature we do not know. (Kant is clear about this advantage of neutral monism, in the particular form in which he espouses it.) If we knew its nature (and our own), it would be easy for us to see why it should appear to creatures like ourselves in the way it does. It would be easy to see why it should appear to us to involve two things that seem so utterly disparate: experiential reality and nonexperiential reality. There would be no more of a felt problem about how it could possess the features that make it appear to us in the way that it does than there is a felt problem about how a thing can have mass and extension.

Neutral monism is a position worth noting, but there is a simple reason why it seems better to call oneself an *agnostic* monist. There is no need to adopt the radical neutral monist view that we have definitely not managed to attain any sort of knowledge of the nature of reality in our use of our actual categories of the mental and the physical. In fact, it seems clear that our belief in the reality of experience cannot be a complete error or illusion. Hence the term 'agnostic monism' is preferable to the term 'neutral monism': if acknowledgment of our ignorance drives us to agnosticism, we should also be agnostic about the extent of our ignorance.

Insofar as I am any sort of materialist, then, I am an agnostic materialist: our current conception of the physical is fundamentally incomplete on its own terms. Quite independently of the mind-body problem, it is a commonplace that there is a sense in which our ordinary concepts of space, time, and matter are profoundly inadequate and partial representations of the nature of the reality to which they are a

---

Spinoza would presumably have been more inclined to classify himself as a positive equal status monist than as a negative one.

Nagel (1986, 30, 48) notes a possible affinity with Spinoza and speculates that "mental and physical aspects of a process [may possibly be] manifestations of something more fundamental," "essential components of a more fundamental essence."

response. Our difficulty with the mind-body problem is just one more aspect of the proven inadequacy and partiality of our conception of matter.

Is agnostic materialism so uncommitted as to be vacuous? Does it turn the word 'material' (or 'physical') into nothing more than a descriptively empty synonym for 'real'? Is an agnostic materialist really just a "?-ist"? Not quite. I will return to this question briefly at the end of the chapter.

4.6 A Comment on Eliminativism, Instrumentalism, and So On

Whatever their differences, theories like neutral monism and panpsychism have a common virtue: they are appropriately radical responses to the enormity of the mind-body problem. I will now consider another view that possesses this virtue, even if it possesses no other.

I have suggested that materialism ought to be explicitly agnostic. But many materialists may now object that I have not given any good reason to suppose that all the blame for the intractability of the mind-body problem should be laid on the inadequacy of our current conception of those phenomena that are traditionally called 'physical'. They may say that at least part of the reason why the mind-body problem appears intractable lies in the inadequacy of our current conception of those phenomena that are traditionally called 'mental' (although they are just as physical as those that are traditionally called 'physical', according to materialism). They may go further and claim that progress with the mind-body problem, if it is going to be made at all, is not going to be made as a result of any radical and currently unimaginable extension or modification of the descriptive scheme of current physics, of a kind that would bring it into theoretical homogeneity (section 4.3) with experiential predicates. Rather, it is going to be a matter of rethinking our current concepts of the mental.

Obviously, my inclination is the other way. For the mental includes the experiential; and whatever faults there may be in our conception of the experiential, our acquaintance with the experiential simply doesn't leave room for us to make a mistake about its basic nature of such a fundamental kind that exposing the mistake could entirely dissolve the mind-body problem without there being any change in the descriptive scheme of current physics. None of the oddities and indeterminacies of experience detailed in Dennett's *Consciousness Explained*, for example, so much as touch the validity of our basic grasp of the nature of the experiential, as we acquire it in everyday experience of eating falafel, having hot baths, and doing modal logic.

Nevertheless, I will now say a little about the suggestion that it is the term 'mental' rather than the term 'physical' that ought to give way or be changed. And in discussing this issue, which is a debate between materialists, I will sometimes use 'mental' and 'physical' in the traditional way—as if they were opposed in a way in which they cannot be, according to materialists.

The current dominant view is still that mental notions will give way. Somehow they will be entirely subsumed under nonmental notions, or entirely reductively characterized in terms of nonmental notions, or entirely *eliminated* in favor of nonmental notions. Somehow or other we will be able to give, at least in principle, a full and satisfactory account of the general nature of reality using only those notions that we already deploy in "contemporary physical science" (Dennett, 1991b, 40; see also Edelman 1992, 113). But when one reflects on the point just made—[a] that mental phenomena include experiential or what-it's-like-ness phenomena, [b] that there is a crucial sense in which current physics lacks the resources for either describing or explaining experiential or what-it's-like-ness phenomena, [c] that (b) is still true even after everything that we have discovered about the structure and function of the brain (and the atom)—this view seems astonishing. It is a very great act of faith.

It is unclear what eliminativism amounts to, but here are three possibilities. First there is [1] eliminativism with respect to beliefs and desires, according to which no one ever really believes anything or desires anything. On one weak version of this view, the claim is that although the terms 'belief' and 'desire' have a conventional and perhaps even respectable everyday use, they will not feature at all in the best scientific account of human (or any) mentality.

This is, perhaps, a relatively mild form of eliminativism. But it does claim that it is, strictly speaking, false that you believe that grass is green or that you ever want to eat anything, and it must presumably expand into [2] eliminativism with respect to all propositional attitudes, according to which no one ever really fears anything or intends to do anything or hopes for anything or regrets anything or longs for anything, and so on.

This is perhaps amazing, but some have gone further. Some have apparently endorsed global eliminativism, [3] eliminativism with respect to all mental properties, sensations, moods, and emotions, as well as propositional attitudes. According to this view, all concepts like "the concepts of . . . belief, desire, sensation, pain, joy, and so on—await [the] fate" of the concepts of phlogiston and caloric. That is, our terms 'belief', 'desire', 'sensation', 'pain', 'joy', and so on, are going to turn out to be terms for things that *simply do not really exist*. In the case of caloric, "it was finally agreed that there is *no such thing*," and the same is going to happen to beliefs, desires, pains, and all other sensations, according to global eliminativism (Churchland 1984, 44). So no one ever really feels anything. No one ever really imagines anything. No one has any sensations or feels depressed. There is nothing it is like, experientially speaking, to eat an avocado or give birth to a child. (It is a moral relief to know that there is no pain in the universe.)

Eliminativists who accept anything like (3) do seem to be out of their minds. But if they exist, they have one virtue. They have an accurate sense of the size of the problem. They have seen the size it has for materialists, given the nature of our current conception of the physical, on the one hand, and the facts of experience, on the other hand. They have seen that the problem is so enormous, given the standard assumption that our current conception of the physical is basically on the right lines and liable to undergo only essentially conservative extensions, that denying the very existence of sensation, and of experience in general, does not seem like a disproportionately radical response to the problem. And they are quite right. For although the response is crazy, in a distinctively philosophical way, and although it would be better to admit that our current conception of the physical is fundamentally incomplete, it is undoubtedly a response of the right size.

The same might be said of the response of becoming an idealist, but idealism is far less implausible than outright eliminativism. It is interesting that modern eliminativists appear to concur with the seventeenth-century view that the physical (matter in motion) cannot possibly be the realizing ground of conscious experience, as ordinarily understood. This led many in the past to believe in immaterial substance as a realizing ground for experience. Now it seems to lead some philosophers to deny the existence of experience. Things have clearly gone downhill in the last three hundred years. Then as now Locke was right: since we do not understand the essential nature of matter, we have no good reason to suppose that it cannot be the realizing ground of experience (1975, II.xxiii.28–32, and IV.iii.6, one of philosophy's great paragraphs).

Perhaps no one really holds position (3). Or perhaps there is a way of formulating the doctrine of eliminativism that makes it sound much more reasonable, according to which it does not claim that there is really nothing that we are talking about when we talk about pains, feelings of joy, tastes, beliefs, desires, and so on. It allows that these terms refer to something real but insists [a] that we fundamentally misconceptualize the reality in question, and [b] that a correct and fully adequate conceptualization of the nature of this reality will not need to make use of anything more than neuroscience and computational science, both of which are ultimately reducible (in the sense of chapter 3, note 1) to physics.[9]

The trouble with this view is that it is obviously false. It is false, given current neuroscience, computational science, and physics, and it will continue to be false until there is a revolution in all three. This revolution will be needed to make (b) true. But in making (b) true, it will, I believe, have to cast doubt on (a). For consider (once again) your experience now, and what it's like, and the silence of physics on the subject. Consider its reality and the reality of all the other streams of experience on the planet. As a materialist, one may assume that experiences have, in addition to an experiential description, a nonexperiential description in the terms of physics (although one is not obliged to assume this by materialism). The old point remains: when we have given this description (with or without further, higher-level nonexperiential descriptions

9. See Rorty 1979, 117–118: "We can say that although in one sense there just are no sensations, in another sense what people *called* 'sensations', viz., neural states, do indeed exist. The distinction of senses is no more sophisticated than when we say that the sky does not exist, but that there is something which people call the sky (the appearance of a blue dome as a result of refracted sunlight) which does exist." What is remarkable here is the belief that the sky analogy, which makes use of the fact that certain sensations may lead us to believe in the existence of something that doesn't exist, can be applied to sensations themselves.

in neurophysiological or computational-science terms), we have still said nothing about the experiences considered specifically in respect of their experiential character.

Some may think that this does not matter very much. They may have made a conscious decision not to say anything about experiential phenomena, because they are pursuing the project of eliminating experience-describing terminology from their account of the world. But then they are simply deciding to leave part of reality out of their scientific account of reality. They are just giving up on the great philosophical-scientific project of giving a unified account of the whole of reality, so far as we are acquainted with it and so far as we are able. For if one thing is clear, it is that experience is as real as rabbits and rocks. Indeed, its reality is still, in this post-post-Cartesian age, the thing we can be most certain of. So 'eliminativism', on this last understanding of the term, has now become the name of the doctrine that we can and indeed should, as scientifically inspired philosophers, ignore one of the most dramatic and puzzling aspects of reality that there is.

Those who think that our sense of the difficulty of the mind-body problem flows (partly or wholly) from our mistaken view that we fully understand the nature of mind are all antirealists of some sort with respect to the mind—whether they are (Dennettian) instrumentalists, (Davidsonian) interpretationists, (Wittgensteinian or "Wittgensteinian") philosophical behaviorists, eliminativists, or covertly or overtly reductive functionalists. The present objection to their approach is simple: even if it has some plausibility in the case of propositional attitudes, or more generally in the case of all aspects of the mental that do not obviously and necessarily involve experience, it has none in the case of experience. Even if we are in some way ignorant of the nature of the experiential, even if our everyday and philosophical language for talking about the experiential is problematic or inadequate in various ways (see section 3.6 and Dennett 1988, 1991b), there is a sense in which we cannot be wrong about experience that has no parallel in the case of the nonexperiential.

This sense in which we cannot be wrong is not the one that is usually considered when it is claimed that some of our judgments about our own mental states and occurrences (and in particular our experiences) are "incorrigible." It is not necessary for present purposes to claim that one cannot be wrong about the experiential character of at least some of one's experiences.[10] It suffices to claim that if it really seems to one that one is having an experience then one must indeed be having some experience or other. One can try the thought that the state of affairs of one's having rich and complicated mental experience might not really obtain but only seem to obtain. But it is self-refuting in Cartesian style, because for it genuinely to seem that such a state of affairs obtains is already for such a state of affairs to obtain.

4.7 Conclusion

Our existing notions of the physical and the mental or experiential cannot possibly be reconciled or theoretically integrated as they stand. One or both of the two sets of notions will have to be radically modified if we are going to be able to understand how monism is true. Some eliminativists think that the source of the problem lies in our notions of the mental and experiential, and that these notions will ultimately be discarded in a perfected philosophy or science of mind. With their more moderate allies, these eliminativists still appear to represent the majority view in contemporary philosophy of mind: they hold that the principal cause of the intractability of the problem lies in the defective nature of our existing concepts of the mental or experiential. I have suggested that it is the other way round: that it is the descriptive scheme of physics that will have to change dramatically if there is to be an acceptable theoretical unification with the mental scheme. (The problem of the lack of a vocabulary for an objective phenomenology, raised in section 3.6, remains untouched.) If the eliminativists or instrumentalists claim that the best *predictive science of behavior* will not have any use for experiential notions, then we may concede the point cheerfully, if only for the sake of argument, because what then becomes clear is that this predictive science of behavior is going to say nothing about the hard part of the mind-body problem—the problem posed by the existence of experience, given the current terms of physics. This predictive science of behavior

10. In fact, this much assaulted claim is plausible and is not put in doubt by the fact that one can be very wrong about the causes of one's experiences, their realizing grounds, their similarity to one's previous experiences, their correct description in the language one speaks, and so on.

will perhaps be useful, powerful, and stylish, but it will shoot straight past the hard part of the mind-body problem.

Having built a heavy Lockean element of agnosticism into the term 'materialist', I continue to call myself a materialist. According to agnostic materialism, the idea that the mind-body problem is particularly perplexing flows from our unjustified and relatively modern faith that we have an adequate grasp of the fundamental nature of matter at some crucial *general* level of understanding, even if we are still uncertain about many details. Agnosticism seems called for because it seems so clear that this cannot be right if materialism is true. As things stand, the best we can do is to take James Clerk Maxwell's advice and try to maintain ourselves in that state of "thoroughly conscious ignorance which is a prelude to every real advance in knowledge" (Maxwell 1877, 245–246).

Why do I call myself a materialist, rather than a "?-ist"? My faith, like that of many other materialists, consists in a bundle of connected and unverifiable beliefs. I believe that experience is not all there is to reality. I believe that there is a physical world that involves the existence of space and of space-occupying entities that have nonexperiential properties. I believe that the theory of evolution is true, that once there was no experience like ours on this planet, whether panpsychism is true or false, and that there came to be experience like ours as a result of processes that at no point involved anything not wholly physical or material in nature. Accordingly, I believe that however experiential properties are described, there is no good reason to think that they are emergent, relative to other physical properties, in such a way that they can correctly be said to be nonphysical properties. Finally, with Nagel (1986, 28), I believe that one could in principle create a normally experiencing human being out of a piano. All one would have to do would be to arrange a sufficient number of the piano's constituent electrons, protons, and neutrons in the way in which they are ordinarily arranged in a normal living human being. Experience is as much a physical phenomenon as electric charge.

5

Mentalism, Idealism, and Immaterialism

5.1 Introduction

What part does reference to nonmental phenomena play in a satisfactory account of mental phenomena? Chapters 3 and 4 responded in one way to this fundamental question. They focused on experiential mental phenomena and accepted the standard materialist assumption that all experiential mental phenomena are intimately existentially related to nonexperiential nonmental phenomena (for reasons independent of the fact that specification of their content often requires reference to nonmental phenomena). These chapters then argued that we are crucially ignorant of the nature of this relation.

In this chapter I drop the standard materialist assumption and address the fundamental question directly, by asking whether the mental (or experiential) is provably or necessarily related to the nonmental (or nonexperiential) in some way. This raises the question of whether any idealist theory of mind is coherent. The answer to this question is probably 'Yes'. But there is a more important question to which the answer may be 'No'. This is the question whether any idealist theory of mind is both coherent and interestingly distinct from a materialist theory of mind. Those who are uninterested in either question may still wish to read section 5.12.

In view of the philosophical preoccupations of the 1990s, it may be worth repeating a point made in section 2.5 before beginning. This is the point that there is no quick "argument from content" (p. 37) to the conclusion that reference to the nonmental is indispensable in a satisfactory account of the nature of the mental. If carrots are nonmental mind-independent things, as we ordinarily suppose, and if a particular belief is a belief about a carrot, then reference to the nonmental is obviously necessary in a satisfactory account of the nature of the belief, for all beliefs about carrots are necessarily beliefs about carrots. It does not follow, however, that reference to the nonmental is central or indispensable in a satisfactory account of the essential nature of the mental, any more than it follows that reference to carrots is. It does not follow, from the fact that some actual beliefs and thoughts are about nonmental things, that thoughts, beliefs, experiences, and so on, cannot possibly exist unless nonmental things exist.

I will start by distinguishing three things that are often identified—mentalism, idealism, and immaterialism—and then try to explain why idealists are pulled between strict-mentalist or pure-process views of the mind, on the one hand, and apparently nonmentalist, immaterial-stuff views of the mind, on the other hand. I think it is worthwhile to reflect on these matters even if one is committed to materialism. Taking them seriously is part of a proper response to the general metaphysical agnosticism that was held to be unavoidable in the last two chapters.

5.2 Mentalism

Strict mentalism, to begin, is the doctrine that absolutely everything is mental, including everything that we ordinarily think of as physical. There are no existents or goings-on that are not entirely mental in every respect. The existence of mental goings-on does not involve the existence of any nonmental goings-on of any sort. It does not, for example, involve any nonmental physical goings-on in the brain, in the way that materialists ordinarily suppose. No doubt there are lesser varieties of mentalism—the word has been used in many ways—but this is strict mentalism. I will call it 'mentalism', occasionally prefixing '(strict)' as a reminder.

Obviously enough, we do not really know what mentalism is until we can say exactly what constitutes being mental. And this seems very hard to do. We can consider various suggestions, but we face the fact that the concept of the mental is an "essentially contestable concept."

I will consider some rival views about the extent of the mental in chapter 6. Until then I will continue to suppose that we have a reasonably determinate idea of what counts as mental, firmly grounded in ordinary use and sufficient for present purposes. Among mental phenomena, there are experiential phenomena, occurrent experiential episodes, like sensations, perceptions, consciously entertained thoughts, emotional feelings, and so on. And then there are dispositional, nonexperiential states, like beliefs and desires. I will speak mainly of experiential phenomena, partly for historical reasons, partly because they are the ones that prove to be difficult when it comes to the mind-body problem, and partly because the reality of things like beliefs and desires can be seriously disputed in a way in which the reality of experiential phenomena cannot.

For the moment I will also assume that all truly and distinctively mental phenomena are essentially mentally *contentful* phenomena. They may have sensory content or conceptual content or both, and there is no need at present to go into the question of whether there are any other kinds of content (see further pp. 163–164 below). I take it that our everyday experience furnishes us with intimate knowledge of the nature of both these kinds of content and thereby provides us with an understanding of the notion of mental content sufficient for the purposes of this chapter. It may be thought that our everyday-experience-based knowledge of the nature of sensory content is superior to our everyday-experience-based knowledge of the nature of conceptual content. But all those who understand this sentence are deeply familiar with the phenomenon of cognitive or conceptual mental content. They know very well what it is, in the sense that matters at present.

Strict mentalism has *total* and *partial* versions. Total mentalism has already been described. It is a *monist* doctrine. It holds that there is a fundamental sense in which there is only one kind of thing, one kind of stuff, in reality.

Traditional *dualists* cannot be total mentalists, because they hold that things—entities, objects, phenomena, occurrences, states, events, processes—are of two fundamental and mutually exclusive types: mental and physical. Nevertheless, they can be partial mentalists, because they can be mentalists about the mind: they can hold that the existence of mental goings-on does not involve the existence of any physical goings-on, even though physical phenomena do exist. I will mean total mentalism when I talk simply of 'mentalism', but the partial option is always worth bearing in mind.

These mentalist views contrast with materialist views in an obvious way. As a monist theory, mentalism is directly opposed to strict materialism, a monist theory that holds that there is a fundamental sense in which everything is physical, including everything that we ordinarily think of as mental. Strict materialism holds that there are no existents that are not entirely physical in every respect.

Obviously enough, we do not really know what materialism is until we can say exactly what constitutes being physical. And this may be very hard to do. But for the moment we may suppose that we have a reasonably determinate idea of the physical. We certainly have paradigm cases of physical phenomena, with which we take ourselves to be familiar: rocks, seas, neurons, and so on.

Here, then, is the traditional framework, rapidly introduced, according to which *mental* and *physical* are the two options for monists and dualists alike. There are various other exotic possibilities, but I will stick to the traditional framework for the purposes of this discussion.

What relations hold between mentalism, idealism, and immaterialism? Here are six suggestions, which I will try to clarify in what follows. Strict mentalism appears to entail idealism, as this is ordinarily understood. That is, it appears to entail the view that what we think of as the physical world (of tables and chairs, etc.) is in some sense constituted entirely out of ideas—whatever exactly they are. And it also entails immaterialism, given that there cannot be material phenomena without there being nonmental things. I take it, however, that these three positions do not all entail each other.

There may be one further entailment to be had, for it looks as if idealism (as ordinarily understood) entails immaterialism. But this entailment may fail, on a less ordinary understanding of idealism. Moreover, immaterialism does not entail idealism, given the various possible ways of taking the name 'idealism' (Berkeley is an immaterialist, but he is not a strict idealist, because he does not think that everything is made of ideas). Nor does immaterialism entail mentalism (for one can believe in immaterial stuff, or "soul substance," without thinking that it is itself intrinsically mentally contentful or that it is entirely mental in every respect). Nor does idealism entail mentalism (for one can be an idealist about the external world and believe in immaterial stuff without thinking that this immaterial stuff is entirely mental in every respect).

Rapidly stated, these claims are very hard to assess, and they are open to various abstruse objections. The best way to try to explain them is to say some more about idealism.

5.3 Strict or Pure Process Idealism

Idealism has several significant varieties, and it seems best to begin with *strict* idealism. This is the doctrine that everything (but everything) is constituted of ideas—or perceptions in Hume's idiom, or thoughts in Descartes's idiom, or experiences or experiential or mental goings-on in a seemingly more neutral modern idiom. (I will often talk simply of ideas.) When people talk of idealism, they usually think of it as a thesis about what we think of as the physical world. But to be a *strict* idealist is also to be committed to the bundle theory of mind, according to which minds as well as everything else are constituted entirely of ideas or experiences.[1] Or in another idiom, strict idealists are committed to the view that the existence of a mind consists entirely in the existence of a stream of ideas or experiential goings-on.

One can also express strict idealism in terms of Cartesian Thoughts.[2] It is the view that, so far as a given mind and its Thoughts are concerned, there is no substance or existent that is ontically distinct from the Thoughts, and of which the Thoughts are attributes or properties. There is just a pure process, an essentially mentally contentful mentation process, the Thoughts process.

One could call this the pure process theory of the mind. According to this theory, the Thoughts process or experience process is all that exists, so far as the mind is concerned. It is the substance, if there must be a substance where there is a mind. We tend to think of experience as a nonsubstantial phenomenon that stands in need of a substance. But if we are going to talk of substance at all, then, as Hume pointed out, it seems that we have no good reason to reject the idea that experience itself can be a substance—a substance process somehow incorporating

1. This may make it look as if strict idealism entails mentalism. If position (I3) (p. 122 below) is coherent, however, this is not so.

2. I capitalize 'Thought' and 'Thinking' when translating Descartes's special wide use of *cogitatio*. He took the term to cover all commonly recognized occurrent mental phenomena: sensings, thinkings, willings, imaginings, doubtings, rememberings, and so on.

both experiences and a subject of experience and standing in no meta-physical need of anything other than itself in order to exist (Hume 1978, 233, 634; the pure process theory is not really distinct from the bundle theory, but the word 'bundle' seems particularly unhelpful).

It may be doubted whether this pure process theory is any sort of Cartesian position, but in section 5.8 below I will suggest that it corresponds to something important in Descartes's thought, even if his dominant idea is that there is, in the case of a given mind, an immaterial mental continuant that is ontically distinct from all its particular Thoughts.

5.4 Active-Principle Idealism

Berkeley is not a strict idealist, because he does not hold that ideas or experiences are all that exist. He also holds that minds exist, and he rejects the strict idealist bundle or stream or pure process theory of mind, according to which minds are entirely constituted out of ideas.

He considers the bundle theory of mind in his *Philosophical Commentaries:*

577 The very existence of Ideas constitutes the soul.

578 Consciousness, perception, existence of Ideas seem to be all one.

579 Consult, ransack y^r Understanding w^t find you there besides several perceptions or thoughts. W^t mean you by the word 'mind' you must mean something that you perceive. . . .

580 Mind is a congeries of Perceptions. Take away perceptions & you take away the Mind put the Perceptions & you put the mind.

581 Say you the Mind is not the Perceptions. but that thing wch perceives. I answer you are abus'd by the words 'that' and 'thing' these are vague empty words w^{th}out a meaning.[3]

He seems tempted to adopt this view. But in the end he clearly rejects it. In the "Third Dialogue" Hylas charges Berkeley's spokesman Philonous with adherence to the bundle or pure process theory, saying, "In consequence of your own principles, it should follow that you are only a system of floating ideas, without any substance to support them."

---

3. Berkeley 1975, 307. I have added quotation marks where words are mentioned rather than used, put in a small amount of punctuation, and spelled out the odder abbreviations.

Philonous replies, "How often must I repeat that I know or am conscious of my own being; and that I myself am not my ideas, but somewhat else, a thinking active principle that perceives, knows, wills, and operates about them" (1975, 198). And in the *Principles* Berkeley writes as follows: "Besides all [the] endless variety of ideas . . . , there is . . . something which knows or perceives them, and exercises divers operations . . . about them. This perceiving acting being is what I call *mind, spirit, soul,* or *myself.* By which words I do not denote any one of my ideas, but a thing entirely distinct from them, wherein they exist" (*Principles*, section 2).

Berkeley, then, is an *immaterialist*, and he is an *idealist* with respect to the physical world. But he is not a *strict* idealist in the present sense.

It is very natural to suppose that Berkeley is also a *mentalist*, because he holds that all that exist are ideas, which are entirely mental things, and minds, which are presumably also entirely mental things. It is arguable, however, that mentalism properly understood entails *strict* idealism. On this view, mentally contentful ideas or experiential goings-on are, strictly speaking, the only truly mental things there are, because they are the only truly mentally contentful things there are. So mentalism must entail strict idealism and hence a thought-stream or pure process theory of mind. In this case Berkeley cannot be a mentalist, strictly speaking, because he is not a strict idealist.

It may be replied, however, that Berkeley can be counted as a mentalist, because there is another way of taking mentalism, according to which ideas are not the only (purely) mental phenomena there are. On this second view, there are perhaps two sorts of things that are not ideas but that are entirely mental in nature. First, there are mental *acts*—of willing, thinking, and so on—that are not themselves "passive," as ideas are in Berkeley's view, and that are therefore not themselves ideas. These, however, are contentful occurrences that one may reasonably assimilate into a wider understanding of the word 'idea'. Second, and more important, there is the mind itself, conceived of as the source of these mental acts—as an "active principle" that, in itself, is entirely mental in character and ontically distinct from its ideas.

It seems, then, that we may after all say that Berkeley is a (strict) mentalist. He is a (strict) mentalist, although he is not a strict idealist, because he holds that the mind is not constituted out of ideas but is rather an active principle distinct from its ideas. There are, of course, great difficulties raised by the question of what exactly this amounts to, some of which I will consider.

It is an interesting question whether Berkeley considers this active principle to be ontically distinct not just from its (passive) ideas but from *all* its mental occurrences, including its acts or acting. In his *Philosophical Commentaries* he writes as follows: the "Substance of a Spirit is that it acts, causes, wills, operates, or if you please (to avoid the quibble that may be made on the word 'it') to act, cause, will, operate."[4] Here Berkeley strikingly eliminates the grammatically substantival 'it' in favor of the nonsubstantival verbal infinitives, which are, in a sense, mere or pure-process terms. To make such a move is to suggest that there is nothing—no thing—that acts, causes, wills, operates, and is ontically distinct from these doings, which are themselves just occurrent mental phenomena, on Berkeley's view. So here he appears attracted by some sort of pure process view, although his later and official position, as recorded in the quotations from the *Dialogues* and *Principles* given above, is usually held to involve the view that the "active principle" is to be distinguished not only from its (passive) ideas but also from its acts—being *something* that acts, something distinct from its acts.[5]

5.5 Stuff Idealism

This suggests a third possible view about Berkeley, according to which he, along with other idealists and dualists, is committed to the idea that there is some kind of immaterial stuff that is the realizing ground of mental goings-on *but that is not necessarily itself intrinsically mental in every respect*, insofar as it is not intrinsically mentally contentful in every respect. I doubt that Berkeley would have accepted this way of putting things, and it seems clear that it cannot be Descartes's official view, but the idea that this is what *dualism* involves is arguably to be found in Locke. It may be, implicitly if not explicitly, the received view about both standard idealist and standard dualist conceptions of mind: both these

4. *Philosophical Commentaries*, sec. 829. See also sec. 701: "The substance of Spirit we do not know it not being knowable. it being purus actus."

5. For a trace of this change in the *Philosophical Commentaries*, see secs. 615 and 615a. In section 5.8 below I will argue that one finds the same hesitation in Descartes, and I will try to explain why it is natural.

conceptions of mind are commonly taken to involve some appeal to an immaterial "soul-substance," or immaterial stuff, while the question of whether this immaterial stuff can be said to be itself intrinsically and entirely *mental* in character is simply elided. On the whole, immaterial substance is presented as something whose essential nature is not known: all that is known about it is that it is, by its nature, intrinsically well fitted to be the realizing ground of mental goings-on.

Consider Locke. Contrary to Descartes, he holds that Thinking is not an essential property of a mind. It is therefore not a property that a mind must have at all times but is rather one of its operations, something that it may or may not be engaged in at any given moment. On his view, there may be times at which there is no Thinking going on at all. Thus he holds that Thinking—mentally contentful process in general—stands to mind as motion, rather than extension, stands to physical body (*Essay*, II.i.10). And this view invites the idea that the mind, as continuously existing immaterial substance, or soul stuff, must have some intrinsic *nonmental* essential property or mode of being. For it must have some mode of existence even when there is nothing mentally contentful going on in it. One could, of course, adopt this Lockean view and simply *stipulate* that the immaterial stuff is to be thought of as intrinsically and entirely mental in every respect. But it is no longer clear what positive grounds one would have for saying this. This is a point on which Locke was very clear, and to which I will return.

A general route to this same conclusion can be constructed within the classical seventeenth- and eighteenth-century debate, even if it is not explicitly stated there. The first step is to take it [1] that the class of truly or wholly mental things is to be identified with the class of experiential goings-on—conscious, occurrent, intrinsically mentally contentful episodes. These are what we know of the mental. They are (therefore) what define 'the mental' for us. The next step is to suppose [2] that such conscious, occurrent, mental episodes need some realizing ground distinct from them, something in which they can "inhere" (not to mention some subject to whom they can belong). It is widely (but not universally) held to be obvious [3] that this realizing ground cannot possibly be physical: physical substance, matter in motion, just isn't the sort of thing that can be the basis of mental goings-on. It follows [4] that the realizing ground must be nonphysical, or immaterial. But it now seems [5] that this immaterial thing cannot itself be wholly mental in character: it cannot be itself entirely composed of conscious, occurrent mental episodes, for those were the very things for which a substantial basis or realizing ground was being sought. But by (1), they are the only truly or wholly mental things. So although the realizing ground of mental episodes must be *immaterial*, it will not itself be entirely mental in character.

I record this line of thought without comment. As remarked, I do not think it is explicit as a line of thought. In fact, I think that there is a lot of understandable blurring on this question, and this is something to which I will return.

So far, then, we have a distinction between three idealist views which tend to run into one another. First, there is strict idealism, which contains as a necessary part a bundle or pure process theory of mind. One might also call this *pure process idealism*. It is a form of absolute idealism, and it is perhaps correctly attributable to F. H. Bradley, although the holistic and Hegelian elements in his thinking make it hard to be sure.

Second, there is the view that I take to be Berkeley's, subject to the reservations expressed above. One could call it *active-principle idealism*. It claims to be a (strict) mentalist view, but it is not a strict idealist or pure process view; at least in its standard version.

Third, there is the version of idealism that posits the existence of some immaterial stuff that is not intrinsically and entirely mental in every respect. (It is not known to be, at least, and there is a difficulty about how it could be, since it is introduced specifically as something that is ontically distinct from—as the indispensable realizing ground of the conscious, occurrent mental episodes that are the only things known to be intrinsically mentally contentful.) This view is neither strict idealism nor (strict) mentalism, but it is nonetheless immaterialist, and it is perhaps the view that is most commonly (if obscurely) thought of as being "idealist." I have suggested that one might call it *stuff idealism*. Stuff idealism has certain clear advantages when compared with other idealist theories, and stuff-idealist elements may well feature implicitly in the thought of many idealists. The danger it faces, as will become apparent, is that it runs the risk of being unable to distinguish itself sufficiently from materialism.

In defining 'stuff idealism' in this way, I don't mean to suggest that all those who have thought it acceptable to talk of immaterial stuff or immaterial substance have thought of this immaterial stuff or substance as something that is intrinsically nonmental in some respect. Some of those who have talked of immaterial stuff or substance have probably supposed, however vaguely, that it is entirely mental in every respect—although they may not have thought very hard about what exactly its mentalness consists in, given that it is something ontically distinct from the mentally contentful goings-on it "supports."

The next thing for me to do is to say some more about immaterialism, but I will first very briefly record a fourth possible version of partial idealism. One might call it 'vat idealism'—for it is idealism adopted with respect to the "objects" that make up the "physical world" in which a person (say Louis) whose brain is a brain in a vat takes himself to live. Obviously, it is part of the brain-in-a-vat hypothesis that the story of how Louis comes to have the experience he has may be given in materialist terms. Nevertheless, the naturalness of giving an idealist account of the apparent physical objects that he confronts—the "Paris" he inhabits—is clear. The objects he sees and touches are not really there. Nor is the space he moves through. There is a computer, some wiring, and so on. His world is an ideational construct.

Note that this last version of idealism is one variety of a whole species of partial-idealist theories. They have in common the idea that we ourselves may be objects of a kind quite unlike what we ordinarily suppose, given our everyday experience of things, while the world of objects we take ourselves to inhabit is, in some clear sense, a mere ideational construct arising from an interaction between ourselves, whatever we are, and something else, whatever it is. So described, this species of views includes Kant's transcendental idealism and neutral monism.

5.6 Immaterialism

It is perhaps already clear that immaterialism does not entail mentalism. For to take an immaterialist view of something is simply to take the view that it is not material or physical. After a normal training in philosophy, we may tend to think of the term 'immaterial' as having some sort of obscure but nonetheless positive descriptive force, but it has none. All it means is 'not material', and there is no good reason to think that anything nonmaterial is ipso facto mental. (Is antimatter material?) Stuff idealism of the sort described above is an immaterialist theory, but it is not a mentalist theory. And whatever the nature of the positions that have historically been called 'neutral monism', outright neutral monism claims that reality is neither physical nor mental, as we ordinarily conceive of these things; in which case reality is immaterial, but not mental. So immaterialism does not entail mentalism.

Nor does immaterialism about the mind entail strict idealism about the mind. For stuff idealism, once again, is an immaterialist theory, but it is not a strict idealist theory. It holds that there is some kind of immaterial substance that is the realizing ground of mental states and occurrences, although it is not itself intrinsically and entirely mental in character and is not constituted of ideas or experiences.

Active-principle idealism is also immaterialist but not strict-idealist, insofar as it involves the view that the mind is nonmaterial but is not itself constituted of ideas or experiences.

No doubt many immaterialists have supposed that the immaterial stuff they posit is itself entirely mental in every respect, and have accordingly taken themselves to be true mentalists. But it is important to see what this claim involves, in the context of the classical debate. The point has already been made. The paradigm examples of mental goings-on, in the classical debate, are just occurrent mentally contentful goings-on or experiential goings-on, ideas or experiences: thoughts, willings, decidings, dreamings, and so on. It is our experience of these intrinsically mentally contentful things that gives positive content to our idea of what the mental is. So if we suppose that there is any *other* kind of mental thing, i.e., immaterial substance, we have to grant that there is a sense in which we know nothing about its nature, apart from the fact that it is, somehow, the source or ground or basis of the familiar occurrent mental goings-on.

If this is right, then someone who thinks that immaterial substance is itself entirely mental in every respect is under some pressure to suppose that the existence of immaterial substance does consist entirely and exclusively in the existence of the familiar occurrent mental goings-on, although this amounts to the pure process view. The alternative is to claim that we can know immaterial substance to be entirely mental in every respect in spite of two rather large problems. First, we know nothing about its nature when we consider it independently of the occurrent mental goings-on of which it is supposed to be the ground. Second, our positive conception of the mental derives entirely from these familiar occurrent mental goings-on, and immaterial substance is, precisely, supposed to be ontically distinct from these goings-on.

It seems, then, that only the unsupported stipulation that immaterial substance is entirely mental in every respect can keep this position distinct from stuff idealism, which is not a mentalist position at all. And if this is right, it helps to explain why the desire to be a mentalist, partial or total, pushes one toward a pure process view of the mind (as Descartes surely realized).

It may again be said that there is a stable, fully mentalist position situated between pure process idealism and stuff idealism. All one has to do is to assert the existence of the ex hypothesi entirely mental self or soul or mind, taking comfort in the grammatical substantivality of these three words. One may then say that there is, in addition to the occurrent mental phenomena, a self or mind, a thing that is simply stipulated to be entirely mental in every respect. But this answer begs the question, for reasons already given. For one then needs to know what the self or mind is, over and above the particular indubitably mental episodes of willing, sensing, and so on, that are attributed to it. Even if one simply assumes that the self or mind exists as something irreducibly over and above the occurrent mental goings-on, the question arises as to what *grounds* one has, and indeed as to what grounds one can have, for supposing (or ruling) that it is definitely "entirely mental in every respect." Why should the stuff-idealist *or even the materialist* account of its nature not be correct? As soon as one suggests that the existence of mental substance may not consist entirely in the existence of occurrent mental goings-on and that mental substance may be like physical substance in having some sort of unknown "real essence," one really has no defense against someone who says that its real essence, for all one knows, may not be wholly mental and may indeed be material. (It is true that the argument can be run equally well by the mentalist against the materialist. But it is the mentalist who is on the defensive at the moment.) This problem arises immediately for the active-principle view, insofar as it claims to be a strict mentalist view while insisting that the active principle is distinct from its occurrent mental episodes.

It seems to me that Berkeley, Descartes, and Locke are vividly aware of these problems, more so than many today who seem prepared to accept the idea that when we are trying to understand what a coherent idealist theory might be like, we can simply *assume* that immaterial substance is some sort of ground of mental states and episodes that is ontically distinct from them and is also intrinsically and entirely mental in character in spite of this ontic distinctness. At one point, at least, Berkeley suggests that there is an inescapable sense in which the ultimate nature of the mind is unknowable, insofar as it is distinct from ideas or occurrent mental goings-on in general, even if we can know *that* it exists and *what* it does. He seems aware that the only way to avoid this conclusion (on the terms of the classical debate) is to accept a bundle or pure-process view of the mind.

It is arguable, then, that Berkeley was not in a position to rule out the idea that the mind might not be entirely mental in every respect. He thought that he could know it must be entirely immaterial, because he thought he could show that the notion of matter was incoherent. But he was in no position to claim to know that it was entirely mental.

5.7 The Positions Restated

Let me now try to order the options more carefully, setting out a table of positions according to whether they are immaterialist (Imm), mentalist (M), or strict idealist (Id), or any two or these, or all or none of them.

The eight possible positions are [1] +Imm, +M, +Id, [2] +Imm, +M, −Id, [3] +Imm, −M, +Id, [4] +Imm, −M, −Id, [5] −Imm, +M, +Id, [6] −Imm, +M, −Id, [7] −Imm, −M, +Id, and [8] −Imm, -M, −Id. But positions (5) to (8) are impossible or of no present concern: (5) to (7) are impossible, since both mentalism and idealism entail immaterialism (p. 110), and (8) is materialism.[6] That leaves (1) to (4). In this way, then, we get four possible monist idealist positions on reality, (I1) to

---

6. Strictly speaking, materialism is just one example of a position of type (8). Some versions of neutral monism are also of type (8), and there are other possibilities.

Table 5.1
Correspondences between immaterialist monist theories of reality and dualist theories of the mind

Immaterialist monist theories of reality	Characterization	Dualist theories of the mind
I1	+Imm +M +Id	D1
I2	+Imm +M −Id	D2
I3	+Imm −M +Id	D3
I4	+Imm −M −Id	D4

Imm = immaterialist, M = mentalist, Id = strict idealist.

(I4), and four closely corresponding dualist positions on the mind, (D1) to (D4) (table 5.1).

The most important positions are already familiar from the foregoing discussion, but I will restate them, and in order to present them I will introduce three idealist conceptions of the nature of ideas or experiences. I am not claiming that these three conceptions of ideas are astoundingly clear, any more than the various idealist conceptions of reality are, and I will sometimes register uncertainties in the course of stating them.

First, there are *non-self-subsistent* ideas or experiences, or ideas$_1$. These are ideas conceived of as entirely dependent on minds, which are ontically distinct from them. They are mentally contentful events in, or states or modifications of, such minds. Being ontically distinct from ideas, these minds can presumably continue to exist when there are no ideas or experiences occurring. (Note that the materialist view of ideas or experiences, and of their dependence on the brain, is essentially similar to this.)

Second, there are two conceptions of ideas or experiences as *self-subsistent*, ideas$_2$ and ideas$_3$, which I will take in reverse order. Ideas$_3$ are not only entirely self-subsistent entities. They are also pure mental contents. They have no content-transcendent ontic nature or mode of being whatever. They are, if you like, immaterial substance, or they are constituted of immaterial substance. But immaterial substance is just mental content.[7]

7. It is "purely experiential content" in the sense of section 1.6. This may well be what Hume has in mind at certain points in his *Treatise* (1978, 233, 634).

Ideas$_2$ are perhaps the strangest. They are entirely self-subsistent, but they are not just mental contents like ideas$_3$. For they have some ontic aspect or mode of being over and above their having the content they have. They are not just contents but are also immaterial, content-possessing *vehicles* of content. They have some content-transcending nature, ontologically speaking; they are constituted of some kind of content-carrying, but ontologically speaking content-transcendent, immaterial stuff.[8]

Now for the eight positions. I will sometimes add details to them, for historical reasons, that are not obviously essential to them on the terms of table 5.1.

[I1] Pure process (or bundle-theory) idealism This position is strict-idealist, for ideas are all that exist. It is mentalist, hence the ideas are ideas$_3$.[9] A person or mind cannot exist in the absence of ideas. It must always be Thinking, in Descartes's terms.

[I2] Active-principle idealism Reality does not consist only of ideas in Berkeley's sense. There are also purely mental "thinking principles" distinct from ideas, and also from any mental acts. Ideas are presumably ideas$_1$.

Someone who holds a position like (I2) can immediately allow for mental continuity through dreamless sleep or complete unconsciousness. (Note that if the thinking principle is *not* thought of as distinct from its mental acts, as in the last paragraph of section 5.4 above, then (I2) turns into a form of (I1).)

[I3] Version 1 of stuff idealism All there are are ideas, but it follows from +Imm and −M that they are ideas$_2$.

This very strange version of stuff idealism could be called 'stuff-bundle idealism'. It is not likely to be a popular option.

[I4] Version 2 of stuff idealism Ideas are not all that exist (−Id), for there are immaterial minds, which are ontically distinct from their ideas. Furthermore, although these minds are constituted of immaterial stuff (+Imm), this immaterial stuff is not intrinsically and entirely mental in every respect (−M). Ideas are presumably ideas$_1$.

8. Compare pictures and their pictorial content. See Strawson 1989b, 37–38.
9. They cannot be ideas$_2$, given +M, and they cannot be ideas$_1$, given +Id.

Clearly, (I2) and (I4) need have no difficulty with the idea that a mind or person persists during unconsciousness or dreamless sleep, whereas (I1) and (I3) do. I think (I3) is uninteresting. The others have a certain dynamic connectedness. Thus I have suggested that Berkeley exemplifies a natural pattern in that he is drawn to (I1), rejects it for (I2), but then finds that he cannot on his own principles rule out (I4). This is a dangerous position for him to be in, since those who cannot rule out (I4) are open to the charge that they cannot rule out materialism either. Descartes may fit the same pattern with respect to (D1), (D2), and (D4).

5.8 The Dualist Options

The dualist theories of the mind closely follow the idealist monist theories of reality, but I will set them out using 'Thought' and 'Thinking' as often as 'idea', with Descartes in mind.

[D1] The radical stream theory or pure process view of the mind Immaterial substance *is* Thought or Thinking. The *res is* the *cogitans*. Just as all that is essential to body is extension, on Descartes's unusual view, so all that is essential to mind is Thinking, on this view. The parallel is exact. Clearly, a mind or person must think continuously for as long as it exists. Thoughts (ideas) are ideas$_3$.

[D2] The mind as an active thinking principle The immaterial mind (+Imm) is not identical with its Thoughts (−Id) but is nevertheless entirely mental in every respect (+M). It is an active "thinking principle" or "soul-substance" ontically distinct from its Thoughts. Thoughts (ideas) are presumably ideas$_1$.

One could add to the description of (D2) the idea that the active thinking principle may in fact be unable to exist without thinking, although it is not actually entirely constituted by its thinking (just as one might suppose that matter cannot exist without being extended, although it is not entirely constituted by its extension).

[D3] Version 1 of the immaterial-stuff view of the mind The mind— the substance of the mind—is entirely constituted of Thoughts (or ideas), but these Thoughts (or ideas) are ideas$_2$. They are not entirely mental in every respect.

Perhaps no one has ever held (D3).

[D4]   Version 2 of the immaterial-stuff view of the mind   The mind is constituted of immaterial stuff. This immaterial stuff is intrinsically well fitted to being the realizing ground of mental goings-on (unlike physical stuff), but it is not entirely mental in every respect. The mind is ontically distinct from its Thoughts. Thoughts (ideas) are presumably ideas$_1$.

Like (I2) and (I4), (D2) and (D4) have no difficulty with the idea of mental continuity through unconsciousness or dreamless sleep.

I think Descartes hesitates between (D1) and its alternatives, and I will consider this idea in some detail because the hesitation seems natural and instructive. It reflects a central uncertainty or difficulty that occurs both in monist idealist theories of reality and in dualist theories of the mind. It is arguable that there are good reasons why such theories should be attracted to type 1 pure process positions and at the same time pulled toward type 2 active-principle positions. It is also arguable that once one has felt the pull from a type 1 position to a type 2 position, one risks being pulled from a type 2 position to a type 4 stuff-idealist position. If so, it may be best, given a starting allegiance to an immaterialist account of reality, or at least of the mind, to stick firmly to a type 1 pure process position, because a type 4 stuff-idealist position may have difficulty in differentiating itself from a materialist position. At the same time, there are also great difficulties in a type 1 position, so it is hard to know where to come to rest. (There are also great difficulties in the materialist position, of course. This is the old metaphysical gavotte.)

Let me first briefly make the case for attributing a non-(D1) view to Descartes. On this view, he holds that Thinking is an essential property of a mind, and indeed the only essential property of a mind. But it is just that: *a* property *of* a mind. That is, Thinking is a property of a mind or substance in such a way that the mind or substance is ontically distinct from the property and is not just the Thinking. All particular Thoughts are "modes" of a mind, or modes existing in a mind, and the mind is not simply identical with the continuous stream that they jointly constitute. According to (D1), in contrast, a mind is just a continuous stream of Thoughts that do not in any sense inhere in something distinct from them.

Descartes seems to have a non-(D1) view in mind when he writes in reply to Arnauld that episodes of Thinking like "understanding, willing, doubting etc. are . . . attributes which must inhere in something if they are to exist; and we call the thing in which they inhere a substance" (1985, 2:156–157). Replying to Hobbes, he notes "that we cannot conceive of thought without a thinking thing," that "a thought cannot exist without a thinking thing," and that if confusion has arisen in the interpretation of his position, it is because "'thought' is sometimes taken to refer to the act, sometimes to the faculty of thought, and sometimes to the thing which possesses the faculty." The implication seems to be that these three references are references to distinct things: there is a *thing* (*res*), which possesses certain *faculties*, and accordingly performs certain sorts of *acts*. Descartes further insists that he does not "deny that I, who am thinking, am distinct from my thought, in the way in which a thing is distinct from a mode" (1985, 2:123–125).

So much for attributing a non-(D1) view to Descartes. Two things in particular suggest some allegiance to (D1). The first arises from the conjunction of his seemingly eccentric claim [1] that "the nature of . . . body . . . consists . . . simply [or solely] in . . . extension" and his view [2] that there is an exact parallel between the relation of the property of extension to matter and the relation of the property of Thinking to the mind.[10] From (1) and (2) we can derive the claim [3] that the nature of mind consists simply (or solely) in Thinking. And to make claim (3) is apparently to say more than that thought is an essential property of the mind. It seems that it is to claim that the nature of mind consists entirely in Thinking, so that there is nothing more to it than Thinking. In the *Principles* (I.53; 1985, 1:210) Descartes writes, "Each substance has one principal property which *constitutes its nature and essence*. . . . Thus extension in length, breadth, and depth, constitutes the nature of corporeal substance, and Thinking [or Thought] constitutes the nature of Thinking substance." Elsewhere he talks of "our soul or our

10. *Principles* II.4. Cottingham (1988, 122–123) notes that this view of matter is "extraordinarily austere" and comments that for Descartes, "matter . . . is really no more than what we might call 'dimensionality' or 'spreadoutness'." He goes on to remark that Descartes seems nevertheless "to have believed that a three-dimensional conception of extension implies solidity and impenetrability" (p. 123, n. 12), which makes the view less strange.

Thought" in such a way that it seems that he is treating the two terms as strictly interchangeable (Preface to the *Principles*; 1985, 1:184). And he writes, seemingly unequivocally, that "Thinking . . . must be considered as nothing else than thinking substance itself . . . , that is, as mind" (*Principles* I.63; 1985, 1:215).

The second source of support for the view that Descartes accepts (D1) is that it immediately makes perfect sense of his insistence (which Locke and many others thought peculiarly perverse) that a mind must always be Thinking. If Thinking—the Thinking process—wholly constitutes a mind's nature or essence or mode of existence, then a mind cannot survive any interruption of its Thinking. For a Thinking process to be interrupted is for the mind that it constitutes to cease to exist.

It may be replied that Descartes insists on this not because he holds (D1), that Thinking is all there is to mind or immaterial substance, but simply because he has ruled, as part of a (D2)- or (D4)-type view, that Thinking is an essential property of a mind: one that a mind must have by definition, although there is more to it than just being a continuing realization of the property of Thinking. And yet some allegiance to (D1) would explain Descartes's insistence (in the face of considerable opposition) that a mind is always Thinking, in a way that attributing to him the mere ruling that Thinking is an essential property of a mind would not.

This is too quick, because the ruling is not a mere ruling. It is not theoretically unmotivated. Furthermore, it is arguable that it is motivated by something other than allegiance to (D1), so that we can see why he accepted it, and therefore committed himself to the view that a mind is always Thinking, without having to suppose that he was tempted by (D1). According to this view, the deep source of the ruling is the thought experiment performed when trying to establish the "Real Distinction" between mind and body, which is supposed to deliver the conclusion that Thinking is all that is essential to mind.

But what is it to endorse this conclusion? Is it not to hold (D1) after all? It may be objected that it is not, and that although Descartes suggests that Thinking is all that is *essential* to mind, he does not hold (let alone therefore hold) (D1), that Thinking is all there *is* to mind.

But what is it, exactly, to say that Thinking is not only an essential property of mind or immaterial substance but is its only essential property?[11] Can one really claim this while holding (D2), that a mind is a *substance* that necessarily has the property of Thinking, although it is *not* itself just Thinking—i.e., although its ontic nature is not exhausted by its being a realization of this property? The problem seems to be this: a mind must have some property or mode of being other than Thinking if its ontic nature is not exhausted by, or wholly constituted by, Thinking. But then either this other property is essential, in which case this is no longer Descartes's view, or it is not essential, which presumably is Descartes's view. But if it is not essential, then the mind can exist without it. But in this case, it seems deeply consonant with Descartes's whole approach to say that what follows is that the Thinking is really all there is to the substance—which seems to be (D1).

It is arguable that Descartes was flustered by objections into endorsing a non-(D1) view, but that (D1) is, in fact, truer to the essence of his metaphysical thought (for a further problem, see note 15 below).

5.9 Summary

I have tried to describe some varieties of idealism and dualism, but I think that there are ineliminable obscurities in the subject. These produce a curious circling movement. Reasons why a view is indefensible or dubiously coherent tend to emerge as difficulties in expounding it. These difficulties of exposition are then taken as evidence that the view has not found its best expression and has therefore not been refuted or otherwise discredited.

And yet it seems that we can continue to make some sort of sense. And the next question is, Why should one not opt, perhaps with Bradley, and perhaps with half of Descartes's indivisible mind, for (I1) or (D1)? Why should one not opt for a type 1 pure process view, according to which all there is to reality[12] is Thinking or experiencing—so that reality is just *occurring mental content*?

11. That is, its only essential property apart from properties that it shares with material substance, like duration and the substance-defining property of "being a thing which depends on no other thing [except God] for its existence" (*Principles* I.51; 1985, 1:210).

12. Or at least to the mind—but I will now concentrate on the monist idealist theory of reality rather than the dualist theory of the mind.

One general tactical reason for adopting a type 1 pure process position, as opposed to a type 2 active-principle position, has already been
noted but is worth a final restatement. In the classical debate, mental
phenomena are standardly identified with occurrent experiential phenomena. It is held that we know their nature. Our acquaintance with
them is the basis of our understanding of the nature of the mental (so
far as we have any positively contentful conception of it). It follows that
to suppose (as in a type 2 view) that there is something entirely mental,
an active principle, whose existence does *not* consist in the existence of
experiential goings-on (Thoughts or experiences or a stream of such
ideas or Thoughts or experiences) is already a potentially problematic
step. For it may oblige one to say that one does not and cannot know
the nature of the mind, insofar as it is distinct from—something more
than—its Thoughts and experiences. To grant this, however, is to face
the challenge that one cannot know, after all, that one's type 2 active-
principle view should not in fact be a type 4 stuff-idealist view—a view
according to which the mind or active principle is constituted of immaterial stuff that is not in fact entirely mental in every respect. And to
grant this is to face the further challenge that this unknown stuff,
allowed to be unknown and yet held to be definitely immaterial, may
in fact be material, for all one knows.

Classically, this last challenge was met by the claim that material stuff
is just not the sort of thing that could possibly be the ground of
experiential goings-on—conscious mental occurrences. And this reaction
is very understandable, for it is true (it is still true) that we have no real
idea of how matter, as we conceive it both in everyday life and in
physics, can be the basis of, or realize, or be, experience. But it relies
on the profoundly dubious (false) view that the nature of material stuff
is fundamentally well understood. And the challenger (preceded, in
essence, by Arnauld) may go on to say that matter may very well have
properties of which one has no idea and that can indeed be the basis
of, or realize, or constitute, experiential goings-on. This move is hard
to counter.

The danger for the idealist or substance dualist is clear: once you
abandon a type 1 view for a type 2 view, it is arguable that you postulate
an unknown essence of the mind, and that such a postulation places you

on a slide at the bottom of which you face the challenge that you have no good reason to suppose that materialism is not true after all.

5.10   Frege's Thesis

A type 1 pure process view seems to be the purest form of idealism, the form most secure from the charge that it cannot be decisively distinguished from materialism. This might seem to be a reason for adopting it if one wants to be an idealist. But perhaps there are also good reasons for not adopting it. In sections 5.11 and 5.12, I will consider three suggestions to this effect, partly because I think that discussing pure process idealism provides a good way of considering some issues that arc of importance to materialists. First, though, I want to discuss a truism. I will call it Frege's thesis, although many have explicitly held it both before and after him and many others have probably thought it too obvious to need saying.

Frege's thesis   "An experience is impossible without an experiencer" or subject of experience (Frege 1967, 27).

This is a necessary truth. Its appearance of necessity is not the product of some kind of grammatical illusion, and it holds equally for man and mouse. But perhaps it is too obvious to see clearly, so it may be useful to try to develop it a little way.

There cannot be experience without a subject of experience, because experience is necessarily *for* someone or something—an experiencer or subject of experience. Experience necessarily involves experiential what-it-is-like-ness, and what-it-is-like-ness is necessarily what-it-is-like-ness *for* someone or something. Whatever the nature of this experiencing something, its real existence cannot be denied. One can insist on this point while agreeing that our natural use of individual-substance-suggesting noun phrases like 'an experiencer' and 'a subject of experience' risks being misleading when we talk about these very basic issues.

Many would concede without question that if there is an experience-occurrence, there must be someone or something whose experience it is. They would briskly claim that there must be a *physical* (or psychophysical) thing—a man or a mouse, say—that is the subject of experience. And this claim is, of course, compatible with Frege's thesis. But the truth of Frege's thesis is prior to and independent of any such claim. It follows immediately from the notion of experience and does not depend on any commitment to materialism or, more generally, to the view that experiential goings-on must be grounded in or realized by nonexperiential goings-on of some sort. It is a truth available and required at the "purely experiential level of description" (section 1.6) before there has been any talk of physical beings or nonexperiential goings-on.

Consider an experience-occurrence e at the purely experiential level of description. The fundamental question is, What must exist, given that e exists? Call anything nonmental or nonexperiential that has to exist if e exists 'o'. Some idealists hold that 'o' denotes nothing. Stuff idealists hold that 'o' denotes certain immaterial but nonmental phenomena. Materialists hold that 'o' denotes various physical things or processes.[13] And so on. Many will be inclined to point to their favored candidate for o when answering the question of what the subject of experience is. But according to Frege's thesis, when one considers e at the purely experiential level of description and tries to answer the question 'What must exist, given that e exists?' one has to grant that the subject of experience must exist before one has made any other assumptions about the general nature of reality (e.g., that it is partly or wholly physical in nature or that the mental depends on the nonmental in some way).

Let e be a mouse experience, for mice may be thought to provide an objection to the claim that reference to the notion of the subject of experience is ineliminable when one considers an experience. It may be said that although we suppose that mice have experience (experience that necessarily has a certain qualitative character), we do not have to discern anything as grand as a subject of experience, at the purely experiential level of description, in the case of a mouse. The physical mouse, or the mouse considered as an integral psychophysical whole, may perfectly well be called a 'subject of experience'. But when we give a full account of what exists when e exists, and *restrict ourselves to the purely experiential level of description*, we do not have to introduce the

13. More precisely, they hold that it denotes nonexperiential physical processes or things or nonexperiential aspects of physical processes or things. This qualification is prompted by the point that experiential goings-on themselves have to be thought of as wholly physical phenomena by serious materialists (see p. 57 above).

notion of the subject of experience; and indeed we should not do so. Speaking at the purely experiential level of description of what must exist given that *e* exists, we need and should speak only of the experience itself, or of experiential content; we need not and should not also speak of a subject of experience.

Frege's thesis denies this. It claims that even when *e* is a mouse experience and even when one restricts oneself to the purely experiential level of description, one is obliged to distinguish the experiencer or subject of experience from the experiential content of the experience in giving a full account of what there is, given that there is *e*.

The objection recurs: If one restricts oneself to the purely experiential level of description, a full account of *e* is necessarily nothing more than an account of the experiential content of *e*. That is all there is to be found, at the purely experiential level of description, when an experience occurs, in a mouse, say. There isn't some other kind of mental object or phenomenon: the Subject of Experience. According to this objection, Frege's thesis is asking us to hunt once again, and at the purely mental or experiential level of description, for the thing that Hume was sup-posedly, and famously, unable to find—and in a mouse.[14]

In reply, let me reexpress Frege's thesis. It claims that if a particular experience-occurrence *e* occurs, then what exists must be acknowledged to be essentially complex in a certain way, even when one restricts one's attention to the purely experiential level of description. It may be complex simply in virtue of its experiential content: it may be an experience as of seeing (or hearing), simultaneously, a complicated array of different colors (or sounds). But Frege's thesis claims that even if *e* does not involve complexity in any of these other ways, still, what there is, given that there is *e*, must be complex, in the sense that its full description at the purely experiential level of description will require the distinction between experiencer and experience (or experiential content): *e* cannot exist without the dual polarity of subject of experience and experiential content.

14. Hume 1978, 252. Hume never said he could not find the self, only that he could not discern it independently of discerning particular experiences. See Shoe-maker 1986.

Once again, this is not to say that the experiencer, who is distinguished from the experiential content, cannot in the case of mice or men properly be identified with the physical thing, the mouse or the man. On the contrary. If mice and men exist in the way we ordinarily think they do, then it is clearly acceptable for us to identify the experiencer, as the thing that must be distinguished from the experiential content of *e*, with the physical or psychophysical thing, the mouse or the man considered as a whole. The present point is just that we have to distinguish the experiencer from the content of experience in order to say what is necessarily involved in the occurrence of *e*, even when we consider *e* at the purely experiential level of description. It certainly does not follow from this that we must think of the experiencer as ontically distinct from the being whose experience *e* is, given that the being is indeed a physical being.

My point is simpler than this, and I will state it once more. Consider an experience of pain. If there is an experience of pain, then there must obviously be someone or something that feels the pain. There cannot be just an experiential content. An experience is necessarily experience *for* someone or something. We must discern at least this much structure or complexity in the world when we say that there is an experience (e.g., of pain), even if we think that reality is purely mental. Perhaps it is awareness of this point that partly underlies continued resistance to reductionist accounts of the self (or person) that seek to characterize experiential reality, considered at the purely experiential level of description (i.e., independently of the question of whether it also has some nonexperiential substantial realization), as nothing more than the occurrence of experiences and thoughts with certain more or less complex contents. (Compare Parfit 1984, section 79.)

The claim, then, is not that an experience, being a *process* or *event*, necessarily requires some sort of *substance* that is in some way distinct from it, in which it can go on or occur. Frege's thesis is independent of any such thesis that process or event entails substance. It holds good even if it is intelligible to suppose that there might be nothing but "pure process," and indeed pure mental process, in the universe. The ineliminability of the subject of experience at the purely mental or experiential level of description is just a simple consequence of the essential "for-someone-ness" of experience.

The for-someone-ness of an experience *e* is not, of course, part of the *content* of *e*; it is not something that is necessarily apprehended by the being whose experience *e* is, when *e* occurs. Equally, representation of the subject of experience needn't be—and standardly isn't—part of the experiential content of *e*. Rather, it is something that we, considering *e* from the outside, as it were, are obliged to discern in saying what exists, even when considering the overall experience-occurrence *e* at the experiential level of description.

The present point is thus a very low-level point. A subject of experience is not something grand. It is simply something that must exist wherever there is experience, even in the case of mice or spiders—simply because experience is necessarily experience-for. One could put this by saying that if, per impossibile, there could be pain experience without a subject of experience, mere experience without an experiencer, there would be no point in stopping it, because no one would be suffering.

The sense in which a subject of experience is not something grand can be illustrated in another way. Consider the following (arguably Parfitian) suggestion. 'If we consider things at the purely experiential or purely mental level of description, it is not clear that we can identify anything that persists over long stretches of time as a single experiencer, whether in the case of cats or bats or human beings. It must, of course, be granted that "an experience is impossible without an experiencer." But maybe the best thing to say, when considering a succession of experiences that we naturally think of as the experiences of a single being at the purely experiential or purely mental level of description, is that each involves a different experiencer. This may be best, although we can certainly also say that they all involve a single experiencer insofar as we are considering them as the experiences of a single persisting physical thing, like a human being.'

Whatever one makes of this suggestion, it is compatible with Frege's thesis as understood here. Many people who have sought to defend the reality of the mental subject of experience have been very concerned to establish its long-term continuity. They have perhaps wanted to show that it can be (and should be) thought of as something that persists over long stretches of time even when it is considered at the purely experiential or purely mental level of description (i.e., even when the idea that a subject of experience is a long-term continuant as a physical thing has been put to one side). Whatever the plausibility of this view, it receives no direct support from Frege's thesis as understood here, for Frege's thesis makes a point at a much more basic level. It says only that where there is an experience, there is an experiencer.

Some think that our subjective experience of the continuous flow of consciousness counts against the view sketched in the penultimate paragraph. But as far as I can see, introspection supports the view, rather than counting against it. The human stream of consciousness has very little natural phenomenological continuity or experiential flow, if mine is anything to go by. "Our thought is fluctuating, uncertain, fleeting" (Hume 1947, 194). It is bitty, scatty, and saccadic. It skips and jinks. It is always shooting off, shorting, and fuzzing. It is "an alternation of flights and perchings" (James 1950, 1:243). It keeps slipping from mere consciousness into self-consciousness and out again. It is not a matter of flow, and this is especially so when one is just thinking, rather than watching some continuous process in the external world, like a football game, which lends it greater continuity. My experience of consciousness is of repeated returns to consciousness from a state of complete, if highly transitory, nonconsciousness. This is most clear when I am alone and thinking. Consciousness is continually *restarting*. The (invariably brief) periods of true experiential continuity are radically disjunct from one another. There isn't a basic substrate (as it were) of continuous consciousness interrupted by various lapses. Rather, there is, in waking life, a (nearly continuous) series of radically disjunct irruptions into consciousness from a substrate of nonconsciousness.

5.11 Objections to Pure Process Idealism

So much for Frege's thesis. I will now consider three objections to (I1), or pure process idealism, or 'PPI' for short. The first two I will deal with briefly; the third will take more time.

It may first be argued that there is something incoherent in the whole notion of a pure process view of anything. If there is a process, it may be said, there must be something in which it goes on. If something happens, there must be something to which it happens, something that is not just the happening itself. This is not a mere grammatical illusion.

It is easy to sympathize with this view. It is a view standardly grounded in a commonsense understanding of the nature of the physical.

And yet physicists seem increasingly content with the view that physical reality is itself a kind of pure process. The idea that there is some ultimate stuff *to* which things happen has increasingly been replaced by the idea that the existence of anything worthy of the name 'ultimate stuff' consists entirely in the existence of fields of energy—consists, in other words, in the existence of a kind of pure process that is not usefully thought of as something happening to a thing distinct from it. (Chronic philosophical difficulties with the notion of substance may provide important negative support for this view, even if it remains hard to know exactly what it amounts to.)

Although this response is very sketchy, it does seem to pose a difficulty for any immediate rejection of a pure process view of anything. It is not clear that materialists, for example, can object to the pure-process aspect of PPI, given contemporary physics.

The second objection to PPI appeals to Frege's thesis and brings with it the difficulties that attach to the notion of the subject of experience. According to the objection, experience requires an experiencer, and a pure process cannot itself be an experiencer. Nor can any part of a pure process be an experiencer.

This may seem plausible at first, and Frege's thesis is a necessary truth. But the objection doesn't have much force, given the point just made. If physicists are right that it is intelligible and accurate to think of the physical world as pure process in some sense, then *materialists* are on weak ground if they suppose there is a direct argument from Frege's thesis to the falsity of any pure process view. Materialists posit a brain and a body in giving their account of the subject of experience, or of the phenomena that incline us to talk in terms of such a thing. But brain and body themselves may best be seen as a matter of pure process, in the present (unclear) sense.

If one is particularly concerned with the question of how there could be such a thing as a *continuing* subject of experience, given a pure process account of the mind, then one should consider that the physical world provides our paradigm cases of continuing things, and that if a pure process view of physical continuants is possible, it is very hard to see why a pure process account of the continuity of the subject of experience should not also be possible.

It seems, then, that Frege's thesis does not provide good grounds for rejecting a pure process view of the mind. I turn now to the third objection to PPI.

5.12 The Problem of Mental Dispositions

It is arguable that experience like our own cannot possibly exist unless nonexperiential and indeed nonmental phenomena also exist: even if there is no physical world, and even if a PPI view of the mind can be correct for some minds, it cannot be correct for minds like ours. There is an argument from memory and a related argument from thought. Both claim that we have to attribute mental dispositions to minds like our own, and that the existence of these dispositions cannot be satisfactorily accounted for by PPI.

I will take the second claim first, and I will consider Louis as a representative human being. In order to achieve a useful theoretical neutrality, I will sometimes speak in terms of the portion of reality that consists of Louis, and I will call this 'the L-reality', for short. This is obviously a rough notion: as a physical being, Louis is enmeshed in wide-reaching physical interactions, and cannot be neatly separated out as a single portion of reality. But it is a serviceable notion nonetheless.

My central point is simple. Even if a pure process view of the mind is possible, it does not follow that a pure-process-*idealist* or (I1) view of the mind is possible. There seems to be something impossibly thin about any PPI account of the mind as nothing but occurrent experiential phenomena. Since PPI considers Louis to be an entirely mental pure process, rather than a physical being, it is natural to wonder what account it can give of what we think of as his mental dispositions: his memories, preferences, beliefs, character traits, and so on. What account can it give of the phenomena that lead us to talk in terms of such things?

The view that such dispositions exist is part of commonsense psychology, and the idea that they are purely mental phenomena seems at first readily intelligible. So perhaps PPI can accommodate them. Perhaps it can think of a disposition as a purely mental structure or process, existing at time t, that is not just a matter of whatever experiential phenomena are occurring at t, although it is nonetheless purely mental in every respect.

There is, however, a problem with this picture, which can be stated as follows. As soon as one attributes dispositional properties to any thing or process X, one seems bound to hold that X must have some other, "categorical" properties whose possession is the *ground* of X's possessing the dispositional properties. For if it is true without qualification that X is now disposed to act or react or change or develop in a certain way, there must be something about X *in virtue of which* it is now so disposed. A dispositional property is essentially a property which a thing or process has in virtue of its possession or actualization of some other property or properties. (If this is held to be metaphysical prejudice, I am happy to own up to it, and in what follows I will use 'categorical' to qualify 'phenomena' as well as 'property'. Note that categorical properties entail dispositional properties as surely as dispositional properties entail categorical properties.)

In the present case, in which we are trying to make sense of the PPI idea that a mind (i.e., Louis) is something with no nonmental aspect, it seems that the only categorical phenomena available are experiential phenomena. There are no other mental categorical phenomena to be had in the L-reality, for there are no other essentially mentally contentful categorical phenomena to be had in the L-reality (recall the assumption that all truly mental phenomena are mentally contentful phenomena). So it seems that the categorical grounds of all of Louis's mental dispositions at a given time—all his beliefs, preferences, memories, character traits, and so on—can only be whatever experiential phenomena are occurring in him at that time. On this view, the grounds of your present knowledge of English or French, or of the rules of chess or bridge, are just your present conscious experiences—the ones you are having right now.

This picture may not be immediately incoherent, but it is certainly incredible. For one thing, even when Louis's conscious experience at time t_1 is very simple, it will have to be the ground of thousands of mental dispositions. For another, the vast bulk of Louis's mental dispositions will have to remain constant from t_1 to t_2 even while the course of his conscious experience changes dramatically (for our experience often changes dramatically while the vast bulk of our dispositions remains the same). But Louis's conscious experience between t_1 and t_2 has to be the whole ground of his mental dispositions between t_1 and t_2, as well as being the experience it is, and it is then deeply mysterious that the vast majority of his mental dispositions should remain unchanged while his course of experience changes so dramatically (perhaps he is riding on a roller coaster). One way out of this is to postulate other courses of experience, and hence other subjects of experience, in the L-reality; to suppose that there might be experiences and subjects of experience in the L-reality of which Louis is not conscious but that provide the categorical grounds of his thousands of dispositions. But this step is ad hoc. It has no independent motivation, it raises many further problems, and I will say no more about it.

The present line of argument can be summarized as follows: There is strong pressure on the pure process idealist to postulate dispositional mental properties. Dispositional properties require categorical properties to ground them. The only such properties available to the pure process idealist are experiential properties. These experiential properties cannot plausibly be supposed to ground dispositional mental properties. Hence there is pressure on the pure process idealist to admit the existence of nonexperiential and indeed nonmental categorical properties, and so to abandon pure process idealism.

I will shortly consider the suggestion that the categorical properties in question may be nonexperiential and yet still mental, so that one cannot simply infer 'nonmental' from 'nonexperiential'. First, though, I will approach the point just made in another way. Consider the case of memory in slightly more detail. It seems that Louis has many memories and sometimes consciously recalls episodes of his past life. The question arises as to where and how the apparent memories are preserved through time, on the PPI view, since they are not part of Louis's stream of occurrent experience. (I am assuming that the pure process idealist is a realist about time, and it should be noted that not all idealists are.)

One reply tries to avoid the problem altogether. It observes that it is logically possible that these apparent conscious memories are really no such thing. Perhaps they are just experiences with a certain distinctive character, experiences that are suffused with Russell's "feelings . . . of pastness" and "feelings of familiarity" (1921, 163) but that do not in fact represent the past in such a way that we have to suppose that there are nonexperiential processes that have somehow preserved knowledge of the past through times when nothing remotely relevant to such knowledge was figuring in Louis's stream of experience. If, however, these seeming memories are real and time is real, then it seems that PPI faces an insuperable problem.[15]

Various more or less exotic replies can be made to this, but I will move on to consider the problem posed for PPI by the existence of concept-structured thought (many memories involve concept-structured thought, so this difficulty merely expands on the last one). As before, the claim against PPI is that there must be nonexperiential (and hence nonmental) aspects to the mind. It has been claimed that this must be so because of the nature of memory; now it is claimed that it must be so because of the nature of things like concept-structured thought.

The basic point is again familiar, although it is not easy to state sharply. It seems that we cannot make sense of what it is for Louis to have and understand a thought at *t* without thinking of the thought understanding as situated in a network of other possible thought understandings; or, equivalently, as constitutively connected with possession of beliefs that are correctly attributable to Louis at *t* but are not in any way present to his consciousness at *t*, not part of his occurrent mental reality; or, again equivalently, as drawing on resources of concept possession that are not exhaustively displayed or deployed or activated in his occurrent mental goings-on. (See, e.g., Searle 1992, chap. 8.)

Like us, Louis can grasp the sense of Goldbach's Conjecture. He can have rich trains of conscious thought. He can have the experience of responding with immediate understanding to sound experiences that he experiences as utterances in a language that he understands. And so on. But no being like Louis can grasp the sense of Goldbach's Conjecture, at a given time, unless he then has many beliefs that are in no way

---

15. Descartes is well known to have located memory in the folds of the brain. But he also found himself obliged to postulate a distinct kind of memory that he called "intellectual memory" and described as "altogether spiritual" (1991, 3:151), holding it to be dependent "on the soul alone" (1991, 3:146), and hence not on the body. This may be thought to count against attributing to Descartes any type 1 or PPI theory of the mind, given that intellectual memory must be supposed to preserve content (e.g., knowledge of the meaning of words—see 1991, 3:336 f.) through times at which it is not present to consciousness. An alternative suggestion, however, is that he did not really face the problem under discussion in the text.

present to consciousness. Louis cannot have rich trains of thought or understand Goldbach's Conjecture unless he possesses a number of concepts. So there must be something about him in virtue of which he possesses these concepts and beliefs (all those concepts and beliefs whose possession is necessarily involved in knowing what a prime number is, what an even number is, what one number's being the sum of two others is, and so on). And this something—so the argument claims—cannot be just his stream of occurrent experience.

It appears to follow that Louis must possess many nonexperiential properties, as well as experiential properties. For we must attribute certain dispositional mental properties to Louis (he has beliefs, possesses concepts, and so on). It follows that there must be categorical properties in virtue of which these dispositional properties are possessed. All properties are mental properties according to PPI, and experiential properties are the only categorical mental properties that there are. But it is utterly implausible (perhaps not even coherent) to suppose that Louis's experiential properties are the full and sufficient ground of his dispositional mental properties, although these experiential properties are categorical properties and mental properties. So there must be some other, nonexperiential categorical properties, that ground the dispositional mental properties. (Here again I assume that Louis's mental dispositional properties cannot be plausibly thought to be categorically grounded by experiential processes within him of which he is unaware.)

Does this argument prove that there are mental properties that cannot possibly be instantiated unless certain nonmental properties are also instantiated? Does it allow one finally to return a definite positive answer to the nonmentality question (pp. 23–24), which asks whether reference to the nonmental is essential in giving an adequate account of the nature of the mental?

Not yet. Even if the argument works, it only shows that there are mental properties that cannot be instantiated unless certain categorical *nonexperiential* properties are also instantiated. And it may now be argued that although these properties must be nonexperiential properties, they may still be properly counted as *mental* properties.

I will consider this move shortly. Note first that it is not open to pure process idealists, for they assume that no phenomenon is properly counted as a mental phenomenon unless it is an intrinsically mentally contentful phenomenon (see sections 5.2 above and 6.6 below). And experiential phenomena provide their only positive model for intrinsically mentally contentful categorical phenomena. Indeed, they hold that all truly mental categorical phenomena are experiential phenomena. They must therefore grant that proof that the existence of certain mental phenomena requires the existence of nonexperiential phenomena is immediate proof that the existence of certain mental phenomena requires the existence of nonmental phenomena.

So far, then, it may seem plausible to say that there are aspects of the mental that we just cannot make sense of without supposing that there are nonmental phenomena. The argument cannot be made secure, however, because of the vagueness of the term 'mental', which I will discuss in chapter 6. And one possible reply to the argument, in which distinctions between 'mental', 'mentally contentful', and 'experiential' become important, is as follows.

'It may be true that (many) intrinsically mentally contentful phenomena—call them C phenomena—cannot possibly occur in Louis, or in the L-reality, unless certain other phenomena exist or occur that are not intrinsically mentally contentful in every respect—call them N phenomena. And we may suppose that it is true. We may suppose that it is true because of the argument just given: certain C phenomena (e.g., the phenomenon of consciously wondering whether Goldbach's Conjecture is true) presuppose the existence of dispositions in the L-reality, and these, it seems, must be categorically grounded by N phenomena, because [1] they can't plausibly be supposed to be grounded by experiential phenomena and [2] experiential phenomena are the only categorical C phenomena there are. Alternatively, we may suppose that C phenomena require N phenomena simply because we are materialists who are convinced that it is a fact about the universe that no C phenomenon can possibly occur without certain N phenomena also occurring (i.e., phenomena that have physics descriptions that make no use of mental-content-specifying terms). Alternatively, we may have more a priori reasons for taking this view. We may, for example, hold that certain intrinsically mentally contentful phenomena or C phenomena can't exist at all unless there is a subject of experience that takes what happens to it in one way rather than another, and that this "taking" cannot itself be intrinsically mentally contentful, on pain of regress.'[16]

'Suppose, then, that certain C phenomena can't occur in the L-reality unless some N phenomena also occur in the L-reality. Does it follow that the C phenomena cannot occur without the occurrence of *nonmental* phenomena? It seems not. For if the occurrence of the N phenomena is bound up with the occurrence of the C phenomena in some metaphysically intimate way, then the N phenomena may themselves be said to be truly mental phenomena, even if they are not intrinsically mentally *contentful* in every respect. Thus, for example, the activity of the subject just mentioned—the activity of taking what happens to it in one way rather than another—is arguably a truly mental phenomenon even if it is not in itself an intrinsically mentally contentful phenomenon. So too the brain processes that realize the C phenomena according to materialists may be said to be, in themselves, truly mental phenomena, in spite of having N-phenomenal aspects.'

On this view, being a truly *mental* phenomenon does not entail being a mentally *contentful* phenomenon, or an experiential phenomenon. Something may be counted as a truly mental phenomenon simply by virtue of the intimate way in which it is bound up in the occurrence of intrinsically mentally contentful phenomena, even if it is not itself an intrinsically mentally contentful phenomenon. It seems to me that this view cannot be proved false, given the indeterminacy of the word 'mental'. I conclude that one cannot actually prove that the existence of mental phenomena requires the existence of nonmental phenomena, even if one can prove that the existence of certain sorts of experiential phenomena (e.g., rememberings or conscious thoughts) requires the existence of nonexperiential phenomena.

Can this second claim be proved? It is a more interesting and more determinate claim than the claim about mental and nonmental phenomena. I have argued that there are strong reasons for thinking it to be true. These reasons derive from the need to postulate mental dispositions

16. Compare section 5.10 above. For a succinct statement of the point as applied to the phenomena of thinking and understanding, see Stroud 1991, 245. I am ignoring the currently unimportant case in which a C phenomenon essentially depends on an N phenomenon simply because the C phenomenon is, e.g., an experience of an N phenomenon, like Hampstead Heath or a hiccup.

in order to give an adequate account of the nature of much of our experience, including our experience of remembering things and thinking concept-structured thoughts. I can, however, imagine a direct denial of the need to postulate such dispositions, and I will conclude by saying how it might go.

'You (G.S.) have stressed the problem posed by concept-structured thoughts, and so on. In this way you have implied that purely sensory experiences do not pose the same problem, and that there is no insuperable difficulty in a PPI conception of a mind that has nothing but purely sensory experiences. Let us suppose that this last thing is indeed so. The following objection then arises: experiential episodes of thinking concept-structured thoughts are like episodes of sensory experience in a fundamental respect, so you should take the same attitude to the former as you take to the latter. For in both cases there is content, more or less rich, given in the experience. In the case of the merely sensory experiences, you do not feel a need to postulate some nonexperiential background network of beliefs, and so on, that make the experiences possible. So why must you postulate this nonexperiential background in the case of things like thoughts? Why exactly is it supposed to be metaphysically *impossible* for an experiencer to experience complex thought as contentful, just as we experience our thoughts, although nothing exists other than an intrinsically mentally contentful pure-process stream of experience?'

It is arguable, in other (still not very clear) words, that the difference between purely sensory experience and the experience of concept-structured thought is just one of degree, degree of richness and complexity of content; and that if one can make sense of a PPI account of basic sensory experience, then there can be no straightforward incoherence in the idea of a PPI account of cognitively complex experience. If one does not have to attribute mental dispositions in the first case, then it cannot be proved that one has to do so in the second case, however natural it may seem. It is a familiar idea that there is a defensible sense in which sensory experience, considered just in its experiential aspect, is just a matter of qualitative character. One of the thoughts behind the present suggestion is the less familiar, more difficult, but correct idea that the same is true of cognitive experience: *considered just in its experiential aspect*, it too is just a matter of qualitative character (see section 1.4

above, and chapter 7 below). In this respect the difference between sensory experience and cognitive experience is just a matter of degree. (Questions about whether intelligent behavior requires dispositions are not relevant here, since the PPI hypothesis is that reality is just a matter of occurring mental content.)

There is more to be said here. (I will return to the point about cognitive experience in section 7.4.) The problem posed by genuine memory experiences, for example, is not solved by the suggestion in the last two paragraphs, and it may be said that we have to postulate dispositions with nonexperiential categorical grounds even in the case of sensory experience, if we are to make sense of its occurrence. Connectedly, it may be argued that a subject of experience cannot itself be a merely experiential phenomenon, and therefore that Frege's thesis also strongly supports the view that experiential phenomena are not possible without nonexperiential phenomena. On the other side, some may even wish to challenge the basic metaphysical thesis that statements attributing dispositional properties must be true in virtue of the truth of statements attributing distinct categorical properties.

I will go no further, however. As materialists and lay neurologists, we are convinced that the intrinsically mentally contentful goings-on of conscious experience have massively complicated nonexperiential underpinnings. But a doubt may yet remain as to whether the existence of experiential phenomena can actually be proved to require the existence of nonexperiential phenomena, and I have already conceded that the existence of mental phenomena cannot be shown a priori to require the existence of nonmental phenomena, given the vagueness of the word 'mental'.

This vagueness is the subject of the next chapter. In conclusion, let me say that the case of memory (and concept-structured experience in general) is an important one. Even if we simply assume that there is no such thing as the physical world, we still have reason to think that there are experiential phenomena whose existence necessarily depends on the existence of nonexperiential phenomena. For this reason, I suspect that stuff idealism is the least implausible version of idealism and that there may be no genuinely workable version of idealism that is interestingly distinct from (agnostic) materialism.

6

'Mental'

6.1 Introduction

So far I have relied on our ordinary understanding of the word 'mental'. I have talked of experiences, emotions, sensations, thoughts, beliefs, and desires, taking it that these things are paradigm examples of mental phenomena even if there are other, very different candidates for the title. On the whole, we use the term 'mental' very confidently. And yet there is considerable uncertainty surrounding the term.

'States', 'events', 'processes', 'occurrences', 'phenomena', 'abilities', 'properties'—these are some of the main general words with which 'mental' couples. I will also apply it to 'beings' and speak of mental beings. By this I will simply mean beings that have mental properties, and I will assume, in accordance with materialism, that all such beings are physical beings.

One example of the uncertainty surrounding the term 'mental' was given in 2.3: many philosophers think of publicly observable behavioral phenomena as entirely nonmental in character (as "mere" bodily movements), but some are inclined to count such behavioral phenomena as mental phenomena on account of the fact that they are standardly caused by, or constitutively "informed" by, things like beliefs, desires, hopes, fears, and so on. I will not discuss this (relatively unusual) sort of suggestion, however. Instead, I will take it that all the main candidates for the status of mental phenomenon are "in the head" (even those whose content cannot be specified without reference to things outside the head). Even if one restricts one's attention to what is in the head, there are plenty of problems.

It is sometimes said that *intentionality* is the fundamental mark of the mental, intentionality being the property that a thought, for example, has insofar as it is a thought about something, like justice or the city of Florence. I think this is a mistake, but I will leave intentionality until the next chapter.

6.2   Shared Abilities?

Machines that we take to be experienceless appear to share many abilities with us. They appear to be able to play chess, perform calculations, detect and distinguish the shapes and colors of things, sort circles from squares, estimate distances, judge size, and so on. When we consider ourselves, we think of these abilities as mental abilities or at least as abilities that involve mental abilities.[1] And obviously we take it that to possess a mental ability is to possess a mental property. But when we consider machines, most of us are very strongly disinclined to call the abilities they have 'mental abilities' or to think that they possess any mental properties at all. And the main reason why this is so is that we suppose that machines are experienceless.

I will assume that we are right about this. It would be foolish to claim that no artificial machine could ever have experience, and such a claim is no part of my present position. In what follows, however, I will consider only machines that are experienceless (no doubt these include all currently existing machines). And I will call the properties that we and experienceless machines appear to share the 'X properties'.

Here are five possible responses to the problem the X properties appear to pose.

First response. [A] We are mental beings. [B] We and experienceless beings have the X properties in common. [C] We count the X properties as mental properties in our own case. Hence [D] we must count the X properties as mental properties in the case of experienceless beings. For

1. There are thousands of abilities, such as the ability to drive a car or walk a tightrope, that involve mental abilities although they are not just (or even primarily) mental abilities. One can group these abilities and any more "purely" mental abilities together under the single heading of 'mental or mental-ability-involving abilities', or 'MOMAI abilities' for short.

if [E] the X properties are correctly considered as mental properties in some cases, then [F] the X properties are correctly considered as mental properties in all cases. Hence [G] experienceless beings can have mental properties.[2]

Second response (extends the first). Given (A) through (F), it follows [G] that experienceless beings can have mental properties. Hence [H] we should count experienceless beings as mental beings. For [I] having a mental property is sufficient for being a mental being.

Third response (contraposes the argument in the second response). Since [not H] experienceless beings are obviously not mental beings, it follows that [not G] they cannot have mental properties, for [I] having a mental property is sufficient for being a mental being. So assuming that it is indeed true that [B] we and experienceless beings have the X properties in common, it follows that [not E] the X properties are not mental properties after all, properly speaking.

Fourth response (rejects the reasoning shared by the second and third responses, as well as part of the reasoning in the first). [A] We are mental beings. [not H] Experienceless beings are not mental beings. It is true that [C] we count the X properties as mental properties in our own case. But it does not follow that [D] we must count the X properties as mental properties in the case of experienceless beings. For (E) does not entail (F). It does not follow, from the fact that [E] the X properties are correctly considered as mental properties in some cases, that [F] the X properties are correctly considered as mental properties in all cases.

Rejection of the move from (C) to (D) (and hence of the move from (E) to (F)) need not sound completely counterintuitive, although it cheerfully violates Leibniz's Law. It may naturally be said that my ability to play chess is (obviously) a mental property that I possess, whereas the computer's ability to play chess is (obviously) not a mental property that it

2. This view is not without supporters, for the ability to think is presumably a mental ability if anything is, and Leiber (1991, 46) asserts that Turing was the first to emphasize "the most basic claim of cognitive science: that thinking is thinking whether realized in human neurology or microchips or whatever."

possesses. On this view, both the machine and I can play chess, but it only counts as a mental ability in my case.

Fifth response (arguably just a variant of the fourth). It is true that [F] the X properties are mental properties tout court. But it is false that [B] we and the experienceless beings have the X properties in common. That is, it is in fact wrong to suppose that the X properties are really properties of such a kind that the experienceless machine and I both possess them. The machine cannot really play chess at all, or tell the difference between circles and squares—not in the sense that I can. To play chess is necessarily to have (or to be disposed to have) certain experiences, in addition to making certain moves, following certain rules, and so on. Leibniz's Law is preserved.

6.3 The Sorting Ability

None of these positions looks fully satisfactory, but for the moment I will leave them without comment and consider some possible machines. Machine M_1 has no electronic circuitry. It has two holes: one circular, the other square. The diameter of the circle is slightly larger than the length of the side of the square. Suitably positioned circular shapes and square shapes pass over the holes, the former falling only through the circular hole, the latter only through the square hole. The machine sorts the shapes into two boxes.

In this case it may possibly be said that M_1 can "distinguish between circles and squares." And the same may be said of other experienceless machines—like a clockwork machine, M_2, that is active in a sense in which M_1 is not, because it is triggered (by placing the shapes in a certain receptacle) to manipulate the shapes into the positions in which they can be sorted, or a machine, M_3, that tells the difference between circles and squares on the basis of information electronically transmitted from a prehensile sensor arm or from a light-array-sensing device.

There is a vast spectrum of possible experienceless beings. At the sophisticated end of the spectrum, the basis of the ability to tell the difference between circles and squares may be physically (or at least structurally) similar to the basis of our ability to do so, except for the fact that it does not involve or give rise to any sort of experience. Seeking to move as close as possible to our own case, on the spectrum of experienceless beings, we can imagine a living, experienceless being with high-quality "blindsight": it has the ability to sort circles and squares presented at a distance on the basis of its sensitivity to their light-reflection properties, but it has no visual experience.[3] We can imagine that the blindsighted being is naturally like this, and not because it has suffered some sort of damage, and that the physical basis of its ability to do what it does is similar to whatever continues to function well in the case of a damaged human being with high quality blindsight. (One can construct parallel cases for the other senses.)

We and all these other entities have what one might call 'the sorting ability' in common: the ability to sort out the circular shapes from the square ones. We are strongly inclined to say that the sorting ability is or involves a mental ability in our case, but not in their case. Why is this? Is it simply because we are experiencing beings? Very large numbers of our apparently mental abilities, such as our speech-interpretation abilities, seem to be grounded in entirely nonexperiential goings-on. Indeed, Lashley's famous remark that "no activity of mind is ever conscious" seems entirely accurate (1956, 4; see Jackendoff 1987, 45 f.). A question therefore arises as to whether our inclination is defensible. Here are a number of questions and responses.

Question 1. Would it be right to suppose that the sorting ability is always a MOMAI ability—a mental ability or a mental-ability-involving ability—when it is possessed by an experiencing being, say B_1?

Response. Surely not, for B_1 may be an experiencing being and have auditory experience, for example, while its possession of the sorting ability is grounded in a physical set-up just like that of machine M_1; so that its capacity for experience has absolutely nothing to do with its ability to sort circles and squares.

Question 2. If the sorting ability is to count as a mental ability in an experiencing being B_2, is it sufficient that it be physically grounded in

3. Some might want to say that the being has no *conscious* visual experience, but I am using 'experience' in such a way that this is pleonastic (see section 1.2; contrast Rosenthal 1991). For a discussion of blindsight, see Weiskrantz 1986.

something that is part of B_2's "central control system," something that involves processes that are physically or at least structurally similar to the electrochemical goings-on that occur in central control systems like ours?

Response. In this case, the sorting ability may conceivably be grounded in goings-on similar to those involved in the functioning of our autonomic nervous system, which we naturally think of as nonmental. More generally, it may be grounded in goings-on in B_2's central control system that are in no way directly related either to any of the processes that are thought of as "subserving" B_2's experiential states (in the way that the subexperiential computational processes postulated in the computational theory of vision are thought of as subserving our visual experience) or to any of the processes that are thought of as directly realizing any of B_2's experiential states. And some will be inclined to say that in this case we do not have any very good reason to count the sorting ability as a specifically mental ability possessed by B_2.

Question 3. Is the sorting ability correctly called a mental (or MOMAI) ability in the case of a naturally blindsighted being, B_3, that possesses the ability to sort circles and squares on the basis of its blindsight and that is an experiencing being (it has auditory and olfactory experience) but that has, in fact, no *visual* experience, nor any other capacity for experience that is in any way connected to its possession of the sorting ability?

Response. Opinions may differ. We may insist that the sorting ability is not correctly counted as a mental ability in the case of experienceless machines like M_1 to M_3, or indeed in the case of any entirely experienceless being, and we may be sure that it is correctly counted as a mental (or MOMAI) ability in our case. We may also, however, doubt whether it will be possible to find any clear principle that will sort out all possible intermediary cases, like that of the naturally blindsighted being B_3, into those in which the sorting ability is correctly or appropriately called a mental ability and those in which it is not.[4] More important, it doesn't seem to matter much—a point to which I will return.

---

4. Jackson (1993) suggests that one might be able to distinguish between experienceless machines that have a prima facie claim to *intelligence* and those that do not by reference to differences in their internal processing structures.

Question 4. If the sorting ability is to count as a mental ability, must possession of the sorting ability somehow directly depend on, or at least be somehow directly connected with, possession of the capacity to have certain sorts of experience?

Response. This is what the previous questions have been leading up to, but it is not clear that the word 'mental' allows us to return a definite 'Yes' to the question. One problem is this: Imagine a human being who loses normal vision while retaining high-quality blindsight. In this case some may want to say that the sorting ability no longer depends on an experiential capacity but is still a mental ability. Others may be inclined to say that it never really depended on an experiential capacity. They may say that such a case of blindsight suggests that an experiential capacity is never really essential (in any human being) to the apparently visual-experience-based possession of the sorting ability, although the sorting ability is still properly counted as a mental ability. Others again may say that the sorting ability started out as a MOMAI ability but ceased to be one when visual experience was lost.

The conclusion seems clear: we may not always be able to say whether or not it is best or appropriate (let alone correct) to call certain abilities, properties, states, or phenomena *mental*. This is not because of any failure of insight or lack of information on our part, but simply because there is no single right answer. Such is the nature of the term 'mental'.

Some theorists see mental phenomena as forming a great continuum. The continuum stretches from the most complex human experiential episodes down to the nervous-system activity that goes on in seaslugs, or enables *Cataglyphus*, a desert ant, to go straight back to its nest in the dark without any environmental cues after pursuing a zigzag out-ward path. (It is as if it has done some complicated trigonometry.) These theorists see no line to be drawn on this great natural continuum of *behavioral-control-system activity*. They see no interesting line that sharply divides truly and distinctively mental activity from nonmental activity on this continuum. And they add, forcefully, that we don't really need to use the word 'mental' at all, or to determine its extension precisely. We can say all we want to say without using it.

Others, at the other extreme, propose to restrict the domain of truly mental phenomena to experiential phenomena—to the surface phenomena of the mind, as it were. Those who take this second view hold that none of the extremely complex subexperiential brain processes that subserve the stream of experience are to be counted as mental phenomena, *sensu stricto*. Only experiential phenomena (including brain processes that can be literally identified with experiential phenomena) should be counted as mental phenomena. Everything else is mere mechanism, ultimately nonmental process. These theorists may offer an analogy: plays are not possible without a great deal of activity behind the scenes, but none of this activity is, strictly speaking, part of the play.

These two opposing sides will obviously differ on the question of whether there was mental life in the universe before there was experience. The first group will say that there was, the second will say that there was not. The first group may well grant that something very important happened when experience began, something quite new. But they will not agree that it was the beginning of mental life, the beginning of *mind*, a sudden switching on of the mental light. Mind, they will say, was already there.

They may add that the theory of evolution shows that the line between the mental and the nonmental cannot be sharp. For behavioral-control systems originally arise simply because certain randomly arising movement-tendencies turn out to have survival value, and hence tend to be preserved in succeeding generations. Thereafter, of course, things increase enormously in complexity, and at some point in this process of increasing complexity, some of the internal causes of the movement-tendencies come to be such that we find it natural to dignify them with the title of 'mental processes'. But it is indeed only a question of what we find natural, and our intuitions are not grounded on any precise criterion that makes a clear cut between the mental and the nonmental. The basic facts of natural history and evolution show that it is foolish to think that there could ever be a sharp answer to the question of when the title 'mental process' becomes appropriate.

A third group are happy to proceed with the philosophy of mind, and the science of psychology, without any attempt at a tight definition of the term 'mental', making do with our ordinary, more or less philosophically informed, more or less science-assisted, general consensus on the question of the proper subject matter of psychology and the philosophy of mind. This third group may be right that it doesn't matter much how we put things, so long as there is some terminology or other in which we can agree on what we are talking about.

6.4 The Definition of 'Mental Being'

Now, however, I am going to define 'mental being' in such a way that it does draw a sharp line, by linking it with another term that draws a sharp line (it is sharp, although we cannot be sure where it runs).

The term in question is 'experiential' or 'experiencing': B is a mental being, according to the present definition, if and only if B is an experiencing being, that is, a being of such a kind that there is something it is like to be it, experientially speaking. Or rather—since experiencing beings may be unconscious or in dreamless sleep—a being whose current state or structure makes it now capable of experience, given appropriate stimulation, say. (This qualification raises problems of detail, since the question 'Capable given what?' arises. But the general idea is clear: an experiencing being is one that currently possesses all the equipment necessary for experiential states, whatever exactly that equipment is.)

'Mental being', then, is an all-or-nothing term. It draws a sharp line. It inherits this property directly from the term 'experiencing'. For it seems very plausible to say that any being either is or is not, at any given moment, in an experiential state (in a state given which there is something it is like to be it, experientially speaking), or in a state of such a kind that it is currently capable of being in an experiential state (given appropriate stimulation)—whatever we can or cannot know about the matter. Just as any number greater than zero is unequivocally a positive number, however small it is, just as any object that emits any photons is unequivocally a source of light, so any experience, however faint or rudimentary, is unequivocally an experience. Whatever the epistemological indeterminability of the question of whether there is experience going on in certain cases, it seems plausible that there can be no objective indeterminacy in the matter. We can't be sure where the line between experiencing beings and experienceless beings runs. We cannot be sure where experience begins on the evolutionary scale, as we consider progressively larger living organisms—viruses, bacteria, paramecia, amoebas, grubs, insects, and so on. But there is, nevertheless, a fact of the matter.

It is true that the line between mental or experiencing beings and others may look unimportant from the point of view of animal ethology and general biology, which study the behavior of all living organisms without any regard to experience. The fact remains that it is a line of great importance. It is arguably the most important theoretical line to be drawn in the whole of reality. It is of great theoretical importance in the philosophy of mind (although some instrumentalists would deny this); the how and the why of its existence is one of the great unsolved problems of science; and it is of supreme moral importance.

I take it to be true by definition that only a mental being can have mental properties (be in mental states, etc.). It follows from the definition of 'mental being' just given, that only experiencing beings can have mental properties (be in mental states, etc.). Now it may well seem that any definition of 'mental being' ought to depend on a prior definition of 'mental' as applied to states, properties, and so on. On this view, a mental being is simply one that can have mental properties, etc., where the set of mental properties has already been determined. But I do not think we can do this, because of the particular way in which the word 'mental' is indeterminate. I do not think that we can fully determine the set of mental properties before settling the question of which beings are mental beings. Instead, it looks as if the best answer to the question of whether or not it is appropriate to count a certain property possessed by being B as a mental property may sometimes depend on whether or not one already has independent reason to think of B as a mental being, on the grounds that B has the key property of being an experiencing being.

The basic idea here is very simple: experience is crucial. (I am expounding an intuition, not offering an argument.) A being is a mental being just in case it is an experiencing being; only a mental being can have mental properties; so only an experiencing being can have mental properties. And when we ask which, if any, of the properties of a mental being, other than its experiential properties, are mental properties, the answer may be no more than a matter of convenient theoretical or terminological decision.

Equipped with this definition of 'mental being', one may attempt to choose between the five responses to the problem of the X properties raised in section 6.2. The first and second responses both claim that it is possible for experienceless beings to have mental properties, and are now ruled out. The third response is to be rejected because of its seemingly unacceptable conclusion that properties like the ability to perform calculations or play chess are not properly counted as mental abilities, or MOMAI abilities, in any case at all.

Nevertheless, the explicitly stated initial premises of the third response are plausible; the unacceptable conclusion is reached only by assuming the correctness of the move from (E) to (F)—the move from 'The properties in question are correctly considered as mental properties in some cases' to 'The properties are correctly considered as mental properties in all cases'. It is the validity of this move that is rejected in the fourth response, and I will now consider the fourth and fifth responses as offering two versions of the only tenable position left.

According to the fourth response, it is perfectly acceptable to say that we and the experienceless beings may add and multiply, play chess, differentiate circles from squares, and so on. The reason why this raises no problem is that it is also acceptable to say that in our case the abilities are correctly considered as mental (or mental-ability-involving) abilities, whereas in the case of experienceless beings, this is not so. This way of putting things may seem natural to some and hopelessly unsatisfactory to others, but it begs no substantive questions, for all parties to the dispute about the best use of the word 'mental' can fully agree about the facts of the case when they are stated, as they can be, without reference to the question of how best to use the word 'mental'. So everything is above board. On the present view, the primary anchor of all decisions about what should or should not be called 'mental' is the ruling that only experiencing beings are mental beings and that only mental beings can have mental properties. But this ruling is only a first step. It leaves plenty of room for dispute about exactly which of the properties of mental beings should be counted as mental properties.[5]

5. If the property of being thought about is a mental property, then experienceless beings can certainly have mental properties, but I will ignore this suggestion.

One can also express this general position (and respect Leibniz's Law) by endorsing a version of the fifth response according to which there is a crucial sense in which we can play chess, etc., but in which experienceless machines cannot really do so at all. One kind of case in which this sort of proposal seems very natural is this: Suppose there are two experienceless machines that ask and respond to personal questions, one of which is "kind" and the other of which is "heartless." (Such machines are not hard to construct.) We are strongly inclined to say that the "kind" machine is not *really* kind at all and that the "heartless" machine is not *really* heartless at all. The "kind" machine's verbal output may be like that of a kind human being, but the machine is not really kind, simply because its behavior lacks the necessary backing of genuine mental attitudes or experiential episodes. The problem is simply that there is no one there, no subject of experience, and what the fifth response does, plausibly or not, is to suggest that our natural response to the case of the "kind" and "heartless" machines is much more generally appropriate: it is appropriate not only in the case of kindness and heartlessness, but also, if less obviously, in the case of playing chess.

Let me ward off two objections. First, I have claimed that only experiencing beings can have mental properties. It needs to be stressed that this is not to claim that all mental properties are experiential properties. It is not even the weaker claim that the instantiation of any mental property somehow necessarily involves experiential occurrences. It is no objection to the present view to say that some of the properties that we normally think of as mental—e.g., the property of believing that wine is wet or the property of liking olives—are nonexperiential in character, insofar as their possession at a given time usually has nothing to do with any experiential goings-on. On the present view, properties like these can count as fully mental properties even if they are nonexperiential properties, so long as they are possessed by experiencing beings. (We have, of course, a powerful intuition that they can only be possessed by an experiencing being, that only an experiencing being can correctly be said to believe anything, or like anything, or fear or hope or understand anything.)

Second, the present view does not prevent one from saying

[A] that the subexperiential processes that directly subserve our experiences are themselves mental processes, given that they go on in mental beings and have the function they do.[6]

It does, however, require one to grant

[B] that none of the processes that subserve the ability of an experienceless being to detect, e.g., the color and shape of objects are mental processes,

even if these processes are *very strikingly similar* to subexperiential processes that go on in us, and, e.g., involve sensitivity to objects' light reflection, absorption, and emission. The present view requires one to maintain (B) even when the experienceless being in question is a naturally blindsighted, organic experienceless being and the processes that subserve its blindsight capacity are physically very similar to some of the vision-subserving processes that go on in us. It requires one to maintain (B) even when one supposes that these two sets of processes are as similar as they can possibly be, given that the experienceless being is indeed entirely experienceless.

This may not seem satisfactory, but one has to choose between options already described. There are three: [1] One may insist on (A) and also accept (B), although this position feels rather unstable. [2] One may accept (A) and then feel that considerations of theoretical smoothness force one to reject (B), on account of the functional, structural, and/or physical similarity of the physical processes in the experiencing being and the experienceless being—so that one ends up granting that experienceless beings can host mental processes and hence have mental properties. [3] One may acknowledge the force of the considerations of theoretical smoothness that seem to lead straight from (A) to the denial of (B), and so deny (A) in order to accept the undeniable (B). In the

---

6. 'Directly subserves' is vague, but in trying to say which nonexperiential processes are mental processes, one has to distinguish between the (arguably mental) processes studied by the computational theory of vision and the processes involved in the maintenance of the brain's blood-sugar supply. (Nonmental processes outside the brain, e.g., all the processes essentially involved in the maintenance of life, are also necessary for visual experience, and hence subserve it indirectly.)

present context, (3) may look preferable to (1), and both are preferable to (2). But I think that in other contexts, (1) can look preferable to (3).

It may be that a balanced position will seesaw. It will oscillate between accepting that there are reasons for saying that no nonexperiential processes are truly mental states or processes, in accordance with (3), and accepting that there are reasons for saying that there are certain nonexperiential processes that should themselves be counted as genuinely mental processes, in accordance with (1).[7]

6.5 Mental Phenomena

Suppose it is now assumed, contrary to (3) above, that at least some nonexperiential states and processes are correctly counted as mental states and processes. Is it possible to say exactly which ones? Is it possible to specify which (if any) of the properties of mental beings, other than their experiential properties, should be counted as mental properties?

An attempt to answer this question amounts to another shot at the general question of what the word 'mental' means. I'm not sure how important the general question is, for it seems that we can say everything we want to say without using the word 'mental' at all. And yet the frequency with which the word is used in books and articles about philosophy of mind makes the question seem worth considering. As in previous chapters, I will speak of Louis, and of the Louis-reality or L-reality.

So we are now concerned only with experiencing or mental beings like Louis. The question is, Which of their properties, other than their experiential properties, are mental properties? If we shift (I think usefully) from talk of properties to talk of phenomena, the question be-

---

7. Objection: If there are true identity statements asserting identity between nonexperiential brain processes and experiential processes, then it follows immediately that some nonexperiential processes are correctly said to be mental processes. Reply: There can be no such true identity statements. If a process is indeed an experiential process, then that is what it is, and it is not identical with any nonexperiential process. Rather there is a single process that has both experiential and nonexperiential features; and it is still open to someone who thinks that only experiential phenomena are mental phenomena to deny that the nonexperiential features are properly called mental features.

comes, Which of the phenomena in the L-reality, other than the experiential phenomena, are mental phenomena?

One answer to the question is, 'None. Experiential phenomena are the only true mental phenomena there are. *Mental reality* is just experience, everything that features as part of the conscious stream of experience of a mental being like yourself: sensations, perceptions, consciously entertained thoughts, felt moods, and so on. Mental reality is the surface. None of the subexperiential processes that make it possible are part of mental reality, insofar as they could conceivably go on without there being any experience. Even if there were nonexperiential processes that were causally sufficient for the existence of experience, so that they could not possibly occur without there being experience, they would not be part of mental reality. Not even the phenomena of subliminal perception and peripheral vision are part of mental reality, if they involve no experience.'

On this view, mental reality is like the play mentioned earlier: none of the backstage activity that makes the play possible is actually part of the play. This view has the attraction of simplicity and corresponds to at least some of our intuitions. Ordinarily, however, we allow that there are also nonexperiential mental phenomena. Many agree with the following. [1] It can be true at time *t*, simply true, true *sans phrase*, that Louis believes that water is wet and likes raspberries. [2] Truths like those mentioned in (1) are truths that record, and are made true by, the existence of real mental phenomena at *t*. [3] This is so even though Louis's believing that water is wet and his liking raspberries are not experiential phenomena (he may be in a dreamless sleep at *t*).

To accept (1) through (3) is to accept that there are nonexperiential mental phenomena as well as experiential mental phenomena. The next taxonomic step is to ask whether members of these two classes of phenomena either can be, or must be, *occurrent* or *dispositional*, considered specifically as mental (and mentally contentful) phenomena.[8]

The first part of the answer is easy. *Experiential* mental phenomena are necessarily occurrent. There are no dispositional experiential phenomena.

---

8. Every occurrent phenomenon may be said to have dispositional features, but the distinction will do for present purposes.

That leaves *nonexperiential* mental phenomena. These need a more extended discussion. It is widely held that there are *dispositional* nonexperiential mental phenomena, like beliefs and pro-attitudes, and that these have exactly as much claim to be counted as mental phenomena as experiential phenomena do. And if this is right—it will be questioned below—the only remaining question is whether there can really be said to be *occurrent* nonexperiential mental phenomena. Should we count as mental phenomena at least some of the many nonexperiential processes currently occurring in Louis's brain as he has a visual experience, or tries to work out whether $17 \times 19 = 323$, or whether q follows from p, given that $[p \to r]$ and $[\neg q \to \neg r]$? I will begin with this question, although I will shortly raise a doubt about its formulation.

No one wants to count all the occurrent nonexperiential processes that occur in the brain as mental processes—including all the processes involved in the maintenance of sufficient blood supply, the upkeep of axon myelination, and the manufacture of neurotransmitters. In fact, it seems plausible to suppose that few or none of the continuously occurrent nonexperiential processes in the brain on which the persistence of the belief that p depends should be counted as mental phenomena. These processes are best seen as processes that have no distinctively mental description, over and above their physics (or neurophysiology) description. They include intraprotonic and other nuclear processes, other subatomic processes, molecular-bonding processes, and so on, up to processes for maintaining the blood-sugar level and processes for the physical upkeep of the neuronal network.[9]

So the question is this: where exactly do the nonexperiential processes that count as mental processes begin? The problem may be difficult, but it seems clear. We want to hold that some of the nonexperiential processes in the brain are mental processes, and we cannot plausibly hold that all of them are. So we have to draw a theoretically well motivated line between those that are and those that are not.

But now it looks as if this isn't the right way to put the question. For many of the nonmental, nonexperiential processes just mentioned (e.g., the nuclear and interatomic processes) are in fact integrally involved in

9. It is arguable that all states are processes on the materialist view, since everything is in time and the constituent parts of matter are constantly in motion.

everything or almost everything that goes on in the brain. So in supposing that there may be occurrent, nonexperiential processes going on in the brain that do deserve to be thought of as mental processes, one obviously cannot be supposing that one is dealing with a set of processes that are entirely ontically distinct from all the nonexperiential processes that do not deserve to be called mental processes. Rather the situation is this: One is confronted with the total reality of a living brain persisting through time, and there are a great many different ways of picking out and describing processes going on in this brain. That is, there are ways of describing what is going on that deliver process descriptions, and these, by a reificatory turn of phrase that is harmless so long as one recognizes it for what it is, may be called descriptions of processes. The mistake to avoid, with this count-noun talk of processes, is the mistake of supposing that all these processes are entirely ontically distinct from each other. The truth is that many different process-identifying descriptions are being used to talk about the same portion of reality in different ways: in computational terms, electrochemical terms, experiential terms, subatomic terms, and so on.

Once we are clear on this, we can continue to talk in terms of processes. We can say that process-identifying descriptions couched in computational terms pick out computational processes, process-identifying descriptions couched in electrochemical terms pick out electrochemical processes, and so on. In the same way, we can say that process-identifying descriptions couched in nonexperiential terms pick out nonexperiential processes, and restate the present suggestion: some nonexperiential processes deserve to be called mental processes, given the nature of the description that identifies them, whereas others do not. They deserve to be called mental processes although it is also correct to call them nonexperiential processes, given the description that identifies them. More particularly, many of the subexperiential processes that subserve vision, calculation, and so on, deserve to be called mental processes. They deserve to be called mental processes even if we assume that they are distinct from the brain processes that realize the experiential processes of visual experience, conscious calculation, and so on. These subexperiential processes are of course physical processes, on the materialist view, and have a physics description. But they are also held to have a description given which they have a claim to be called mental processes, in spite of the fact that they are nonexperiential processes. This description may be some sort of computational or "program" description. It may even be some description that naturally employs the same sorts of term as those we use to describe or refer to the content of indubitably mental processes, like sensations or conscious entertainings of thoughts.

We now have three possible positions before us:

[1] Only experiential phenomena (E phenomena) are truly mental phenomena.

[2] The class of mental phenomena also includes dispositional, nonexperiential phenomena (DN phenomena), such as beliefs, pro-attitudes, and memories, in addition to E phenomena.

[3] In addition to E phenomena and DN phenomena, the class of mental phenomena also includes certain occurrent nonexperiential phenomena (ON phenomena), such as the subexperiential processes that subserve vision, mental calculation, and so on.

There is, however, a fourth possible position:

[4] The class of mental phenomena includes E phenomena and ON phenomena but not DN phenomena.

Position (4) might appeal to someone who is inclined to take an eliminativist attitude to propositional attitudes, and indeed to mental dispositions in general, but who wishes to take a fully realist attitude to the existence of both experiential phenomena and subexperiential mental goings-on.

6.6   The View That All Mental Phenomena Are Experiential Phenomena

Need we choose between these positions? I don't think so. It's enough to get the options reasonably clear and to have some sense of the considerations that count for and against each of them. I will try to take things a little further by considering some of the arguments in favor of position (1). Ordinary talk appears to favor (2) and, I think, (3) over (1) and (4), but the attempt to defend (1) may help to clarify some important parts of our thought about the mental.

Here, then, is an enriched statement of position (1). It begins with the following assumption:

[a] All truly *mental* phenomena are intrinsically mentally *contentful* phenomena; such mental contentfulness is necessary and sufficient for being a mental phenomenon.

I will take this assumption for granted in expounding position (1), and consider a doubt about it at the end of the chapter. It raises the long question of what kinds of mental content there are, but I will say as little about this as possible. There is undoubtedly sensory content, and there is undoubtedly conceptual or cognitive content, and for the purposes of argument I will inquire no further. It may be doubted whether emotional-feeling content can plausibly be supposed to reduce to sensory and conceptual content, and there are reasons to doubt whether the distinction between sensory and conceptual content is exhaustive as well as exclusive (i.e., there are reasons for thinking that there is such a thing as nonsensory, nonconceptual content; see Peacocke 1992, 76–90). There are also questions to be asked about the distinction between "broad" and "narrow" content, and so on. But I will not address such questions. Instead, I will start from the simple fact that we know a great deal about the nature and varieties of mental content simply by having experience in the way we do, and I will take it that this knowledge sufficiently grounds our understanding of the notion of mental content, so far as the purposes of the present discussion are concerned. It gives us a strong fix on what mental content is. This is so even if we are ordinarily unable to put much of this knowledge into words; even if we vary among ourselves more than we realize; even if there are also many things we do not know about the nature of mental content; and even if there may be ways in which mental content can exist in reality that are unlike the ways in which it exists when experiential phenomena occur.

Some may claim that appeal to the acquaintance with mental content delivered by ordinary experience is unhelpful in a discussion that aims to address the real issues and difficulties in the theory of content. I think that any such claim would indicate serious confusion, but there are many sorts of problem in the theory of mental content, and it is sufficient for present purposes that it be granted that there is some solid sense in which we know a lot about what mental content is simply in having experience in the way we do.

Position (1) may now be articulated as follows.

[a] All *mental* phenomena are intrinsically *mentally contentful* phenomena.

[b] All *experiential* phenomena are intrinsically mentally contentful phenomena.

[c] No nonexperiential phenomena are intrinsically mentally contentful phenomena.

Hence,

[d] no nonexperiential phenomena are mental phenomena.

That is,

[e] all mental phenomena are experiential phenomena.

I take (b) to be self-evident. The crucial claim is obviously (c), and the intuitive idea behind it may be expressed as follows: Consider Louis in a dreamless sleep at time t. He is in a completely experienceless state. Ex hypothesi, there are no experiential phenomena in the L-reality.[10] The question is then this: are there really any intrinsically mentally contentful mental phenomena in the L-reality at t? According to position (1)—the view that all truly mental phenomena are experiential phenomena—there are not.

The principal objection to this has already been mentioned, and goes as follows: Louis is a normal human being, and the following things are true of him at t: he believes that water is wet, he likes sunshine, he intends to go to Paris next week, he prefers black to green olives, he possesses the concepts of addition and adultery, he is witty, modest, and melancholic. According to the objection, the statements attributing these properties to him are not just part of our "best current theory" for explaining and predicting Louis's behavior, if this is supposed to amount to something less than truth. They are, quite simply, true.[11] It would

10. On the assumptions, which I am happy to make (see p. 138), that Louis is the only experiencer in the L-reality, and that there are no subsystems within Louis or the L-reality that are also subjects of experience.

11. This strong realist claim can only strengthen position 2, which I am currently arguing against on behalf of position 1.

seem to follow immediately that these statements *truly describe part of mental reality, at t.* After all, they state part of the simple truth about how things are in the world at *t*, and they employ indubitably mental terms to do so.

This sounds plausible. And yet there seems to be a deep difference between the truth conditions or "reality grounds" of the truth of statements attributing experiential mental phenomena to the L-reality (call these E statements) and the truth conditions or reality grounds of statements attributing nonexperiential but allegedly genuinely mental dispositional phenomena (beliefs, preferences, knowledge of French) to the L-reality (call these DN statements). In the case of each type of statement, the question is, What is there, existing now in the world, that makes the statement true now? On the standard materialist view, nonexperiential neural arrangements and goings-on are among the reality grounds of the truth of both sorts of statement. But in the case of E statements, intrinsically mentally contentful goings-on, i.e., the experiential phenomena themselves, are also among the reality grounds of their truth, whereas in the case of DN statements, only nonexperiential neural arrangements and goings-on feature among the reality grounds of their truth—physical arrangements and goings-on that can be described by physics and have no intrinsic mental contentfulness. This is shown by the fact that DN statements can be true of Louis at *t* when there are no experiential phenomena in the L-reality. On this view, although it is true that Louis in his dreamless sleep believes that water is wet and likes black olives, this is not because of the existence of any intrinsically mentally contentful mental phenomena in the L-reality at *t*.

It will be objected that this just begs the question about what intrinsic mental contentfulness is, but my present aim is to articulate an intuition, not to argue for it. The analogy is perhaps imperfect, but the sense in which there is a certain mental reality at *t*, with certain specific characteristics, as Louis sleeps dreamlessly on with all his beliefs, preferences, and so on, is a bit like the sense in which there is music in the world, and specifically Beethoven's quartets, even if no one is playing any music, but there is a set of compact discs of Beethoven's quartets loaded in a CD player. In this case there is complete silence. No music is to be heard. But there is a sense in which music, specific music, can be said to be part of reality now—a sense that one has fully understood when one knows about CDs and CD players. The sense in which music is part of reality in this case arguably closely resembles the sense in which something mental is part of the L-reality as Louis lies in his dreamless sleep, utterly experienceless but with all his beliefs, preferences, and so on.

To change the analogy, suppose that we have a computer program that is used to model the Panamanian economy with histograms and pie charts. We may come to think that it is intrinsically about the Panamanian economy. But—a familiar point—it may work equally well when the shapes that appear on the computer screen are given a different interpretation, and it is employed to model wind flow round the Outer Hebrides. The program, as it runs, is no more intrinsically about the one thing than the other. Considered merely as a computational structure or process, it has no intrinsic (mental) content at all. I suggest that exactly the same may be said of the nonexperiential processes going on in Louis's brain—all those in virtue of which it continues to be true to say of him that he believes that p, likes c, and so on.

One can carry the analogy back into Louis. Suppose that we can maintain him indefinitely in a state of dreamless sleep—a completely nonexperiential state—while leaving everything else about him completely normal. In this state he has thousands of beliefs, preferences, and so on, just as he does when he is in natural dreamless sleep. His brain processes continue just as they ordinarily do when he is in natural dreamless sleep. But now we detach his brain from his body and install it in a machine that drives a light show device on the basis of the neural structure and neural activity it detects. In the same way, we could put a CD of Beethoven's fifteenth string quartet in a CD player adapted to drive a light-show device on the basis of the patterns cut in the surface of the CD. As it sits there, a physical object with a complex structure, the CD is not *intrinsically* musically contentful. It is no more intrinsically musically contentful than it is intrinsically light-pattern contentful. Nor are our brains intrinsically mentally contentful, on the present view, when considered as physical systems in which no experiential processes are going on. They can no more be said to be intrinsically mentally contentful, on the basis of the typical behavior and experience they produce when normally sited and connected in a human body, than they can be said to be intrinsically light-pattern contentful on the basis of the typical light-show effects that they produce when installed in the light-show device. Nor can their individual causal history (or long-term evolutionary history) be appealed to in arguing that they are intrinsically mentally contentful, on this view.

Certainly, so far as facts in the L-reality are concerned, we suppose that it is something about the physics-describable physical arrangement of the brain that makes it true to say that Louis believes that water is wet (the point of the clause 'so far as facts in the L-reality are concerned' is that this truth also depends on causal facts about Louis's past acquaintance with water). Nevertheless, belief states (i.e., states of a being in virtue of which it is true to say that it believes that p or that q) are not states of the brain, or of Louis, with intrinsic mental content. They are not states or structures that have intrinsic mental content, although they standardly sit in the dark of nonconsciousness. On the present view, it is no more true to say that there are states of the brain, or of Louis, that have intrinsic mental content, when Louis is in a dreamless and experienceless sleep, than it is true to say that there are states of a CD that have intrinsic musical content as it sits in its box.[12]

It follows that there are no truly mental phenomena in the L-reality as Louis sleeps dreamlessly on. It is true of Louis that he believes that water is wet and likes black olives, just as it is true of this CD that it is a CD of Beethoven's fifteenth string quartet. But there are no mental phenomena in the dreamless L-reality, just as there is no music in the room as the CD sits on the shelf. For there are no intrinsically mentally contentful phenomena in the L-reality, and mental phenomena are intrinsically mentally contentful, on this view. Everything else is nonmental. It is experienceless structure, mechanism, or process. It is something that can exist in experienceless beings that are not mental beings at all and have no mental properties. That is the intuition. It is only an intuition, but it has a natural place in a discussion of the word 'mental'. The conclusion it leads to is that there are, strictly speaking, no dispositional nonexperiential mental phenomena.

12. Here the present position coincides with certain aspects of tough functionalist and instrumentalist views, and even limited eliminativist views. Differences remain in that the present position involves a commitment to two things in particular: outright realism about the experiential and the idea that ascriptions of propositional attitudes can be simply true. Searle (1992, chap. 7) argues differently for a related position.

It may be objected that I am making two incompatible claims: [1] Louis is in a state of such a kind that it is true to say of him that he has a contentful belief, a belief *about water.* [2] There is no state of sleeping Louis that is contentful, or about anything. In reply I can only repeat the CD analogy. Consider a CD of Beethoven's Opus 132. It is a physical object, and nothing about it is intrinsically musically contentful. So too nothing about Louis's brain at *t*—about the L-reality at *t*—is intrinsically mentally contentful. When certain things happen to the CD, there is music of a certain kind. When certain things happen to Louis's brain, there is mentally contentful experience of a certain kind. This is why we say that this is a CD of Beethoven's Op. 132, and this is why we say that Louis believes that water is wet. I take this to be in accord with Searle's claim that what are going on in the brain are neurophysiological processes and consciousness and nothing more (1992, back cover).

Having said this, Searle holds out (p. 158) for the view that beliefs are unconscious, intrinsically mental, intentional states, whereas I deny this. It is arguable, however, that this is just a (nonnegligible) difference of emphasis. Searle later stresses that "the ontology of mental states, at the time they are unconscious, consists entirely in the existence of purely neurophysiological phenomena" (p. 159), and it may be that when he talks of "purely neurophysiological phenomena," he means phenomena that cannot really be said to be intrinsically mentally contentful, considered in themselves, any more than a CD can be said to be intrinsically musically contentful, considered in itself. If this is right, then we are in agreement.

So far I have defended the view that there are no dispositional, nonexperiential mental phenomena, strictly speaking. A question remains as to whether there are *occurrent* nonexperiential mental phenomena. That is, are there any occurrent, nonexperiential phenomena that can be thought of as intrinsically mentally contentful? Here are two suggestions that support the view that there are.

First, it is Tuesday, and one has been given a posthypnotic command to leaf through every book in the room the following Sunday. On Sunday one has a strong desire to do so, and one does. In this case one is very likely to have acquired the conviction that one has left something important inside one of the books. For one will be under heavy pressure to be able to cite a belief that will permit one to make sense of one's action both to oneself and to others. Where does the belief come from? Presumably some nonexperiential process has gone on in one and has generated a belief that allows one to make sense of one's urgent desire and consequent behavior. The question is, How has the nonexperiential process managed to produce such a perfectly appropriate belief? It is natural to suppose that such a perfectly appropriate belief can be produced only by a process that, although nonexperiential, somehow involves the entertaining of the content that one wants to leaf through every book in the room. That is, it seems natural to think of the belief-forming process as involving occurrent and nonexperiential, but essentially mentally contentful, goings-on.

Here is the other case. One is stuck on some problem. One thinks that p is surely the case, but one does not see how, for q is certain, and $[q \rightarrow \neg r]$ and $[p \rightarrow r]$. One puts the problem aside for a few days and goes on holiday. Returning to the problem with a sinking feeling, one finds that something has shifted. One is no longer stuck, one can see how to go on. As before, p and q are indeed the case, and $[q \rightarrow \neg r]$. But it is not true after all that $[p \rightarrow r]$. Rather, $[p \rightarrow r]$ is true only if s is (i.e., $[[p \rightarrow r] \rightarrow s]$), and s may not be true. This is what one has come to see. Here it seems natural to suppose that the reason why one is no longer stuck is that one has worked something out entirely nonexperientially (it was no part of the course of one's experience while on holiday, for one was swimming and walking from dawn to dusk, and gave the problem no thought at all). And if one supposes that this is so, then it also seems natural to suppose that what must have occurred was a mental process with a certain specific conceptual content, a process that, at the very least, involved some sort of entertaining of the originally problematic propositions. And this seems, at least prima facie, to suggest that there are occurrent, nonexperiential processes that can naturally be thought of as intrinsically mentally contentful.[13]

Another familiar experience is this: a useful new thought, perhaps about a philosophical problem, flashes up out of nowhere when one is

13. Nelkin (1993) uses a similar example for essentially the same purpose. He suggests that blindsight and hemineglect also provide cases in which occurrent nonexperiential processes have intentionality, and hence mental content.

engaged with something else. This again suggests that one has been thinking about the problem in some sense, but nonconsciously or non-experientially, or at least that thought processes have been occurring that concern it, and that therefore have specific mental content.

In fact, there is nothing special about these cases. The same sorts of nonexperiential process go on every time we have a conversation and speak cogently in reply without any conscious process of formulating a reply. Writing this sentence, I do it simply by waiting for the appropriate words to come up into consciousness as a result of some process of which I know nothing except its results (it is this sort of thing that motivates Lashley's remark that "no activity of mind is ever conscious"). So if there is a good case for supposing that intrinsically mentally contentful, nonexperiential processes are possible at all, there is probably a good case for supposing that there are a huge number of them. The well-known phenomenon of driving while absorbed in conversation is also worth considering in this connection.[14]

Others who think that there are occurrent nonexperiential mental phenomena may do so because they take a realist attitude to the Freudian unconscious and its operation. But this idea adds nothing essential to the cases I have already considered.

All these suggestions have a common purpose. They seek to show that even if one holds that a truly mental phenomenon must be an *intrinsically mentally contentful* phenomenon, one is not obliged to conclude that it must be an *experiential* phenomenon. But they do not amount to anything as strong as an argument against (e) on p. 164, the view that only experiential phenomena are genuinely mental phenomena, and those who hold (e) will be unmoved. They will insist with Searle (1992, 187) that "the only occurrent reality of the mental as mental is consciousness" or experience. They may say that the nonexperiential processes that underlie the phenomena described in the last five paragraphs

14. See Jackendoff 1987, 280. Consider also the phenomenon of one's mind wandering radically while one continues to look at a scene. In this case it might be argued that the mentally contentful, mental visual field persists as a nonexperiential content. It persists even though there is no visual experience being had by anyone—no visual experience of the sort that there would be if conscious attention were to be paid to the contents of the mental visual field. See Lockwood 1989, 162–168; Dennett's discussion of the game of Hunt the Thimble (1991b, 334–335); and Rosenthal 1991.

are no more intrinsically mentally contentful than the processes that go on in a pocket calculator. They will take the same attitude to occurrent nonexperiential phenomena as was taken above to dispositional nonexperiential phenomena. They will hold to (c) on p. 164 above, the view that *mentally contentful* implies *experiential*, and it is hard to see how they can be argued out of this position.

Clearly there is nonexperiential processing of information in some sense. But this is not *mental* content, according to the present view. It is no more mental content in the case of processes in your brain than in the case of processes in a pocket calculator. The two cases are fundamentally identical. Suppose that the capacity for experience were permanently and cleanly subtracted from your brain (perhaps by interfering with the reticular activating system) so as to leave almost everything else untouched. In this case complicated nonexperiential processes might continue. The nonexperiential process that would have resulted in your having the experience of suddenly seeing how to solve a philosophical difficulty might continue without ever giving rise to that experience. But it would not be correct to say that the process had intrinsic mental content. Linked to a light-show device, it would do one thing. In your untampered-with brain, it would have done another thing. In a music-generating device, it would do a third thing. Considered in itself, it cannot be said to have intrinsic mental content. That is the intuition.

One may go further. There is an important sense in which Lashley's remark that "no activity of mind is ever conscious" appears to be true (1956, 4). Jackendoff gives good reasons for supposing that the best way to think of those linguistic-image-involving processes that we naturally call processes of conscious thought is just as "experiential evidence" that operations of thought (in themselves nonexperiential) are or have been going on (1987, p. 288). On the present view, none of these occurrent nonexperiential processes or activities of mind are themselves intrinsically mentally contentful. They could conceivably go on in an experienceless light-show device. Yet the present view does not threaten us with [1] the conclusion that we are somehow helpless passengers of our machinery, or [2] any puzzle about how mental content can appear to be causally efficacious.

As for (2), it is true that I have presented reasons for saying that there is no "true" mental content outside consciousness or experience. But (roughly and rapidly) there are also clear and conclusive reasons for saying that everything that matters about content, causally speaking, can be present without consciousness. There really is no "problem of mental causation," given materialism. This is the (by now extremely familiar) lesson of universal Turing machines and, more concretely, of pocket calculators, computers, and other artificial intelligence devices—things that show how rational and practical-rational procedures, for example, can be embodied or realized by physical structures and processes that know nothing of rationality (see Fodor 1992). Nature in her wisdom (natural selection) has ensured that we and other animals contain and host such structures and processes (see Hume 1975, 55).

As for (1), the claim that we risk turning out to be helpless passengers of our machinery: it is false, because we are our machinery. There is *no* threat to our autonomy in, e.g., Libet's claim to have shown that conscious decisions to perform actions may occur after the processes that lead to the execution of those actions have been initiated in our brains (Libet 1985, 1987, 1989). For even if this claim is true, it doesn't threaten anything that matters to us. My decisions are not less my own because the processes that lead to them are nonexperiential. They are not, for this reason, less rational or less mine; they are not less expressive of my wishes or personality. If my conscious thoughts are best thought of as "experiential evidence" that (nonexperiential) operations of thought are or have been going on in me, it does not follow, and is not in any sense true, that the thought that goes on in me is for that reason not really my own thought.

I will end this section by raising a doubt about the so far unquestioned condition of intrinsic mental contentfulness (condition (a) on p. 164).

It may be objected that we have to recognize, as truly mental, certain brain operations—call them B operations—that are not themselves intrinsically mentally contentful, although they involve the manipulation of items that we do think of as intrinsically mentally contentful. An example might be the operation of moving from $\neg q$ and $[p \rightarrow q]$ to $\neg p$. Searle gives a general argument that we have to recognize such B operations (Searle 1992, chap. 8; see also the exchange in Stroud 1991 and Searle 1991).

Once this objection is raised, it may look as if a whole new area of debate and uncertainty is about to open up. In fact, however, the objection leads back to issues already discussed. For various descriptions of these operations will be available, and one can say the following. If [1] the B operations are described in such a way that they could conceivably go on in experienceless beings, then it is open to those who hold that all truly mental phenomena are intrinsically mentally contentful, and that intrinsically mentally contentful phenomena can never occur in experienceless beings, to insist that the B operations are not rightly thought of as essentially mental in character. A computer "programmed" by a burst of radiation from outer space can seem to be as keen on modus ponens and modus tollens as the best of us. There is a natural way of describing the capacity to engage in modus ponens that does not require one to attribute intrinsically mentally contentful states to the entity that one ascribes this capacity to.

If, alternatively, [2] the B operations are described in such a way that they cannot possibly be supposed to go on in experienceless beings, then presumably this can only be because their full description involves ineliminable reference to intrinsically mentally contentful happenings after all; in which case they do not constitute a potential counterexample to the view that intrinsic mental contentfulness is a necessary condition of mental phenomenonhood.

Objection: The 'presumably' in the last paragraph is unwarranted. Perhaps [3] the B operations are not intrinsically mentally contentful in themselves but are nevertheless causally sufficient for the occurrence of intrinsically mentally contentful experiential phenomena, so that they cannot be supposed to go on in experienceless beings. Reply: The case may be granted, but it changes nothing essential. Some may think that it provides further reason to say that some occurrent, nonexperiential, and indeed noncontentful phenomena may themselves be counted as mental phenomena, but others will disagree.

A better case, for those who wish to say that there are some operations that are truly mental even though they are in themselves noncontentful, is perhaps the case of "grasping" a content or representation in thinking or understanding. It may be said [4] that this grasping is necessary for mentally contentful conscious thinking or understanding to occur and that it cannot itself be thought of as something mentally contentful, on pain of regress (see Stroud 1991, 245). Grasping may therefore be proposed as an example of a B operation that is indubitably mental, although it is not itself intrinsically mentally contentful.

Some, however, may doubt the genuineness of the distinction between an episode or operation of grasping and a conscious, experiential episode of understanding. The former, it may be said, is an integral part of the latter. Alternatively, it may be said that if one stresses the necessity of episodes or operations of grasping, then one will have to be prepared to attribute experienceless versions of these graspings to computers that respond appropriately to commands, or to questions about London, say. It may then be insisted, with this parallel in mind, that automatic nonexperiential physical processes underlie grasping as much in the human case as in the computer case, that these processes, considered in themselves, are not distinctively mental in character, and, once again, that it is only the actual occurrence of experiential phenomena that is a distinctively mental occurrence.

Many complications are possible, but the basic set of options remains the same. One can continue to hold out for the view that all truly and distinctively mental phenomena are experiential phenomena. Or one can adopt a compromise position (see the fourth response on p. 147, and position (1) on p. 157) and say that even when B operations are described in way (1), they can still be counted as truly mental in cases where they go on in experiencing beings—even if relevantly identical processes can go on in experienceless beings and are not correctly counted as mental when they do. Or one can make a radical move in the opposite direction and allow that mental processes can go on in experienceless beings. Or one can simply refused to get involved in debates about the meaning of 'mental'.

Two main claims have been considered in this section. First, that *mental* implies *intrinsically mentally contentful*. Second, that *intrinsically mentally contentful* implies *experiential*. Both claims can be challenged, both can be defended. In the end, the view that the only distinctively mental phenomena are experiential phenomena deserves serious respect. For many purposes, it is a very good way of putting things. But the word 'mental' pulls in several directions.

I have no remedy for this indeterminacy, but no remedy is needed. It is enough to have some sort of map of the tendencies of the word. If this seems unsatisfying, it is worth remembering that the notion of the experiential is much more important than the notion of the mental when it comes to the mind-body problem, and that the notion of the experiential has none of this indeterminacy.

7

Natural Intentionality

7.1 Introduction

It is sometimes said that *intentionality* is the fundamental mark of the mental and offers us a primary lead in understanding its nature.

According to one currently central use of the word 'intentionality', the property of intentionality is the property of "aboutness." It is the property that a thought has when it is a thought about something—say the city of Rome. But in this use it seems clear that intentionality is not a universally fundamental feature of mental phenomena. Sensations are among the clearest examples of mental phenomena, and they are not necessarily about anything at all. Sensations of pain, for example, are not about anything in the relevant sense. So it is misguided to suppose that a solution to the supposed problem of intentionality is the key to an understanding of the notion of mind.

It may be replied that it is *a* key even if it is not *the* key. And it may be said that intentionality is peculiarly puzzling or problematic. Here, however, I wish to exercise the intuition that there is no deep problem or puzzle of intentionality that is genuinely distinct from the problem or puzzle of experience, so far as the task of giving a naturalistic, materialistic account of mind is concerned. I will call this the *no-problem thesis*. Even if the case for the no-problem thesis fails, or has the consequence that the no-problem thesis is trivial if true, I think it provides a useful frame for discussion.

The qualification about the task of giving a naturalistic account of mind may be important: it may allow some to agree with the basic idea expressed in this chapter while insisting, quite correctly, that there are some distinctive further problems raised by the notion of intentionality.

Truth in philosophy, "although not to be despaired of, is so complex and many-sided, so multi-faced, that any individual philosopher's work, if it is to have any unity and coherence, must at best emphasize some aspects of the truth, to the neglect of others which may strike another philosopher with more force" (P. F. Strawson 1985, viii). Here I have hardly mentioned some of the problems that others think central. Nor have I tried to *prove* that experience is necessary for intentionality. This is not something that can be proved, given the indeterminacy of the word 'intentional'. My primary purpose is to examine an intuition, not to convince those who reject it that they are wrong.

I will call the intentionality or aboutness that mental states and occurrences have when they are about something real or existent 'E intentionality', and the intentionality that they have when they are said to be about (or "about") imaginary or nonexistent objects 'N intentionality'. E intentionality subdivides into E/C intentionality—intentionality with respect to concrete objects like platinum or Mount Fuji—and E/A intentionality—intentionality with respect to abstract objects like the number π. It is arguable that N intentionality can also be divided in this way: N/C-intentional thoughts may be about (or "about") nonexistent concrete objects like imaginary cats, platinum coat hangers, or unicorns, while N/A-intentional thoughts may be about, or may purport to be about, nonexistent abstract objects like round squares or the square root of the largest number. As will later become clear, indefinite thoughts like 'If a human being were to go to Mars . . .' have N/C-intentional content insofar as they are not about any particular person, and E/C-intentional content insofar as they are about the human race. If one wished to give telling names to the three types of intentionality that will be of concern in this chapter, one might call them 'rock intentionality' (E/C intentionality), 'π intentionality' (E/A intentionality), and 'unicorn intentionality' (N/C intentionality). I will stick to the more formal names, however, and when it does not matter or is clear which I am talking about, I will omit or abbreviate the prefixes.[1]

1. Insofar as it is possible at all, N/A-intentional thought must be about (or "about") logically impossible things, because logical possibility is a sufficient condition of existence, in the case of abstract objects.

Other complications arise in the case of N/C intentionality, but I will not pursue them. It may, for example, be thought that N/C-intentional thoughts must con-

I will begin with a simple case of E/C intentionality. And so far as types of mental state and occurrence are concerned, I will begin with experiences and comment later on propositional attitudes. At various points this chapter will presuppose familiarity with the discussion of understanding-experience in section 1.4.

7.2 E/C Intentionality

Consider two human beings, X and Y. Both are having qualitatively identical experience—call it 'S experience'. It is experience as of thinking about, and perhaps visualizing, a statue. In fact, it is just like the experience someone might have if he or she were thinking about, and perhaps visualizing, a certain real statue S on Easter Island.[2] And in fact X's S experience has normal causal links to seeing S or pictures of S, reading about S, and so on, although X has no memory of where S is. Y's S experience is caused by a freak brainstorm.

X's S experience is correctly said to be *about* S; it has classic E/C intentionality. In contrast, Y's S experience is not about S at all. It is not about any real concrete object, although Y thinks it is. So the two experiences differ dramatically in their E/C aboutness. But the only relevant difference between them lies in their causes. It does not lie in their intrinsic qualitative character. Nor is there any relevant difference between X and Y so far as their neurally grounded behavioral dispositions or mental or neural dispositions are concerned—their BMN dispositions, for short. It is the difference in the causes of their experiences that makes the difference in respect of E/C intentionality.[3]

---

cern things that could possibly exist, like platinum coat hangers. Unicorns then raise special problems: given that they are fictions, it is unclear whether anything that could come to exist in the future, either by evolution or genetic engineering, could ever count as an example of what we meant when we talked of unicorns, even though we would doubtless call it a unicorn.

2. Recall the discussion in section 1.4: experience includes conscious entertainings of thoughts and understanding-experience, such as you are having now, as much as sensations, perceptions, and so on.

3. It has been argued that a being can think about an object only if it possesses "discriminating knowledge" of that object, knowledge that would enable it to distinguish the object from all others (see e.g., Evans 1982, chap. 4; for a doubt,

Complications arise, of course, complications that are routine in causal accounts of things. Thus one's thought about S is not about the neuronal happenings that directly causally precede and precipitate the thought. Nor is it about the light waves and optic-nerve electrical activity that are causally involved in one's coming to know about S by seeing it or reading about it. But there is nothing especially philosophically problematic about these complications (in the same way, photographs and sound recordings are only of things located at a certain stage in their causation), and they certainly don't constitute a difficulty peculiar to the present account of intentionality.

The very existence of experience is a mysterious matter from the materialist perspective. We don't understand how experience itself can be a physical thing, given our current physics. But the phenomenon of its E/C intentionality is not a further mystery. I think that this becomes clear when one asks why X's S experience is about S and Y's experience is not, because it is so obvious that the difference between them can only be a matter of the difference in their causes. Furthermore, the causal difference that explains why X's S experience has this aboutness and Y's S experience does not is not itself mysterious. It is not significantly different from the causal difference that explains why this picture is a picture of Z (it is a photograph of Z, or a portrait of Z), whereas this qualitatively identical picture is not, since it has been randomly generated by an image generator or is a work of pure imagination. It is not significantly different from the causal difference that explains how a work of pure fiction can be indistinguishable from an accurate work of fact without being about the person the work of fact is about.

People say 'How can a thought be about an object?' or 'How can one thing possibly be *about* another at all?' as if there were some further deep difficulty. But once one has subtracted the problem of experience, it is arguable that there is as much mystery remaining in the E/C

---

see Fodor 1990, 119). Here it may be noted that there is ex hypothesi no difference between X and Y in virtue of which X but not Y possesses such knowledge, other than the difference between the causal origins of their (real or apparent) thought experiences. Both may describe the thing they think they are thinking about, both may be told that is on Easter Island, both may look through a book of photographs and say, of one of the statues depicted, 'That was the one I had in mind.'

aboutness of some thought of an object as there is in the fact that a mirror or an expanse of water can carry a reflection of an object other than itself. Both X's S experience and Y's S experience are puzzling from the materialist perspective just insofar as they are contentful experiential episodes. But they are equally puzzling in this respect, and X's thought does not have some further deeply puzzling feature in being truly about S. Intentionality is not a supernaturally unbreakable string that connects X's thought to S. It is just a matter of routine causation as it affects a certain sort of representational system. It is, admittedly, a representational system of a rather special and (to us) puzzling kind, insofar as it involves experience. But once this is granted, there is no more mystery in the fact that X's thought is indisseverably about S than there is in the fact that this normally exposed roll of camera film is, necessarily and for as long as it exists undecayed, a roll of camera film of S.

We are struck by how creatures like human beings can *intend* or *target* a particular concrete thing (especially an absent thing) in thinking consciously about it, and part of the puzzlement about E intentionality may be expressed by the question 'How does the mere act of thought— the merely mental episode—make and secure a connection to the thing?' (In fact, there need not be any sort of act, for there is intentionality in dreams and in involuntary thoughts of Georgia.) The answer is that it doesn't, that no mere act or episode of thought can do this. In the imagined case, X and Y are identical in respect of the fact that it seems to them that they are connecting mentally with a particular thing. Both have the same experience of subjective conviction that a particular object is targeted in thought. But only X's thought really has E/C intentionality, given its causes. Nothing about the total current experiential character or the total current nonexperiential neuronal character of X's thought episode makes it connect unerringly with the thing that it purports to be about, for in that case Y's thought episode would have E/C intentionality, just as X's does, and it does not. None of X's relevant nonexperiential BMN dispositions make the difference, for Y's are the same. It is (once again) mere causal history that makes the difference and makes it true that X's thought connects to S while Y's does not.

As remarked, conscious thought may seem especially puzzling, considered as a representational medium. It may be thought to be puzzling even independently of the general problem of how experience is possible.

For it may be thought to be puzzling in a way in which sensation, say, is not. My claim is just that its actually having E/C aboutness should not be thought to be part of why it is puzzling. The puzzle, whatever it is, is all there in the case of Y.

One important reason why conscious thought is puzzling, considered as one of the varieties of experience, is that it can seem so abstract and insubstantial—intangible and diaphanous—while still being indubitably part of the course of one's experience (see section 1.4), and while seeming to be determinately contentful. One could speak of the diaphaneity property of conscious thought, and also of the determinacy property, where the determinacy property of conscious thought is the *experiential* property it often has of seeming (sometimes veridically, no doubt) to have highly determinate conceptual content. To get an idea of how these two properties coexist, consider your experience of understanding this not very interesting sentence. I will briefly say something about each of them before continuing with the main line of thought.

'The diaphaneity property' is a vague and metaphorical phrase for a vague thing. The point is not only that language-borne conscious thought seems intangible relative to sensory experience, or even vivid imagining. It also seems that one may be having no clear sensory imagining or presentation, and may not even be clearly entertaining words subvocally in one's mind, and yet still be such that thinking about Z is the principal feature of one's current course of experience. (That, perhaps, is part of the reason why analogies with rolls of film or photographs can seem unsatisfying. They are, however, adequate for the limited job that they are intended to do.)

To stress diaphaneity is not to deny that the experience of understanding a sentence can have a character of great determinacy as it occurs. It can, as already remarked. Consider this sentence. Consider the sentence 'The mass of the moon is just over one percent that of the earth.' The experience of understanding such sentences can have a character of great determinacy, even while seeming profoundly diaphanous and unpindownable. (The notion of understanding-experience is discussed in section 1.4.) It has this latter character, I think, partly because we can't get at it or present it in other terms. The only way in which we can try to convey the content of the experience of understanding such sentences to each other is simply by repeating them:

'Consider this sentence.' 'The mass of the moon is just over one percent that of the earth.' As we do this, we cannot know how we may differ among ourselves specifically with respect to the understanding-experience we have on being confronted with the sentence. (We may, of course, differ with respect to the inessential phenomenological accompaniments of understanding experience—see p. 8.) But this does not mean that the experience of understanding such sentences cannot have the determinacy property. Nor does it mean that the experience of communication with others is or may be somehow illusory. Apart from all our obviously practically successful communication with each other, we can and do make and experience and communicate extremely fine and abstract distinctions in philosophy and in other areas of life. There are great rewards in doing so, in hearing others do so, and in having the experience of seeing exactly what others mean. The experience of communication about difficult things is moving.

There is, then, no conflict between the diaphaneity property and the determinacy property. The fact that thought experience has both these properties is easily confirmable by unprejudiced reflection. (Think of this sentence.) The two properties are not very amenable to theoretical elaboration or manipulation, however, and the vital and unassuming task of philosophy, here as elsewhere (see p. 12), is simply to acknowledge them adequately so as to avoid being misled by them and by the shadows they cast. "It is remarkable concerning the operations of the mind, that, though most intimately present to us, yet, whenever they become the object of reflexion, they seem involved in obscurity" (Hume 1975, 13), but the main present point remains unaffected by the diaphaneity property and the determinacy property. For although they are both part of what makes conscious thought seem so remarkable as a representational medium, any problems that they may seem to raise for a naturalistic account of mind are part of the problem of experience, not part of any supposed further problem of intentionality.

In some moods, then, we may think that it is an extraordinary thing that X's thought experience can be and is directed at an (absent) object, and thus possesses E/C intentionality. But on the present view, there is an analytic perspective onto the thought experience that discerns just three principal things. The first is a certain kind of causal-origin property that

X's thought shares equally with a photograph and does not possess in any way in which a photograph does not also do so. The second is a neurally grounded set of BMN dispositions (p. 179) that *X* has in common with *Y*. The third is a certain kind of "narrow" or "purely experiential" content property (see section 1.6), the content in question being the overall experiential quality that *X*'s thought experience has for *X*. This it shares equally with *Y*'s apparent thought experience about S, and does not possess in any way in which *Y*'s apparent thought experience does not also do so. The first thing, the causal-origin property, is in no way obviously mysterious (unless one is worrying about causation generally). The second thing, the neural structure that grounds the BMN dispositions, poses no deep puzzle for naturalistic materialism, except insofar as it grounds dispositions to have certain sorts of experience. The third thing, the experiential property, *is* deeply puzzling relative to materialism and current physics, just as an experiential property, but there is no other source of puzzlement in the phenomenon of *X*'s thought experience.

"Externalists" or "anti-individualists" about content should not think that the reference to narrow or purely experiential content means that they can ignore this argument. The legitimacy of the present simple notion of narrow content has already been granted by anyone who accepts that the story of how *X* and *Y* come to have apparently identical experience is even so much as intelligible.

So here, I propose, we have a fundamental case of intentionality: the case of experiential states or occurrences and their intentionality with respect to real, concrete things in the world. Little needs to be added if one goes on to consider dispositional, nonexperiential states like beliefs, desires, and propositional attitudes in general, and allows, in spite of the proposals made in section 6.6, that they too can be thought of as intrinsically contentful states that can have E/C intentionality. For the existing story of *X*'s and *Y*'s experiences adapts immediately to the case of their propositional attitudes. Thus we may suppose that *X* has a set of beliefs about S, formed as a matter of normal belief-forming processes. By all available (non-backward-looking) tests, *Y* appears to have exactly the same set of beliefs, but has them as a result of a freak brainstorm. (Some may insist that *Y* doesn't really have any beliefs at all in this case, because there is nothing his apparent beliefs are about [see Evans 1982, chap. 4]. If one accepts this, one can put the present point by saying that although X and Y are not the same with respect to apparently S-related beliefs, they are the same with respect to apparently S-related *beliefs**, where beliefs* are either beliefs or are like beliefs in all the respects in which Y's apparently S-related states are like beliefs without actually being beliefs. I will use the asterisk sporadically.)

In the case just described, we judge that X's beliefs(*) have E/C aboutness, while Y's beliefs(*) lack it, just as we judged that X's S experience had E/C aboutness, while Y's lacked it, and our reasons for the judgment are the same. Three main things were relevant in the case of X's and Y's S experiences: a causal-origin property, a structure of BMN dispositions, and a (narrow) content property. The same is true in the case of X's and Y's apparently S-related propositional attitudes. In the case of the experiences, I argued that X's and Y's experiences differed in respect of E/C intentionality because they differed in respect of causal origin, although they were the same in respect of (narrow) content and the structure of relevant BMN dispositions. The same goes for the beliefs(*).

It may seem much harder, in the case of belief, to separate out a clear narrow-content property. But this is unsurprising on the present view: given the proposals in section 6.6, a state of Louis that makes it true to say of him that he has a certain belief is, unlike one of his experiential episodes, a dispositional state that has no intrinsic mental contentfulness. So one shouldn't really assign the state a content property at all, let alone a narrow content property. If, however, one is determined to assign genuine content to dispositional, nonexperiential, propositional-attitude states, one can give clear and sufficient expression to the idea that X's and Y's apparently S-related beliefs(*) have the same (narrow) content by considering the ways in which X and Y are similarly disposed: the conscious-thought experiences and subexperiential neural reactions they are similarly disposed to have, the ways in which they are similarly disposed to behave, and so on. As remarked, they both appear by all available (non-backward-looking) tests to have exactly the same beliefs.

Intuitively, then, X and Y are the same with respect to apparently S-related beliefs(*). But in X's case the apparent beliefs have E/C intentionality, and in Y's case they do not, and this difference, once again, is entirely due to a difference in causal origin.[4] Varying the CD analogy in section 6.6, one might compare X's beliefs about S, as X lies (for our theoretical convenience) in dreamless sleep, to a videotape that is magnetically patterned in the way that it is as the result of the normal functioning of a video camera—or a chance-assembled object identical to a video camera—pointed at S in daylight. Y's apparently S-related beliefs are then a videotape that has been identically magnetically patterned as a result of exposure to a burst of freak radiation. Neither of these metal and plastic objects is intrinsically intentionally contentful, or even light-pattern-contentful, in its mode of existence. Both could drive a music-generating device, or govern the motions of an automated car. Both behave identically when placed in a VCR, of course, and they behave in such a way that the X tape, given its origins, may be said to be about S, while the Y tape cannot be said to be about S.

In sum, one may insist (as is common) or deny (as in section 6.6) that propositional-attitude states are intrinsically mentally contentful states that can, as such, be genuinely intentional states. In either case, they raise no problems, so far as intentionality is concerned, that are not equally raised by experiential states and occurrences (including conscious thoughts). One may therefore concentrate on the latter when discussing intentionality. This conclusion is not undermined by the plausible-sounding suggestion that the only way to make adequate sense of the idea that conscious thoughts are contentful in the way that we ordinarily take them to be is to suppose that they are episodes that occur in beings that possess many dispositional properties, properties of having certain beliefs, concepts, Searlean "background" capacities, and so on.[5]

7.3 The Experienceless

Having allowed that nonexperiential states can be intentional states, one may go on to consider whether entirely experienceless entities can be

4. In the standard Twin Earth case (Putnam 1975) there is E/C intentionality in the case of both twins, but different E/C intentionality due to difference in causal origin.

5. For this view, and a doubtful doubt, see section 5.12, pp. 139–144. Some may vaguely feel that propositional-attitude states somehow have a *better* claim to be counted as intentional states than occurrent experiential episodes. Here is an

said to be in intentional states. I think not, but it is not as if there is a simple right answer. It depends on how one interprets the word 'intentionality'. It depends on how one embeds it theoretically, and it will be useful to discuss the experienceless. We may note straightaway that if intentionality is thought to be properly attributable to experienceless beings, this will raise no difficulty for, but rather will strongly support, the no-problem thesis that is my main concern (according to which there is no deep puzzle of intentionality distinct from the puzzle of experience, so far as the task of giving a naturalistic, materialistic account of mind is concerned).

When a dog chases a cat it "locks onto" the cat, and we readily grant that its representation of its target has E/C intentionality and is about the cat. What do we say when a heat-seeking missile locks onto its target? Does its representation of its target have intentionality? I will briefly consider three responses.

First, if we allow aboutness to the dog's representation of its target but not to the missile's, this strongly suggests that the dog's capacity for experience is making the difference for us: we hold that true intentionality is found only in the case of experiencing beings.

Second, if we allow aboutness to the missile's representation of its target specifically because it was designed by humans to do what it does, this again suggests (although it does not show) that the humans' status as experiencing beings somehow makes the difference for us. This view is commonly expressed by saying that the missile has only "derived" intentionality, and that true or original or intrinsic intentionality is found only in the case of experiencing beings.

Third, if we allow aboutness to the missile's representation of its target independently of the fact that humans designed it—so that we would allow it equally in the case of an object that came into existence by fluke and was qualitatively identical to the heat-seeking missile—then we clearly detach the existence of intentionality from any considerations

---

impressionistic diagnosis of this (indefensible) intuition: *Propositions* are the paradigm possessors of intentionality. They are not real things in the world, and to that extent do not concern us here, but *beliefs*, in their dignified dispositional silence, can seem to have more of the character of propositions than occurrent *experiential episodes*, even when the experiential episodes are episodes of conscious thought.

about experience. But in so doing, we endorse the no-problem thesis. For we endorse a notion of intentionality according to which there is a fundamental respect in which intentionality is no more philosophically puzzling than the fact that an object like a heat-seeking missile can have complex internal structure of such a kind that it can latch onto an object in the way that it does. And this fact is not philosophically puzzling at all (within the philosophy of mind—see p. 94). We can fully explain it in the terms of current science. It is no more philosophically puzzling than the fact that a pool of water can reflect a tree.

Reflection on the pool suggests that our intuitions about whether or not an experienceless entity's representational states can be said to have intentionality are very powerfully and apparently irrationally influenced by whether or not the entity can behave in certain ways, e.g., move around and pursue things. Suppose that there is a robot that incorporates a television camera. Programmed not by us but by a freak burst of radiation, the robot tracks the one blue cube in the room on the basis of information received from the camera. The robot retrieves the cube wherever we put it. Some will be inclined to say that the robot has formed a representation of the blue cube and is capable of being in a genuinely E/C-intentional state. But they may be unwilling to say this of an ordinary television camera pointed at the cube or a mirror that reflects it. They will be hugely swayed by the fact that the robot can do something with the representation, that it can use it in some way. On this view, certain sorts of behavior can be sufficient for the ascription of genuine intentionality even in an entirely experienceless (and undesigned) machine.

One possible difficulty for this view derives from the fact that a capacity for (large-scale) behavior does not seem to be a necessary condition of a capacity for intentional states—this being shown first by the case of a completely paralysed animal (canine or human), and second and more dramatically by the possible cases of the Pure Observers and Weather Watchers (see chapter 9 below), who have beliefs, perceptions, a complex mental life, but are constitutionally incapable of any sort of behavior and have (I argue) no dispositions to behave in any way. The difficulty is this: given that a capacity for behavior is not a necessary condition of a capacity for intentional states, as seems to be the case, those who claim that behaviorally complex (and undesigned) experienceless beings can have intentionality may find it hard, in the end, to explain exactly why they deny intentionality to a pool of water.[6]

7.4 Intentionality and Abstract and Nonexistent Objects

X and Y are concept-exercising human beings and deploy concepts in their real or apparent thoughts about S, but it may be said that the discussion of E/C intentionality in section 7.2 does not help much in understanding the intentionality involved in the possession of concepts. It may be said that intentionality is relatively easy to understand when it is a matter of relation to a particular concrete object, and that the really puzzling features of intentionality have not yet been mentioned. First, there is our ability to have thoughts that seem to be about "abstract objects" like justice or the set of prime numbers (these are E/A-intentional thoughts, as opposed to E/C-intentional thoughts about concrete objects). Second, there is N intentionality. Y's apparently S-related beliefs or experiences have N intentionality or N aboutness although they are not about anything real, for N intentionality corresponds to the use of 'intentionality' according to which even beliefs or thoughts about nonexistent objects have intentionality—beliefs or thoughts about unicorns or mile-high skyscrapers or round squares or an imagined cat that is no actual cat.

A simplification can be made here. For when one is concerned with the nature of intentionality, there is no interesting difference between N/A intentionality and E/A intentionality. Indeed, it may be argued that there is no such thing as N/A-intentional thought, either on the grounds that a putative thought about an impossible object is not really a thought at all, or on the grounds that there are no nonexistent abstract objects, because impossible things like round squares have as much claim to

6. If such people agree that no behavioral condition is necessary, they will presumably claim that a certain sort or degree of complexity of internal organization makes the difference. But how much is enough? And why, in any case, should this sort of thing be thought to be sufficient for genuine aboutness? It seems that those who deny that experience is necessary for intentionality would do best to give up the idea that there is a fact of the matter about intentionality and opt for antirealist or Dennettian "instrumentalism" with respect to attributions of intentionality (see Dennett 1987).

reality as the set of prime numbers, once one attains the rarefied realm of abstract objects. For present purposes it does not matter whether these views are defensible. Thus even if it is reasonable to suppose that there is a distinct class of nonexistent, logically impossible abstract objects, it suffices to consider more straightforward cases like π or the set of prime numbers. That is, one may ignore putative cases of N/A-intentional thought and stick to cases of E/A-intentional thought.

A further simplification may be suggested. It may be claimed that there is no crucial difference between E/A-intentional thought about abstract objects and N/C-intentional thought about unicorns and imaginary cats, on the grounds that there is a corresponding abstract object for every imaginary unicorn or cat. I will, however, continue to treat the cases separately. In what follows, therefore, I will consider E/A intentionality and N/C intentionality.

Can the experienceless be said to be capable of N/C intentionality and E/A intentionality? Consider two experienceless machines. The first is a robot that can be tuned to search for different types of object. At present it is set to seek out a three-inch blue cube, although there isn't one. It scans each object in the room for the favored properties. If such a cube were present, it would retrieve it. The suggestion is that it has a representation that has N/C intentionality, a representation of a type of object that it has never encountered and that does not (we may suppose) in fact exist.

The second machine is a mathematically powerful computer set to calculate the set of prime numbers from 2 up and display them on a scrolling screen. It may be said that its operations have E/A intentionality—that it is set to represent an abstract object.

As before, some may be inclined to say that these experienceless machines have derived intentionality, since they were programmed to do what they do by creatures like ourselves. The important question, however, is whether experienceless entities can be said to have underived intentionality. One way to make the question vivid is to imagine that unprogrammed versions of the two machines are struck by a burst of radiation. At first, we may suppose, it sends them haywire. Then they settle reliably into doing exactly what the original machines do. (We can further imagine that the new machines are fluke assemblages, junkyard analogues of the "Swampman." See Davidson 1987.)

Do we still have examples of E/A intentionality and N/C intentionality in this case? Or did those judgments depend, in the original case, on our knowing that the original machines had been programmed? In the case of the irradiated computer, there seems to be no good reason to say that there is any sort of E/A intentionality. It is just that the prime-numbering machine's operations *happen to be interpretable* as a calculation of the set of prime numbers. Similarly in the case of the blue-cuber, there seems to be no good reason to say that it has any N/C intentionality. It does certain things as a result of the burst of radiation. It reacts in complex ways to the light-reflection properties of objects. What it does is interpretable in certain ways. But it is mere convenience to say that it has N/C intentionality. It no more has intentionality than a Venus flytrap or a coin-operated vending machine or a pool rippling under the impact of a stone.

I think this is the best response. Even if one were tempted to say that an experienceless entity could have full E/C intentionality with respect to a particular object in its environment that it could track and interact with, one might be quite unprepared to claim that it could ever be said to have E/A intentionality or N/C intentionality. We may find attribution of the latter two types of intentional content intensely natural when considering certain operations in the experienceless and undesigned, but it is still unjustified, on the present view.

This raises the large question of how experience can make the difference. There is no doubt that it can make the difference, but it is not clear how much one can say about this fact—a point that I will return to.

Having taken up this position, I should make it clear that I have no present quarrel with those who insist that the experienceless can have E/A intentionality and N/C intentionality, because their view simply confirms the no-problem thesis. Consider N/C intentionality first. To say that experienceless entities like the blue-cuber can have N/C intentionality is to suggest that an entity can have full-fledged N/C intentionality solely in virtue of its possession of properties and modes of operation that are fully adequately explicable by current physics and completely unproblematic from the point of view of naturalistic, materialist

philosophy of mind. (Perhaps the entity is structured in the way described in Dretske 1986, sec. 5.) It is also to suggest that if we find the
existence of N/C intentionality puzzling in our own case, this is probably
because we are confused. We are confused by the nature and richness
of our experiential representational capacities into supposing that N/C
intentionality is more than it is, and that it is something intrinsically
puzzling, whereas it is in fact the nature and richness of experience that
is puzzling.

The same line may be taken about E/A intentionality. Consider the
irradiated prime-numbering computer. If it is said to be capable of E/A
intentionality, then certain forms of E/A intentionality, at least, are no
more problematic, from the standpoint of philosophy of mind, than the
existence of the computer doing what it does. (I say 'certain forms'
because one cannot yet set a computer to determine the structure of
justice in the way that one can set it to determine the value of π.)

Obviously, the capacity of the experienceless to have intentionality can
be further debated. But whether or not E/A intentionality or N/C
intentionality is attributed to the irradiated machines, the currently
relevant outcome is the same: in both cases the machines offer no
challenge to the no-problem thesis. For if they are correctly said to have
this sort of intentionality on the basis of what they do, then there is a
fundamental sense in which this sort of intentionality is not deeply
problematic, so far as the task of giving a naturalistic, materialist
account of mind is concerned. It is just a matter of possessing certain
nonexperiential BMN (behavioral or mental-or-neural) dispositions. Or
rather, since experienceless machines are now included among the intentional, it is just a matter of possessing certain nonexperiential behavioral
or control-system dispositions—BCS dispositions, for short.

If, on the other hand, these experienceless machines are not correctly
said to have either of these sorts of intentionality, then they confirm the
thesis that the problem of intentionality is inextricably bound up with
the problem of experience. In this way they offer some support to the
stronger no-problem thesis, according to which there is no deep problem
of intentionality distinct from the problem of experience.

The no-problem thesis is not the false claim that there is no difficult
work to be done in trying to give an adequate account of nonexperiential
aspects of the conditions of intentionality within a naturalistic materi-

alist framework. When one tries to specify the structure of BMN or BCS dispositions that is needed for correct attribution of a more or less semantically determinate concept to an individual, one encounters tricky problems of detail. This has been the subject of some important recent discussion (see Fodor 1990, chaps. 3 and 4; see also Millikan 1984, Dretske 1986). The no-problem thesis readily grants this. It merely claims that there is no extra deep *puzzle* about intentionality, over and above the puzzle posed by experience.

So much for the experienceless. Turning now to experiencers, I will restrict attention to their experiential states and episodes and ignore their dispositional propositional-attitude states. In section 6.6, I argued that there is a sense in which such propositional-attitude states are not intentional states at all. But this is controversial, and the present justification for putting them aside is rather the argument above (pp. 184–186) that even after their claim to be called intentional states has been granted, they raise no special difficulties or issues, so far as intentionality is concerned, that require that their case be treated separately from the case of experiential states and episodes. I will continue to take it that this is so, and I will begin by rehearsing a familiar point about experience, after making three further preliminary remarks.

First, the restriction of attention to conscious thought is a matter of convenience, since conscious hopes, desires, fears, and so on, all display the same intentionality features.

Second, the restriction of attention to conceptual features of experiential content is also a matter of convenience, for even if purely sensory elements of experiential content raise no intentionality issue, nonconceptual elements of experiential content may do so (see, e.g., Peacocke 1992, chap. 4).

Third, some may favor a conception of experiential content according to which such content is not something that can be thought to have intentionality in itself. On this view, experiential content is not intentionally contentful until some sort of interpretive attitude has been taken to it, and the interpretive attitude is not itself part of the content. Suppose that one accepts this view and calls the uninterpreted content that it postulates 'content*'. One can then reply by saying that for present purposes the word 'content' denotes the end product of taking the interpretive attitude to content*. The end product is content that is intentionally contentful in the way that we ordinarily suppose our thoughts to be. If anyone wants to think of this content as the result of the taking of an interpretive attitude to content*, so be it.

7.5 Experience, Purely Experiential Content, and N/C Intentionality

It may well be that any experience is a physical event and that it has, as such, nonexperiential properties as well as experiential properties. But we can consider an experience just in respect of its experiential properties, and so consider it just as something that has a distinctively experiential *qualitative character* of some kind, whether it is cognitive or sensory, thought or pain.[7] The tendency of the last fifty years of analytic philosophy has been to separate the notion of conceptual content sharply from the notion of experience, and this fact, combined with the *diaphaneity property* of conscious thought, may make it seem odd to many to say that the experience of seeing red and the experience of now seeming to understand this very sentence, and of thinking that nobody could have had different parents, are alike in respect of having a certain qualitative character. And yet they are. They all fall into the vast category of experiential episodes that have a certain qualitative character for those who have them as they have them. They fall into this category however much they may also differ among themselves. One can measure how fully someone has absorbed the crucial (and ostensibly widely acknowledged) point that experience is as much cognitive as sensory, by considering whether that person has really ceased to have difficulty with the idea that the experience of thinking consciously that nobody could have had different parents is, considered just as an experience, just a matter of qualitative character. I tried to debug this idea in the discussion of understanding-experience in section 1.4. I think that it remains a very difficult idea in the current climate of philosophical thought and requires reflection. (Attacks on the idea tend to assume that all experiential qualitative character must be akin to sensory qualitative character; as a

---

7. The phrase 'distinctively experiential' is necessary, strictly speaking, because anything that exists has qualities and therefore has some qualitative character.

result they have little trouble in making it appear ridiculous. See Nelkin 1993, Wittgenstein 1980, 70.)

One of the difficulties we feel with the idea is that we are aware of the *semantic evaluability* (i.e., assessability as true or false) of such thoughts, and this (combined with the diaphaneity property and the determinacy property as defined in section 7.2) may lead us to suppose that even when conscious thought experiences are considered just with respect to their experiential character, their nature and content essentially transcend qualitative character. Some, indeed, may think that philosophers who insist on the richness of the purely experiential content of episodes of conscious thought are subject to illusion, an illusion that arises because they surreptitiously and illegitimately smuggle the richness of the external world into their conception of such purely experiential content. To combat this, one needs to make suitably vivid the fact that the richness of experiential content is something that it has just as "purely experiential content."

One good way to appreciate the richness of purely experiential content is to consider someone like Instant Louis. But it suffices to consider the old fact that it is conceivable that one has oneself just come into existence—either fully embodied or as a "brain in a vat." It is conceivable that there is no world of the sort one believes to exist. One's current experience may be of lying in the dark at night. One thinks about one's childhood, the disagreeable character of the Democratic and Republican conventions, the operation of the international money markets, Auden's poem for Yeats ("You were silly like us"), and *Terminator 2*. None of these exist. There is no such thing as the English language. There is only one's stream of experience, with all the extraordinarily complex (and apparently world-involving) content that it has for one as one has it. It is conceivable that it should exist without the existence of the world that it appears to be about. It is ontologically independent, in its intrinsic richness of content, of everything apart from itself (other than any nonexperiential realizing grounds that it may have). The point must, I think, be conceded even by philosophers who claim that in this case one's freak causal history means that one doesn't really have thoughts or sensations or even experiences, as they understand these terms (for the case of thoughts, see Davidson 1987, 444). For whatever *words* are permitted or forbidden in the description of the case, the nature of what is going on is sufficiently and dramatically indicated by saying that it could conceivably be one's actual situation now.

Episodes of conscious thought, then, are contentfully rich considered just in respect of their purely experiential content, and hence considered wholly independently of their causes. And this richness is, in the end, just a matter of qualitative character. It is just a matter of experiential what-it's-like-ness for a subject from moment to moment. This what-it's-like-ness is indubitably real, whatever other real things there are. And it is (by definition) all there is to episodes of conscious thought considered just in respect of their purely experiential content. We are familiar with sensory modalities, but it looks as if these need to be subsumed under a more general category of experiential modalities. Each sensory modality is an experiential modality, and thought experience (in which understanding-experience may be included) is an experiential modality to be reckoned alongside other experiential modalities. We have, so far, no explanation of how the systems of the eye and brain give rise to the phenomenology of color experience in the particular way that they do (leaving aside partial "abstract morphology" explanations like the Churchland-type explanation mentioned in section 4.2). In the same way, we have no explanation of how the systems of the brain that underlie or realize thought give rise to, or involve, conscious thought experience in the way in which they do. The fact remains that our cognitive lives are, as such, experientially rich. This is perhaps never more apparent than when one is lying in the dark thinking of one thing after another, unable to sleep. (Insomnia has philosophical uses.)

The situation is then this. One can speak of the purely experiential content of episodes of conscious thought. Even when considered solely in respect of their purely experiential content, such episodes are rich in their cognitive complexity as conscious thought, conscious desire, cognitive understanding-experience. And one natural way of characterizing the undeniable and conceptually complex contentfulness of what is going on in the case of Instant Louis or Instant you is to say that there is a stream of experience that is replete with N/C-intentional content although it has no E/C-intentional content, no link to anything real.

When *we* have N/C-intentional thoughts about platinum coat hangers or aging hippogriffs, we take the elements of our imaginings from the real world, and to this extent our N/C-intentional imaginings have E/C intentionality. Because of the concepts they deploy, they have indirect E/C intentionality, even when they are about nonexistent objects like hippogriffs. But this is a contingent consequence of the source of our concepts (or mental contents). It is not an essential feature of any possible N/C intentionality, on the present view. If Instant Louis's internal disposition is identical to ordinary Louis's, and if he can have thought experiences that are experientially identical to N/C-intentional thought experiences that we have, we may say that his thought experiences also have N/C-intentional content. This, I propose, is one natural way to take the notion of N/C-intentional content.

First objection: If there is just this *experience*, it may be illusory, like any experience. In particular, its appearance of having N/C-intentional content may be illusory.

Reply: Not on the present conception of N/C-intentional content. Suppose that one has just come into existence and that one is not in fact normally embodied, or located where one thinks one is, and that none of one's thoughts or experiences have the E/C intentionality that they appear to have. So far, with a bit of imagination, so good. Now try to imagine that even the *appearance* of one's thoughts' and experiences' having rich and specific content is somehow a total illusion. This one cannot do. (If you doubt it, try it—bearing in mind that even your attempted thought that all your other thoughts don't really have any content really has no content.) Here one hits some sort of Cartesian bedrock. Even if one supposes that one has just come into existence, it is an inescapable fact that at least it seems to one that one is thinking of something right now, or seeing something that one is inclined to think of as familiar. In this sense one's thoughts and experience indubitably have N/C-intentional content, even if they have no E/C-intentional content.

Second objection: This last statement is not indubitable. In fact, apparent thoughts about platinum coat hangers (e.g.) cannot be said to have any genuine N/C-intentional content unless they are composed of genuinely E/C-intentional elements. On this view, ordinary Louis's conscious imagining of a platinum coat hanger, or of a cat that is no actual cat, is a genuinely N/C-intentional thought, whereas Instant Louis's experientially identical apparent conscious thought is not N/C-intentional at all.

Reply: Those who wish to take this line may do so, but then they will simply have to recognize the existence of a new type of content, a type that can be attributed not only to Instant Louis but also to themselves as they formulate this view, since it is conceivable that they have just come into existence and that their thoughts have content only of this type. It will then be hard for them to offer plausible resistance to the (by now familiar) suggestion that for ordinary Louis to have an N/C-intentional thought about a platinum coat hanger or an imagined cat is (1) for him to be like Instant Louis with respect to the purely experiential content of his thought episode, and with respect to his neurally grounded BMN dispositions (his behavioral dispositions and general mental or neural dispositions), and (2) for him to stand in certain causal relations to platinum and coat hangers and cats that Instant Louis does not stand in. The remaining issue will then be terminological. Is one to say that Instant Louis has genuine N/C-intentional content, and that Louis has something more (i.e., E/C-intentionality-involving N/C-intentionality)? Or is one to say that only world-connected Louis has genuine N/C-intentional content, and that Instant Louis has something less? One can choose. The important point is that whatever Instant Louis has, it may be all that you have, and it deserves a decent name. I will continue to say that Louis's and Instant Louis's thoughts of platinum coat hangers and possible cats are equally examples of N/C-intentional thought, having noted the difference between them. One could mark the difference by saying that Instant Louis only has N/C* intentionality (before he begins to acquire connections to the world).

7.6 Concepts in Nature

So much, for the moment, for N/C intentionality. On the present view, Instant Louis provides us with a case of a stream of experience replete with N/C(*) intentionality but with no E/C intentionality.

It also appears to be true that Instant Louis can think about prime numbers and justice, just as we can, lying in the dark, unable to prove that we have not just come into existence. He appears to be capable of fully fledged E/A intentionality. Our innate capacity for E/A intentionality is fostered by our causal interaction with the world, but E/A-intentional thought does not require causal connection to the things it is about, unlike E/C-intentional thought, for there is no such causal connection to be had. (Abstract objects don't sit in Plato space, a bit like chairs in ordinary space, accessible to thought via a paracausal mechanism that allows one to treat their case as strongly analogous to the case of thoughts about concrete things. To think about the set of prime numbers is not a matter of hitting a Plato thing with a superluminal thought beam, or of being struck by a form of ideoradiation emanating from it.)

So how is it done—by us, or by Instant Louis? Books can be written answering this question, but I will limit myself, in defending the no-problem thesis, to two or three extremely sketchy remarks.

How is it done? The first answer is that we have certain concepts or contents that enable us to do it. On this view, the natural phenomenon of E/A intentionality, as well as that of N/C(*) intentionality, *consists* in the natural phenomenon of the deployment in thought of certain concepts or thought-contents by certain creatures.[8]

What is it for us to have and deploy such concepts or contents? One can first ask how we acquire them. This is a key question for anyone who hopes to give a full naturalistic account of intentionality. But it is not a question about the necessary conditions of any possible acquisition of such concepts or thought contents, for Instant Louis acquires them by cosmic fluke, on the present view, and it is extremely important that this is an intelligible possibility.

'Instant Louis acquires them by cosmic fluke'—this prompts a recurrence of the objection considered at the end of section 7.5. It may again be doubted whether Instant Louis can really be said to have such concepts or thought contents at all, given his (lack of) history. But he is, by hypothesis, the physical and (hence) experiential double of a real person, and his knowledge of mathematics does not depend on causal connection to the world. He may be able to run a passionate and original seminar on algebraic topology ten seconds after coming into existence. He may prove a new theorem, and he will experience his thought just as ordinary Louis does. Materialists who claim to doubt the intelligibility of the Instant Louis hypothesis must consider the fact that Instant

8. As before, an extension may be made to include dispositional states like belief states in the class of E/A-intentional and N/C(*)-intentional states.

Louis is a wholly physical thing, experiences and all, on their view, and that any physical thing is potentially perfectly duplicable. They can engage him in detailed and informative conversation about the moon, learn a lot, apply what they learn to the actual moon, and still know that Instant Louis is not really talking about the moon. But they cannot similarly dismiss his claim to knowledge after an equally useful conversation about logic or mathematics. What is it that he doesn't know?

It may be objected that even if Instant Louis must be allowed to possess concepts like the concept *square*, he can't be said to possess concepts like the substance concept *diamond* so long as he lacks any appropriate contact, direct or indirect, with diamond. This is a dubious objection unless 'indirect' is given a very wide interpretation.[9] But one may grant it for present purposes and then say that he possesses not the concept but the concept* *diamond*, and that possession of the concept* *diamond* is the same as possession of the concept *diamond* in all respects in which it is possible for it to be the same, given the lack of any appropriate connection with diamond on the part of the possessor of the concept*. This point can be animated in a familiar way by saying that if the real Louis were eliminated from the world and Instant Louis were dropped into his place, Instant Louis would experience things and behave just as real Louis would have experienced things and behaved. Clearly, the concept* *diamond* is a genuine mental content of some sort, even if it is not a genuine natural-kind concept. It is a genuine content element with a distinctive role in the experiential, inferential, and behavioral economy of Instant Louis's thought, just as the concept *square* is. The point can be put by saying that when the E/C-intentional content of the concept *diamond* is removed, rich N/C(*)-intentional content is left, and this is what Louis has.

Having defended Instant Louis, I return to the previous question. How do creatures like ourselves come to acquire *concepts*—those apparently

9. The objection is dubious because an alien scientist familiar with ordinary carbon could work out that diamond (or buckminsterfullerene) is possible, and name it and predict its properties, on a planet (or in a universe) where no diamond existed. If diamond then came to exist, the scientist could say 'This is diamond.' At a greater remove, a creature familiar only with elements other than carbon could hypothesize the existence of diamond, just as human scientists hypothesized the existence of germanium and predicted its properties in advance of discovering it.

remarkable things? It is a big question, but it only requires a very general answer in the present context, an important part of which can be given in a routine way by reference to the theory of evolution by natural selection. The theory of evolution lays the foundation of an answer, insofar as it can provide an explanation, in terms of random mutation and survival value, of how sensory-intellectual mechanisms for detecting, representing, classifying, and ordering features of the environment can come to exist and can then come to be of increasing sensitivity once they have come to exist.

Objection: The theory of evolution cannot yet directly explain why experience should have developed at all, since it seems that sophisticated survival-promoting detecting, representing, classifying, and ordering mechanisms can exist in the absence of experience. It is reasonable to assume that experience has survival value, but in the absence of a direct explanation of why this is so, the theory of evolution can be said to explain the existence of these detecting, representing, classifying, and ordering mechanisms only insofar as they are conceived of independently of the fact that they may involve experience.[10]

Reply: This is true, but it doesn't undercut the point that the theory of evolution can provide a partial naturalistic account of the existence of increasingly complex thoughts and concepts. This initial account can then be expanded in various ways. It can be enriched—to move very rapidly—by more detailed theories of individual developmental psychology, human and nonhuman. To these may be added theories of the way in which the development of language and imagination furnishes a medium and environment for thought that allows thought to take itself as an object and build on itself and complicate itself in remarkable ways—until it is hard (at least for us) to imagine how it could take place without the assistance of some such medium and environment. If we consider numbers and justice, it is not hard to see how these ideas arise in creatures like us. Children of three have a vivid if egotistical sense of

10. A revolutionized experience-integrating physics of the sort envisaged in chapters 3 and 4 might reveal this apparent problem for the theory of evolution to be a pseudoproblem. Waiting for the revolution, one can say that there may be as yet unknown biological reasons why experience provides a uniquely efficient way of integrating information from different environmental-feature-detecting organs, and so has survival value.

what is or is not fair. Numbers and numerical relationships present themselves in the manifest multiplicity of things like fingers and sheep. This is extremely perfunctory, but it is where we start from.

At this point questions about experience start to reassert themselves, questions about the contribution that experience is supposed to make to concept possession in particular, and intentionality in general. I am still deferring these questions, about which I will have remarkably little to say. In the meantime, it is important to stress the point that even when one restricts oneself to discussing nonexperiential aspects of the conditions of intentionality, various difficulties of detail arise, not only within the disciplines mentioned in the last paragraph but also, and especially, within philosophical theories of conceptual intentionality in the manner of Dretske, Fodor, and Millikan.

There is, however, no reason to think that any of these difficulties raise doubts about the no-problem thesis. That is, they do not suggest that there is some special deep puzzle in the existence of intentionality that is distinct from the puzzle of experience, so far as naturalistic materialism about the mind is concerned. The goal of these philosophical theories is precisely to show that conceptual intentionality is naturalistically tractable when considered apart from the question of experience, and a further part of their claim is that intentionality *should* be considered apart from experience, because it does not necessarily involve experience. In Fodor's theory, for example, the property of semantic or intentional "determinacy" or "univocality" or specificity of content (1990, 110, 129) that may appear to be possessed by a concept possessed by an individual is wholly accounted for by reference to a nonexperiential structure of reactive (BMN or BCS) dispositions in that individual, plus or minus some facts about the etiology of these dispositions (for the minus, see Fodor 1994, Appendix B).

Whether this kind of theory can satisfy all our intuitions about the nature of human concept possession is very unclear. A question remains about the place of experience. It seems that we can build experienceless machines that can do almost all the things that we may at first think of as requiring intentionality. They can track objects doggedly through space. They can be very good at distinguishing water (e.g.) from anything that is not water. They can pour forth the decimal expansion of π.

And each of these designed machines has an exact and undesigned fluke counterpart that can do anything that it does. For many, it is the undesigned counterparts that drive home the intuition that genuine intentionality is essentially bound up with experience. When an undesigned machine processes a sample of liquid and prints 'This is (not) water', it seems profoundly implausible to say that it is exercising the concept of water. That is the intuition.[11]

7.7 Intentionality and Experience

The last section shoots across a highly complicated area, but the questions we come back to are simple. Why exactly should experience be thought to be necessary for intentionality? What exactly does my conscious experience add to my computation of, e.g., the set of prime numbers, relative to the computation and search of (irradiated or humanly programmed) machines? What exactly does my conscious thinking about a three-inch blue cube add to whatever it is in the machine that guides its search for a three-inch blue cube? (In considering experiencing beings, I am still restricting attention to their experiential states and episodes, for reasons of simplicity given on p. 186.)

Many are inclined to say, 'My thought is *really* about the set of prime numbers, I really have a three-inch blue cube in mind, whereas the machine's operations are not really about the set of prime numbers, it does not have a three-inch blue cube "in mind" at all. Only in the experiential case are there truly contentful states that are truly about anything.'[12]

11. The machine may be more sophisticated. It may be the fluke counterpart of a machine belonging to a legally wary firm. It may print 'Sample A is just like water (passes all available tests for being water) but may not be water'—as if, like us, it had a concept of water that transcended its discriminatory capacities. But still, it is not exercising the concept of water. That, to repeat, is the intuition. The example gives the same result if the words 'a perfect circle' are substituted for 'water' and does not exploit a peculiarity of natural-kind terms.

12. As I remarked, this can seem less clear in the case of E/C intentionality with respect to an individual object than in the case of E/A and N/C intentionality. A missile can track—appear to hunt—a plane. A bug-eyed robot can indefatigably pursue a human being, maintaining a respectful two-meter distance. And so on.

This is a very powerful intuition. And if we ask how exactly experience is supposed to make the difference, the alarming answer seems to be that all it adds, in bringing about the presence of intentionality, is itself. Experienceless entities can have everything else that could possibly be needed, so far as qualifying for intentionality is concerned. All that is really relevantly extra in the world, in the case of the experiencing beings, is just the occurrence of experience that has a certain complexly contentful (and more or less diaphanous) qualitative character. This is my central claim.

It may be denied that experience is all that is 'relevantly extra'. It may be said that our behavioral dispositions are also relevantly extra. And those who say this may propose that in considering the objection we understand 'behavior' in a very wide sense—a sense that will become important in chapter 10—according to which behavioral dispositions include not only [1] dispositions to large-scale, ordinarily other-observable behavior, but also [2] what one might call 'microbehavioral' dispositions, dispositions to brain activity or, in more neutral terms, central-control-system activity.

The reply is immediate, however. The experienceless machines also have behavioral dispositions of types (1) and (2), so the presence of such dispositions is not what makes the difference. It is true that we differ from the experienceless insofar as our microbehavioral dispositions include dispositions to have experience. But to say that this difference is crucial is again to endorse the view that it is experience that is crucial in making the difference in respect of intentionality.

It may be said that our microbehavioral dispositions are fundamentally differently structured in some way, and that it is this fundamental difference of structure that makes the difference in respect of intentionality. But so long as this difference of structure is not essentially tied to our capacity for experience, it may be mimicked by experienceless entities. And if it is essentially tied to our capacity for experience, this once again suggests that it is, after all, experience that makes the crucial difference in respect of intentionality.

Next objection: One crucial fact about us is that when we have a particular thought, we exercise capacities that are necessarily part of a larger network of capacities to have other thoughts, and our possession of this larger network of capacities is something that is relevantly extra.

Reply: It seems that experienceless machines may match us in this, in the relevant respects, when they search for a blue cube or calculate the set of prime numbers. They may also be capable of many other complex mathematical operations and many other search-object specifications. They may spontaneously switch from one task or search to another, and may be designed in such a way that their (microbehavioral) capacity to perform one sort of operation is an integral part of a larger capacity, or network of capacities, to perform many other sorts of operation. So this sort of microbehavioral disposition does not emerge as something relevantly extra. The point made at the end of the last paragraph can be repeated: so long as the microbehavioral disposition is not essentially linked to a capacity for experience, it can presumably be mimicked in an experienceless being.

This prompts a relatively complicated objection. Perhaps there is some structure s_1 of microbehavioral dispositions or capacities of which the following things are true: [1] s_1 can only occur in experiencing beings; [2] s_1 is crucial for intentionality; [3] what makes (2) true of s_1 is independent of what makes (1) true of s_1. So [4] only experiencing beings can have intentionality, but [5] it is not the case that experience is all that is relevantly extra, when experiencing beings are compared with (microbehaviorally complicated) experienceless beings.

To this the best reply is, What might be an example? If what makes (1) true is indeed independent of what makes (2) true, as (3) requires, it seems plausible that a structure s_2 can exist that shares with s_1 that which makes (2) true of s_1 while failing to share with s_1 that which makes (1) true. But in that case, s_2 can exist in an experienceless being, and the objection loses its point, which is to show that (5) can be true even if (4) is.

I suggest, then, that all that is relevantly extra, in the intentionality-involving case, is the presence of experience—purely experiential content that has a certain qualitative character. (I am still deferring the question of what sort of character.) When there is experience with this qualitative character, in addition to all the various relevant nonexperiential properties, capacities, and dispositions that we and the experienceless may have essentially in common, there is E/A intentionality and N/C* intentionality. And—to take one crucial further step—this is not because such intentionality is somehow emergent with respect to, and somehow irreducible to, the total phenomenon of [a] experience with a certain qualitative character taking place in an entity that also possesses [b] all the various relevant nonexperiential properties, capacities, and dispositions that we and experienceless machines may have essentially in common. The existence of intentionality simply *consists* in the existence of the total phenomenon (a) + (b), on the present view, and does not in any way transcend it. This *just is* intentionality (E/A intentionality and N/C* intentionality), considered as a natural phenomenon. What else might one suppose there to be?

If this is right, the no-problem thesis is upheld. For the total phenomenon that constitutes the existence of E/A intentionality and N/C* intentionality (N/C intentionality that does not involve E/C-intentional elements) consists of (b), which is complicated but not fundamentally problematic from the naturalistic point of view, and (a), whose existence raises no problem other than the problem of experience. And all we have to add, in order to include E/C intentionality, is the requirement on E/C intentionality [c] that states that are candidates for E/C intentionality also have certain causal-origin properties.

No further difficulty is raised by the fact that one may sometimes need to refer to causal-origin properties when specifying the conditions of existence of N/C-intentional thoughts that involve E/C-intentional elements (e.g., the thought of a diamond mountain). Clearly, thought of diamond is an E/C-intentional element in the N/C-intentional thought of a diamond mountain, and empiricism seems to be right in implying that all human N/C-intentional thought will have such E/C-intentional elements. It is Instant Louis, or Instant you or I, who illustrates the sense in which N/C-intentional thought or experience need not involve E/C-intentional elements. Obviously, Instant Louis cannot think about a diamond mountain, for reasons given earlier. But he can have conscious-thought experience, which is, as experience, just like the experience real Louis has when thinking about a diamond mountain; and in this case Instant Louis's experience has N/C(*)-intentional content, as currently defined, although it does not have E/C-intentional content in the way that Louis's does. If one doubts that Instant Louis's experience really has content at all, one should reflect once again that one cannot prove that one is not an Instant person oneself, now. More moderately, one should reflect that even if one has normal biological origins, one's current and apparently patently contentful thought about diamond may be the result of a brain disorder that has led one to think, quite erroneously, that there is something hard, shining, and transparent called 'diamond'.

In this way, then, I attempt to defend the no-problem thesis: to argue that if the phenomenon of intentionality poses a deep problem for naturalistic materialism, then it is at bottom just part of the problem posed by the existence of experience. It may be suggested that the kind of experience necessary for there to be intentionality is a special kind of experience, one that raises special problems within the problem of experience even though its nature is ultimately just a matter of qualitative character, like all other experience. Perhaps, perhaps not. The present point is just that there is no fundamentally separate puzzle about aboutness. Put experience aside, and everything else about aboutness is a matter of naturalistically tractable causal relations and nonexperiential structures. The ruling thought of this chapter could perhaps be expressed by saying that meaning or intentionality is a less deep phenomenon than is often supposed. It falls out rather lightly from the existence of beings that have evolved the capacity to discriminate, classify, represent, and order their environment, and that do this in experiential or conscious mode.

To say that the existence of intentionality consists in (a) and (b) plus or minus (c), is not to deny any traditional controls on what can count as such thought. Not only can we judge that creatures who claim to be thinking about diamond are doing no such thing, given their causal histories; we can also judge that creatures who claim to be thinking about justice or the set of prime numbers or a three-inch blue cube are doing no such thing, given what they say or otherwise do when asked about these items.[13] This connects with the familiar idea that thoughts are what they are partly in virtue of their position in a network of other possible thoughts; in virtue of the way in which they arise from the exercise of a general (dispositional) capacity that is necessarily a capacity to have other related thoughts.

13. There is an analogue of this in the case of experienceless machines, in as much as their operations may be very naturally interpretable as concerning prime numbers or blue cubes, although these interpretations later require us to charge them with error or inconsistency.

7.8 Summary with Problem

I will take a final run at the topic, and raise a long-deferred problem.

1. Suppose that it is insisted that experienceless machines can reasonably be said to be in intentional states, or to have intentionality, for short. We may then say that they can at most have what could be called 'behavioral intentionality', intentionality that is attributable essentially on the basis of their behavior and causal interactions as they move around or compute things. (The case of undesigned machines is the best one to consider.)

2. If this behavioral intentionality is counted as a case of full intentionality, then there is no deep problem of intentionality, so far as the task of giving a naturalistic, materialistic account of mind is concerned. On this view, intentionality can be correctly attributed to certain experienceless (and undesigned) entities simply on the basis of the way they behave. The no-problem thesis is therefore upheld: facts about intentionality are reducible without residue to facts about experienceless mechanism, disposition, and behavior that are not deeply problematic for a naturalistic, materialist philosophy of mind. According to this view, some creatures also have experience, and there is indeed a problem about experience, given materialism and current physics, but the *intentionality* properties of these experiencing entities are not deeply problematic, and are indeed independent of the fact that they have experience.

3. Like many others, I think that mere behavioral intentionality can never amount to true intentionality, however complex the behavior, and that one cannot have intentionality unless one is an experiencing being. I think this is the best way to use the word, but that it is also important, if one is to attain a true view of things, that one should be very impressed by the respects in which the experienceless can seem to have intentionality. After this necessary episode, an old and rightly irrepressible thought should reassert itself. This is the thought that there is a fundamental sense in which there is no meaning at all, and hence no intentionality, in a world in which there is no consciousness or experience.

The word 'meaning' has many meanings. The one that matters here is the one according to which meaning is always a matter of something meaning something *to* something. In this sense, nothing means anything in an experienceless world. There is no possible meaning, hence no possible intention, hence no possible intentionality, on an experienceless planet on which the words of the Bill of Rights exist, perfectly formed in 120-point Palatino, as part of the growth of a fungus; nor in a universe in which behaviorally complex organisms have evolved and pursue intricate survival strategies in interacting with their environment but are experienceless. There is no entity that means anything in this universe. There is no entity that is about anything. There is no semantic evaluability, no truth, no falsity. None of these properties are possessed by anything until experience begins. There is a clear and fundamental sense in which *meaning, and hence intentionality, exists only in the conscious moment*—although the conscious moment is a most unsatisfactory item, from the point of view of theory. One cannot get very far in thinking about intentionality without a vivid appreciation of the sense in which this is true, even if one then goes on to define 'intentionality' in such a way that it can be ascribed to the experienceless.

If one goes the other way, and restricts intentionality to experiencing beings, one can still make a concession. One can acknowledge the sense in which meaning exists only in the conscious moment while endorsing a theory that attributes intentionality to some of the nonexperiential states of experiencing beings (e.g., their dispositional propositional-attitude states and some of their occurrent, nonexperiential mental processes—see section 6.6). The primary case of meaning or intentionality remains the case of occurrent, experiential episodes.

4. The line of thought set out in (3) above connects with the view put forward in section 4.4, where it was argued that experience is the only hard part of the mind-body problem. Experienceless beings can mimic the behavior of sensorily and conceptually sophisticated experiencing beings; they can behave *just as if* they had concepts and concept-involving (or concept-constituting) recognitional capacities. Clearly, the same goes for intentionality. Experienceless (and undesigned) beings can behave just as if they had intentionality.

Accordingly, some are inclined to say that experienceless beings do have intentionality, as in (2) above. They thereby endorse the no-problem thesis, and I will say no more about them. Others insist that one can't have intentionality unless one has experience, or at least a capacity for experience, as in (3) above. But they too can endorse the no-problem thesis—the thesis that there is no deep puzzle of intentionality distinct from the puzzle of experience, so far as the task of giving a naturalistic, materialistic account of mind is concerned. They insist on the importance of experience. But all that (a), experience, really brings to the world, in addition to (b), all the nonexperiential conditions of intentionality that can be fully fulfilled in its absence, is itself: experiential what-it's-like-ness, experiential qualitative character that may seem relatively plain and simple (i.e., pain or color experience) or highly complicated and curiously unpindownable (i.e., thought experience like that involved in understanding this sentence). When (a) and (b) are in place, there just is intentionality (certain causal conditions, (c), must also be fulfilled in the case of E/C intentionality). This is my claim, together with the claim that intentionality is not something radically emergent with respect to (a) and (b) ($\pm$(c)). Rather, the existence of (a) and (b) ($\pm$(c)) *constitutes* the existence of intentionality. If it is objected that these things together cannot be supposed to secure or constitute determinacy of content for thoughts that purport to be about things, then the reply is simple: it is an illusion to suppose that there is any kind of determinacy of content above and beyond what can be secured or constituted by the existence of (a), (b), and (c). (Compare Schiffer 1987, chap. 3.)

5. A long-deferred objection erupts. It is not as if any experience will do. Imagine a sophisticated creature k that has complex behavioral or "as if" intentionality. Imagine further that k has genuine and wholly internally caused color experience, and no other sort of experience, and that its color experience plays no part in its capacity to behave just as if it had intentionality. Here the mere presence of experience is not enough to justify the attribution of genuine intentionality. This is obviously not a satisfactory case of (a) + (b) $\pm$ (c).

What is? What must (a), the experiential component, be like in the case of any particular conscious, intentional episode? How exactly does (a) contribute to intentional content? How exactly must (a), the experiential component, relate to (b), the nonexperiential component, in the case of a particular intentional episode?

I do not think these questions can be answered in any detailed or interesting way. Consider a case in which Louis looks at a rock and mistakes it for a horse. His subsequent conscious thought about it is about a rock, although it deploys the concept *horse*. A dog can make the same sort of mistake, and it is a familiar point that a being's conscious thought or perception of an individual thing X may have full and genuine E/C aboutness in spite of being a hopelessly inaccurate representation of X, relative to that being's normal way or ways of representing things like X. (Among the experienceless, a life-saving robot may misidentify a tree stump as a human being and initiate human-being-protection routines.)

This immediately raises another question. What about the conceptual intentionality involved in Louis's mistaken deployment of the concept *horse* in thinking about the rock? Suppose that we have some account of the causal and nonexperiential conditions sufficient (so far as causal and nonexperiential conditions are concerned) for one to count as possessing the concept *horse* (e.g., on the lines of Fodor 1990, chap. 4). What do we then say about experience? What sort of cognitive experience (see section 1.4) must conscious deployment of the concept *horse* involve? What is the lower bound on acceptable forms of experience?

Here it is very unclear what to say. It is entirely unclear how one might go about trying to produce a general account of what it is that distinguishes cases of conscious thought that most would recognize as cases of genuine deployment of the concept *horse* from cases, like the case of the creature k, in which there is experience of some sort, and the right sort of "as if" or behavioral intentionality, but no genuine intentional deployment of the concept *horse*. (One would also need to take into account unclarities that derive from the fact that children grow into concepts and, more generally, the fact that there are various ways in which one can have thoughts involving concepts that one grasps only incompletely; see, e.g., Burge 1979, Greenberg forthcoming.)

One doesn't have to study these obscurities for long to see why analytic philosophy has wished to separate the issue of conceptual intentionality sharply from the issue of experience. The fact remains: experience is a necessary condition of genuine aboutness. There is a fundamental sense in which experienceless entities cannot have intentionality. A pool of water reflecting a tree in the wind does not have intentionality. Some experienceless entities are so constituted that their interactions with their environment are mediated by highly complex internal processes, but these can never make them mean anything. If any experienceless entity can have intentionality, a pool of water can.

If this is just the expression of a terminological preference, so be it. It is a terminological preference that marks a profoundly important difference. Think of the Eiffel Tower. You have just done something no experienceless creature can do—not just (trivially) by being the host of an experiential episode, but also by being the host of an occurrence that is truly and intrinsically about something. This is a hard fact, if an elusive one. It is a characteristic if inconvenient feature of the philosophy of mind that some of its central, proprietary facts are like this one. No one can get to first base without admitting such facts. The main reason why such facts get sidelined in contemporary analytic philosophy is that they sit uneasily with a patently inadequate conception of materialism and don't lend themselves to theory building.[14]

At this point those who champion intentionality for the experienceless may feel that they have the dialectical advantage, because their opponents seem unable to give any precise or interesting specification of the sorts of experience that are allegedly necessary for intentionality, either in general or in any particular case. And their opponents, who continue

---

14. With regard to terminological preference, consider three propositions about states or occurrences and five reactions.

Proposition A: intentional → mental
Proposition B: intentional → experiential or conscious
Proposition C: intentional → exists or occurs in an experiencing or conscious being

Reaction 1: Searle accepts (A) and (C) and rejects (B) with a qualification he calls the "Connection Principle," according to which "all unconscious [or non-experiential] intentional states are in principle accessible to consciousness" (1992, 156).

Reaction 2: I favor all of (A) through (C) with certain reservations.

Reaction 3: Fodor rejects (B), without any qualification like Searle's, and expresses strong doubts about (A) and (C) (see 1990, 130: a "good theory of content might license the literal ascription of [underived] intentionality to thermometers").

Reaction 4: A harder cognitivist line rejects all of (A) through (C) outright.

Reaction 5: A variant of reaction 4 that accepts (A), simply because it takes a liberal view about what is mental, and continues to reject (B) and (C).

to insist that only experiencing beings can have intentionality, may feel their position to be worryingly fragile or theoretically thin. They may feel that they cannot reasonably maintain it unless they can give a more substantive answer to the question raised in section 7.4: how exactly does experience contribute to the constitution of the intentional content of thoughts or representations in particular cases?

I believe that this is a philosophical mistake. There is no need to worry (compare p. 12 above). When we insist that experience is necessary for aboutness, we cannot go far in giving a general description of what experience of the right sort is, either in general or in any particular case. But the shining truth remains that we have cognitively rich experiential lives. We think consciously and precisely about particular things: justice, lemon trees, philosophers, and π. Whatever the differences between us, each of us knows, from his or her own case, what the experience of conceptually rich, genuinely object-directed conscious thought is like. We have such experience almost all the time we are awake, and often when we are asleep. The phenomenon in question is as real as any other natural phenomenon, and it just is the natural phenomenon of intentionality. And yet all there is relevantly to be found in the natural world is behavior (and behavioral dispositions) and experience (and experiential dispositions) and nonexperiential central-control-system processes (and central-control-system-process dispositions).[15]

7.9 Conclusion

So when we consider intentionality as something that threatens to create a problem for naturalistic materialism, we find nothing that creates a deep problem other than the problem of experience. This is what becomes clear when we consider what experienceless entities can do (i.e., almost everything). They play a useful analytic role. They strip away experience, leaving causal connections to the world, complex internal nonexperiential processes, behavioral and microbehavioral competences

---

15. As before, some may wish to go on to ascribe intentionality to certain dispositional states of experiencing beings, and indeed, to certain of their occurrent, nonexperiential mental processes. In chapter 9, I will give reasons for thinking that reference to behavior is not in fact necessary in the specification of the conditions of intentionality.

(p. 204), and so on—things whose existence is unproblematic from the point of view of naturalistic materialism in the philosophy of mind, although there are many problems of detail. Having stripped away experience, they offer us a choice. Either there is true intentionality here, in which case intentionality is no problem for naturalistic materialism, or there is no true intentionality here, because only experiencing beings have true intentionality. I have argued that if the second view is correct, it is not because intentionality arises out of experience in such a way that it creates a problem for naturalistic materialism that is distinct from the problem of experience. The only deep puzzle for naturalistic materialism is the old puzzle. It is the scientific (rather than philosophical) puzzle posed by the very existence of experience, given present-day science.

Beside the experienceless stand the instant people, the (Russellian) adult neonates, Instant Louis, Instant you, Instant I, even the instant person who turns out to be a brain in a vat. They also play a useful analytic role. They strip away the causal connections to the world and leave experience, together with certain behavioral competences and dispositions, which, in the vat case, may be merely microbehavioral, involving only mental activity or brain activity. They show that E/A intentionality and N/C(*) intentionality can exist fully fledged even in these extreme conditions of sudden creation. It is a philosophically illuminating fact that we cannot prove that they are not ourselves at this moment, as we continue to live our lives, our experiences as thickly intentionally contentful as they are at this moment.

8
Pain and 'Pain'

8.1 Introduction

What is pain? We all know what it is. Unfortunately, nothing could be more simple. But many philosophers think that it is not so simple.

Whatever pain is, it is what the word 'pain' means. So it looks as if the question 'What is pain?' is the same as the question 'What does the word "pain" mean?' But when one asks the question about the word rather than the thing, one runs into some distinctively philosophical difficulties. And many philosophers think that it is very important to ask the question about the word, instead of asking the apparently more direct question about the thing, because one then finds oneself compelled to admit something very surprising: one finds oneself compelled to admit that reference to certain publicly observable occurrences—typical observable *causes* or *correlates* of pain and typical observable behavioral *effects* or *expressions* of pain—enters essentially into any satisfactory account of the meaning of the word.

If this is correct, then given the fact just noted—the trivial fact that whatever pain is, it is what the word 'pain' means—it appears to follow that reference to publicly observable occurrences must also enter essentially into any satisfactory account of the nature of pain itself. But this distinctively philosophical view seems incorrect. It conflicts directly with the ordinary view that 'pain' is simply a general term for a certain class of unpleasant physical sensations, considered just as such, i.e., considered just as sensations and hence considered entirely independently of their typical causes or typical behavioral effects or expressions. Obviously, the ordinary view includes awareness of the fact that pains tend to have certain typical observable causes and effects or expressions (from now on I will not always include reference to expressions in addition to effects, although the difference between them is a philosophical issue in itself). But it is absolutely clear that the word 'pain' is just a word for a certain type of unpleasant sensation. That is all it means. (I say 'a certain type of sensation' because 'pain' does not cover all unpleasant physical sensations; nausea is extremely unpleasant but is not usually classified as pain.)

The ordinary view about pain is certainly correct. It is not the case that a few philosophers know the meaning of the word 'pain', while billions of nonphilosophers are wrong in hundreds of languages. If so, the distinctively philosophical view must be incorrect. And yet there seem to be some powerful arguments in its favor. Among them are arguments offered by Wittgensteinians and functionalists. The former are likely to focus on the explicitly linguistic question about the word 'pain' in arguing for the distinctively philosophical view, but many functionalists fully agree with the distinctively philosophical view without making any direct appeal to facts about the acquisition and use of words.

I think the distinctively philosophical view is incorrect not only in the case of the word 'pain' but also in the case of many other words for mental states and occurrences, including even words like 'desire' and 'belief'. But in this chapter I will stick to the case of pain. I will proceed in a mildly polemical manner and concentrate on the claim about effects rather than the claim about causes, although parts of my argument generalize from one to the other.

8.2   The Neobehaviorist View

Restated in general terms, without particular reference to pain, the claim about effects comes out as follows: for almost any (type of) mental state or occurrence M, reference to the typical observable behavioral effects of (instances of) M is necessary in a full and satisfactory account of the nature of M, and hence in a full and satisfactory account of the meaning of terms for M. Or, to reverse the order of argument, reference to the typical observable behavioral effects of (instances of) M is necessary in a satisfactory account of the meaning of terms for M, and hence in a satisfactory account of the nature of *M*. (Functionalists prefer the former order, Wittgensteinians the latter.)

After a certain amount of philosophy, this general claim, run one way or the other, may come to seem both natural and attractive. It may come to seem inevitable. And some philosophers do not see how one can avoid advancing from the present claim that reference to publicly observable occurrences enters essentially into a satisfactory account of 'pain', and hence pain itself, to the much stronger claim that reference to publicly observable occurrences is all that enters essentially into a satisfactory account of 'pain' and hence pain. I will stick to the weaker form of the claim, which admits the extraordinary stronger form as the limiting case, for it is arguable that even in its weaker form, the claim constitutes the greatest single error of recent philosophy of mind, and that even after all these post-(logical-)behaviorist (and now post-classical-functionalist) years, the mainstream tradition in the philosophy of mind still misjudges the place of reference to observable behavior in a correct account of the nature of the mental.

In the terms of this book, the mainstream tradition is no longer (logical) behaviorist, but it is still *neobehaviorist*: it supposes that reference to observable phenomena, and in particular to observable behavior, enters ineliminably into the correct account of the fundamental or essential nature of all or almost all types of mental state or occurrence: emotions, sensations, thoughts, beliefs, desires, and so on.[1]

In section 8.5 below I will tell a short story about pain in order to try to cast doubt on one argument in support of neobehaviorism. In the next two sections I will restate and vary the argument to be challenged. It is due in essentials to Wittgenstein, or at least to followers of Wittgenstein. Because I'm not sure which, I will call its supporters 'W theorists'. It has many variants, and I will try to state it in a general way.

I will also take it for granted that the sense in which a sensation of (physical) pain is a mental occurrence is clear. Thus, consider a case in which the experience of pain is hypnotically induced and to that extent

---

1. The claim may be thought to generalize from these familiar sorts of mental state and occurrence to many of the subexperiential states and occurrences recognized as mental by cognitive science, but I will not consider the point here.

"merely mental" (perhaps the hypnotist has told the subject that he has been punched in the stomach). The experience of pain in this case may be just the same as in the case in which the experience of pain has a normal physical cause. To that extent the pain sensation, considered just as such, is merely mental, even in the normal case.

One recurrent reaction to what follows may be that the points made only count against inaccurate accounts of Wittgenstein's views, not against correctly sophisticated accounts. I am sure this is partly true. I hope it is entirely true, and that Wittgenstein would not have objected to my main conclusions. The fact remains that his views have many false relatives, and these are worth attacking. If one can raise objections to them that do not count against Wittgenstein's own view, then one can contribute to the attempt to work out what his view really is.

It may be thought that this whole chapter is blurringly question-begging, since it regularly uses the word 'pain' in the way held to be illegitimate by the distinctively philosophical or W-theoretic view. But there is no real problem here. I do regularly presuppose the defensibility of our common understanding of the word. But this does not make it difficult—let alone impossible—to formulate the distinctively philosophical or W-theoretic view. Some W-theorists hold that the supposedly commonsense alternative to the W-theoretic view cannot even be stated, because the attempt to do so involves the assumption that the word 'pain' (or 'sensation' or 'experience') has a meaning that it cannot possibly have. It would, however, be disingenuous of the W theorists to claim that they really do not understand what the proponents of the alternative view are trying to say about the word 'pain' in using the words 'sensation', 'experience', and so on, as they do. They need only recall how they thought before they started philosophy. So the debate can at least get started.

Another assumption that I will make later, and that may be thought to be somehow question-begging, is the assumption that two people, receiving a painful injection, can intelligibly be supposed to have experiences that are different or similar in respect of their qualitative character. Some think that this supposition is dubiously intelligible, on the essentially verificationist ground that there is no point of view from which their experiences can be compared, or because subjective points of view are for some other reason intrinsically incomparable. I disagree.

The supposition is clearly intelligible. It is surely *intelligible* to suppose that identical twins receiving identical injections may have qualitatively similar or identical experiences. It is something that could possibly be true (see pp. 62–64 above). But those who feel that questions are being begged could read the following more as a description of the structure of a certain realist view of things than as a direct argument against their own view.

8.3 A Linguistic Argument for the Necessary Connection between Pain and Behavior

The W theorists' argument goes something like this: 'We have to learn words like "pain" from others. And if we are to learn the word from others, there must be publicly observable circumstances—circumstances observable both by us and by those from whom we learn the word—that are held to be circumstances in which it is right (or appropriate or correct) to apply the word, and in which they duly apply the word in such a way that we are able, following their example, to pick up on the circumstances of appropriate or justified or correct application of the word.'[2]

'It follows from this that even though a word like "pain" is a word for a mental state or occurrence, a word for a sensation, certain sorts of publicly observable behavior on the part of a being must be granted to constitute grounds that are standardly sufficient for applying the word correctly to that being. There is this sort of essentially *noncontingent* connection, at least, between giving a satisfactory account of how we learn the meaning of the word "pain", and of what it is to know the meaning of the word "pain", on the one hand, and reference to behavior, on the other. Hence there is also a noncontingent or "logical"

2. Here many may want to say, commonsensically, that the reason why certain publicly observable circumstances are deemed to be circumstances of correct application of a word like 'pain' is simply that they are circumstances in which people typically have unpleasant physical sensations, sensations whose qualitative character—which is that in virtue of which they are pains—is not publicly observable and is in that unproblematic sense "private" (see section 8.4 below). Many W theorists, however, seem to hold that all such facts about people's private sensations "drop out of consideration as irrelevant" to the question of the meaning of the word 'pain'. (Compare Wittgenstein 1953, sec. 293.)

connection between pain and behavior and, indeed, between pain and publicly observable behavior.'

(Interpolation: Strictly speaking, the claim in the last paragraph does not follow from the claim in the paragraph before it, and there is a considerably weaker form of neobehaviorism, which does not really deserve the name at all—it could perhaps be called the necessity-of-outward-criteria view—according to which the key neobehaviorist claim can be weakened from 'There is a noncontingent connection between pain and behavior' to 'There is a noncontingent connection between pain and publicly observable occurrences'. Thus there could be creatures that merely changed color when in pain, or the air temperature might change around them, or the local birds might sing differently in their presence, and some might say that none of these things are really behavior but are sufficient for use of the word 'pain' to evolve normally. Having noted this, I will continue to speak in terms of behavior, with a further proviso in note 3.)

'This connection between pain and publicly observable behavior is of a rather special kind. For it is, on the one hand, *essentially loose*, in the sense that no sort or amount of behavior is ever strictly necessary or sufficient for pain in any particular case (for on one side there is the stoic, who conceals all pain, and on the other there is the actor, who falsely appears to be in great pain); but it is also *essentially noncontingent,* for the reasons given in the last paragraph but one. And so it seems that reference to observable behavior does indeed enter ineliminably into any satisfactory account of the essential nature of mental states and occurrences like pain.' End of the W-theoretic argument.

What happens here? We move in a familiar way from the claim that reference to publicly observable circumstances will enter essentially into any satisfactory account of the *correct circumstances of use or application* of the word, to the claim that it will therefore enter essentially into any satisfactory account of the *meaning* of the word, to the claim that it will enter essentially into any satisfactory account of the essential *nature* of what the word is a word for. The transmission conditions of the word essentially involve reference to publicly observable phenomena—and to nothing else, on the extreme view. The same must then be true of its correct-application conditions or truth conditions. Thus the publicly observable, and only the publicly observable, on the extreme view, enters essentially into what one might call the semantic essence of the word. (Note that to claim [1] that reference to publicly observable occurrences enters essentially into a satisfactory account of the nature of pain is not necessarily to say [2] that it does so because it is reference to part of what pain *consists in*, although some may hold that this is so. For one may make claim (1) simply on the grounds that reference to the typical *effects* of pain must enter into a satisfactory account of the nature of pain, and simply deny (2).)

Essentially similar if somewhat more complicated applications of this argument produce similar conclusions for other mental terms, including very general terms like 'sensation', 'experience', and 'feeling'. The general W-theoretic conclusion seems plain: the notion of behavior is central and indispensable in discussing the nature of the mental, simply because it has a central and indispensable place in any correct analysis of the nature of our *language* for the mental.[3]

It is worth noting that the reference to the learning of language does not seem to be indispensable. For one thing, it seems that we may imagine beings whose knowledge of language is fully innate. And whether such beings are possible or not, the general thesis can be equally well expressed without reference to learning, as the thesis that the meaning of a word is "logically tied" to publicly observable features of circumstances that are generally held (there is a necessary vagueness in this phrase) to constitute sufficient grounds for its correct application. Nevertheless, I will continue to refer to the facts of language learning from time to time.[4]

3. As stated here, the conclusion depends on the assumption that the publicly observable circumstances necessary for acquiring of mental terms will in all cases involve behavioral phenomena that are *effects* (or expressions or typical concomitants) of mental states or occurrences, whether or not they also include publicly observable occurrences that are *causes* of mental states or occurrences. This assumption can be challenged: it is arguable that publicly observable causes alone might suffice for such acquisition. I will not challenge the assumption here, however, since it is usually shared by those who propound the W-theoretic argument.

4. The possibility of fully innate knowledge of language may seem doubtful: it may be thought that one cannot be truly participant in a language unless one has been initiated into it by some process of learning. Wittgensteinians, however, ought to find it particularly hard to reject the possibility of a fully innate

8.4 A Challenge

This W-theoretic argument may seem simple and powerful, but it is hard to pin down its implications with exactness. One challenge to it goes as follows: Although the argument does give a basically correct account of how we acquire a grasp of mental terms, and indeed of the ordinary conditions of use of those terms in a mature human language practice, it simply does not follow from this that some form of neobehaviorism is true. That is, it simply does not follow that reference to behavior enters essentially into the correct account of the essential nature of all or almost all types of mental state or occurrence (emotions, sensations, thoughts, imaginings, fantasies, rememberings, beliefs, desires, etc.). Epistemological facts about the publicly observable evidential circumstances in which human beings individually acquire and communally sustain a (public) means of communication about mental phenomena just cannot be supposed to dictate answers to questions about the fundamental nature of mental phenomena in this way. And this is so although these epistemological facts are key facts about the circumstances of acquisition (and conditions of continuing circulation) of the *very words in which the questions about the fundamental nature of mental phenomena are posed*, and although it seems natural to suppose that key facts about the circumstances of acquisition (and conditions of continuing circulation) of a word must have some essential or constitutive place in an account of the meaning of that word.

In its crudest form, the claim to be challenged is this: that the *epistemological* facts about the necessarily public evidential circumstances in which a given mental term is acquired and used determine the *semantic* facts about the meaning of the term, and hence determine the *ontological* facts about the thing the term is a term for—since to know what a term *means* just is to know what the thing it is a term for *is*.

---

language. For the admission of such a possibility appears entirely consonant with Wittgenstein's 'This is just what we do' approach to the question of the basis of linguistic meaning, according to which there is no further fact about linguistic meaning over and above the given fact of agreement in usage. It seems that Wittgenstein once considered and admitted the force of the suggestion, but later came to doubt it (1969, 12; see Pears 1988, vol. 2, 375–377).

This claim can sound very plausible, but it is mistaken: to suppose that these epistemological facts about the publicly observable circumstances of language acquisition and use do in this way dictate answers to questions about the nature of the things we talk about is (as far as I can see) to misunderstand the nature of language and the nature of reality and the nature of possibility. I think it is to misunderstand the scope and nature of philosophy, and to reduce it to a covert or indirect form of anthropology. (The opposing polemical remark is that it is hubristic folly to suppose that it can be anything more than this.)[5]

The semantics of words like 'pain' and 'gold' are, of course, different, and for a variety of reasons, but consideration of natural-kind terms like 'gold' has sufficed to convince many that arguments that run from epistemology to semantics to ontology in this way do not have general application, whatever their attraction in the philosophy of mind, and that it is not in general true that the meaning of a word cannot in any way transcend what is available for inspection in the publicly observable circumstances in which transmission of mastery of its use takes place. Thus it is widely held that a word for a natural kind is a word for a thing whose essential nature is certainly not wholly revealed or accounted for in an account of what we take to be the correct circumstances of use of our word for the thing.

In fact, and as remarked, once one has accepted the W theorists' argument that reference to publicly observable occurrences enters essentially into any satisfactory account of the meaning of the word 'pain',

5. The attraction of the old empiricist argument from epistemology to semantics to ontology also explains the phenomenon of phenomenalism (Carnap once wrote a paper called "Empiricism, Semantics, and Ontology"), and many have supposed that Hume makes this move in his discussion of causation, moving from the claim that regularity is all we *know* of causation to the claim that regularity is all that we can possibly *mean* by 'causation' to the claim that regularity is (definitely) all there *is* to causation. But he does better than this, because he allows that his famous two "definitions" of cause are "imperfect" and do not in fact purport to say what causation is. They simply state what it is to us, given our limitations (they state what the word 'cause' means, insofar as it has any positively descriptive content for us). As Hume says, "we cannot attain [any] more perfect definition" of 'cause', given our limitations (1975, 76–77, 92). Connectedly, he allows that the word 'cause' or 'power' may be understood to *refer* to something whose nature is in certain fundamental respects unrevealed, not publicly accessible, in the circumstances in which we learn to use the word.

it may be hard to see how one can stop the slide into the view that reference to publicly observable occurrences is all that enters essentially into any satisfactory account of the meaning of the word 'pain'. And then one is faced with the wonderful conclusion that language is utterly incapable of talking in any way about pain. It is utterly incapable of talking about the things we know are pains: these sensations that you and I have, and that are, as sensations, entirely private, in a natural and wholly defensible sense of the word 'private'. (The word 'private' is a battleground, but certain simple facts remain: that only I have my sensations, that only I know that I have many of my sensations, and, most importantly, that only I can know, corrigibly or not, the particular qualitative character that my sensations have as I have them. The claim that only I have my sensations is often dismissed as a useless logical triviality, but the point of it in this context is just that my sensations of pain are, in respect of their qualitative character, publicly unobservable, and in this simple sense private.)

This conclusion seems absurd—the conclusion that language can't talk in any way about pain.[6] And yet many may be unable to resist the general argument that has already been given. It deserves a final recapitulation: '[1] When we are concerned with the essential nature of the mental, we are (obviously and necessarily) concerned with the essential nature of what we are talking about when we employ mental vocabulary. [2] We cannot properly determine what we are talking about when we employ mental vocabulary without referring to the sorts of public circumstances in which such vocabulary is mastered (and subsequently employed) by us. [3] For these circumstances have a *constitutive* or *definitional* role when it comes to asking about what we *mean* when we

---

6. Wittgenstein appears to endorse this conclusion in sec. 304 of the *Philosophical Investigations*: "'Again and again you reach the conclusion that the sensation itself is a *nothing*.'—Not at all. It is not a *something*, but it is not a *nothing* either! The conclusion was only that a nothing would serve just as well as a something about which nothing could be said." The penultimate sentence of the quotation is pretty odd (it is not clear whether Wittgenstein would have been happy to grant that the sensation was something although it was not *a* something), but the currently relevant point is that in the last sentence Wittgenstein seems to suggest that even if the sensation with its publicly unobservable qualitative character were allowed to be something, it would still have to be admitted to be something about which nothing could be said.

employ mental vocabulary and hence when it comes to asking about the essential nature of what we are *talking about* when we employ mental vocabulary, i.e., what we are *really* talking about, whatever we *think* we are talking about, when we employ mental vocabulary.'[7]

This is the W theorist's argument. It can appear very plausible. And yet I think it fails to provide good reasons for endorsing the neobehaviorist view (the view that reference to publicly observable behavior enters ineliminably into a satisfactory account of the essential nature of all or almost all types of mental state or occurrence). In fact, as already remarked, I think that the neobehaviorist view is false, and that this is so even though a general attack on it must defeat not only the W theorists' argument, but also the latest varieties of sophisticated (neobehaviorist) functionalism, which make no appeal to the thesis about language use and acquisition.

The W theorist's argument seems to show that it is not possible for us to have what we evidently do have: a word, like 'pain', that is nothing more and nothing less than a word for a certain class of sensations considered just as such—i.e., just as experiential episodes with a certain (unpleasant) character—and hence considered completely independently of any typical causes or effects (let alone any *observable* causes and effects) that they may have. It raises the question, How is it possible to have such a word in a language? And it is usually thought to show that we do not really have such a word after all. It is thought to show that the nature of the word is fundamentally other than we suppose. But we do have such a word—this is the fact from which we must begin.[8]

7. McGinn once compressed this widely endorsed line of thought into an epigram: "The epistemology of mind is constitutive of its nature" (1982, 7). Note that it has another version that does not appeal primarily to considerations about language learning but insists rather that our attributions of mental states to others, and hence our whole language of mental states, must be seen as part of our general practice of making sense of people on the basis of their behavior. According to this "interpretationist" view, the whole point and purpose of such attributions resides in this general practice of interpreting behavior. Hence questions about the meaning of the mental terms that feature in these attributions will be resolved without remainder simply by giving an account of their function in this general practice. Davidson (1984) has proposed something like this view for the case of propositional attitudes, at least.

8. Comparison of 'pain' with words like 'red' is instructive. It seems that there is a sense in which W-theoretic arguments may require us to revise our ordinary

I will now tell the story promised earlier. I don't much like such stories, but I do not see how to avoid them in philosophy.[9] After considering various complications in sections 8.6 to 8.9, I will try, in section 8.10, to state what I take to be the fundamental reason why it is possible for us to have such a word.

It may be thought that the story is not the best story for making the point, because it offers a number of unnecessary hostages to defenders of the position it attacks. But this is intentional; it helps to articulate the discussion. The story is initially designed to support the claim that there may be a community in which pain is never accompanied by any observable behavior. Some will think it redundant, on the grounds that it is obviously logically possible that there could be creatures who had highly unpleasant sensations although they were constitutionally incapable of any behavior at all.

8.5   The Sirians

The Sirians are a red-skinned alien race who turn white once a year when their moon is full.[10] This phenomenon, call it X, is a taboo subject for them, and it is talked about as little as possible. Even to think about X is held to be wrong, and no one would admit to doing it. And yet all of them do it. They dwell on X in imagination, for it is an enjoyable thing to do. They find it hard to resist, and each suspects that the others do it too.

But it has a price: whenever the Sirians think about X, they subsequently experience very severe pains in the head. And this happens only after they have thought about X, for they are not subject to any other sort of pain in any other circumstances. And yet they never talk about these pain sensations—we may call them 'S sensations', for they have no word for them—because they don't want to admit to having performed the shameful act. Each knows that S sensations occur only

---

understanding of 'red' in a way that has no parallel in the case of 'pain', because of the greater generality of the latter word. (See Strawson 1989a.)

9. Wittgenstein told them constantly, although usually very briefly. Lewis (1983) tells a story that contrasts usefully with the one told here.

10. Lewis (1983) has permanently co-opted the Martians for the purposes of discussing pain.

after thinking about *X* in its own case, and each naturally supposes that others are the same. (Their supposition is reasonable enough, in spite of the standard objections to the "argument from analogy", given their grasp of the basic principles of biology and their awareness of the great extent and complexity of the similarities between themselves and other members of their species.) So each of them takes it that to try to convey any knowledge of S sensations would be tantamount to admitting to having thought about *X*.

In imagining this, one does not have to suppose that the S sensations of the Sirians are qualitatively identical from individual to individual, any more than we have to suppose this about human pain sensations. 'S sensation' denotes members of a class of sensations that may be defined as follows: they are sensations [1] that, among the Sirians, follow (and are in fact caused by) thinking about *X*, and [2] that are unique among the Sirians' sensations in being unpleasant for them ((2) suffices to identify the class). This definition obviously allows for the possibility that the Sirians' S sensations may possibly differ qualitatively from individual to individual, just as your and my pain sensations may possibly differ qualitatively, even when we receive outwardly identical pain stimuli—say gammaglobulin injections in the buttock—and even when we are inclined to report our pain sensations identically.[11] When Sirians think about *X*, and experience S sensations, most of them unreflectively suppose that what it is like for them, qualitatively, is much the same as what it is like for others, just as most people ordinarily suppose this about things like toe stubbing. But more reflective Sirians may wonder (as some human beings do) whether what others feel might not be qualitatively unlike what they feel, although still highly unpleasant.

It may be said that sensations like nausea can be highly unpleasant without being painful, and it may be asked how we can be sure that the

---

11. Some philosophers question the coherence of this idea, often on verification-ist grounds, but I will take it for granted. Human beings vary qualitatively in respect of all their features, and it would be very extraordinary if they could not vary in their experiences of pain in respects that simply did not show up in their reports of pain, especially in light of the relative crudity of our language for describing pain.

Sirians' unpleasant S sensations fall within the range of what we would call pains. For the moment we may settle this by stipulating that if we were to experience them as Sirians do, we would classify them as pains.

The next feature of the story is this: S sensations have no other-observable typical *cause* and no other-observable behavioral *effects*. As for the cause, thinking about X is a purely mental performance, a matter of dwelling on something in imagination, and there is nothing in particular that sets it off. (S sensations may be correlated with some distinctive type of neural activity, but the Sirians have no neuroscience.) As for effects, the Sirians never talk about S sensations, nor do they behave in any characteristic nonverbal way on experiencing S sensations. No instinct prompts them to move in any way. We tend to be less inclined to move our heads when we have a headache. Other creatures may be inclined to shake their heads violently. The Sirians are not inclined to behave observably in any way different from the way in which they would behave if they had no headache at all. This is how they are and how they naturally suffer. One may suppose that pain is simply added to whatever else is going on for them (perhaps they are capable of multitrack attention).

This completes the first part of the story, according to which there could be creatures whose pains have no observable causes or observable behavioral effects. It may be said that their pains must have causes and effects that are in principle other-observable, just insofar as they are, or are realized by, macroscopic physical processes (e.g., neural processes) that must have macroscopic physical causes and effects. To say this, however, is to assume the truth of materialism; and while one may be happy to do this, neobehaviorist arguments (functionalist or Wittgensteinian, instrumentalist or interpretationist), to the effect that reference to publicly observable occurrences, and in particular to behavior, enters essentially into any satisfactory account of the nature of pain, are meant to be entirely independent of any such assumption, in such a way that they remain undisturbed by the assumption of dualism.

The second part of the story tries to go further. It proposes that the Sirians could acquire a *word* for pain even though their pains had no observable causes or effects. The point of trying to show this should be clear: success would further undermine the W theorists' argument for neobehaviorism given in section 8.3.

Before beginning on this task, I should note that S sensations not only have a typical cause—thinking about X—but also have a typical effect, for the Sirians are standardly aware of having just experienced pain after they have done so. And this suggests that a key idea of functionalism is preserved in this story. For functionalism does not have to commit itself to the claim that mental states and occurrences must have (standardly) *observable* causes or behavioral effects (although it always does so in practice). It can retain the thesis that mental states and occurrences (necessarily) have typical causes and/or effects and drop the public-observability requirement. It can happily allow that there could be immaterial minds in which, e.g., occurrences of the thought q tend to be caused by occurrences of the thoughts $p \rightarrow q$ and p, and, in conjunction with an occurrence of the thought $q \rightarrow r$, tend to cause occurrences of the thought r and so on. It can take involvement in causal relations of these sorts to be partly constitutive of what it is for a thought, to be a thought without supposing that there need ever be any other-observable behavior anywhere.[12]

8.6 N.N.'s Novel

The Sirians live their lives as described until N.N. writes a scandalous novel whose protagonist lives a normal life, thinks about X from time to time, and subsequently experiences S sensations. N.N. coins a word to refer to these S sensations, calling them 'S' and noting how they begin after thinking about X.

There are many possible versions of what N.N. says about S sensations, having first identified them merely as occurrences that follow thinking about X. In one, N.N. calls them 'bad' (the Sirians have such

12. Any mental state can come to be partly constitutive of a disposition to behave observably in certain ways when suitably conjoined with other states. Thus it is possible to imagine the lifting of the Sirians' taboo and, further, that the Sirians might become positively disposed to talk about S sensations on experiencing them. I do not deny this point (I return to it in section 8.7). The fact remains that the Sirians never talk about S sensations after generation, and are not now disposed to behave observably in any way on experiencing S sensations.

a word and apply it to ugly things). In another, the protagonist wants to think about X but is afraid to because it knows it will experience S (there are things of which the Sirians are afraid, like death, although they have no unpleasant physical sensations other than S sensations). In another, N.N. introduces the word 'S' and continues, 'about which I will say nothing more, for you know all too well what it is like'.

The novel is published by a small press and is immediately banned. N.N. is silenced, but copies of the original book circulate illicitly. Nearly all of the Sirians read it, although none of them can bring themselves to talk about it, and each of them suspects that nearly everyone else has read it.

What do they make of the term 'S'? All who read N.N.'s novel naturally and unquestioningly take it that they *know what 'S' means*. They take it that it refers to unpleasant sensations experienced after thinking about X. It never crosses their minds that this might not be so.

It seems to me that they are right. They do know what 'S' means on coming across it in NN's book. They know what it means in at least the sense in which we can all be said to know what 'pain' means, and to mean the same thing by it, in spite of the real if unverifiable possibility that we may differ significantly among ourselves so far as the overall qualitative character of our pain experiences is concerned. (Perhaps the Sirians are vividly aware of the possibility of qualitative variation because they are all disposed to have two or three different kinds of painful sensation when they think about X, depending on other features of their internal condition. Or perhaps N.N.'s protagonist explicitly remarks on the fact that its S sensations vary from time to time.)

Certainly there is scope for uncertainty. But it is a fact—it is part of the story—that each of them simply assumes that it knows what 'S' means. Each of them assumes that it *knows what N.N. is talking about*. And in this way language—unruly, opportunistic, and contagious—takes off without a backward glance at the suggestion that it is somehow inadequately grounded because it is not tied to publicly observable circumstances. Language leaps without looking and lands on its feet.

Some may object to this on the grounds that 'S', introduced by N.N. in this way, can only be a name for sensations that are qualitatively just like N.N.'s own unpleasant sensations, even though N.N. explicitly intends 'S' to refer also to the (possibly qualitatively different) unpleasant sensations that N.N. believes others feel. There is some irony in the fact that this objection may be advanced in defense of the W theorists' view, since it seems to appeal to something like a private act of naming of the sort W theorists repudiate. But in any case, the objection seems wrong. What actually happens is simply that the Sirians' universal and unhesitating assumption that they all know what 'S' means lifts 'S' ipso facto into the position of a mutually understood (if unused) word—given that they all do in fact have sensations that they experience as highly unpleasant after thinking about X. If one of the Sirians suddenly ignored the taboo and talked openly about thinking about X, and then went on to use the word 'S', the others would immediately understand (know) just what it meant. That is, they would be sure they understood, and they would, I suggest, be right. They would be astonished to hear the matter discussed, but their conviction that they knew what was being talked about would be immediate and complete.

It seems, then, that the Sirians possess a word for pain. If N.N.'s novel were to be translated into English, it would be correct to translate 'S' as 'pain(s)' or with some phrase containing the word 'pain' or 'painful'. And yet their grasp of the meaning of 'S', together with the fact that this unused word has, in effect, become a word of their (shared) language, does not depend in any way on their having learned it in a context involving publicly observable causes or effects of S sensations.

At this point it may be objected that grasp of a word or concept necessarily involves the existence of some sort of "rule following." But all that follows from this, I think, is that any version of the rule-following view that finds itself in tension with the claim that the Sirians possess a word for pain will have to adjust itself to accommodate the claim. (It might also be said that their *not* talking about their pains is itself intentional behavior. But this cannot provide any sort of publicly detectable indication or criterion of the presence of pain.)

Certainly the description of the conditions under which they come to acquire a word for pain adverts to other things of which they are aware: to X and to thinking about X. (In section 8.8, I consider a case that severs such connections.) And it is, of course, important to the story that the Sirians already have some sort of language of sensation in place (a point to which I will return). It remains true that the story of their acquisition of the word 'S' makes no reference to any publicly observable causes and effects of S sensations. The central fact to which it appeals is simply that there exists a certain kind of general, interpersonal, de facto congruence in the character of the Sirians' (private) experience: all of them experience these highly unpleasant sensations in certain circumstances.

I suggest that the central fact is the same in our case when it comes to understanding the word 'pain'. The real force and point of those of our practices that involve use of the word depend, above all and essentially, on the simple fact of the existence of a certain kind of general, interpersonal congruence in the character of our (private) experiences. This is the fundamental realist claim about pain and the language of pain. It is, of course, compatible with granting that the point and force of our use of the word do not depend only on this general interpersonal similarity, since our pain has links with publicly observable occurrences.

Recall that this interpersonal congruence with respect to experience need not be supposed to involve any sort of close or complete qualitative similarity of experience. It is just a matter of our being similar in an essentially *general* respect: in respect of the fact that we are creatures who are naturally so constituted that we have experiences that are, for us as we have them, highly unpleasant in a certain way. Apart from this, our pain experiences may differ qualitatively in every way in which it is possible for them to do so, given their general similarity in respect of being experienced as unpleasant.[13]

13. Here I imagine the following objection. It is not as if the use of the word 'unpleasant' can give one unproblematic access to a strongly realist, language-and-behavior-independent notion of pain, for familiar sceptical problems arise: how can I know that a sensation that you find unpleasant is not a sensation that I would find pleasant if I were to have it?

Taken in one way this idea is innocuous. I may like seeing green, and you may hate it, even though my color experience when I look at something green is in fact qualitatively identical to yours. But the objection goes further. Perhaps some sort of pleasure-spectrum inversion is possible, similar to color-spectrum inversion (see, e.g., Locke 1975, II.xxxii.14–15; Shoemaker 1984); so that if, per impossibile, I could be you for a time, while still somehow retaining my own point of view, I might discover that even the *total* character of your experience, on occasions when you were having experience that you found unpleasant and disliked, was of such a kind that I found it pleasant. That is, I would not only have the same basic sensory experience (say of greenness) that you have, but would also have the whole accompanying affective experience that constituted

The qualification 'in a certain way' marks the fact that we do not count all unpleasant sensations as pains. This may be thought to introduce great uncertainty into the discussion of pain, and in a way it does: it may be very hard to say exactly what distinguishes pains as a subset of unpleasant physical sensations. But this just shows that the word 'pain' is indeterminate in a certain way. It does not undermine the idea that 'pain' is just a word for a class of (private) sensations, considered just as such, and hence considered independently of any publicly observable causes and effects.

---

your finding it unpleasant. And, having all this, I would find the experience a pleasant one, although you found it unpleasant.

I don't think that this pleasure-spectrum inversion is a real possibility. Certainly I can find pleasant almost everything you find unpleasant (and vice versa). But the experiences of pleasure and unpleasure themselves can't be switched or inverted. Let 'X' name an experiential state that you are in at a certain time and that is pleasant for you. Let 'X' be a name for it considered in its *total* character. If I am then in an experiential state just like X, I can't find it unpleasant. The word 'total' rules out my taking an attitude to the experiential state that is different from yours, for any such attitude would be part of the total character of my experiential state at that time. So an experience of pleasantness on your part (considered in its total character) can't be qualitatively just the same as an experience of unpleasantness on my part (considered in its total character).

The objection may be restated. It may be held that your liking can be my disliking (and vice versa). But like and dislike can't flip or invert in this way. The range of things that I like and dislike can be very peculiar, from your point of view. But there is—to be blunt—a fact of the matter about what dislike is, considered as a real and entirely naturally occurring phenomenon, given which we cannot coherently suppose that *liking* for you might actually be what *disliking* is for me, in the way in which we can coherently suppose that your experience of red might be my experience of green (in the sense that your experience, when looking at objects generally called 'red', might be qualitatively just like my experience when looking at objects generally called 'green'). One could say that experience of dislike has an essence, considered as a general type of experiential phenomenon, in a way that experience of red does not, given that the story of color-spectrum inversion makes sense.

Your red can be my green (to speak crudely). The sensations you dislike or find unpleasant can be the sensations I like and find pleasant. But your like can't be my dislike. Variation analogous to the variation imagined in the case of color-spectrum inversion is coherently imaginable only for particular types of qualitative sensation considered independently of essentially more general attitudes that may be taken to them, such as liking or disliking them. If this is thought to be mere assertion, so be it. I'm not sure that argument between realists and W theorists can go further on this issue.

It is important that I don't claim to be able to *prove* this claim about the de facto general congruence of human beings with respect to unpleasant sensations. I take it for granted, acknowledging the traditional problem of other minds (or rather, other experiences) to be, strictly speaking, insoluble. If I am wrong about this de facto general congruence—if, for example, I am in fact the only human being that there is "something it is like to be," experientially speaking—then I am wrong about what 'pain' means. (A human being brought up by two experienceless humanoid robots that produced sounds just like normal English would make this mistake.) It is crucial to the realist approach that it makes the meaning of the word 'pain' sensitive to the presence of this unprovable, de facto congruence. (For a good discussion of this, see Craig 1982, esp. pp. 552–558.)

The W theorists' account, by contrast, seeks to liberate questions about the meaning of the word 'pain' from the uncertainty that connection with this unprovable de facto congruence brings with it; and so it loses sight of pain in its account of 'pain'. It is arguable that it makes an excessively skeptical move in doing this, rather than a skepticism-defeating move. In the same way, it is arguable that the Wittgensteinian account of other minds, which claims to defeat skepticism, achieves this appearance only by covertly endorsing the skeptical doubt and building it into our terms for mental states and occurrences. The mistake is to attempt to defeat skepticism. To think that skepticism must be defeated is to accord it too much force. To acknowledge that it is irrefutable is to keep it in proportion.

We have, then, this large, simple, immoveable, unprovable truth: that we are in fact similar in that we have sensations that are wholly private in a wholly unproblematic sense and that are, for us as we have them, highly unpleasant. This, just this, is the central datum that one needs to bear in mind when one attempts to give a satisfactory answer to the question, How is it possible for creatures like ourselves to have a word like 'pain', given that it is a word for a class of sensations considered just as such and hence considered entirely independently of any of their typical publicly observable causes and effects or expressions? I will take this point further in section 8.10. But first I will consider an objection, make some further remarks about the Sirians, and consider a variant of their story.

8.7 An Objection to the Sirians

According to the objection, the connection between pain and pain behavior that is essential from the W theorists' point of view is not put in question by the story of the Sirians, for two things remain true. [1] To be in pain is necessarily to be disposed to engage in some sort of pain-avoidance behavior, ceteris paribus. [2] To have the *concept* of pain is necessarily to know (1): it is necessarily to be aware of the necessary connection between feeling pain and being disposed to engage in pain-avoidance behavior, ceteris paribus. The neobehaviorist conclusion is that reference to behavior must after all enter into a full and satisfactory account of what it is to be in pain, and hence of the concept of pain.

This objection may be applied to the case of the Sirians. As for (1), it may be claimed that if one of the Sirians is in pain then it must have an *indirect* behavioral disposition, at least, for it must be so disposed that if it did think that there was something it could do to avoid pain, then it would thereby be disposed to do that thing on experiencing S sensations, other things being equal.

As for (2), the Sirians' possession of the concept of pain: suppose that S sensations came to be talked about freely, and that it came to be generally believed that head shaking prevented S sensations from following thought about X. The objection would hold that if the Sirians *really* had a word for pain—if they really had the concept of pain—then they would have to realize that those who expected to feel S sensations would thereby be disposed to shake their heads, other things being equal.

I am prepared to grant both these claims for the moment, and it is true that the objection sounds plausible. Nevertheless, I think it is incorrect. It is incorrect even after one has taken some account of masochism (which may be thought to be insufficiently covered by the ceteris paribus clause) by dropping the claim that there is a necessary link between being in pain and being disposed to engage in *avoidance* behavior, in favor of the claim that there is a necessary link between being in pain and being disposed to engage in behavior of some sort or other.

Consider the following four points. First, even if there were a necessary connection between being in pain and being disposed to engage in some sort of (avoidance) behavior, it would not follow that there was a "logical" connection between pain and behavior of such a kind that 'pain' was not just a (somewhat indeterminate) word for certain types of sensation, considered just as such, and hence considered entirely independently of any typical causes or typical behavioral effects. (That is, even if (1) were true, (2) need not be.)

Second, even if there were a necessary connection between being in pain and being disposed to engage in some sort of (avoidance) behavior, it would not follow that there was a necessary connection between being in pain and being disposed to engage in *publicly observable* behavior, so that the one thing could not exist without the other. The way to avoid S sensations after thinking about X might not involve any publicly observable behavior. It might be discovered that the way to do it was to think about Y before thinking about X. (That is, even if (1) were true, it would not follow that there was a link between pain and publicly observable behavior of the sort generally insisted on by W theorists.)

Third, in fact it seems that there is no necessary connection between being in pain and being disposed to behave in some way. (That is, (1) is false.) For there may be sentient creatures—the Weather Watchers— that have sensations of pain although they are naturally and constitutionally incapable of any sort of (intentional) behavior and cannot even be said to be disposed to behave in any way at all, given their overall mental makeup. I will argue that such creatures are a genuine possibility in the next chapter.

Fourth and finally, I do not think that one has to believe that there is a connection between pain and a disposition to (avoidance) behavior, in order to possess the concept of pain, for one can have the concept of pain without having the concept of behavior at all. (That is, (2) is false.)

It may be objected that one must have the concept of behavior to have a mental life rich enough for it to be plausible to talk of one's having the *concept* of pain at all, rather than just of one's knowing what pain is because one has experienced something that is in fact correctly classified as pain. But why should possession of the concept of behavior be indispensable to the concept-exercising life? It seems very unlikely that it is, and I will argue that it is not in the next chapter. In general, it seems plausible that if creature C experiences pains, fulfills whatever very general conditions there are for being a concept-exercising creature, and can (e.g.) have thoughts about experiences of pain in their absence, then it has a concept of pain, even though it may not be a behavioral being at all and may have no concept of behavior.

Some may grant this and then object that C can't really be said to have *our* concept of pain, because our concept is so intimately connected with the concept of (avoidance) behavior. To this the blunt reply is that whatever the intimacy of connection between my ordinary human concept of pain and the concept of (avoidance) behavior, my concept of pain is still a concept of just—pain. Unlike C, I know pains tend to cause (avoidance) behavior in behavioral beings, but my concept of pain—even acquired, as it is, in interaction with others—is just a concept of unpleasant sensations like the one I now have in my back, and in this it is entirely like C's concept.

A quite different sort of objection goes as follows: concept-exercising creatures like the Sirians can't really be said to have exactly our concept of *pain*, rather than a more general concept of *unpleasant physical sensation*, even if all their unpleasant sensations are such that we would count them as pains if we had them ourselves. To have our concept of pain, it may be said, it is at least necessary that they should be inclined to distinguish, as we do, between unpleasant sensations that are pains and those (like nausea) that are not.

Now this may be conceded, given the description of the Sirians so far, for they do not make this distinction. We might very well have had a word denoting unpleasant physical sensations in general, but in fact the English word 'pain' is not like this. So the Sirians do not have exactly our concept of pain. This is a very minor objection, however. What we may still say is that they have *a* word for pain, just as we may say this about all the different human language-using groups on earth, even though the words in human languages that are best translated by the English word 'pain' probably don't all have exactly the same extension. Recall that the Sirians have the conceptual resources to think that there could be highly unpleasant sensations qualitatively unlike the ones they experience themselves.

8.8   The Betelgeuzians

Simpler than the Sirians are the Betelgeuzians. Their only pains are fearful headaches that have no typical observable causes or nonverbal behavioral effects. They are freely speaking creatures, and it seems clear that they will, somehow or other, come to be able to communicate with each other about these things, although they lack the public observabilia that are supposedly necessary for any language of pain to evolve. One reason why it seems clear is that the alternative is so implausible. It is completely implausible to suppose that freely speaking creatures who are in fact all alike in encountering such headaches as a vivid part of their experience will *necessarily* be utterly incapable of talking about them in any way. In a case like this, language will find a way. It will be subject to uncertainties, but then it always is.

There may be more scope for deception in their case than there is in ours. But they may have no reason to deceive, or they may be incapable of lying. There are many possibilities, and the Betelgeuzians cannot be simply dismissed with the insistence that "an inner process stands in need of outward criteria"—at least if this remark is taken to carry the implication that merely verbal behavioral effects are not enough in the way of outward criteria for inner processes.[14]

One may further suppose that the Betelgeuzians are at first not subject to any form of pain. The tendency of their species to suffer from these apparently randomly occurring headaches begins suddenly and spreads steadily. (Perhaps the unknown and unsuspected cause of their new susceptibility lies in some unobservable change in their sun.) In this case the claims of the first few sufferers will be ill understood and doubted. But not for long—as the phenomenon spreads and pain becomes a fact of common experience. As this happens, they will undoubtedly become able to talk about it, in spite of its lack of any typical observable causes or (nonverbal) behavioral effects or expressions.

14. The quotation is from Wittgenstein (1953, sec. 580) and it may well be thought to carry this implication, for one of the ideas behind it seems to be that a genuine practice of talking about some particular inner process cannot possibly get going in the absence of any nonverbal publicly observable causes, effects, expressions, or reliable concomitants of that process.

It may again be said that a peculiar uncertainty will afflict their apparent talk about pain, because they will be unsure that they are really talking about the same thing. But the same is true of our talk about pain. When one undergoes what is outwardly the same painful experience as other people, one can never be sure whether it is the same for them as it is for oneself. And if they go on about it more than one does oneself, one can never be sure whether they are suffering more or complaining more.

8.9 The Point of the Sirians

All the Sirians have suffered pain. In that sense, at least, they all know what pain is. Reading N.N.'s novel, they all immediately take it that they know what 'S' means, what N.N. means by 'S'. I have proposed that they are right about this, although S sensations have no publicly observable (i.e., Sirian observable) causes or effects. The fact that language has the kind of looseness that makes this possible—the fact that a word for pain can take off like this, among the Sirians, in spite of the possible interpersonal differences in the character of their sensations—is one of the things that Wittgenstein (along with Quine) has done much to render vivid. It may be objected that the Sirians' acquisition of a word for pain may depend on their having already evolved some sort of language for talking about mental phenomena, and on their having done so in the normal, observable-circumstance-embedded way in which we have done so. But this point has already been granted. The Sirians have a strictly limited point to make: They are invoked to show that a word for a phenomenon like pain can be acquired in a community in which pains have no typical observable causes or nonverbal behavioral effects or expressions. They challenge one argument for the claim that each general type of mental phenomenon must always be constitutively bound up with some type or types of observable phenomenon in the way that neobehaviorism standardly supposes.

So far I have set out the case against neobehaviorism in a fairly polemical fashion, and various conciliatory moves can be made. Neobehaviorism can be weakened in a number of ways, relative to its standard formulations (functionalist or W-theoretic). One possible weakening, the necessity-of-outward-criteria view, was mentioned on p. 220.

There are others. It is an interesting question whether any sufficiently weakened version of neobehaviorism could fully accommodate the story of the Sirians.

So far as the story of the Sirians' acquisition of a *word* for pain is concerned, it may again be insisted that they cannot acquire it in the way described unless they already have some language of sensation or mental states in place. It may be said that the existence of this language of sensation presumably does depend on the existence of connections between sensations (or other mental states) and publicly observable circumstances that are taken to constitute standardly sufficient grounds for attributing the sensations (or other mental states). This may then be taken as grounds for saying that there is, after all, an essential (non-contingent) connection, albeit an extremely indirect one, between 'S' (the Sirian word for pain) and publicly observable circumstances. For there is an essential connection between 'S' and those publicly observable circumstances that are criterially linked with any sensation word or mental-state word whose prior possession was necessary for the Sirians to be able to acquire the word 'S' from N.N.'s book in the way described.

All this may be granted. It does not in any way support the idea that pain itself must necessarily have typical publicly observable causes or concomitants or effects or expressions. Nor does it challenge the claim that 'pain' is just a word for certain types of private unpleasant sensation, considered entirely independently of their possible causes and effects.[15]

8.10   Functionalism, Naturalism, and Realism about Pain

I don't think that the conclusion of the story of the Sirians should be controversial. In fact, I think that it is obvious that the connection between pain and (observable) behavior, is strictly speaking, a contingent

15. Derek Parfit and Ingmar Persson have pointed out that the story of the Sirians can be more easily told by substituting, for pain, some odd and highly distinctive sensation that the Sirians would all be inclined to describe in a similar way and that is unlike pain in that we have no reason to expect it to have any strong links to nonverbal behavior, such as avoidance behavior. Parfit and Persson are right, but it seems profitable to try to tell the story for the more difficult case of pain.

one, and that one can see this as soon as one puts aside one's philosophical training for a moment. The connection is contingent because pain can exist in the complete and permanent absence of any (observable) behavior and of any disposition to (observable) behavior, not only in the case of a particular individual but also in the case of a whole population, and indeed a whole universe (the claim about dispositions will be further supported in the next chapter). Pain, as such, is just a matter of unpleasant sensations of certain sorts. It does not have to have any publicly observable causes or correlates or effects or expressions in order to be pain. It does not have to have any *function* in order to be pain.[16]

I have used the phrase 'publicly observable' freely, and in a standard way. Obviously, it raises the question, Which observers, and which public? The usual assumption is that the public is composed of human beings, or of the other members of the species whose claim to pain is in question. The motivation for the second of these assumptions is clear if one is interested in the question of how a *word* for pain is acquired by members of a species and accepts a W-theoretic view about the necessary conditions of such acquisition. But if one is concerned only with the more fundamental question of what it is to *be* in pain, it is again not clear why any considerations about publicly observable phenomena should be thought to be relevant.

Defenders of the neobehaviorist view may still insist that such considerations are relevant, and argue as follows: [1] All pains have causes and effects. [2] For any thing that exists, and a fortiori for these causes and effects, one can imagine a possible creature (a member of the actual or logically possible galactic public) that can observe it. Hence [3] all pains have observable causes and effects after all. In reply: even though (1) is questionable, one may grant it and concede the whole case to the neobehaviorists, if this is what they mean by 'publicly observable'. For

16. This claim about contingency of connection is fully compatible with species-specific modal claims of the form 'Necessarily, if a creature of type *X* has a pain of type *Y* and is in state *Z*, then it will behave in way *W*'. Note that even if one accepts the false suggestion that a creature's capacity to feel pain has to have some sort of *adaptive function* or survival value in order for what the creature feels to count as pain, this gives one no reason to suppose that its pains have to have causes and effects observable either by us or by other members of its own species.

now their view comes down to nothing more than claim (1), the claim that all pains have causes and effects. Others may argue that it follows from the truth of materialism that pain will always have causes and effects that are in principle observable. But materialism cannot be invoked in this way in support of what is supposed to be an a priori claim about the nature of pain. A better move for functionalist neo-behaviorists, one that is unavailable to W-theoretic neobehaviorists, is simply to reject the requirement of observable causes and effects as *entirely inessential to the ruling idea of functionalism* (see section 9.4).

One bad objection to the story of the Sirians derives from what one might call 'logical naturalism' or 'conceptual naturalism'. On this view, 'pain' can only refer to something that has evolved naturally in a nonmagical universe, and the Sirians' pain cannot be supposed to have done this. But first, the universe may be extraordinary without being magical. Second, no one has yet given a satisfactory, direct evolutionary explanation of the existence of experience, let alone of pain. Third, this claim absurdly rules out as logically impossible the spontaneous coming into existence of a creature capable of feeling pain. Fourth, the claim is simply not required by a generally naturalistic approach in philosophy. There is no tension between accepting the conclusion of the story of the Sirians (and Betelgeuzians) and noting the facts of pain on earth.

Here is another bad objection: The story does, in a way, aim at something that is logically possible, but describes it wrongly. The story describes it wrongly because the (human) word 'pain' is not in fact correctly applied in this case. This is because the (human) word 'pain', given its origins, is correctly applied only to sensations that are con-nected with (publicly observable) behavior in a way that is familiar to us on earth. So we need another word, say 'bain', to describe the real, unpleasant physical sensations of the Sirians. And bains are not pains. They are not pains even though they are sensations that are highly unpleasant for those who have them and even though they have a qualitative character that would make them properly counted as pains if they occurred in creatures like ourselves and, so occurring, had certain typical publicly observable causes and effects.

I think this is hopeless, but I share the objectors' sense that the problem is a real one. We do face the question, How can we possess a word like 'pain' that allows us to state the truth that the connection between pain and (publicly observable) behavior is contingent in the sense set out at the beginning of this section? How is this possible, given the correctness of Wittgenstein's observations about the transmission conditions of the word 'pain'—his observations about language learning and his apparently highly plausible views about the constitutive connection between the (publicly observable) circumstances in which a word is learned and used and the meaning of the word?

Replying, one can concede for the sake of argument that a vocabulary of mental terms cannot normally get going, or continue to exist, in the absence of any links between any mental terms and publicly observable circumstances of the sort stressed by Wittgensteinians; some mental terms, at least, must have such links.[17] This done, one may still insist that this very general point about the conditions of natural genesis and continuing existence of a genuine vocabulary of mental terms does not really settle any questions about the meaning of particular mental terms. And one may then go on to make the indispensable realist move: whatever the conditions of the acquisition and existence of language, and in particular of a vocabulary of mental terms, the possibility of our possessing the word 'pain' that we actually do possess—the word about which billions of nonphilosophers have a correct view in hundreds of languages—is fundamentally grounded in the simple fact of the existence of a certain sort of interpersonal congruence in the character of our (private) experience. It is grounded in something quite independent of any facts about behavior: the fact that we have experiences that are, for us as we have them, unpleasant in a certain way. We may grant that language can only serve as a means of communication about matters of common experience. But *the* PRIVATE *experience of pain is itself (and specifically as private) a fact of* COMMON *experience.* This private experience is the fundamental given fact, so far as our own language of pain

17. The concession may be made, but one still has to consider various apparent possibilities, e.g., the possibility of a fully innate language, mentioned in section 8.3, and the possibility that creatures could communicate with each other telepathically while their minds existed in the way that immaterialist idealism supposes. Even if these apparent possibilities are combined into a case in which there are few, if any, links between the use of mental terms and nonmental, publicly observable circumstances, it seems that language—or at least a de facto reliable and successful mode of communication, if this is different—could still exist and flourish.

is concerned. This is the fact that we access with our talk of pain, however we acquire the ability for such talk.

As things are, it is important that we are also observably similar in the way in which we typically react to pain, and again in respect of the things that typically occasion pain in us. But things can be important without being essential. We could have varied enormously with regard to what typically caused us pain but have been highly predictable, with respect to such causes, when considered individually. Or our episodes of pain might have occurred apparently randomly, relative to the outwardly observable circumstances of our lives. In this case, we might have been very similar in our nonverbal observable behavioral expressions of pain, or we might have been very different in this respect as well; or we might have lacked any natural, nonverbal, observable behavioral expressions of pain while also lacking any motive (or ability) to claim falsely that we were in pain. There are many possibilities, and one can increase the force of factors that seem to introduce uncertainty into an apparent language of pain until one may be unsure whether there is a language of pain at all. But if freely speaking creatures are in fact similar in regularly having (private) experiences that are, for them as they have them, highly unpleasant in a certain way, then this fact of common experience will be something that language will be able to reach out to and speak about, even in cases in which pain has no typical observable causes, effects, or expressions.

It seems a somewhat oblique way of putting the point—to say that the fundamental fact, so far as our joint possession of our actual word for pain is concerned, is the fact of our similarity in having experiences that are, for us as we have them, unpleasant in a certain way. I adopt it only to avoid use of the word 'pain'. When the word 'pain' is used, the blushing simplicity of the point can no longer be concealed: it is just a fact—strictly speaking, an unprovable fact—that we all (or nearly all) do experience sensations of pain, and it is true of these sensations, considered entirely independently of their causes and effects, that they have a certain highly unpleasant qualitative character that is publicly unobservable, and in this sense private. Having pain is thus a fact of common experience, and would continue to be even if language suddenly ceased to exist. Unsurprisingly, we manage to have a common word for a fact of common experience—whatever the vagueness of the boundaries of what counts as pain, and whatever intersubjective variations there may be in the qualitative character of pain. In the end, it must be unsurprising that we manage to have a common word for this common fact of private experience.

I say this and once again face the objection that this is just not the sort of thing that language ("public" language) can get to be about. But it can. What we learn is that language is a looser and more powerful thing than the W theorists' arguments allow. It breaks the rules that the arguments claim that it must keep. What are the "facts about use" with which Wittgensteinians and W theorists are so concerned? The facts about use are that we intentionally use the word 'pain' as a word for nothing more (and nothing less) than a certain class of unpleasant (private) sensations, considered entirely independently of any causes and effects that they may have. *This is what we do*, as W theorists say. This is what we mean and intend. The publicly observable is not all that is shared among us. We are not only fundamentally similar in general observable physical form. We are also, no doubt, fundamentally similar in respect of the general character of our private experience. The reality of private experience is also something shared among us, in such a way as to be available to be talked about in the way that it is.

It is worth noting that the present argument has no difficulty with the fact that human beings who cannot feel pain can be fully competent with the word 'pain', although it will be true to say that there is something they do not know about pain. If, however, one of the Sirians does not feel pain, it will be in the dark when it reads N.N.'s novel and comes across 'S'. If another of them has only wonderful sensations after thinking about X, it will be completely mistaken in its view of what 'S' means. It is important for my position that such errors are possible. They are impossible according to some W theorists because the nature of an individual's sensation "drops out of consideration as irrelevant" when it comes to giving an account of the meaning of a sensation word.

In my use and understanding, then, and in the use and understanding of virtually every human being, the following is true:

[P] The word 'pain' is just a word for a certain kind of unpleasant sensation, considered entirely independently of any of its behavioral or other publicly observable causes and effects.

I have argued that two further theses follow from (P):

[Q] The meaning of the word 'pain' transcends what is available for public inspection in the circumstances in which mastery of the word is standardly transmitted.

[R] No reference to what is available for public inspection in the circumstances in which mastery of the word 'pain' is standardly transmitted is essential in a correct account of what pain is.

The best summary account of things may then be something like this. [1] One is exposed to a public language practice involving the word 'pain'. [2] There appears to be a respect in which some kind of W-theoretic account of the meaning of this public word is inevitable (we can take it that commitment to the falsity of (P) is the essential feature common to all W-theoretic accounts). [3] If (2) is granted, it must then be stressed that the W-theorists' account of the word is not the whole story; that is, if (2) is granted, it must also be granted that one also evolves, on the basis of one's private experience of pain together with one's exposure to the public language practice, a non-W-theoretic, essentially private-experience-informed take on the meaning of the word 'pain'. [4] This take is essentially general. That is, it does *not* follow from (3)—from the fact that one evolves one's understanding of the meaning of the word partly on the basis of one's own experience—that one is obliged to suppose, or inevitably does suppose, that all pain is qualitatively like one's own. For we are immediately able to understand the idea that another being's pain might be qualitatively very unlike our own while still being highly unpleasant for that being.

This sort of account of things is commonly proposed by students when they are first confronted with the problem of pain, in the context of the "problem of other minds." It is the commonsense response, and it is clearly correct. For this is what actually happens. The word 'pain' kicks away the ladder of the publicly observable circumstances that allow it to get going, and takes on its actual meaning as a word that refers only to experiences—yours, mine, theirs—that are entirely private in an unproblematic sense of the word. It is securely underpinned, in this transition, by the fundamental similarity that exists in fact, if un-verifiably, among people's publicly unobservable (and in this sense private) experiential lives. And so it comes to mean, and mean only, the publicly unobservable (and in this sense private) sensations that in fact, if unverifiably, almost invariably occur when the things generally recognized as the publicly observable concomitants of pain occur. Thus the public word comes to be a word for a species of private phenomenon. And we return to the truth of common sense.

The difficulty of this issue can seem rather beautiful, and I don't claim to be able to resolve it finally. The fact remains: 'pain' is just a word for a certain class of unpleasant sensations, considered just as such, and hence considered independently of any observable causes, correlates, effects, or expressions that they may have. This is not something we have to argue for, and it is not something we can prove. It is something we know, and so we have to think about how it is possible. We know it before we begin to do philosophy, and we know it again when we close our books, even if philosophy has made us doubt it in between.

8.11 Unpleasantness and Qualitative Character

This section can be omitted. It raises a point of detail about the notion of our interpersonal similarity with respect to experience of pain. As remarked, such similarity need not involve any sort of complete qualitative similarity. It is simply a matter of our being similar in respect of the fact that we have experiences that are, for us as we have them, highly unpleasant in a certain way (the phrase 'in a certain way' provides a necessary element of vagueness). Apart from this, the experiences may differ qualitatively in every way in which it is possible for them to do so, given this general similarity or congruence. And here we should not only consider human variation, but also that of the Sirians and other aliens, who may have unpleasant sensations that are indeed very different from ours but are nonetheless correctly counted as pains.

I'm not sure that anything more precise can be said, but there is another question worth considering. Suppose that two human beings X and Y are both experiencing highly unpleasant but qualitatively different physical sensations. (If Louis experienced both sensations, he would classify them as very different.) One may express the fact that they are similar in respect of having unpleasant physical sensations by saying that they are U-similar. The question is this: can their U-similarity itself be thought of as a kind of *qualitative* similarity between their respective experiences? If one says that two beings who are similar in respect of the qualitative character of their experience are Q-similar, the question is whether U-similarity entails, by being a form of, Q-similarity.

It is arguable that U-similarity must be a form of Q-similarity. After all, the unpleasantness of pain is something *experienced*. That is, it is itself part of the qualitative character of experience. For what else could it be? So if two people are similar in respect of the fact that thay are having experiences that are, for them as they have them, highly unpleasant, it follows immediately that there is a qualitative respect in which their experience is similar. U-similarity is indeed a form of Q-similarity.

Is this claim correct? Consider two rough models of pain, one of which may be thought to cast doubt on the claim. According to the first, we may distinguish, within a given pain experience E, a core experience e with qualitative character q, and a certain attitude a to that core experience e—an attitude of finding e unpleasant in a certain way—given which E is an experience of pain. We are not naturally inclined to distinguish a from e, according to the model, because to have e and to have a toward e just is for it to seem to one that it is just e—e on its own—that is the pain. This model appears to fit well with the cases reported by Dennett (1978a, 208) in which subjects who are administered a certain analgesic report that although the pain is still there, as intense as ever, they do not mind it at all. The model accounts for this by claiming that they have e but not a. (In this case, one may be strongly inclined to say that they are not really in pain, on the grounds that pain is essentially unpleasant. And one can insist on this while agreeing that it is entirely natural and reasonable for the subjects to report the character of their experience by saying that the pain is still there although they do not mind it at all. For, as remarked above, to have e and to have a toward e just is for it to seem to one that it is just e that is the pain, and this view of e may then naturally persist in the absence of a.)

This model is neutral with respect to the claim that X's and Y's U-similarity is, in itself, a form of Q-similarity. In the terms of the model, their case is correctly described as follows. [1] X has experience E_1 consisting of core experience e_1 with qualitative character q_1 together with a certain attitude to the core experience given which E_1 is a highly unpleasant experience. [2] Y has experience E_2 consisting of core experience e_2 with qualitative character q_2 together with a certain attitude to the core experience, given which E_2 is a highly unpleasant experience. [3] Ex hypothesi, Y's q_2-type core experience is qualitatively different from X's q_1-type core experience. The truth of (3) may at first suggest that they are U-similar but not in any way Q-similar. But in fact the difference stipulated in (3) is compatible with the claim that they are similar in respect of part, at least, of the qualitative character of their experiences, *simply* insofar as they are U-similar, similar in respect of the fact that each is having a highly unpleasant experience.

A second model of pain rejects the two-part picture just described and attempts to cast doubt directly on the claim that U-similarity entails (or is a form of) Q-similarity. According to this second model, there are many qualitatively different types of pain. There is A-type pain, B-type pain, C-type pain, and so on. All pains have unpleasantness in common, but we must distinguish A unpleasantness from B unpleasantness, B unpleasantness from C unpleasantness, and so on. There are different forms of unpleasantness that are constitutive of the qualitative character of the various types of pain in such a way that U-similarity does not obviously entail Q-similarity. Thus, according to the second model, one cannot really abstract unpleasantness as itself a *qualitative* characteristic that all pains have in common and say that X and Y are Q-similar simply because they are U-similar. Thus if you have a very bad backache and I have a second-degree burn on my hand, then we are, of course, U-similar, but we are not thereby Q-similar. This view may perhaps be reinforced by the suggestion that Sirians may feel pain, and that although it must be unpleasant for them if it is pain, nevertheless the overall qualitative character of Sirian pain may be so different from that of human pain that it need not follow, from the fact that we and they are U-similar, that we are Q-similar in any way. (Compare U-similarity with *C-similarity*, defined not as similarity in respect of one's current color experience but merely as similarity in respect of the fact that one is currently having some color-experience or other. Is C-similarity a form of Q-similarity? Consider a case in which X is currently experiencing blues and greens, while Y is currently experiencing reds and oranges, and assume that X and Y have identical color vision, in the sense that they respond identically to given objects, experientially speaking.)

This second model may at first seem preferable because simpler. In having pain, we are not naturally aware of a distinction between a core experience and an attitude toward it. Furthermore, the first model may seem implausible when one considers nonhuman animals. But the fact that we do not naturally draw a distinction does not show that it is not correctly drawn, and the second model may have trouble with the cases reported by Dennett. What is more, there seems to be no good reason to believe that the first model is implausible for nonhuman animals. After all, they might very well have the same experience as Dennett's human subjects, if they were administered the analgesic reported to leave the feeling of pain but to stop one minding about it. On these grounds, the first model may appear preferable after all.

There are various possible blends of the two models, and no doubt there are other models. I don't want to decide finally between them. Nor do I want to decide finally between the claim that U-similarity entails Q-similarity and the claim that it does not. All pain is (necessarily) similar in being unpleasant, and it is very hard to see what could count as a *proof* that such similarity could not possibly be held to be a form of Q-similarity.

We are left, then, with two pictures. The first, to summarize, has it that the unpleasantness of pain is to be thought of as essentially qualitatively typed—into A unpleasantness, B unpleasantness, C unpleasantness—in such a way that it is plausible to say that X and Y can be U-similar without really being Q-similar. The second has it that unpleasantness must itself be thought of as an aspect of the qualitative character of experience, so that for X and Y and a Sirian to be U-similar is necessarily and ipso facto for them to be Q-similar. Unpleasantness is thus a kind of higher-order qualitative characteristic of experience, but a genuine qualitative characteristic of experience nonetheless. For what else could it possibly be supposed to be?

Although this last question is a good one, I will leave the matter open. Both pictures are worth having, even if one accepts that U-similarity is necessarily a form of Q-similarity. The second allows that we can know something about what it is like to be a bat, if bats can suffer; but this does not count against it.[18]

18. See Nagel 1979. I am grateful to Sebastian Gardner for prompting me to write this section.

9

The Weather Watchers

9.1 Introduction

The Weather Watchers are a race of sentient, intelligent creatures. They are distributed about the surface of their planet, rooted to the ground, profoundly interested in the local weather. They have sensations, thoughts, emotions, beliefs, desires. They possess a conception of an objective, spatial world. But they are constitutionally incapable of any sort of behavior, as this is ordinarily understood. They lack the necessary physiology. Their mental lives have no other-observable effects. They are not even disposed to behave in any way.

Are the Weather Watchers impossible? They are if neobehaviorism is true. In this chapter I will try to show that they are possible, and that neobehaviorism is therefore false.

In the next chapter I will discuss the word 'behavior' and propose a nonstandard understanding of it. But in this chapter I will continue to understand the word in the standard way and take it to mean observable behavior. (I will sometimes retain the qualification 'observable'.)

Is neobehaviorism true? First, is it true that one must actually behave observably in certain ways if one has mental properties? Most would be prepared to concede that this is not the case, citing the example of a completely paralysed human being. Is it true, second, that one must at least be *disposed* to behave observably in certain ways if one has mental properties? Many would insist that this is so—that it is impossible for there to be a being that has mental properties but is not even disposed to behave in any way. One may call this the *dispositional thesis*.

According to the dispositional thesis, *mental* beings—by which I simply mean beings that have mental properties (section 6.4)—are necessarily *behavioral* beings, i.e., beings that are at least disposed to behave in certain ways.

Some may think that the dispositional thesis is too strong. They may be prepared to admit the theoretical possibility of a creature whose mental life is limited to having color experiences and auditory experiences, say, although it is neither able nor disposed to behave in any way, given its makeup. But even those who take this conciliatory line are likely to insist that no mental being with anything like the mental complexity attributed to the Weather Watchers could possibly fail to be a behavioral being. I will argue that this is not true and that neobehaviorism as a whole is false, given our ordinary understanding of 'behavior'. The argument does not depend on the Weather Watchers, but they help to animate it.

Can the Weather Watchers act, and can they have intentions? This question is not settled by saying that they do not behave in any way and are not disposed to behave in any way, for it seems that there can be (intentional) action without behavior, given the ordinary understanding of 'behavior'. There can, for example, be mental action like mental arithmetic. Hence there can also be intention without behavior (or dispositions to behavior). So the Weather Watchers could act without behaving in any way, given the ordinary understanding of 'behavior'.

This is one possible version of their story, but I will concentrate on a more radical and potentially more revealing version, according to which the Weather Watchers cannot act in any way at all, although they have sensations, thoughts, emotions, beliefs, and desires. Nor are they disposed to act in any way at all. Nor do they have intentions, nor any dispositions to form intentions. It may be said that nothing can have an interestingly complex mental life without having intentions. But this is not obvious, and this chapter offers an argument by description to the effect that it is not true.

Do the Weather Watchers possess the *concept* of intentional action? I will take it that they may possess it or lack it. In the first case, they are able to have thoughts about what it would have been like if they could have acted to further the fulfillment of their desires about the weather. (They do not mind that they cannot influence the weather—they would not have it otherwise.) In the second case, they simply lack the conceptual resources to think about intentional action. The weather just happens as it does. This they know. But they do not think about it in any way that requires possession and exercise of the idea that they (or anyone) might have been able to do anything about how it happens—or indeed about anything else. It may be objected that beings that cannot act or behave in any way cannot possibly possess the concept of action. It is not clear why this might be thought to be so, but even if the objection were granted, it would only mean that one had to restrict attention to the second of the two proposed cases.

As so far imagined, then, the Weather Watchers may or may not possess the concept of action (depending on which of the two possibilities is being considered at the time). They do not and cannot act or behave in any way at all, and are not even disposed to act or behave in any way at all, on the ordinary understanding of 'behavior'. One immediate objection is that thought itself necessarily involves (mental) action, or at least possession of a capacity for a certain kind of mental action. But why should this be thought to be so? It seems that there could be a purely passive observer and knower, whose thoughts just happened. In our own case, nearly all our thoughts just happen. Even when they are appropriate to our situation and our needs as agents, action and intention usually have little or nothing to do with their occurrence. Most thoughts just spring up. The process is largely automatic and largely involuntary. Consider what happens when one engages in conversation. One does not act to generate material for one's reply. It just comes, and it's interesting that one often knows it's there, and that its content is appropriate, before one knows in detail what its content is.

Beginning in section 9.5, I will consider a number of attempts to show that the story of the Weather Watchers is incoherent. I do not think they succeed. When we think about these things, we risk being overwhelmed by our own case. We are also tempted to confuse genetic or evolutionary questions, about how minds can develop in a nonmagical universe of the sort we take ourselves to be familiar with, with conceptual or analytic questions about what sorts of minds are conceivable.

9.2 The Rooting Story

It follows from the description of the Weather Watchers that we never have any good reason to attribute mental states to them. But it does not follow, from the fact that we never have any good reason to attribute mental states to them, that such attributions cannot be true. I take this to be self-evident, since it is absurd to suppose that what exists, or can exist, is bounded by what we can have good grounds to suppose to exist. Those who doubt this should read the following as an attempt to show that such attributions make sense by offering a description of the Weather Watchers that—if successful—reveals itself as making sense as it goes along.

It may help to imagine that the Weather Watchers are members of a race whose natural course of development leads them from an active, mobile youth to a state of immobility, rooted to the ground, in which they retain basic sensory and intellectual capacities. Perhaps they have fixed compound eyes, indistinguishable from the rest of their surface, and look to us like lichen-covered standing stones. Being of a happily adaptive disposition, they progressively lose all desire for what they cannot have—action—and although they retain many desires about how the weather should go and about the naturally shifting scenery, these are desires about things they were never able to affect even when they were active. Their memory span is limited, and as time goes on, all their memories of their former capacity for action fade away. Their thoughts fall into different patterns. It is very hard for us to imagine what it is like to be them, because we are so profoundly action-oriented. But by the time we reach them, they are long settled in their rooted form of life. They are motionless meteorologists, and no trace of their former agentive or behavioral capacities remains. We may even suppose that they have lost the concept of intentional action.

This story of origins may be called 'the rooting story'. It is not a necessary part of the description of the Weather Watchers, but it may aid the imagination. It is not a covert concession that the existence of beings as complicated as the Weather Watchers is unintelligible without some reference to action or behavior. Logical possibility immediately provides for the possibility that they should simply have come into existence as they are, by some astonishing rearrangement of existing particles.

9.3   What Is It Like to Be a Weather Watcher?

A Weather Watcher lives the rooted life, but there are many respects in which its mental life is like ours. It sees the sky and hopes the clouds are bringing rain. It watches a seed lodge in a gap between two rocks by the edge of the river. It forms the belief that a tree may grow there before long, and hopes that it will. It sees a second seed settle near by and hopes that it will not germinate, since it dislikes the species of tree in question.

I make this second suggestion in order to consider an objection: surely, if it dislikes the second sort of tree, it must, ipso facto, wish it could (act to) prevent the second seed from germinating, and must thereby, ipso facto, be disposed to act or behave in some way?

Why should this be thought to be true? It is simply not true that if one wants something not to happen, one ipso facto wishes one could stop it from happening. If we find this hard to see, it is because we are deeply habituated to action and action-thinking (not to mention wishful thinking and magical thinking). It is not part of the *logic* or *essence* of desiring that something should happen, that one should wish that one could bring it about—even in a case in which one thinks it is unlikely to occur. If a Weather Watcher is not only constitutionally incapable of action but doesn't even possess the concept of intentional action, there will obviously be no necessary link between its wanting something not to happen and its wishing it could do something about it. The link may also fail in the case of babies and nonhuman animals. It seems that it may also fail in the case of a being that possesses the concept of intentional action, e.g., in the case of one's desires about the outcome of the World Chess Championship. I'll return to this question later.

This Weather Watcher is also given to more philosophical reflections. (It is not a Peripatetic philosopher but a Static one.) It reflects on the nature of its mental life. It has come to realize that things are not always as they seem: sometimes it misperceives things, and realizes its mistake only as the things in question get closer. It has been struck by the idea that many of its beliefs and concepts are automatically deployed in its perceptual experiences, and it sees that one cannot adequately characterize the nature of many experiences without attributing certain concepts and beliefs to those who have them. It has noticed how its beliefs and other propositional attitudes interact—how one belief, hope, or expectation tends to lead to another. And it has been attracted by the thought that this way in which they interact is partly constitutive of their nature. That is, it has entertained the thought that part of what it is to believe that if p then q is to tend to form the belief that q when one forms the belief that p, say on the basis of some perceptual experience.

Clearly, I am taking it that the Weather Watchers can entertain their beliefs and desires in some conscious mode of thought. This will presumably be a mode of thought that is structured in something like the way in which language-articulated thought is structured. It may be said that possession of such a languagelike mode of thought entails possession of the ability to act, or at least of the concept of action. I will later reject this suggestion.

9.4 The Aptitudes of Mental States

To some, the story of the Weather Watchers seems an evident possibility. And yet the claim that it is intelligible is likely to prompt objections other than the broadly speaking Wittgensteinian objections considered in chapter 8. Some of these are motivated by the anthropocentric bias that philosophers tend to reveal when they try to address general questions about the conditions of possessing concepts or abilities.[1] Other objections lay claim to greater generality.

I will try to consider the principal objections, but I will ignore any that are motivated by "public-domain positivism" or *evidentialism*, according to which a hypothesis that something exists or might exist simply lacks any content in the absence of an account of what would count as publicly available evidence for its existence. This claim raises

---

1. This is arguably the principal defect of Evans's analyses of the conditions of possessing certain abilities and concepts in *The Varieties of Reference*. They fail to achieve maximal generality by overconcentrating on the human case. Kant is exemplary in the explicitness of his attempt to avoid such anthropocentricity in his account of the conditions that a being must fulfill if it is to possess a conception of an objective world.

well-known problems, but I will not consider them here.[2] Instead, I will take it for granted that philosophy sometimes needs to consider hypotheses that essentially involve the idea that there neither is nor could be any evidence for their truth that is publicly available to human beings or to the beings who are the subject of the hypothesis. As remarked, it follows from the description of the Weather Watchers that there is nothing we can do to establish that they have a mental life, nothing that even gives us any prima facie reason to suppose that they do.

This said, it may be noted that the point of the present story would be unaffected if one supposed that there were observable changes in the Weather Watchers that were not instances of intentional behavior but that could nevertheless be supposed to constitute evidence for their having mental lives. Highly complicated nervous-system-like internal activity might weigh with us, even in the absence of any overt bodily movement plausibly interpretable as intelligent behavior. Or one could even imagine that each of the Weather Watchers, standing in its isolation, regularly and involuntarily produced sounds that it experienced as expressing information about its environment, and that were open to such an interpretation by an external observer. There are, of course, very considerable difficulties raised by the question of how interpretation could get going in the absence of any other form of behavior, but correlations between sounds and salient events might make it possible, on certain assumptions, and might lead observers to believe that the Weather Watchers had a mental life.

Some may say that it is just not clear what the case of the Weather Watchers establishes, because it is underdescribed. The best way to enrich the description is to respond to specific objections, and I will try to do this. First, though, let me try to avoid a misunderstanding. The Weather Watchers' case carries no implication that consideration of the causes and effects of mental states and occurrences is irrelevant or inessential to an understanding of their nature. Examining the (typical or possible) causes and effects of something (if any) is always worthwhile

2. Which public? Evidence for whom? Evidence that could in principle be available to human beings, given time travel, intergalactic mobility, and immortality? Evidence available to some superbeings? (If the superbeings can detect and know everything, the thesis is trivial.)

when one is trying to understand its nature. The Weather Watchers are invoked in order to consider the consequences of the fact that when it comes to things like thoughts, sensations, beliefs, desires, and so on, what is causally typical in the case of one species may not be typical in the case of another.

Certainly mental states and occurrences must have some characteristic causal profile in the case of the Weather Watchers. (I use 'profile' rather than 'role', because 'role' suggests effects rather than causes.) And they do: sensory experiences arise for the Weather Watchers as they do for us, and their mental states and occurrences interact in nearly every way in which ours do.[3] Sensory experiences give rise to beliefs, desires, doubts, wonderings, emotions, and so on. Newly formed beliefs couple with existing beliefs to produce further beliefs, or with existing desires to produce further desires, hopes, and fears. Thoughts give rise to other thoughts. Existing beliefs determine the general character of what happens when a Weather Watcher is puzzled by some problem.

Generally, a Weather Watcher has many *mental-activity* dispositions: emotional-reaction dispositions, desire-formation dispositions, train-of-thought dispositions, automatic sensory-experience-interpretation dispositions. Its thought tends to run in certain ways; it tends to welcome and regret certain things. Things tend to seem to it to be a certain way when events of this or that kind happen in its environment. And these mental-reaction dispositions, which are just like dispositions we possess ourselves, will no doubt need to be referred to in giving a full account of what beliefs a Weather Watcher has, and in speaking of the causes and effects of its thoughts, sensations, and so on. But none of its mental goings-on are intentionally undertaken (surprisingly few of our own mental goings-on are intentionally undertaken), and none of them either constitute or give rise to any action or behavior, as ordinarily understood.[4]

---

3. The main types of interaction they lack, as compared with us, are those that involve intention, as well as any other types specific to (the mental part of) practical reasoning.

4. I continue to mention action in addition to behavior only because there are mental actions, like mental arithmetic, that many are disinclined to count as behavior. If one holds that *all* action is behavior, including non-other-observable action (see section 10.4 below), then the mention of action is redundant.

It is not clear, then, that reference to action or behavior is generally essential in giving an account of the fundamental nature of mental states and occurrences like thoughts, sensations, emotions, beliefs, and desires. It seems that all these mental states and occurrences can exist without any action or behavior, and without any disposition to action or behavior. In other words, neobehaviorism does not follow from the indisputable fact that mental states and occurrences have causal connections. It can perhaps be made to follow on two assumptions that I will defend in section 10.4: [1] that there can be unobservable mental behavior, and [2] that unobservable mental goings-on may count as behavior even if they are in no way intentionally undertaken. But both these assumptions go against the ordinary understanding of 'behavior', which is what concerns us at present. Nor will they help neobehaviorists who have Wittgensteinian loyalties or who feel committed to public-domain positivism of any sort.

One can agree with Armstrong, then, that a mental state is "a state that is *apt to be the cause of certain effects, and to be the effect of certain causes.*"[5] One can even accept that this is a conceptual truth: one can accept that "the *concept* of a mental state essentially involves . . . the *concept* of a state that is apt to be the cause of certain effects, and to be the effect of certain causes."[6] But one can do this while rejecting his answer to the question, What sorts of effect and what sorts of cause? For he seems to hold (with many others) that it is also a *conceptual* truth that "the effects caused by the mental state will be certain patterns of *behavior* of the person in that state."[7]

5. Armstrong 1981, 20; emphasis in the original. Talk of states as causes raises certain problems, but the essential point can be easily translated into other idioms.

6. Armstrong 1981, 20; my emphasis. The ellipsis marks the omission of the phrase "and is exhausted by." Many would agree that this phrase should be omitted simply because it is hard to see how the qualitative character of experience can be accommodated in the pure "causalist" account of mental states that results from its inclusion.

7. Armstrong 1981, 21. In full, this passage runs, "The concept of a mental state is the concept of something that is, characteristically, the cause of certain effects and the effect of certain causes. What sort of effects and what sort of causes? The effects caused by the mental state will be certain patterns of behavior of the person in that state." It is possible to read this passage as falling short of the

According to the present position, this is at best a contingent truth. One could put the point by saying that functionalism does not entail neobehaviorism. Even if all the actual mental states in the universe were implicated in behavioral-disposition-constituting patterns of mental states and characteristically or typically had behavioral effects, it would not follow that it is a conceptual truth about the nature of mental states that they characteristically or typically have behavioral effects, or that they characteristically or typically jointly constitute behavioral dispositions. It would be a contingent truth about our universe. The universe could contain nothing but Weather Watcher mentalities—billions of them. It would then contain billions of mental states and occurrences. But it would not be true to say that mental states characteristically or typically had behavioral or agentive effects. In this universe, mental states would never have behavioral or agentive effects. Nor would any creature be *disposed* to behave or act in any way.[8]

I still haven't defended this last claim, although many think that it is necessarily false. I will start my defence in section 9.7. For the moment, the point is this. One can fully accept Armstrong's crucial causal thesis, his "causal profile thesis," according to which a mental state is, essentially, "a state that is *apt to be the cause of certain effects, and to be the effect of certain causes,*" while rejecting two of his other claims. First, his "strong conceptual causalism"—his view that "the concept of mental state . . . is *exhausted* by the concept of a state that is apt to be the cause of certain effects, and to be the effect of certain causes."

---

conceptual claim and as allowing for the present view, but I do not know that Armstrong would wish to do this. His later claim that "the concepts of perception and belief . . . cannot be elucidated without appealing to the concept of purpose" (p. 23) puts him fundamentally at odds with the Weather Watchers, as does his claim that "there is a very close logical tie between sense-perception and *selective behavior*" (pp. 12–13). Nevertheless, from the present perspective, Armstrong's analysis has the great merit of clearly separating two claims: [1] the claim that a mental state necessarily has certain causal *aptitudes* and [2] the claim that the causal aptitudes are of such a kind that possessors of mental states necessarily possess *behavioral dispositions*.

8. All the oxygen in the universe might be combined with hydrogen to constitute water, but it would not follow that oxygen could not exist without actually contributing to the constituting of water. Here some may again be tempted by the logical naturalism mentioned in chapter 8 (p. 242).

Second, his neobehaviorist claim that the effects of mental states will and indeed must characteristically include behavioral effects. It is particularly important to see that the causal profile thesis and the neobehaviorist claim are not indisseverable. Many, I think, are inclined to conjoin the belief that the causal profile thesis is irresistible with the mistaken view that it entails the truth of some version of the neobehaviorist claim.

9.5   The Argument from the Conditions for Possessing the Concept of Space

Before turning to the central objection to the Weather Watchers in section 9.7, I will consider two subsidiary objections. The first questions whether a creature incapable of intentional bodily movement and, in particular, of moving through space can possess a conception of an objective spatial order.

First reply: it is not, strictly speaking, necessary that the Weather Watchers possess a conception of an objective spatial order, given the intended point of their story. Second reply: the objection that they cannot possess such a conception is implausible, in any case. It is very hard to see how one might go about trying to establish it. Nor does it seem that one has to be able to move in order to grasp the concept-of-space-involving concept of motion. On the terms of the rooting story, the Weather Watchers simply retain their concepts of space and motion after they have lost all capacity for action or behavior (as does a completely paralysed human being). But one could also suppose that they are located on floating islands that move when blown by the wind. They may also have 360 degree vision, or eyes that sometimes move relative to their unmoving heads, although their eye movements are not under their intentional control in any way. They may also have ears, and naturally and automatically interpret what they hear in certain ways—as coming from the left or from the right.

Third reply: suggestions like those in the last paragraph may be thought to provide further support for the supposition that the Weather Watchers possess a conception of an objective spatial world, but none of them is necessary for the intelligibility of the supposition. There is a general objection to all forms of the claim that one needs to be exposed to a certain form of experience in order to acquire a certain concept (or group of concepts. The objection is simply that the concept (or group of concepts) in question may be innate.

This can be put more moderately. Whatever the respective contributions of innate factors and experiential factors to the process of a being's acquiring a certain concept, it is always possible that there should be other beings in whom the contribution of experience is proportionately less and the contribution of innate factors proportionately more. In the present case, it is claimed that one could not possibly acquire a concept of space without experience of moving through space. But one cannot rule out a priori the possibility of creatures who are innately so constituted that they naturally and automatically come to deploy the concept of space when exposed merely to visual experience of the Weather Watchers' sort, although they never have any experience of themselves moving, let alone of self-produced movement. The Kantian question, What are the conditions of the possibility of objective experience (i.e., experience that has, for the experiencer, the character of being experience of an objective order of things that exists independently of the experiencer's experiences)? is wrongly understood when it is taken as a question about what sort of experiential inputs a creature must be exposed to if it is to come to think of its experiences as experiences of an objective order of things. For the answer to this question will always be, It depends on the nature of the creature. The true Kantian question is, Which concepts must be deployed or involved in the having of experience in order for us to be able to say that the experience has, for the experiencer, the character of being experience of an objective order of things that exists independently of the experiencer's experiences? Consider the claim that a necessary condition of the possibility of acquiring or possessing a concept of an objective world is that one's experience should display a certain regularity and order. This is a common claim, but it does not seem to be correct. A creature might be innately so disposed that it thought of itself as having (subjective) experience of an objective order of things distinct from itself and its experience even though the experiences that it took to be experiences of the objective order were completely chaotic in character. It might make mistakes about what was objective and what was merely subjective, but this does not imply that it does not really possess the concept of an objective order. It presupposes that it does.

9.6 The Argument from the Conditions for Language Ability

It may now be objected that the Weather Watchers cannot have beliefs that certain things are the case, or desires that they should be the case, or any other propositional attitudes, because they cannot have a language. They cannot have a language because they have no communication intentions or dispositions (since they have no intentions and no dispositions to action).

On the terms of the rooting story, one can reply to this by supposing that they originally acquired a language in the normal way. Now they are neither able to communicate with each other nor in any way disposed to do so. They have forgotten all about it. They have forgotten that they have conspecifics. Each of them is absorbed in the contemplation of nature.[9] If they have lost the concept of action, they have lost the concept of intentional communication along with it. And yet they still naturally think in language, in the way that we can be said to do. That is, thoughts just occur to them in a linguistic form, as often happens in our own case. Each lives its life wrapped up in itself and its thoughts, hopes, and perceptions of the environment. They are as unreflective about the nature of their linguistically couched thought as most ordinary human beings. They take it to be a fundamental natural fact that thought occurs and is like this. It is a given, like the structure of one's body.[10]

A more general and less conciliatory reply makes no appeal to the rooting story. It insists that when we are concerned with questions about the fundamental nature of the mental, we are (necessarily) concerned with possibility, and it is possible that there should exist beings who are naturally and indeed involuntarily given to apparently language-

9. "La contemplostate de la Nature [l']absorculant tout entier"—A. Rimbaud (1972, 267).

10. One can imagine that Man Friday never turned up and that Robinson Crusoe, troubled in mind, forgot that other people exist, but still went on naturally having thoughts in English.

involving thought, although they have no thought of the possibility of intentionally producing such thought or of intentionally communicating with others.

A third reply challenges the view that there cannot be thought without language. I will not consider this, although there are good reasons for such a challenge (see Jackendoff 1987, 323–325, and Martin 1987). I am supposing that the Weather Watchers can have fully fledged propositional attitudes, and it seems plausible to suppose that one cannot be said to have such propositional attitudes unless one is at least capable of thought that is structured in something like the way in which language-borne thoughts are structured.

9.7 The Argument from the Nature of Desire

9.7.1 The central objection
I think the central objection to the Weather Watchers may be stated as follows: The notion of desire is linked to that of action or behavior in such a way that it is not intelligible to attribute desires (and beliefs) to a creature that is constitutionally incapable of action or behavior. More fundamentally, it isn't really intelligible to attribute desires (and beliefs) to a creature that lacks any disposition to action or behavior.

As remarked, I think that some neobehaviorists may be prepared to let the first claim go. They may grant that it is intelligible to attribute desires and beliefs to creatures incapable of any sort of action or behavior, for they will not wish to say that it is unintelligible to suppose that completely paralysed human beings can have desires and beliefs. They may hesitate for longer over the claim that it is intelligible to attribute desires and beliefs to creatures that are naturally and constitutionally incapable of any sort of action or behavior. But they can insist that to concede this is still to concede very little, for the crucial neobehaviorist claim is the second one. It is the *dispositional thesis* (pp. 251–252) relativized to the particular case of desires (and beliefs). Thus relativized, it says that to possess desires and beliefs is necessarily to be disposed to act or behave in certain ways, even if one never in fact acts in any way at all—whether because one is paralysed or because one is naturally and constitutionally incapable of action or behavior. According to neobehaviorism, the connection between desire and behavior is of such a kind that one can't really say what desire (or belief) is without talking about behavior and dispositions to behavior. This view is my present target.

9.7.2 Belief

I will concentrate on the notion of desire, but many hold that the notion of belief is equally such that it is not intelligible to attribute beliefs to a creature that lacks any disposition to action or behavior.

This is a surprising claim. Why should it be thought to be incoherent to suppose that there could be *Pure Observers*, entirely dispassionate, desireless observers of the world who are constitutionally incapable of any sort of action or observable behavior and who are not disposed to act or behave observably in any way? Why should the existence of such beings be thought logically impossible? It may be that one cannot have desires without beliefs, but the converse is surely not true. The only reason I can think of for claiming that the Pure Observers are impossible is a (more or less sophisticated) commitment to the old evidentialist confusion of epistemology and metaphysics, according to which we are obliged to suppose that possession of beliefs (and desires) is inseparable from possession of dispositions to action or behavior simply because only such action or behavior could provide (publicly available) evidential grounds for *attributing* beliefs to others. (See chapter 8, note 7.)

This view, orthodox for much of the twentieth century, has no plausibility. It is true that to believe something is necessarily to be *set to react* in certain ways. But this reaction setting need not involve any disposition to act or behave in any way, given the ordinary understanding of 'behavior'. To believe that p may be just this: to be disposed to have the thought that p in certain circumstances, to be disposed to experience the world in certain ways, to be (fallibly) disposed to form the belief that q on forming the belief that p implies q, and so on. F. P. Ramsey famously remarked that "a belief . . . is a map of neighbouring space by which we steer" (1990, 146), but the context suggests that he had the space of thought in mind, rather than physical space. And if he was thinking primarily of getting about in physical space, then what he said was at best a truth about creatures like us, not a necessary truth about belief.

It may be said that the Pure Observers would be disposed to act in certain ways if they acquired certain desires, given their existing beliefs. But even if this is true, it does not affect the present point. And in fact, it is implausible, for reasons that I will discuss shortly. (They would probably have to acquire further beliefs as well, if not also the ability to act in certain ways.)

9.7.3   The basic claim

The claim about desire looks more plausible than the claim about belief. It seems extraordinary to say that the notion of a Pure Observer is incoherent; it seems a lot less extraordinary to apply the dispositional thesis to the case of desire and claim that a being could not possibly have *desires* and not be disposed to act or behave in any way.

Nevertheless, it does not seem to be true. It does not seem to be true that we cannot make sense of the notion of desire independently of the notion of action or behavior, or the notion of wanting *to do* something. The central point could not be more simple. In fact, it is a tautology. It is that the fundamental and only essential element in desire is *just*: wanting (or liking) something. It is wanting some thing, or wanting something to be the case. And being in this state does not necessarily involve being disposed to act or behave in any way. No doubt to want something is, standardly, to be disposed to feel satisfied or pleased or happy or contented should one get it (see pp. 280–284 below). But it does not follow that to want something is necessarily to want to do something about getting it, or even to wish that one could do something about getting it. The Weather Watcher philosopher described in section 9.3 would find it quite extraordinary that we should suppose that wanting something did essentially involve any of these things. To want something is not necessarily even to have any conception of the possibility of being able to do something about getting it. Perhaps the case of babies and nonhuman animals may help us to see this. Whether it does or not, there is no contradiction in the idea that even a creature capable of conscious thought with languagelike structure might want something while lacking any conception of the possibility of being able to do anything about getting it.

I think this is immediately clear if one reflects dispassionately about it. Wanting (or liking) is just wanting (or liking). It may be essentially linked with dispositions to be pleased or satisfied in certain circumstances, but it has nothing necessarily to do with action or behavior. Desire, want, need, pro-attitude, longing, love, approval—these things do not necessarily involve the will.

Some may accuse me of laboring the obvious. Others will doubt the point, so I will now try to make some unnecessary difficulties for myself, in the attempt to convince the unconvinced.

9.7.4 Desire as set

The Weather Watchers are said to have sensations, thoughts, emotions, beliefs, and desires, although constitutionally incapable of any action or behavior. It is then claimed that they are not even disposed to act or behave in any way. It is then objected that they are necessarily disposed to act or behave in certain ways, simply insofar as they have beliefs and desires, and even if they are constitutionally incapable of any sort of action or observable behavior. It is objected, in other words, that the force of the dispositional thesis has not yet been fully appreciated. In particular, it is objected that if you have some desire, then even if you never act in any way and may not even conceive of acting in any way, still you are ipso facto disposed to act. In having a desire you are ipso facto *set* or *programmed* in some way. You are set to operate in certain ways should certain conditions be fulfilled. This, it may be said, is partly and essentially constitutive of what it is to have a desire.

There is a sense in which this is true, but it does not follow that the Weather Watchers are disposed to act or behave in any way, given the ordinary understanding of 'behavior'. Two points can be raised about the phrase 'operate in certain ways should certain conditions be fulfilled'. The first picks up on 'operate', the second on 'conditions'.

The first is that there is indeed a sense in which a Weather Watcher is set to operate in certain ways in certain conditions, in having the desires that it has. Thus if it likes rain to fall in circumstances C, it is set to come to hope that it will rain when it believes that circumstances C obtain, and to feel pleased if it does then rain. Similarly, if it wants an X, and comes to believe that Ys lead to Xs, it is disposed to come to hope for a Y. Thus its wants interact with its beliefs and have typical causes and effects. Most simply, in having desires or preferences or pro-attitudes in the way that it does, it is disposed to undergo episodes of consciously desiring that something or other be the case. But none of this involves it in any action or behavior (as ordinarily understood). Nor does any of this inevitably create or constitute any disposition to action or behavior (as ordinarily understood). Whatever is true in functionalism is compatible with the present view, as remarked in section 9.4. It is only *neobehaviorist* functionalism that is incompatible with it.

The second point is this. In having desires, the Weather Watchers are not merely set to operate in certain ways should certain conditions be fulfilled. They are also set to *act or behave* in certain ways, should certain conditions be fulfilled. But it does not follow that they are now disposed to act or behave in any way. This may sound implausible, but one has to bear in mind the Byzantine fact that everything is set to act or behave in certain ways *should certain conditions be fulfilled*. The table in front of me is set to go for a walk, for example, should certain conditions be fulfilled (a radical rearrangement of its subatomic particles). You just have to put enough into the set of conditions.

Everything is set to act or behave in certain ways should certain conditions be fulfilled, but there are obviously limits on the sorts of thing one can plausibly mention as conditions when one claims that something is, *as it now is*, currently disposed to act or behave in certain ways should certain conditions be fulfilled. I will now consider what these limits might be.

9.7.5 An initial case
Consider first the following relatively complicated case:

1. I desire that X should occur.
2. I have the following two beliefs:
   a. I believe that I can bring about Y by ϕ-ing if (and only if) circumstances C obtain.
   b. I believe that if Z occurs, X will occur.
3. If I were to bring about Y by ϕ-ing, Z would occur.
4. I have never thought about the fact stated in (3). But it is true of me now (given my internal state) that if I were to think about it, I would soon realize that it was true; that is, I would come to the conclusion that if I were to bring about Y by ϕ-ing, Z would occur. And this might then couple with my belief (2b) to make me see that I can bring about X by ϕ-ing.

5. I have no objections to bringing about *X* by *φ*-ing. That is, if I had realized that I could bring about *X* by bringing about *Z* by bringing about *Y* by *φ*-ing in *C*, I would be all set to *φ* on forming the belief that *C* obtained (and ceteris paribus).

In other words, *φ*-ing in *C* would give me something I want. I have not realized that this is so, but I already have all the information I need in order to realize it. I have simply failed to put this information together. The question is then this: given that this is so, is there any sense in which I am *now* disposed to *φ*-should-I-believe-that-circumstances-*C*-obtain, other things being equal?

The answer seems plain. I am not. My internal state is such that I could easily *become* disposed to *φ*-should-I-believe-that-circumstances-*C*-obtain. But I am not now disposed to *φ* in *C* (in circumstances I believe to be *C* circumstances). I lack a necessary belief (the belief that *φ*-ing in *C* would give me *X*). The following conditional is true of me: if I were to form this belief, then I would become disposed to *φ* in *C*. So—again—I am now so disposed that I could easily become disposed to act in a certain way in certain circumstances. But I am not now disposed to act in that way in (what I perceive to be) those circumstances.

I set out this case because something similar but more general may be said about the Weather Watchers. They are constitutionally incapable of action or behavior. But it may be said that they are necessarily *disposed to become disposed* to act or behave in certain ways, simply in virtue of the fact that they are creatures with beliefs and desires. (They are certainly further along this road than the table.)

Even if this is granted, however, it does not follow that they are actually disposed to act in any way at all, as they now are, simply in virtue of having beliefs and desires.

9.7.6 Desire and disposition

I will try to reexpress the point. Consider the following schematic description of what it is for being *B* to be disposed to act in a certain way *φ*. If *B* is now disposed to act in a certain way *φ*, then some proposition of the form of the following conditional is necessarily true:

Conditional (C) *B* is now such that *if Q were to happen*, then, other things being equal, *B* would perform, or attempt to perform, an action of kind *φ* (or would behave, or attempt to behave, in way *φ*).

Suppose this is granted. The question is then, What are the possible replacements for Q? I will suggest that there are limits on what can replace 'Q', that there are limits on what one could call the Q *antecedents*; and that understanding why this is so helps one to see that the Weather Watchers are not correctly said to be disposed to act in any way, even though they have beliefs and desires.[11]

In considering cases, I will start with a normal human case and then work toward the Weather Watchers by considering human cases that may be said to approximate progressively to their case, although they all fall short of it.

Case 1: a badly wants gas for her car. So she now has the property that if she were to see an accessible gas station, she would drive into it, other things being equal. Thus she is now disposed to act or behave in a certain way, ceteris paribus. Here the Q antecedent is: a sees an accessible gas station.

Case 2: b has become completely paralysed but does not know it. He wants an orange, and there is one on the table, which he has not noticed. It is now true of him that if he were to notice the orange, he would attempt to reach out and take it, although nothing would happen in the way of large-scale bodily movement. In this case, b is now disposed to act or behave in a certain way, and this is so even if he is in fact unable to act or behave observably in any way at all. Here the Q antecedent is: b sees the orange on the table.

A complication must be introduced before moving to the next case. It arises because completely paralysed people may be able to act not only insofar as they can still perform mental actions like mental arithmetic but also insofar as they may still be able to *try* to perform large-scale physical actions. This is because to try to do something is to act in a certain way—not only in the case when one tries to hit the bull's eye, pulls the trigger, and misses, but also in the case where one tries to move one's arm and finds that absolutely nothing happens, because one has become completely paralysed.[12]

11. I will ignore C. B. Martin's notorious "finkish" objection to conditional analyses of dispositional statements, as it makes no important difference to my present argument (see Martin 1994).

12. Compare Hornsby 1980, 33–43. Hornsby argues convincingly that there is a sense in which all actions are tryings, but denies that all tryings are actions.

It is because to try to act is to act, even in the absence of any large-scale physical movement, that the present sequence of cases, which seeks to take human beings with desires and beliefs to the point at which they can no longer act or behave in any way at all, is obliged to conclude with a case in which a human being loses even the ability to try to act. First, though, an intermediate case.

Case 3: *c* is completely paralysed and knows it. There is still something that, for her, constitutes trying to move her arms and legs, etc. But nothing ever happens when she does try, and so she has given up. At the moment she wants the orange on the table, and the following is true: if, suddenly hoping, she were to come to believe that she might not be paralysed after all, so that it was worth trying to reach out for the orange, she would try to reach out for it. Here *c* is genuinely disposed to act or behave in a certain way. She is disposed to perform the action of trying to reach out for the orange. And here the *Q* antecedent is: *c* comes to believe that it may after all, be worth trying to reach out for the orange.

Case 4: *d* is completely paralysed, and worse off than *c*. For he used to try to act—to move his body—although he knew he was paralysed. There used to be something that, for him, constituted trying to do things. Now, however, he has completely lost contact with his former experience of and capacity for agency, and he finds that there is no longer anything that, for him, constitutes even trying to move his body.

What might this be like? It resembles the experience many people have when they decide to try to move their ears directly, i.e., not by using

---

One argument for the claim that all tryings are actions is that tryings that get nowhere can be morally praiseworthy or blameworthy in just the way in which successful actions can be. Suppose *b* has a button under his finger and knows that pushing it in the next twenty seconds will destroy a city of innocent people. He decides to push it and, with a due sense of the irreversible consequences of what he is about to do, produces (in whatever way we do this) the neural activity that would normally have resulted in his finger depressing the button. Nothing happens to his finger. But he has indeed done something. And what he has done is morally reprehensible. He has performed a morally evil action.

Note that the fact that tryings are actions shows that the story of the "brain in a vat" does not provide any quick support for the present view that desire can exist without any disposition to action or behavior; nor does the apparent intelligibility of immaterialism.

their hands or moving their head, and the experience nearly all people have when they decide to try to make their hair wave around directly. The thought of the attempt simply fails to connect with anything in their action repertoire, even if it causes a tingling feeling on the scalp. I experience this utter blankness when I contemplate trying to wink my left eye, although I can blink and wink my right eye.

It may be added that even d's thoughts just happen, in a stream that he cannot direct. But this is not as bad as it might sound, since most of our thoughts are like this in everyday life, as already remarked. They tend to be mostly to the point, but not because we act to make them so. (This is how it is for me, but it may be less clear for others.)

Suppose that in spite of all this, d finds himself coming to think that there may, after all, be a chance of his ψ-ing—of his moving his body in a certain way. He may then find himself intending to ϕ, where ϕ is: trying to ψ. But he will then once again be confronted with a perfect blankness—the blankness of there being nothing that, for him, constitutes ϕ-ing (trying to ψ). The blank is so complete that it is not even true to say that there is something that constitutes trying to ϕ (i.e., trying to try to ψ), and so on.

In this case, he cannot act in any way at all. The proposed Q antecedent is [1] that d comes to feel that there may after all be a chance of ϕ-ing (i.e., trying to ψ). But the relevant conditional (C) is false, given this Q antecedent: as things are, it is not true that if Q were to happen, then, other things being equal, d would perform, or attempt to perform, a ϕ-type action. For what will happen when Q happens, in the way of action or behavior, is—nothing at all.

If the conditional (C) is to come out true in this case, Q has to be expanded. And the way in which it has to be expanded is highly significant, for it takes us over a crucial line. To the original Q antecedent, (1), d comes to feel that there might after all be a chance of ϕ-ing (trying to ψ), one has to add, [2] d comes to be such that there is once again something that, for him, constitutes ϕ-ing (trying to ψ), and so comes to be such that he is once again *able to act in some way.*

But (2) takes us over the line. The idea implicit in the notion of a Q antecedent is that when we specify such an antecedent, we are considering beings that are *already intentional agents.* Q antecedents are occurrences of such a kind that, when they occur, beings that are already intentional agents then perform, or attempt to perform, actions of certain kinds (ceteris paribus). But with the addition of (2) to (1) in the last substitution for Q, nothing less than the acquisition of the ability to act in some way—acquisition of the property of intentional agent-hood—has been included among the Q antecedents. And to allow this into the Q antecedents is to allow too much. It risks the consequence that everything is disposed to act or behave in some way. If even acquisition of the ability to act or behave can get into the Q antecedents, then the table is now disposed to act in some way. (The Q antecedent is that its subatomic parts get radically rearranged in such a way that it acquires certain desires and beliefs and certain abilities to act. Some may object that these will only be apparent beliefs and desires, not real ones. But it will be hard to maintain this view for long, as the table-agent continues to be situated and active in its environment.)

It seems, then, that Q antecedents cannot include occurrences that actually turn the beings under consideration into agents. One might as well say that a jumbled heap of wood, felt, metal, ivory, and ebony is now so disposed that one can play the *Diabelli Variations* on it, given that it can be assembled into a piano. Returning to d, we get the conclusion that he is not now disposed to act or behave in any way, even though he has beliefs and desires and even though he could relatively easily be turned into something that was disposed to act or behave in certain ways.

I think this case may not convince, but nothing hangs on it. It still falls a long way short of the case of the Weather Watchers, because d is a human being and thinks like a human being and characteristically has desires to do things. Nevertheless, the case is worth describing, and before moving on, it may be worth noting that there are two ways of underpinning the idea that a radically incapacitated human being like d is no longer even disposed to act or behave in any way. The first way involves the idea that there are fundamental physiological and neuro-physiological reasons why there is now, for him, nothing that constitutes even trying to act in any way. This is what I had primarily in mind when discussing d above. The second way involves the idea that the primary obstacle is d's unshakeable *conviction* that there is nothing that, for him, constitutes even trying to act in any way. Some may find this second case more plausible. They may find it more plausible in this case to say that d is no longer disposed to act in certain ways. We may accordingly complete the description of d's case by supposing that he is incapacitated in both the ways just described.

Some may still be inclined to think that d is now disposed to act in various ways simply on account of his possession of ordinary human desires for action: after all, there are things he would like to *do*, things he would like to be able to do, and he would do them if he could. I have suggested that he is not now disposed to act in any way, and that the fact that he has these desires for action makes no difference, given his radical incapacity. But I could simply concede that he is disposed to act, for the crucial point would then emerge more sharply: if d is after all disposed to act, given these desires for action, then it is not the mere possession of desires and beliefs that makes this true but rather the possession of certain particular desires and beliefs with certain particular contents. This point may become easier to see when one takes a further step toward the Weather Watchers and considers e, whose situation is identical to d's in currently relevant respects except for the fact that she has evolved successfully into her paralysed state, like a good radical Epictetian. She indulges in no wishful thinking and has no trace of any desire for what she knows to be impossible. She still wants certain things (she wants the sun to shine, she wants Wimple to beat Ivanov in the World Chess Championship), but she no longer wishes she could bring anything about. She has put her agent past entirely behind her.

But we find the case of e hard to imagine. Our convictions about human nature strongly impede our imagination and encourage us to slip back into thinking that it is after all a necessary truth that to want something is ipso facto to be disposed to do something about it. So I will switch to the case of the Weather Watchers.

9.7.7 Desire and disposition, continued

I have argued that not just anything can go into the Q antecedents of (C) conditionals. If anything could go into the Q antecedents, then even the Weather Watchers would be disposed to act in certain ways. For one could say this: given that Weather Watcher W now very much wants it to rain, the following complex conditional is true: if $W [Q_1]$ were to come to be capable of action, [Q_2] were to come to know or believe this fact,[13] [Q_3] were to come to believe, more specifically, that it could (now) affect the weather by ϕ-ing (e.g., by performing some sort of mental incantation), [Q_4] were, in coming to be capable of action, to come to be capable, in particular, of ϕ-ing, or at least of trying to ϕ,[14] [Q_5] had no stronger desire not to interfere with the weather, etc., then, other things being equal, W would ϕ, or attempt to ϕ.

Perhaps something like this is true. But it does not follow that W is now disposed to act or behave in any way, because too much has been added into the Q antecedents. To say that W is necessarily now disposed to act in certain ways because of the truth of this conditional is like saying that a lump of plastic is now disposed to conduct electricity because its constituent parts could be reorganized to constitute gold. It's like saying that a piece of wet clay is now fragile because it is now such that if it were treated in a certain way (baked in an oven), it would be fragile.

Generalizing away from the Weather Watchers, there are complex conditionals linking desire descriptions and action-kind descriptions, of a sort already considered, that are candidates for being *necessary truths*. There are conditionals of the following form (C^*): if, at a given time, being B [1] had desire D, [2] believed there was something it could then do about satisfying D, [3] believed in particular that ϕ-ing was the best or only way of trying to satisfy D, [4] believed itself able to ϕ, [5] had no equally strong or stronger countervailing desire D' that it believed it could do something about, [6] was in fact capable of action, [7] was, more particularly, able to ϕ, or was at least capable of trying to ϕ, then, ceteris paribus, [8] B would ϕ, or attempt to ϕ.[15] But the fact that such

13. There is an intermediate case in which W comes to be physically capable of action but has no knowledge of this, no proprioceptive inkling. In this case, there is a sense in which W remains as incapable of action as ever, or at least not disposed to act in any way.

14. That is, W would come to have something that, for it, constituted trying to ϕ.

15. This is a human-adapted version of a claim that, if true, presumably applies in some weaker form to all beings correctly held to be capable of intentional action. (The *cetera paria* include all sorts of things: the world running on, B not suddenly succumbing to paralysis, etc. I am continuing to put aside the "fink" objection mentioned in note 11.)

conditionals are true, if indeed they are, provides no grounds for an objection to the Weather Watchers, who may fulfill (1) and (5) and may or may not fulfill (3), depending on whether or not they have the concept of action, but do not fulfill (2), (4), (6), or (7). It would be unwarranted to say that they do really have certain dispositions to action or behavior because of the truth of conditionals of this form.

A more general and very familiar point is this: it is only in specific combinations that beliefs and desires dispose to action. So an agent is not necessarily disposed to act in any way simply because it has a certain desire. The property that a mental state like a desire has of being apt to cause certain sorts of behavior is not one that it has in isolation. It has it only in combination with certain specific beliefs. This well-known fact immediately provides a reason to question the neobehaviorist view that it is essentially constitutive of the nature of desire that it should (actually) dispose to action or behavior, and essentially constitutive of the nature of belief that it should (actually) dispose to action or behavior.

Any desire has the following property: it is necessarily true that there are beliefs with which the desire can combine in such a way as to give rise to, or constitute, a disposition to act or behave in some way.[16] This is a conceptual truth, true even of desires to change the past and desires for logically impossible things. But if I am rightly sure that I could never do anything about satisfying any of my desires about the weather, or lack any conception of the possibility of doing anything to satisfy my desires, then I am not *now* disposed to act or behave in any way simply

---

In a well-known article, Lewis introduces the idea of "mad" pain (1983, 122). A person with mad pain "feels pain, just as we do, [but] is not in the least motivated to prevent [it] or to get rid of it" (p. 122). If there can be mad desire analogous to mad pain, then conditionals like (C*) will be neither necessary nor true (unless this status is preserved for them—at the risk of becoming trivial—by a 'ceteris paribus' clause). What might mad desire be? It cannot simply be to desire X without being in the least motivated to try to get X, for our desires about the weather are standardly like that. One might propose to *define* mad desire as desire that allows (1) through (7) to be true while (8) is false; but it would need some independent characterization.

16. The desire not to act in any way at all may lead self-defeatingly to intentional inaction, which is a form of action, or else to adopting a course of action designed to lead one to cease to act altogether.

on account of the fact that I have certain desires. This is especially clear if I am also constitutionally incapable of any sort of action or behavior.

Oxygen is apt, in certain circumstances and when combined with certain other things, for quenching thirst in human beings who ingest it. Similarly it is apt, when combined with certain other things, to kill human beings who ingest it. It is also apt for causing existing flames to leap up higher and, suitably combined with other things, for quenching flames. Beliefs and desires are like this in their relation to action and behavior. *Given their already existing and independently graspable nature*, they can enter into combinations in which they may be said to constitute dispositions to action or behavior. But this fact is in no tension with the fact that beings like the Weather Watchers can have beliefs and desires and not be disposed to act or behave in any way.

Ignoring difficulties with talking of desires as states and with talking of states as causes, we can say, in the manner of D. M. Armstrong, that the concept of desire is the concept of a state that is apt to be—and is intrinsically suited to be—the cause of certain patterns of behavior, when suitably combined with certain beliefs. But it does not follow that one has to know about behavior in order to know what desire is. If one does not know about behavior, it does not follow that there is any sort of inadequacy or defect in one's notion of desire. It may be true, for us, that "the primitive sign of wanting is *trying to get*" (Anscombe 1972, 68), but again it does not follow that one has to know about behavior to know what desire is. Relationally speaking, the concept of desire is the concept of a state apt to be the cause of certain patterns of behavior when suitably combined with certain beliefs. But you would not fail to know something about the essential nature of desire in not knowing explicitly about this particular aptness, described in this way. Rather, if you did know what desire was and then learned about action and behavior, you would doubtless understand *why* desire was intrinsically suited to be the cause of action or behavior, given what you already knew about desire—about liking or longing or wanting or preferring or approving, considered just as such. The Weather Watcher philosopher who possesses the concept of desire but does not possess the concept of intentional behavior will doubtless understand this aptness if it comes to acquire a grasp of the latter concept, given its prior understanding of the nature of desire.

In general, then, even if desire characteristically or typically causes behavior, it is not true that desire is made to be what it is partly by this aspect of what it typically does. Rather, it is because of what it intrinsically is that this is an aspect of what it typically does. Even if, as a matter of natural fact, all existing desires occur in creatures that are the product of evolution by natural selection, and even if (roughly) desire evolves because it tends to be implicated in the causation of behavior that has survival value, it still does not follow that desire is made to be what it is partly by this aspect of what it typically does (compare p. 40 above). Desire can exist entirely unlinked to any dispositions to behavior.

It may be objected that to grant that conditionals like (C*) may be necessary truths is to concede that it is after all partly constitutive of the essential nature of desire that it can dispose to action or behavior, in combination with suitable beliefs. It is *therefore* also to concede that one cannot give a satisfactory account of the essential nature of desire without reference to action or behavior.

It is this 'therefore' that I dispute. One may grant that the property that oxygen has of being disposed to combine with carbon or uranium in the way that it does is partly constitutive of the essential nature of oxygen. But this property, *specified in this way*, is not constitutive of the nature of oxygen in such a way that you cannot possibly be said to know the nature of oxygen without knowing about carbon (or uranium) and knowing that oxygen combines with it in the way it does. Indeed, one could possibly know about oxygen's atomic structure without knowing about other elements or about the forming of chemical compounds. Somewhat similarly, the property that any desire has of being essentially suited to combine with beliefs in such a way as to constitute dispositions to action or behavior is not a property that you have to know about, under this description (i.e., in a way that requires possession of the concept of action or behavior), in order to know or say what a desire is.

Nothing depends on this analogy, and it may seem unconvincing to some. They should think of the Weather Watcher philosopher longing for rain, with no conception of the possibility of action or behavior. It knows what it is to desire or want or like something, and in this fundamental sense it knows what desire is.

It is not that I believe in some sort of Lego theory of relations among concepts that portrays nearly all such relations as extrinsic. It is simply that our ordinary concept of desire allows that a being may have desires and beliefs without being disposed to action or behavior and, relatedly, that a being may be a concept-exercising creature, experience desire, and come to possess what can properly be called the *concept* of desire on the basis of that experience, without possessing the concept of action or behavior. It may be objected that one's concept of desire must be incomplete or defective in some way if one is ignorant of necessary or a priori truths, e.g., conditionals like (C*), in which the concept figures. But this is incorrect. There seems to be no more reason to think that the Weather Watchers' concept of desire is incomplete or defective, because they do not possess the concept of action or behavior, than there is to think that someone's concept of the number 2 is defective, because she does not possess the concept of a numerical square or cube (or root) and therefore does not even know all the *types* of necessary truths in which the concept of the number 2 figures, let alone all the necessary truths in which it figures.

Consider the special case of pain. Pain may be necessarily connected to dislike in a way that you have to grasp if you have the concept of pain. But dislike is not in turn necessarily connected to being disposed to avoid what is disliked in a way that you have to grasp if you have the concept of pain, or of dislike. One can want something to stop without having any conception of the possibility of doing anything about it.

We ordinarily acquire mastery of the words 'want', 'desire', and so on, in a rich context of attributing actions and behavior to others (which is equally a context of action and behavior on our own part). And no doubt our concept of desire is in some way grounded in this learning experience. But the semantic (or conceptual or "grammatical") consequences of this fact must not be overestimated. Once we have acquired the general concept of desire in this way, we can go on to grasp the idea that beings like the Weather Watchers can have strong desires, although they are incapable of action or behavior, have no disposition to action or behavior, and even lack the concept of action or behavior. Whatever the true story of how we master the concept of desire, we acquire a concept that allows that desiring something to be the case is not indisseverably "logically tied" to doing something about it, or trying to do something about it, or wanting to do something about it, or wishing one could do something about it or even to being disposed either to do something about it or to try to do something about it or to want to do something about it or to wish one could do something about it. As remarked—and leaving aside all facts about the *phenomenology* of conscious episodes of desiring, important as they are—the primary linkage of the notion of desire to a notion other than itself is not to the notion of action or behavior but rather to the notion of being pleased or happy or contented should something come about (or at least to the notion of ceasing to be unhappy or discontented should it come about) and to the distinct but correlative notion of being unhappy or discontented or disappointed should it not come about.[17]

9.8 Desire and Affect

The expression 'primary linkage' is loose. It needs to be loose, because the connection between desire and dispositions to enter into states that one might neutrally call positive-or-negative-affect states (states of pleasure, satisfaction, contentment, happiness, etc., and their opposites) is no more unbreakable than the connection between desire and dispositions to action or behavior, even though it is (I believe) more fundamental. The normal case is clear: the experience of positive or negative affect occurs when the desire is fulfilled or frustrated. But many things can go wrong. Pleasure in the fulfillment of a want may be annihilated by a misfortune, and the moment of satisfying a want can be the moment at which one discovers that one was in fact wrong to want what one wanted.[18] The Weather Watchers are uncomplicated beings who are invariably pleased when their desires are fulfilled, and disappointed when they are not, but

17. Switching a light switch, one does not normally register any experience of positive pleasure when the light comes on as one wants and expects, but one is likely to experience some sort of displeasure if it doesn't.

18. Because we usually regard the link between desire satisfaction and contentment as tight, we naturally express this by saying that what one finds out is that one didn't really want what one thought one wanted. But this may not be accurate. One did want it, but one discovered that one didn't like it. The case of Tigger (Milne 1928, chap. 2) is instructive.

things are not always so simple. Consider three initially plausible claims.
[1] If a wants X to occur at time t, she will, at t, be pleased or satisfied
if X does occur. [2] If a wants X to occur at t, she will, at t, derive pleasure
or satisfaction from the thought that X will occur. [3] If at t, a wants X
to occur she will, at t, believe that she will be pleased or satisfied should
X occur (assuming that she does not in the meantime acquire any reason
for not wanting X to occur). None of (1) through (3) are obviously true.
Suppose that a is standing in the cold outside a phone booth. The booth's
occupant looks at her while conducting an amazingly leisurely conversation. As she stands there, she imagines the hostile remark she will make
when the occupant emerges. After ten minutes, she really wants to make
this remark. But none of (1) through (3) need be true of her.[19]

The connection between desire and affect is a big subject, and largely
beyond my present scope. I will, however, consider one challenge to the
proposal that the primary linkage of the notion of desire to a notion
other than itself is to the notion of affect.

Consider a race of creatures—the Aldebaranians—that have beliefs,
sensations, thoughts, and so on. They are not capable of any affect states
at all, but they are capable of entering into states—call them 'M
states'—given which, and given that they believe what they believe, they
are regularly caused to move in certain ways, and so regularly engage
in what looks like purposive behavior. M states, then, may be defined
as motivating states that are functionally very similar to states that we
normally think of as desire states. They are functionally similar in
respect of the way in which they interact with a being's informational
states to cause it to move in apparently goal-directed ways. Roughly
speaking, specific M states, in combination with specific informational
states, lead to specific movements.

19. I owe the example to Derek Parfit. The present claim is stronger than
Watson's claim that one "may in no way value what one desires," which he
illustrates with "a squash player who, while suffering an ignominious defeat,
desires to smash his opponent in the face with the racquet" (1982, 101). The
squash player may well derive pleasure or satisfaction from what he does not
value. John Heil has pointed out to me that guilt can vitiate desire satisfaction
in another way: one gets what one wants, and although one doesn't discover that
one didn't really want it after all, guilt cancels any pleasure or satisfaction. (See
also Gosling 1969, chaps. 6–7).

Some may hold that these M states should be counted as desire states, given their motivational role, even though the Aldebaranians never feel any sort of pleasure or displeasure on account of having brought about what they have brought about. On this view, the way in which M states combine with informational states to constitute dispositions to engage in movements that look like purposive behavior suffices on its own to show that M states are rightly thought of as desire states, even though there is no connection between 'M-satisfaction or M-nonsatisfaction' and any affect.

Others, however, think that it is not a general truth that states that can combine with informational states to motivate behavior are desire states. They think that this is not a general truth even after unreliable things like nervousness have been ruled out of consideration, and even after the suggestion that beliefs alone can suffice to motivate action has been put aside. (This suggestion is made by some moral philosophers, and its relation to the current framework of discussion may be worth further investigation.) The reason they give is that M states, as defined above, can exist in completely experienceless beings, and that such beings can never truly be said to have desires, given that they are experienceless. This is not because desires or pro-attitudes are themselves necessarily experience-involving, for they are not, but rather because a being's possession of the capacity for experience is at least a necessary condition of its being such that it can correctly be said to desire things, believe things, hope for things, understand things.

The Aldebaranians are in fact experiencing beings, although they lack any affect dispositions. So one cannot reject the claim that their M states are desire states on the grounds that they are experienceless. Nevertheless it may still be argued that they cannot *really* be said to want or desire anything, given that they are incapable of affect.

My sense is that the link to the notion of affect dispositions is internal to and fundamentally constitutive of the notion of desire in a way that the link to the notion of behavioral dispositions is not. It may, however, be suggested that the notion of desire has not one but two principal linkages: one to the notion of dispositions to action or behavior, one to the notion of affect. It may be further suggested that either can suffice in the absence of the other as a reason for saying that something is a desire, although a race of creatures cannot truly be said to have desires if both linkages are severed. On this view, when we tell philosophers' stories, we must rely increasingly on one of the linkages, in proportion as the importance of the other is diminished, in order to be able to go on making sense of the claim that something really is a desire. So the story of the Weather Watchers needs to stress the link with affect, because it cuts the link with action or behavior.

There is much more to say on this subject, but I will limit myself to one further set of rather programmatic observations. So far I have used the word 'desire' in the standard semitechnical way to refer both to certain dispositions—preferences, likes and dislikes, attitudes of favor and disfavour, pro-attitudes and con-attitudes, etc.—and to conscious episodes of desiring, wanting, longing, and so on. But the distinction between these two things—between dispositional desire and occurrent desire—can become important.

As just remarked, some philosophers may opt for a notion of desire according to which [1] appropriate connection with behavioral dispositions is sufficient for something to count as a desire. On this view, M states qualify immediately as desires. Others may hold that [2] appropriate connection with affect dispositions is essential for something to count as a desire, and sufficient even in the absence of (1). A third suggestion may now be made: that [3] a capacity to undergo conscious episodes of desiring or wanting is at least necessary if one is to count as desiring anything, and is arguably sufficient, even in the absence of both (1) and (2). Desire, on this view, can be all there just so long as there is conscious desiring.

Several questions arise about (3). First, is a capacity to undergo conscious episodes of desire really necessary for desire? If we mean occurrent desire, then the answer is obviously 'Yes'. But if we mean dispositional desire, the answer is (I suggest) 'No'. A reliable capacity and tendency to react with pleasure or displeasure to various occurrences may surely be held to be sufficient for the attribution of genuine likings, preferences, or pro-attitudes, even in the complete absence of conscious episodes of desire. The Weather Watchers have conscious episodes of desire, but one of their close cousins might note its affective reactions over time and build up a clear picture of the structure of its likes and dislikes—its desires, in a word—without ever having any conscious episodes of desire.

Second, is exercise of a capacity for conscious episodes of desire sufficient for desire even in the absence of (1) and (2)? I have argued at length that (1) is not necessary for desire. That leaves (2). But the question of whether exercise of a capacity for conscious desire could be sufficient for desire in the absence of any affect dispositions is pre-empted by the question of whether conscious desire is even possible without affect dispositions.

This is part of a more general question: What are the possible forms of conscious desire? Must one at least be capable of affect if one is to undergo conscious episodes of desire? It seems to me that the answer to this question is 'Yes'—that nothing could count as genuine conscious desire in a creature utterly incapable of any sort of affective state. And this reinforces the thought that the primary linkage of the notion of desire to a notion other than itself is to the notion of affect—pleasure or displeasure in the widest sense.

As remarked, there is more to be said here. I will close by noting that although Weather Watchers have no dispositions to action or behavior, their claim to have desires is firmly grounded both in their strong affect dispositions and in their dispositions to have conscious experiences of desiring this or that.

9.9   The Argument from the Phenomenology of Desire

The notions of action, behavior, and desire are intimately linked. It seems plain that reference to the notion of desire (or pro-attitude) enters essentially into a satisfactory account of the nature of action, and action is a species of behavior. I have not questioned this. I have questioned its converse, arguing that reference to action and behavior does not enter essentially into a satisfactory account of the nature of desire. It enters in only secondarily, along with many other things. It enters in only because action or behavior is among the many things that can be or become the object of desire. There are two very familiar cases. [1] Sometimes a being wants Y and believes it can do something, X, that will bring about Y, and hence, doing X itself becomes the object of its desire. [2] Sometimes doing something is the object of a being's desire in its own right, and not because it is a means to anything else.

In this sense, however, anything that can be an object of desire—like sunshine or snow—enters into the elucidation of the notion of desire. Indeed, from this perspective the main difference between desires to do things and desires for sunshine or snow is simply that the former are much more common than the latter (here on earth, at least). If we think that dispositions to act or behave form an essential part of desire, it may be because we happen to live on a planet swarming with agents, a planet on which desires are incessantly involved in the causation of action and behavior. And so we are perhaps led to mistake a causal connection for a constitutive connection, and we may be powerfully reinforced in our conviction by reflections on the evolution or natural history of desire. For the natural history of desire on earth is clear: the existence of desire on earth is inextricable from its role in the causation of action or behavior.[20]

This is one major source of the standard view that to desire is necessarily to be disposed to act or behave in certain ways, but it is not the only one. The primary source of current attachment to the view is probably still a misplaced respect for public-domain positivism. We are, furthermore, heavily committed to attributing desires or pro-attitudes to nonhuman animals just on the strength of their behavior, in such a way that their dispositions to behavior, and actual behavior, can easily come to seem inextricably constitutive of what we *mean* when we attribute desires or pro-attitudes to them.[21]

Another suggestion is that the human phenomenology of desire is an important source of our attachment to the standard view, and in conclusion I will briefly consider this suggestion.

20. This point may again tempt some into the highly dubious "logical naturalism" mentioned in chapter 8 (p. 242). According to logical naturalism, if one has good grounds for thinking that feature F will always be connected to feature G in any creature that can plausibly be supposed to be the product of evolution by natural selection in a nonmagical universe, then one may infer that there is indeed a conceptual or constitutive connection between F and G. In the present case, logical naturalism proposes that desires and beliefs will always be connected with (dispositions to) action or behavior in any creature that is the product of nonmagical evolution, and it concludes that there is a conceptual or constitutive connection between the two things. I have argued that such a conclusion is false.

21. Wittgensteinians offer the same sort of argument (routed through a consideration of the conditions of language learning) in the case of our attribution of desires to each other.

Suppose that one badly wants to be close to some object X but feels it would be unwise to move now. There it is, over there, too far away. One's desire to be close to X seems essentially bound up with one's inclination to act—to move to go over to X or to cause X to come over to where one is. The inclination to act may seem to be part of the desire. And the desire may set up a kind of automatic anticipatory ghosting of appropriate action. There may be a kind of vaguely proprioceptively perceived sketching of movement in one's limbs. In the human case, the experience of desire for X is saturated with the thought of action promoting acquisition of X.

But compare a Weather Watcher. It has the same desire as one has oneself. It too wants to be close to X. It hopes that X will move closer to it. But it has no capacity for action, and there is nothing that, for it, constitutes even trying to do something about it. It has no vaguely sensed movement impulses at all. Either it has the concept of action and knows that it has no capacity for action (in one main version of the story), or it has no concept of action (in the other). Either way, its desire has no action-involving resonances; it sets up no anticipatory kinesthetic hum. There is just the wanting; action is not part of the content of what is wanted, nor is action (or any disposition to action) essentially bound up in the wanting in any more indirect fashion. Perhaps an intense desire that the weather should change can give one some experiential sense of what this might be like. Whether or not it does, it remains true that to want something is, essentially, just to want it. It is not necessarily and ipso facto to be disposed to do anything. In claiming that to want is necessarily to be disposed to do something, we seem like people who have a perfectly good theory of the elements and yet assert that there can be no such thing as pure oxygen because they inhabit a planet on which the ambient conditions ensure that oxygen never occurs except in compounds.

It may be objected that if one desires to be close to X, one must at least wish that one could do something about it. This seems wrong for two reasons. First, one can have such a wish only if one possesses the concept of action, and one may not possess the concept of action, like the Weather Watchers in one of their versions.

Second, suppose that one does possess the concept of action. Does it follow that if one desires to be close to X, one must at least wish that one could do something about it? Is it true that if one possesses the concept of action and desires X to come about and thinks it will not, then one must wish that one could do something about it? We may be tempted to think that this is true, but I do not think that it is true even in the human case. Even here the desire for X does not necessarily involve any wish to be able to do anything to bring X about. When I want Wimple rather than Ivanov to win the World Chess Championship, I do not wish—let alone necessarily wish—that I could affect the outcome. I want something to happen. I do not wish that I could do anything about it. Desire does not necessarily involve the will.

More generally, one may possess the concept of action, know oneself to be constitutionally incapable of action, and be fully at ease with this fact. One may be very rationalistic or profoundly Epictetian in one's outlook. One may just have the desire to be close to X and simply have no sort of thought about actual or possible action. More interestingly, one may very much want to be constitutionally incapable of action. The Weather Watchers who have the concept of action may remember their active pasts, and remember them as times of striving and disappointment, conflict and unhappiness, inextricably linked with the capacity for action. In semi-Buddhist fashion, they may have discovered that peace comes only when action ceases. (Full Buddhist enlightenment appears to involve the complete extinction of desire and affect.)

We may be very unusual creatures. We are very given to wishing that we could do or have things that we know we cannot do or have. But this tendency is not a necessary part of being an agent, still less of being a creature with desires. When we release a dart or a bowling ball, we know we can do nothing about what happens next. Nonetheless, we may lean to the left as we will our dart or bowl to go to the left, seeking to generate and project leftward-movement-producing energy by a strange sort of psychophysical clenching. When we watch an athlete on television, we may tense up violently, as if our doing so could help her on. Even after the ball is kicked, footballers and their spectators try to guide the ball into the net by a strange will-incarnating set of the body. Owners of not very powerful cars, when going up hills, find themselves leaning forward and tense in their seats because they are "willing the car on." Their strong desire for the car to keep up speed automatically and irrationally converts into bodily movement thought of as helping the car on. But these irrational human things are not necessary to any possible form of genuine agency, let alone any possible form of desire. Some active beings may be perfectly easy in their awareness that they can do nothing about the athlete or the dart. They may watch, and passionately desire a certain outcome, without any trace of this strange human behavior. In our case, our life of almost nonstop action (together with our ineradicable tendency to indulge in wishful and magical thinking) deeply determines our experience of desire, to the point at which a felt inclination to act blends with our experience of desire even in many cases in which we know that we can do nothing to further what we desire. And this may indeed be part of the reason why we are inclined to treat a contingent connection between desire and action or behavior as something deeper, as a constitutive connection. As in so many of our researches, we may tend to be overwhelmed by the familiar details of our own case.

I have argued that beings may have desires and beliefs without being disposed to act or behave in any way, and that one can have desires, and have the concept of desire, and know what desire is, without knowing what action or behavior is. Forget the Weather Watchers. The fact remains that desire does not necessarily involve the will. It does not necessarily involve action or behavior, or any disposition to action or behavior. I conclude that standard neobehaviorism is false for the case of desires, beliefs, and propositional attitudes in general, just as it is false for the case of sensations, given the argument of chapter 8.

It seems to me that this conclusion has a curious property. On the one hand, it can be taken on board without too much difficulty by mainstream contemporary philosophy of mind. On the other hand, most recent writings on the philosophy of mind contain statements that are incompatible with it.[22]

22. For an admirably blunt statement of some of the main claims of the last two chapters, see Searle 1992, 65–71. One central point could perhaps be summarized as follows. Many have held that to be in pain, or to have a desire, is ipso facto to be disposed to behave in some way. Adopting a crude symbolism in which 'P' stands for being in pain, 'D' stands for having a desire, and 'B' stands for being disposed to behave in some way, one could write this as follows:

$$[[P \lor D] \to B] \tag{1}$$

I have argued that (1) is false. The first proposed modification is simple: to be in pain, or to have a desire, is ipso facto to be disposed to behave in some way *if one is a behavioral being*, i.e., a being in fact capable of action or behavior. That is, taking 'BB' to stand for being a behavioral being, we have (2):

$$[[P \vee D] \rightarrow [BB \rightarrow B]] \qquad [2]$$

It seems, however, that (2) is also false. For one may be a behavioral being and, as a matter of contingent fact, never actually have any thought of being able to do anything about one's pain, or about one's desires (either some or all of them). More positively, one may believe (and believe truly) of one's pain, or of any one of one's desires (and perhaps all of one's desires), that there is nothing one can do about relieving or satisfying it (or them). That is, if we take 'F' to represent failing to have any thought of the possibility of action or behavior with respect to pain or desires and 'G' to represent believing that there is nothing one can do about one's pain or desires, we have (3):

$$[[P \vee D] \rightarrow [BB \rightarrow [[\neg F \,\&\, \neg G] \rightarrow B]]] \qquad [3]$$

It may then be said that the '$[\neg F \,\&\, \neg G]$' condition needs to be supplemented by a positive condition, call it 'H', which represents actually having some belief in the possibility of being able to do something about one's pain or one's desire, this giving (4):

$$[[P \vee D] \rightarrow [BB \rightarrow [[[\neg F \,\&\, \neg G] \,\&\, H] \rightarrow B]]] \qquad [4]$$

In fact, though, it seems that (5) is true:

$$[H \rightarrow [\neg F \,\&\, \neg G]] \qquad [5]$$

So the '$[\neg F \,\&\, \neg G]$' condition can be dropped to give (6):

$$[[P \vee D] \rightarrow [BB \rightarrow [H \rightarrow B]]]. \qquad [6]$$

Suppose that all this is so. It may then be objected that (6) is a priori, that a further related a priori truth is available, to wit, (7),

$$[BB \rightarrow [[P \vee D] \rightarrow [H \rightarrow B]]] \qquad [7]$$

and that what truths like (6) and (7) show is that there is an a priori connection between pain and desire and behavior of the sort ordinarily supposed. In reply, I am content to accept (6) and (7), but my conclusions remain what they are.

10

Behavior

10.1 Introduction

Most contemporary philosophers of mind are neobehaviorists. They hold—for a variety of reasons—that reference to behavior enters centrally into a satisfactory account of the nature of almost all, if not all, mental states and occurrences. I have argued that this view is false on the ordinary philosophical understanding of the word 'behavior'. But what is this ordinary philosophical understanding?

It isn't easy to say. We use the word with great confidence, just as we use the word 'mental' with great confidence. It rarely features in the indexes of books as something that needs special discussion. There is thought to be a fairly comfortable consensus about its proper use. But it is not obvious that this is true. Like the word 'mental', the word 'behavior' bends with the theories of its users. Even within the philosophy of mind, it lends itself to significantly different uses in different contexts.[1]

I will try, nevertheless, to give a loose, general account of its standard use in sections 10.3 and 10.4 below, for it is relative to this use that neobehaviorism is false. Then, in section 10.5, I will argue that there is a defensible wider notion of behavior that improves the prospects of neobehaviorism. I will say nothing about the familiar point that a taxonomy of types of behavior that employs only conventional

1. For a helpful account of some tensions in the term, from Ryle 1949 to Kim 1982, see Hornsby 1986. For an impressive recent attempt to realign the notion, see Dretske 1988.

physical-description terms is useless if one is trying to establish interesting correlations between types of behavior and types of mental state.

10.2 A Hopeless Definition

The philosophy of mind is obviously not concerned with all uses of 'behavior'. People talk of the behavior of markets, stars, words, viruses, plants, engines, gas molecules. I will offer a definition of 'behavior' that narrows the set of possible instances of behavior in a familiar way. It consists of four arguably overlapping conditions, in which I have italicized terms that are importantly vague.

Definition   To be an instance of behavior on the part of a being B is to be a motion or change, or lack of motion or change, M, that is a motion or change in or of B and that fulfils the following conditions:

[O] M is *ordinarily other-observable*.

[D]   It is correct or reasonable to describe M as something B *does*, rather than as something that just *happens* to B. Or, it is correct or reasonable to describe M as a self-motion or self-change on the part of B.

[I]   The *proximal cause* of M is internal to B.

[C]   The *proximal cause* of M is some activity in the *central control system* of B.

   I hear immediate protests, but let me first note a fifth candidate condition that will be considered and rejected in section 10.3.8:

[F] M has some adaptive function.[2]

Let me also mention and put aside a sixth possible condition:

[M]   The *proximal cause* of M is some *mental* activity.

I will make no appeal to this last condition. It is true that the present discussion of the notion of behavior is part of an attack on neobehaviorism, and it seems that an attack on neobehaviorism need only be concerned with motions or changes that do fulfill condition (M), since

---

2. Millikan (1993, chap. 7) puts (F) at the center of her natural-history-oriented account of behavior.

neobehaviorism is a thesis about the essential nature of mental states and their relation to behavior. Nevertheless, it is best to leave (M) out in a more general discussion of the common conception of behavior. For one thing, many would simply deny the necessity of (M). For another, the extension of 'mental' is as indeterminate as that of the word 'behavior'. (Their indeterminacies are linked.) So I will pay most attention to conditions (O), (D), (I), and (C). Even after (M) and (F) have been dropped, the four conditions may be thought to be thoroughly dubious, and far too restrictive.

In section 10.4 below I consider the other-observability condition, condition (O), and present the main contention of this chapter. Section 10.3 contains nothing very philosophical, and those who wish may omit it after taking a look at the rough definition of 'doing-behavior' on p. 302. It raises a cloud of dust, recording a number of positions without endorsing any of them and without organizing them into any clear taxonomy.

I think all four conditions (O), (D), (I), and (C) have some intuitive appeal, as indeed does (F), and that some philosophers are probably inclined to accept all of them, given what they ordinarily understand by behavior. At the other extreme, there may be some who are inclined to think that (I) alone is sufficient for behavior. This cannot be right, but (O), (D), (C), and (F) are all open to objection. Ryle, one of the fathers of philosophical behaviorism, has no strong attachment to (C) or (F), and seems inclined to deny (O) and (D). And even (I) can be challenged.

So the definition proposed won't do. But it may identify the problem area correctly. In this sense, it may even be said to define the term 'behavior'. It may be said to define the word considered as a general name for a certain heavily disputed area in which different particular conceptions of behavior coexist. It will then be successful to the extent that it is correct in its suggestion that its component conditions, together perhaps with condition (F), are the ones that are centrally disputed when rival accounts of behavior are opposed to each other.

10.3 Difficulties

10.3.1 Vagueness
It may first of all be objected that the expression 'proximal cause' in (I) and (C) is hopelessly vague. Faced with the causal continuum of the

world, we examine it in a more or less fine-grained manner, depending on our practical and theoretical interests. What we count as the proximal cause of an event is relative to our interests.

This is true, but I don't think it matters. The notion of proximal cause appropriate to the discussion is clear enough. One may assume, for example, that all our intentional large-scale bodily motions are correctly said to have their proximal cause in the central control system or CCS—ignoring an obvious narrower use of 'CCS' according to which none of these motions have their proximal cause in the CCS, because of the electrical impulses that must travel down the nerve pathways in order for them to take place. No doubt 'proximal cause' really means little more here than 'cause that appears salient, given our present theoretical interest in the notion of behavior'. But perhaps this fact can be tolerated without too much difficulty, although I will raise a couple more doubts later.[3]

10.3.2 Motionlessness

The motionlessness of the lioness before she springs is an instance of behavior. It is an essential part of her hunting and stalking behavior. That is why some instances of lack of motion or change should be included, as limiting cases, in the class of motions or changes. I will take this inclusion for granted and continue to speak only of motions and changes. (All motions are changes, and it may be said, on materialist grounds, that all changes are motions. Nevertheless, I will use both terms.) Note that motionless behavior is as observable as motion-involving behavior, and that some may find natural a conception of behavior according to which a live animal's motion or motionlessness relative to its immediate environment is always and necessarily a matter of its behaving in a certain way; unless, perhaps, it has been knocked unconscious or drugged. (Motion due to transport or planetary or galactic motion is obviously irrelevant.)

3. See Dretske 1988, 24–25. This rough ruling may help one to handle imaginary cases like the one in which CCS activity is transmitted out to a receiver by radio links, then back directly to the motor nerves in the hand, causing appropriate movements.

10.3.3 Classification

I will use '*M*' to talk about particular motions or changes and also in the plural to talk of sets of motions or changes. Motions or changes can be characterized by means of a bracketed matrix indicating their standing with regard to conditions (O), (D), (I), and (C), although many of these characterizations may be disputable, in particular those relating to (D) and to a slightly lesser extent (C). Thus a wave of the hand may be [+O +D +I +C], the motions involved in a silent mental calculation may be [−O +D +I +C], an antibody's multiplication in the blood may be [−O −D +I −C], a sexual erection may be [+O −D +I −C].[4] I take it that among the motions or changes that we are ordinarily inclined to count as behavior are "fixed action patterns" and displacement activities. These are not the same thing, but they may both, perhaps, be classified as [+O ±D +I +C].[5]

Many would want to exclude purely reflex actions, like knee jerks or blinking at a flash (perhaps [+O −D +I −C]) from the class of instances of behavior. But others would disagree. And even those who want to exclude reflex actions might nevertheless want to include things like snoring or shifting in one's sleep. Bodily motion due to planetary motion is excluded, and also, presumably, motion due to things like tripping over something [+O −D −I −C],[6] the motion involved in the formation of goose pimples [+O −D +I −C][7] or other pimples [+O −D +I −C],[8] the

4. It may be claimed that erections are always +C; it depends on how one defines 'central control system'. Some human beings can achieve orgasm just by thinking about something, but it may be argued that orgasm is not +D in such cases, not something that they do, but something that they make happen by doing something else.

5. ±D because some displacement activities and fixed action patterns seem more like things that happen than things that are done. There can be no precision in these classifications. It may well be that ±C should replace +C for some organisms. There is also a case for ±O, since human displacement activities, for example, may be silent mental routines.

6. Ordinary usage does not help in deciding on the (D) condition, for we naturally talk of things like falling and tripping as things we do, although we also naturally say that these are things that happen to us rather than things we do. The same goes for yawning and sneezing.

7. ±C if scary imaginings can be the proximal cause of goose pimples.

8. ±C if anxiety can cause pimples and be counted as the proximal cause.

motion of circulating blood [–O –D +I –C], muscular tremors, and the peristaltic motion of the gut. Many would also ordinarily be inclined to exclude the physical motions that constitute the electrochemical activity of the brain [–O ±D +I +C],[9] and the motor-nerve innervations that occur in the normal course of large-scale physical action, although the latter might well be held to be parts of processes that are behavioral processes or instances of behavior. It may be that things like shivering [+O –D +I –C] are unclear, although some would find it natural to say that shivering is not behavior and that sweating is even more obviously not behavior. (Sweating and shivering seem like phenomena that ought to be classified similarly, but some feel more inclined to treat shivering as behavior simply because it involves large-scale motion. Once again this shows the looseness of the term 'behavior'.)

There are sixteen possible combinations displayed in table 10.1, ranging from [–O –D –I –C] to [+O +D +I +C]. But only eight or perhaps ten of them are possible cases, since (C) and (D) both imply (I) and (D) may imply (C). Even fewer are viable as examples of behavior: maybe as few as one, perhaps as many as five or six, depending on the conception of behavior that one favors (table 10.1). Cases of type 16 are unquestionably behavior. In section 10.4, I will argue for cases of type 8. Others would include cases of types 11, 12, and 15. Type 4 may be thought to trail some way behind 8, 11, 12, and 15, but in section 10.4, I will suggest that some cases of type 4 should also count as instances of behavior. If types 4, 8, 11, 12, and 15 can provide cases of behavior, then none of (O), (D), and (C) is a singly necessary condition of behavior.

10.3.4 Doings and happenings

Further examples could be accumulated, but I will now consider specific objections to the four conditions. Condition (O), the ordinary other-observability condition, is highly problematic, but for the moment I will take it for granted.

---

9. ±D because it is arguable that some of these motions are (at least sometimes) something we do if the motions somehow *constitute* our thinking and our thinking is (at least sometimes) something we do.

Table 10.1
Types of behavior

Type no.	Characterization	Example
1	[–O –D –I –C]	Cellular change in B caused by gamma ray
2	[–O –D –I +C]	—
3	[–O –D +I –C]	Antibody multiplies in B's blood.
4	[–O –D +I +C]	It strikes B that it's Monday. B's blood-sugar level drops as a result of B's thinking.
5	[–O +D –I –C]	—
6	[–O +D –I +C]	—
7	[–O +D +I –C]	Impossible if (D) implies (C).
8	[–O +D +I +C]	B does mental arithmetic.
9	[+O –D –I –C]	B falls when pushed.
10	[+O –D –I +C]	—
11	[+O –D +I –C]	B sweats or shivers.
12	[+O –D +I +C]	B's hair stands on end when B concentrates.
13	[+O +D –I –C]	—
14	[+O +D –I +C]	—
15	[+O +D +I –C]	Impossible if (D) implies (C) (but see section 10.3.6 below).
16	[+O +D +I +C]	B waves goodbye. The Sphex wasp prepares her burrow (?).

O = observable, D = doing, I = internal, C = central control system.

Condition (D), the 'something the organism does' condition, is obviously vague: some of the examples have already shown that it is not always clear whether it is more natural to say that a given motion M is something B did, rather than something that happened to B. This is one of the central vaguenesses in the notion of behavior, and it must be acknowledged and tolerated. It may well be that one can ignore difficult cases for the purposes of discussing neobehaviorism, and stick to cases that most people find it overwhelmingly natural to classify as cases in which M is something B does. But even these cases may range very widely. They may range from a human being drafting or signing the

Declaration of Independence, down through the whole range of other less sophisticated actions of human and other animals, down through the more or less complex fixed action patterns exhibited by nonhuman animals, right down, perhaps, to the ichneumon larva automatically avoiding the vital organs of the caterpillar when eating the rest of the caterpillar's insides.[10]

Consider a problem case. The freshwater shrimp *Gammarus* normally keeps to the bottom of the stream and spends a lot of time hiding under rocks. This is good and prudent behavior on its part, because there are predators about. But *Gammarus* tends to get infected by a certain parasite, a nematode worm, and then it starts leaping up and down in the water. This is very bad for the shrimp, but it is very good for the parasite, because the shrimp is then much more likely to get eaten by the fish that are the parasite's other main host.

If one saw infected shrimps leaping up and down, one would be naturally inclined to classify what they were doing as behavior and to wonder why they did it. But when one learned that they did it only because of the effect the parasites had on their control systems, one might be inclined to think that this was something that happened to them rather than something they did, and hence not really an instance of behavior. And one might be inclined to think this even given the liberal understanding of 'do' illustrated in the last paragraph, which counted the choosiness of the ichneumon larva when eating out the insides of its host caterpillar as behavior. One might well be inclined to think that what happens to *Gammarus* is like an involuntary muscular tic or tremor in one's eyelid, which does not really count as behavior; the only difference is that it happens to affect *Gammarus*'s whole body.

One party of thought thinks this is the right thing to say. A second party challenges the 'hence' in the second sentence of the last paragraph; that is, it challenges condition (D). Members of this second party think that it sounds unacceptably odd to say 'We thought that this was an instance of behavior, but we later discovered that it is not really an

---

10. It leaves the vital organs until last to keep the caterpillar alive for as long as possible. For further description of this case, which in the nineteenth century greatly troubled those who believed that God designed the world, see Gould 1983.

instance of behavior at all'. They add that there many illnesses that involve characteristic sorts of involuntary behavior, and that this is just one more of them.

Members of a third party hold that a tic in the eyelid is not really behavior, and grant that *Gammarus*'s affliction is essentially similar in character, but still insist that the leaping up and down should be counted as behavior—even though it is more natural to say that it is something that happens to *Gammarus* rather than something it does. They say that the mere fact that it involves the whole body and is internally caused is sufficient to make the term 'behavior' appropriate. And in saying this, they may be correctly reporting a natural use of the word.

It does not seem reasonable to suppose that there is a single right answer to this question. One may insist that behavior (behavior "proper") must be something the organism does, but some will be more liberal than others in their judgments of what count as doings rather than happenings.

10.3.5 Internally caused

Conditions (I) and (C) state further considerations that may be operative when one is deciding whether it is correct to describe some motion or change as an instance of behavior. It is natural to suppose that (C) entails (I), and it may also seem very plausible to suppose that (D) entails (C), although chickens that run around without heads may raise problems. I take it that *B*'s central control system or CCS need not be anatomically single, and that it can possibly be located outside what we assume to be *B*'s main body, as in the story told by Dennett (1978b), in which he imagines his body to be connected by radio links to a detached brain that controls its motions. (C) does not fail in this case, nor need (I) be supposed to fail: for in this story Dennett is simply a widely distributed entity, spatially speaking. Nor need (C) be threatened in a case in which *B*'s central control system is widely distributed in its body, profoundly "modular" in its functional organization, and so on. This case reveals another area of indeterminacy, rather than raising a difficulty of principle.

Condition (I) seems to be the most secure of the four proposed conditions, and (C) simply proposes a restriction on (I). It proposes that only a certain subset of (I)-fulfilling *M*s—the (C)-fulfilling *M*s—are instances of behavior. Some will want to reject the restriction. Certain

ethologists and philosophers may insist that all (O)- and (I)-fulfilling *Ms*
are instances of behavior, and be suspicious of the view that the notion
of a CCS can be made usefully precise. I will consider this view further
below. First let me briefly note a challenge to (I) in the person of Paul.
Paul is literally and entirely puppeted by someone else. He is controlled
by means of some strange body-enclosing force-field device.

Here we may find it natural to talk of Paul's behavior. But it is
arguable that what we discover, when we discover that Paul is utterly
puppeted, is that his apparent behavior is not really behavior (it is
[+O –D –I –C]). Paul behaves, in the widest sense of the term, but only
in the way in which a wooden puppet does, or a pendulum or a body
of gas. And this is no threat to the claim that (I) is a necessary condition
of behavior of the sort that matters to philosophy of mind. Nor is it a
threat if he is controlled by radio links to his brain. In this case, if his
motions are correctly classified as [+O –D +I +C], then they may perhaps
be held to be instances of behavior, although some may take [–D] as
sufficient reason for saying that they are no such thing. Alternatively, it
may be said that the fact that his brain is entirely controlled by a
puppeteer and a radio means that the case should be classified as
[+O –D –I –C] and that his motions should not be counted as behavior
at all. Either way, there is no serious threat to (I) as a necessary condition
of behavior. Condition (I) may also be challenged by the claim that
blinking at a flash of light is behavior and has an external proximal
cause, and here there is no escape from the indeterminacy of 'proximal
cause'. But one may still take it that there is an internal proximal cause
in this case and that (I), in spite of vagueness, is a necessary condition
of behavior.

10.3.6 Doubts about doing

Now consider a mental being *B* and the totality of its (I)-fulfilling *Ms*—
the totality of its internally caused motions or changes. As already
remarked, there is no good reason to suppose that it will always be
possible to achieve complete agreement on which of these motions or
changes are things *B* does, i.e., things which also fulfil (D), even when
all the relevant facts are in. In fact, there is no good reason to suppose
that it would always be possible to achieve complete agreement on which
of them fulfilled (D) even if one had achieved full agreement on what

constituted *B*'s CCS, and could therefore always determine whether or not the (I)-fulfilling *M*s were also (C)-fulfilling *M*s.

I will support this last claim in sections 10.3.7 and 10.3.9. First, though, I want to record an extreme position according to which all (I)-fulfilling *M*s count as behavior on the part of *B*. Some philosophers, ethologists, and experimental psychologists may be initially inclined to accept this, on the grounds that all (I)-fulfilling *M*s must be treated as potential grist for their theoretical mill. But they will be checked by the reflection that even subatomic interactions may then count as behavior on the part of *B*, and this may at first incline them to add the irreducibly vague (O) condition—the condition that the *M*s be ordinarily other-observable—to the (I) condition.

In response to this, it may be wondered why the property of other-observability should be endowed with this sort of theoretical importance. Even if the notion of other-obervability could be made precise—the problems it raises cannot be delayed much longer—a question would remain about why it should be given such a decisive role in sorting out motion or change that is behavior from motion or change that is not behavior. In section 10.4, I will argue that it should not be given this role.

So it is not at all clear that the (O) and (I) account of behavior is tenable. I will raise some more doubts about it later, but the position I want to notice here is not so much the one that claims that (O) and (I) are *sufficient* conditions of behavior but rather the one that denies that (D) and (C) are *necessary* conditions of behavior. It seems that there is undoubtedly a tenable position that rejects (D) and (C), and thereby lets in reflex actions as instances of behavior, whether or not it can get by with just (O) and (I).[11]

The notion of behavior that rejects (D) and (C) is natural for some purposes. Some philosophers take it more or less for granted; others find it highly counterintuitive. One cannot refute either side, but one can introduce terms to mark their difference. Thus one can say that those who reject the necessity of (D) and (C) are interested in "behavior in

11. Someone who denies the necessity of (D) and (C) can agree that (O) and (I) are not sufficient and go on to propose other necessary conditions—such as the adaptive-function condition (F), introduced in section 10.3.8 below.

the broad sense," while those who insist on the necessity of (D) and (C) are interested in "doing-behavior," which may be defined by saying that it fulfills (D), by definition, and also (C), whatever else is true of it.

The insistence on (D) may still not yield a very exclusive notion of behavior, for it may still be thought to let in things like the choosy eating behavior of the ichneumon larva, described earlier. The insistence on (C) may introduce some restrictions, however, for there may be things that we are at first naturally inclined to describe as things that an organism does, although their proximal causes do not lie in (what we are inclined to identify as) its CCS. There is, after all, no reason why evolution (or logical possibility) should feel obliged to involve the CCS in establishing all those adaptive responses that we find it natural to think of as behavior, and as things that the organism as a whole does. It must be possible for the control of adaptive responses that seem like doings to be delegated to systems of the body that are not plausibly thought of as parts of the organism's CCS. Dretske notes a possible example: Sherrington's (1906) description of the way "a fly, settling on a dog's ear, is reflexively flung off *by the ear.*"[12]

There is, however, a natural position according to which it is true by definition that (D) implies (C), so that the fly flinging is best characterized as [+O −D +I −C]. In the end, it comes down to a terminological choice. We may or may not wish to insist that (C) is a condition on doing-behavior. Here I will assume that it is for purposes of exposition.

Is isolating this particular notion of doing-behavior helpful? Condition (D) is irredeemably vague, and condition (C) cannot be supposed to hold out any promise of determinacy either. But once again, this vagueness does not matter. Even if the notion of doing-behavior is vague (just as the standard notion of behavior is vague), it can still be of some use in allowing one to split up uncertainties within the overall notion of behavior into uncertainties at the behavior/not-behavior-at-all dividing line and uncertainties at the doing-behavior/behavior-in-the-broad-sense dividing line.

---

12. Dretske 1988, 24. He also illustrates (pp. 9–11) how natural it is to talk of plant behavior and to distinguish between what plants do and what happens to them.

10.3.7 Doing and the central control system

Every instance of doing-behavior is now by definition a (C)-fulfilling M, but not every (C)-fulfilling M is an instance of doing-behavior, for a (C)-fulfilling M need not fulfil (D), and it can fail to fulfil (D) whether or not it fulfils (O). This gives two categories of Ms caused by CCS activity that are not instances of doing-behavior. Examples of the first ([−O −D +I +C]) might be motions or changes of B's body involved in the drop in B's blood-sugar level, caused by B's doing some hard thinking and not ordinarily other-observable, or neural motions involved in B's dreaming. Examples of the second ([+O −D +I +C]) might be B's eye twitching nervously when B thinks of X, or the motion of Y's hair, given that Y is a member of a race of beings whose hair stands on end when they think hard.

On the materialist view, much activity inside the CCS may fall into a third category, the category [−O +D +I +C], and this too will fail to count as behavior, or doing-behavior, if the condition of being ordinarily other-observable is insisted on. Examples of this might be the motions or changes of B's brain involved in B's mentally calculating the sum of 1485 and 1848, or deciding to ski rather than to swim if offered a choice. Are these motions instances of behavior? Many would say 'No'. And even if they were accepted as instances of behavior, and indeed as instances of doing-behavior, it would still be unclear how much of the activity inside the CCS deserved to be counted as a matter of *doing*. For, first, there are all the motions involved in subexperiential brain processes over which we have no control, so that they arguably do not fulfill (D). Second and more radically, there are good reasons for saying that even thinking, concluding, deciding, etc., are for the most part not so much things we do as things that just happen, so that it is often very questionable whether they fulfil (D). The same is arguably true of most mental activity. What does one actually do when one wants to think about something or work something out? It seems that one somehow sets one's mind in the right direction (perhaps by rapidly and silently repeating key words or sentences to oneself) and waits for something to happen. Then one *has* an idea, it *comes* to one that p, it *occurs* to one that q, it *strikes* one that r, one *realizes* that s, one *sees* that t. That is, something happens; one does not do anything. We naturally talk of thinking, deciding, and so on, as if they were things we do. But that shows very little, for the same is true of sneezing, yawning, dreaming, and tripping over something. Seeing and hearing are also cases that arguably fall into the third, [–O +D +I +C], category. But in their case too, it can be doubted whether they really fulfill (D).[13]

10.3.8   Adaptive function

It may now be suggested that the biologists' notion of *adaptive function* ought to feature in an account of the notion of behavior. A new condition on a motion's being an instance of behavior may be proposed:

(F) M has some adaptive function.[14]

Condition (F) purports to be a general condition on anything's being an instance of behavior, but it will be particularly helpful to invoke it in certain cases, e.g., in the case of motions that we are inclined to think of as behavior but are not inclined to think of as (D)-fulfilling doings. Why? Because an initially attractive suggestion about the notion of behavior is that a motion or change M that is truly an instance of behavior must have an explanation that shows it to have a certain point or purpose; so that when it is not natural to think of M as something done, something that can either be explained in terms of fully fledged reasons for action, or at least in terms of something like reasons for action (e.g., in the case of lower animals), it seems that it must at least be possible to explain M in terms of its possession of some adaptive function.[15]

---

13. In this respect, seeing and hearing may be compared with watching and listening, which clearly fulfill (D). What this shows, once again, is that the boundaries of the notion of doing-behavior are very vague. It also shows that the Weather Watchers are not, strictly speaking, well named (as Nicholas Nathan pointed out to me).

14. More strictly speaking, it is the disposition to make M-type motions in certain circumstances that is selected for, and whose presence in B is explained in terms of its adaptive function. For a development of this view, see Millikan 1993, chap. 7. Note that the disposition to make M-type motions in certain circumstances—call it d—may itself have arisen as a result of the exercise of a more general capacity: the capacity—call it c—to learn various types of behavior. The explanation of the presence of d in terms of adaptive function will thus be mediated by an explanation of the presence of c in terms of adaptive function.

15. Explanation in terms of reasons, or something like reasons, may be said to reduce ultimately to explanation in terms of adaptive function, since possession of the general capacity to act for reasons, or something like reasons, may itself be explained in terms of its adaptive function.

It seems, however, that possession of adaptive function is not a necessary condition of M's being an instance of behavior. For (1) much human behavior has no adaptive function, although it essentially involves the exercise of faculties that do have such a function. (2) Malfunctions may count as behavior—as "behavioral disorders"—but have no adaptive function (consider gesticulations caused by a "brainstorm"). (3) A species could exhibit some highly distinctive behavior pattern that had no adaptive function but rather occurred simply because its cause was accidentally but tightly genetically linked to some other trait that did have an adaptive function. (4) Members of a species could acquire a very distinctive behavior pattern as a result of the influence of chance cosmic radiation.

The fourth objection may be thought to be superficial, but it does provide a counterexample to the proposed condition. As for the third objection, it may be said that one can formulate a disjunctive necessary condition of M's being an instance of behavior according to which M is an instance of behavior only if

[F′] M has a reasons-citing explanation, or an adaptive-function-citing explanation, or occurs because it is tightly but accidentally genetically linked to possession of a disposition that does have an adaptive function.

And I suppose one can. But even the weak claim that possessing adaptive function is some sort of (occasionally defeasible) necessary condition of M's being an instance of behavior seems implausible.

Some may now say that their working notion of behavior is best captured by a definition that insists on (I) and has as its second condition the disjunction (O) or (F). This denies the necessity of other-observability, and also of possessing adaptive function, while ruling out subatomic interactions in B as instances of behavior and ruling in behavioral disorders of the sort mentioned above. But it looks ad hoc, and it still implausibly counts things like the production of antibodies (and indeed anything that has an explanation in terms of adaptive function) as behavior on the part of B.

10.3.9 The place of the central control system
My last comment concerns the notion of a central control system or CCS. As remarked, it is a vague notion. In section 10.3.6, I suggested that M's

being caused by the CCS should be held to be a necessary condition of *M*'s counting as an instance of doing-behavior, but this suggestion does not seem likely to be of much practical or theoretical help in distinguishing doing-behavior from behavior in the broad sense. Suppose that one set oneself the task of trying to establish what counted as doing-behavior on the part of an unfamiliar or alien being *B*. One might well not be able to establish any clear, purely physiological criterion for determining what it was reasonable to count as part of *B*'s CCS, that one could then use to help to determine which motions or changes counted as doing-behavior. That is, one might well be unable to establish any clear criterion of CCS-hood that one could apply independently of one's intuitive judgments about what it was reasonable to count as *B*'s doing-behavior, even if merely structural features of its body were highly suggestive.

There are other difficulties. It seems that there is one important restricted sense of the word 'behavior' (the sense here represented by the word 'doing-behavior') according to which it is correct to say that fulfilling (C)—being CCS-caused—is a necessary condition of being an instance of behavior. But many things that fulfill (C) are not instances of doing-behavior, as remarked in section 10.3.7. And if we take the human brain and central nervous system as the human CCS, then it includes the hypothalamus, which is itself the central control system of the autonomic nervous system, whose activities are not plausibly thought of as instances of doing-behavior. Finally, there is the chicken that runs around after its head has been cut off. It seems that the running is something that the chicken does, although it has lost its CCS.

There are various possible responses to this admittedly unimportant case. Those who accept that (D) entails (C) may say either that what it shows is that a sufficient amount of the chicken's CCS remains, so that the running is [+O +D +I +C], or that it is not really true that the chicken does something in this case. Others may deny that (D) entails (C), as in the case of Sherrington's dog. They may claim that we can have good physiological grounds for identifying *B*'s CCS in such a way that some of the things that deserve to be counted as things that *B* does do not have their proximal cause in the CCS.

This is the same old pattern of disagreement, and the conclusion to be drawn from it is the same old conclusion: there is little hope of achieving precision in this area, little hope of specifying a criterion of what counts as doing-behavior that will deal with every difficult case. There are multiple and divergent pressures on our use of the word 'behavior' in the philosophy of mind, and my present purpose is simply to illustrate this fact.

10.4 Other-observability

I will now discuss condition (O), according to which instances of behavior (and doing-behavior) must be ordinarily other-observable. It is open to two main objections. The first is that it is vague to the point of vacuity; the second is that it is simply incorrect. Neither objection is new, but both are worth restating.

According to the first objection, condition (O) is hopelessly vague because what is ordinarily other-observable depends on who is observing. There may be rational beings whose highly efficient activities we could discern only under a high-powered microscope. It would not be plausible to say that their activities cannot be counted as behavior, because they are not ordinarily observable by us. Nor can we rule out the possibility that there are purposive beings, and indeed rational agents, whose physical activities are so small, or perhaps so big, that they would be unobservable by us whatever extensions of our senses we were able to achieve by artificial means.

What *we* can observe cannot matter. But then, who does matter? Any motion or change in a mental being will be ordinarily observable by some possible being. So if we change condition (O) to 'M is ordinarily observable by some possible being', it will exclude nothing. If we want to preserve condition (O) in any nonvacuous form, we have to draw some line, and perhaps the unexpressed intuition behind the requirement is that the motions should be ordinarily observable by other creatures of the same sort, or perhaps of the same general size, as the creature under study. But there may be creatures with very limited perceptual powers who are almost completely insensitive to each others' behavior, and there is no conceptually necessary relation between a creature's size and the size of the objects it can perceive, even if the laws of physics may impose certain restrictions.

10.4.1 Mental action as behavior

So condition (O) is vague. But a more fundamental objection now arises. Why on earth are epistemological facts about observers thought to have any place at all in an account of what behavior is? Many philosophers have thought that they must have such a place. I will consider two simple cases and argue that this is wrong.

The first case reacts to the fact that the account of behavior with which we standardly operate wrongly excludes mental actions like doing mental arithmetic, on a natural interpretation of the other-observability condition. It may immediately be objected that doing mental arithmetic can be counted as behavior, given condition (O), because it is (somehow) identical with certain neural processes that are potentially other-observable. But this is the wrong sort of objection. There are, I think, decisive a priori reasons for saying that mental actions like mental arithmetic ought to be counted as instances of behavior, and it would be misguided and inadequate to make the truth of the claim that mental action is behavior depend on the possible truth of the materialist hypothesis that mental action is (somehow) identical with potentially other-observable brain activity. If there are good reasons for calling mental actions behavior, they ought to be as compelling for dualists and immaterialists as they are for materialists.

Here is case 1. One is listening to the radio, and the voice says, "Take the number 7. Square it. Add 1. Divide by 2. Multiply by 3. Add 6. Take the square root. Take the square root again. Subtract 3. Multiply by infinity. Subtract 1. Take the square root." What happens? One does what one does mentally. One reaches an answer, step by step. One has certain experiences. But there is, in the standard sense of the word, no behavior involved in what one does mentally, although the way one sits or holds one's head still may be said to be a matter of behavior.

It is fairly mysterious what one does, as the answer comes to one. But whatever it is that just happens, it still seems correct to say that the calculation, taken as a whole, is something one does and does intentionally.[16]

---

16. Those who find this sort of mental arithmetic very easy may find it helpful to take a more difficult example and observe what happens when someone asks them to calculate something like 39×47, or 139×147, in their head. Some calculating geniuses, when they hear a mental-arithmetic question, find the answer coming to them without experiencing any intervening conscious mental

Why, then, exclude intentional actions of this kind from counting as behavior while including other actions? Why draw the Great Behavior Line—the supposedly momentous theoretical line that divides B's behavior, on the one hand, from everything going on in B that is not behavior at all, on the other hand—between doing mental arithmetic and doing other-observable things like scratching one's head and writing figures on paper? Why draw the line between two sorts of thing that ought to be classified very closely together by a good theory of mind, since they differ in a way that is just not very important, theoretically speaking, given that one's interest is in mental beings and all their doings?

It is not hard to explain this drawing of the Great Behavior Line. Recent philosophy of mind has evolved in the context of public-domain positivism, and given public-domain positivism, behavior *must* be (ordinarily) other-observable if the notion of behavior is to play a central role in a satisfactory account of mind. Some philosophers, following Wittgenstein, Quine, and Davidson, have reached this conclusion specifically as a result of reflections on the nature of language (see section 8.3 above). But the philosophical question returns. Why should other-observability be taken to be so important when it is the mind (of all things) and its activities that is in question? It seems overwhelmingly natural to say that if a woman listening to a radio decides to engage in answering mental arithmetic questions, what follows is a certain sort of behavior on her part. She may also be driving a car, but there is no more reason to say that her driving is behavior while her mental arithmetic is not than to say that her mental arithmetic is behavior while her driving is not. She may be lying in a state of complete relaxation when the radio program begins and engage in the mental arithmetic with no perceptible change in her posture. It is still true that what follows is a certain sort of behavior on her part. She is, after all, doing something, in the sense of this loose word that contrasts doing things with things merely happening to one, and it is very natural to suppose that all such doing, other-observable or not, is behavior. To do something just is to behave in a certain way. Even to daydream is to behave in a certain way, and when we restrict attention to intentional doing, the case can only

---

goings-on. There is a good description of this in Gregory 1987 under the heading "Calculating Genius," but it is not the normal case.

be strengthened. (This is the a priori point I mentioned earlier. It is worth noting that it is a contingent fact about us that concentration on mental arithmetic tends to affect our observable behavior in some way. We might have had a capacity for multitrack attention given which this was not the case.)

In sum, mental actions tend not to be thought of as instances of behavior, for reasons that may be traced back to the influence of public-domain positivism. But these reasons are not good reasons from the point of view of philosophy. Nor are they good reasons from the point of view of science: they are not good reasons from the point of view of ethology or the theory of evolution. From the general ethological and evolutionary point of view, a being's mental doings are just as much part of what it is "designed" by natural selection to engage in as its larger-scale other-observable doings. Its mental doings are just as much part of *the overall way it is designed to behave*—as we may naturally say.

10.4.2 Mental activity as behavior

Case 1 questions whether the standard definition of behavior is adequate, given that it excludes certain sorts of mental action, and goes on to suggest that the definition of behavior should be expanded to include mental actions like mental arithmetic. Case 2 suggests that the standard definition should be further expanded to include certain mental goings-on that do not involve action at all.

Here is case 2. Compare the following two stories.

1. X is sitting on a bench and sees Y in the distance. This causes him [1] to start adjusting his clothes, and [2] to start arranging his hair in a semiautomatic fashion. [3] His pulse rate goes up. [4] He crosses his legs, uncrosses them, and crosses them again. [5] His fingers fidget automatically and unconsciously, and [6] his right eyebrow twitches nervously and minutely.

All this, except for (3), may be thought to count as behavior on the part of X (there may be argument about the eyebrow). No doubt some of it, but not all, also counts as action.

2. On a later occasion X sees Y again. He is exhausted and does not move observably, but the sight of Y causes [1] the involuntary onset

of a very vivid and gloomy train of thought. It also causes [2] a powerful feeling of sick depression. It gives rise to [3] a kind of automatic
mental fidgeting, featuring strong images of places and memories of
embarrassing scenes, and [4] once again his pulse rate goes up. We
may also suppose that it causes him [5] to try to turn his thought
away from Y by silently reciting George Herbert's poem "The Pulley."

On the second occasion it seems that there is no canonical behavior
at all. (Those convinced by the discussion of case 1 can allow that (5)
is behavior.) But the two cases obviously have something important in
common: in both cases equally, a perception causes a great deal of
reactive activity in X.[17] Some of this reactive activity is other-observable,
and is called 'behavior', and some of it is not other-observable, and so
is not called 'behavior'. But—once again—is the line drawn by this use
of the word 'behavior' really of importance? All the activity in the two
cases falls equally under the heading of 'reactive activity going on in X
and caused by a perception'. And it is arguable that when one thinks in
general philosophical terms about the mental, about mental states and
occurrences and about their effects, one should make the general category of (CCS-caused or CCS-involving) reactive activity theoretically
primary. One should not concentrate just on those aspects of reactive
activity that happen to be other-observable and are most naturally called
'behavior' for bad reasons derived from an indefensible commitment to
public-domain positivism. One should not invest the distinction between
the non-other-observable mental effects of a perception and the observable, large-scale-bodily-motion-involving effects of that perception with
a theoretical significance that it simply does not have.

In a word, one should not be so fixed on *overt* behavior—to use a
once common adjective that explicitly marks the possibility of recogniz-
ing the existence of nonovert, non-other-observable behavior. The difference between the other-observable finger fidgeting in the first story
and the mental fidgeting in the second story is not much more important
than the difference between observable finger fidgeting and observable
toe fidgeting. In both cases there is a sense in which we have the same

17. I understand the word 'activity' in such a way that there may be *activity*
without any sort of intentional *action* or any *doing*. There is a great deal of
activity in a rumbling volcano.

thing: a certain kind of nervous activity on the part of X caused by the sight of Y.

One may compare this case with the task of giving a comprehensive account of what goes on on the stage at an opera. The distinction between [a] the activity in X that counts as canonical behavior because it is other-observable and [b] the reactive activity in X that does not count as canonical behavior because it is not other-observable seems to be as about as important as the distinction between [a] what a member of the audience sees and [b] what she doesn't see because her view of the stage is partly obscured by a pillar.[18]

10.4.3 Summary

I have three main points. First, the notion of behavior standardly employed in the philosophy of mind is wrongly limited to other-observable behavior. There is no good philosophical reason for this, even if there once seemed to be good scientific and experimental reasons for it. If the notion of behavior is going to continue to incorporate an other-observability condition it should be expelled from its central position in the philosophy of mind. The alternative is to expand it to include mental actions, at least, i.e., non-other-observable goings-on like mental arithmetic, silently reciting poetry, and so on.

Second, the notion of an organism's *reactive activity* is more fundamental than the standard notion of its behavior, when it comes to considering the nature of mind. Reactive activity may or may not be other-observable. To think that the other-observable parts of an organism's reactive activity have some sort of special importance in a philo-

---

18. This discussion focuses on examples of conscious mental reactive activity, but it is fully compatible with the view that most mental reactive activity has no conscious aspect and may nonetheless be properly counted as behavior. Obviously, it is no part of the present position to claim that non-other-observable mental goings-on are ignored by contemporary philosophy of mind. They are explicitly recognized in standard formulations of functionalism, which characterizes types of mental state or occurrence not only by reference to their typical other-observable causes and effects (the "physical-stimulus inputs" and "behavioral outputs") but also by reference to their typical non-other-observable mental causes and effects (their typical relations to "other mental states and occurrences"). It does not, however, normally include any of the latter in the category of behavior.

sophical account of the nature of mind is to give facts about an *evidential perspective* on the mental completely the wrong weight in one's account of the *nature* of the mental. On the present view, behavior as ordinarily understood, i.e., other-observable reactive activity, is of interest only because it is one of the possible kinds of reactive activity. It is of no further special interest. It is a mistake to suppose that its *epistemological* importance, when it comes to attributing mental states and occurrences to others, confers any special *metaphysical* significance on it, when it comes to asking about the essential nature of mind. Realism about the mental denies that there is any valid argument from the nature of language or meaning to the conclusion that other-observable reactive activity has any such special significance. (A Wittgensteinian version of this argument was challenged in chapter 8.) There is no fundamental sense in which "the epistemology of mind is constitutive of its nature" (McGinn 1982, 7), as some followers of Wittgenstein and Davidson, in particular, have held. The strangeness of this view is increased by the fact that many have construed it, more precisely, as the view that it is the third-person, public-domain epistemology of mind that is fundamentally constitutive of its nature.

It may be thought that philosophical *naturalism* somehow supports the view that the standard category of behavior should be given special importance. But naturalism (which we may take to incorporate a commitment to the truth of the theory of evolution) provides no good reason to treat other-observable reactive activity as in any way more important than non-other-observable reactive activity. As far as natural selection is concerned, reactive activity obviously does not have to be other-observable to be selected for. It just has to have survival value. One of the key events in human evolution occurs when human beings begin to get very good at worrying, at imagining what might happen if . . . and at anticipating the mental calculations of others (see Humphrey 1983). What can we say about this? We can say that they begin to engage, with increasing proficiency, in certain new and sophisticated forms of behavior, forms of behavior whose unobservability (at the time of their occurrence) is essential to the selective advantage they confer.

The third point is this: If one is going to extend the term 'behavior' to cover non-other-observable mental goings-on, then there is no reason to restrict it to mental *actions* like mental arithmetic. These are clear instances of intentional doings. So they are doing-behavior if they are behavior at all. But if one accepts that the category of behavior is wider than the category of doing-behavior when one considers the other-observable realm (see p. 301), it seems that one should, in consistency, take the same attitude when one considers the non-other-observable realm, and that one should therefore classify many mental goings-on that are not plausibly seen as actions as behavior—dreaming, for example, or having ideas or worrying unstoppably as one lies awake at night (compare fidgeting). The distinction between motions or changes that count as instances of behavior because they are intentional doings and motions or changes that count as instances of behavior although they are not intentional doings makes as much sense in the non-other-observable realm as it does in the other-observable realm.

Here I am encouraged by Gleitman, who writes as follows in a standard psychology textbook: "Dreams as conscious mental experiences are essentially private; they go on 'inside the individual'. As such dreams can be regarded as a form of behavior that is looked at from within" (1986, 21). Millikan is also happy to talk of "inner behaviors, such as thinking processes" (1993, 133), and Ryle agrees, insofar as he includes such things as "dwelling in imagination on possible disasters" under the heading of behavior (Ryle 1949, 129; see Hornsby 1986, 100) (such a dwelling in imagination may be thought of either as something one does or as something that happens). In fact, this quotation from Ryle's *Concept of Mind* comes from a list of things that one is prone (disposed) to do if one believes that the ice is thin, and there is no proof that Ryle is thinking of it specifically as behavior. But he sometimes talks explicitly of "overt" behavior (pp. 33, 309), and he does not intend this phrase to be pleonastic. Elsewhere he includes dreaming and "suddenly [seeing] in my mind's eye an uninteresting street corner of a town I hardly know" under the heading of behavior (p. 307), and he appears to suggest that for a man "to indulge in roseate daydreams about his own successes, to avoid recalling past failures and to plan for his own advancement" is for him "to behave in certain ways" (p. 83). Clearly, then, the present suggestion is not new, although most current uses of the word 'behavior' conform to a more narrow understanding of the word.

10.5 Neo-neobehaviorism

Having enlarged the notion of behavior in this way, I can come out as a partial neobehaviorist, or neo-neobehaviorist. A vast amount of mental activity is now itself a matter of behavior, and so it is trivially true that we must refer to behavior in giving an adequate account of mind. Thinking, worrying, reasoning, imagining, craving—these are modes of behavior, whether they are doings or happenings. Absent-minded day-dreaming is behavior, as is absent-minded thumb-twiddling. Dreaming is behavior. Mental arithmetic is as much behavior as paper-and-pen arith-metic. The first simple question, when one wants to generate candidate instances of behavior, is 'What is X doing?' While it is certainly not true that all the natural answers to this question deliver instances of behavior (X is tripping over something; X is falling through space), the list of answers that do deliver instances of behavior extends far into the mental realm.

Neobehaviorism is still false for mental phenomena like pain, however. More generally, reference to behavior can be dispensed with in giving an account of what is arguably most distinctive of mind (see further chapter 11), for it can be dispensed with in giving an account of the essential nature of any aspect of the qualitative character of experience. (Unless, of course, having such experience is itself classed as a form of behavior. On this last view, the thesis of neobehaviorism becomes truly trivial.)

I think that the enlarged notion of behavior is theoretically superior to the one it replaces and should be adopted—or much more explicitly adopted—by neobehaviorists as well as everyone else. To do so, how-ever, is to abandon the old motivations for neobehaviorism entirely. It is to abandon the reductionist motivations for neobehaviorism. It is to abandon the idea that a definition of the mental partly in terms of behavior might, as such, be part of a definition of the mental in nonmental terms. It is to abandon an old, deep commitment to public-domain positivism, according to which the reason why reference to behavior is so important in an account of the mental is that an adequate account of the nature of the mental must be given partly or wholly in terms of publicly observable phenomena.

On the present view, behavioral phenomena are not necessarily publicly observable phenomena; nor are they even characteristically or paradigmatically publicly observable phenomena. If reference to behavior is important or essential in an adequate account of the fundamental nature of mind (as it surely is), it is not because reference to publicly observable phenomena is. And if reference to publicly observable phenomena is important or essential in an adequate account of the fundamental nature of mind (a dubious view), it is not because reference to behavior is. Is this obvious? Very well then it is obvious (as Walt Whitman might have said).

11

The Concept of Mind

The nonmental, the publicly observable, and the behavioral as ordinarily understood—these things do not have the place they are commonly supposed to have in a correctly centered account of the nature of mind. This is the main negative claim of this book.

It may be said that this claim is easily established: all one has to do is to prove that idealism and immaterialism are not incoherent, however implausible they may seem. But the negative claim as expounded in this book does not rest on a defense of idealism or immaterialism. It would stand even if it could be shown that some form of materialism is true.

Less has been said about how a positive account of the nature of mind should go. Sometimes it seems that the only thing that is completely clear is that reference to experience must have a central place in such an account. By 'experience' I mean conscious experience, the phenomenon of life's having rich experiential content from moment to moment. The term 'experience' has no theoretical charge. It refers only to something with which every normal human being is profoundly familiar.

Does anything nonexperiential have a similarly central place? Some still think that behavior and behavioral dispositions do. Some go further and say that experience is relatively unimportant in an account of the nature of mind. They go too far. Others go further. They deny the very existence of experience, as ordinarily understood. This is invigorating, and it may perhaps be dialectically aerobic, but it is also mad.[1] One does not have to displace the experiential from a central position in one's

---

1. Here is a theory about why this claim gets made: There really are near-perfect zombies, in the technical philosophical sense. That is, there are experienceless human beings whose general patterns of behavior are nearly but not quite

account of mind to be a sensible and realistic materialist or naturalist. Obviously, there is a ghost in the machine, if to say this is to say that there is experience or consciousness. The correct naturalistic, materialist response to this is not to deny the obvious. It is rather to admit it and to stress that we don't yet understand the machinery of the ghost, given our current theory of the nature of matter. There is no conflict between acknowledging the absolute centrality of the experiential in any plausible account of the nature of mind while making the point that there are very strong, if ultimately inconclusive, reasons for thinking that the existence of mind as we know it depends on the existence of something nonexperiential (see section 5.12). (Note that 'nonexperiential' doesn't entail 'nonmental', a point discussed below.)

Some think that philosophy should look to developments in artificial intelligence (AI) for answers. It is a mistake, however, to suppose that developments in AI support neobehaviorism in any way, or oblige us to admit that the realm of the mental, and of mental beings, is larger than we used to think. The opposite view is at least as plausible: what developments in AI show us is that the realm of the distinctively mental is actually smaller than we used to think, since so many of the abilities or properties that we used to think of as distinctively and essentially mental can now be seen to be possessed by things that are experienceless, and are not mental beings at all. If this is right, developments in AI will not lead progressively to a general recognition that mind has nothing essentially to do with consciousness or experience. On the contrary, they will lend increasingly strong support to the view that the only thing that is distinctively and essentially mental is precisely experience or consciousness.

To adopt this view as a materialist is to endorse a kind of naturalized Cartesianism about the mind. According to naturalized Cartesianism, only experiential phenomena (which are entirely physical phenomena, on this view) are distinctively mental phenomena. This position has many attractions, moderated as it is by the word 'distinctively'. Whatever is

---

identical to those of normal human beings, who have experience. The most striking difference in the zombies' behavior, as compared with that of normal human beings, is this: when they do philosophy of mind, they get attracted to radical eliminativism of one sort or another.

necessary for mind, experience is the only thing that is incontestably *sufficient*.

The core of the position defended in this book may be summarized as follows.

• It accepts commonsense experiential realism outright. It not only insists that there is experience or consciousness—for this is a form of words with which few philosophers would quarrel (the trouble is that some of them then go on to give accounts of the nature of experience or consciousness that amount to a denial of its existence); it also insists that there is a crucial respect in which there is no sort of error or inadequacy in the ordinary person's view of what experience or consciousness is or is like. It insists that this is so even though the scientific story of how experience arises and comes to have the character it does is in many ways highly surprising (Dennett 1991b presents a good survey of cases).

• It accepts "intentional realism." That is, it accepts that statements attributing beliefs and desires (propositional attitudes in general) to human beings can be and often are simply true, even while holding that so-called dispositional mental states are not, strictly speaking, mentally contentful states (section 6.6). It also accepts that explanations of actions in terms of beliefs and desires and other propositional-attitude states can be and often are simply true.

• It rejects neobehaviorism. It rejects the view that mental life is linked to behavior in such a way that reference to behavior enters essentially, centrally, and constitutively into any adequate account of the essential nature of the mental—where 'behavior' is understood in the ordinary imprecise way to mean 'observable behavior'. It holds that even if materialism is true, mind—beliefs, desires, emotions, sensations, thoughts, and so on—can exist in the complete absence of behavior, as ordinarily understood, and in the complete absence of dispositions to such behavior. It holds that the correct account of the meaning of a word like 'pain', for example, does not require one to make any reference to behavior: 'pain' is just a word for a private sensation considered entirely independently of any publicly observable phenomenon. Similarly, it holds that a satisfactory answer to the question 'What is desire?' or 'What is belief?' does not strictly require one to make reference to behavior or behavioral dispositions. (Weather Watcher philosophers who lack any conception of action or behavior do not ipso facto have defective or incomplete concepts of desire or belief, any more than they have a defective or incomplete concept of pain. If we think otherwise, we are blinded by our own case.) Finally, it holds that neobehaviorism fails to be generally true even when the notion of behavior is expanded in the way suggested in section 10.4, so that many mental goings-on come to be counted as behavior.

I take these three claims to be central to a correct account of the nature of mind, and hence to the concept of mind. Mind, I suggest, is very much what ordinary people think it is. I do not, however, take it to be a general truth—still less an analytic truth, as some have believed—that what most ordinary people think must be right when it comes to the analysis of such highly general concepts as the concept of mind. Such a view is clearly false.

The claims just stated are central. Within their scope, however, there is room for disagreement about the minimal case of mind, and this deserves some further comment. As observed in chapter 6, it is helpful to have a view about the entailment relations between three predicates—'mental', 'experiential', and 'mentally contentful'—when trying to delimit the scope of mind, and there are six possibilities:

mental → experiential   [1]

mental → mentally contentful   [2]

experiential → mental   [3]

experiential → mentally contentful   [4]

mentally contentful → mental   [5]

mentally contentful → experiential   [6]

I take it that (3), (4), and (5) are clearly true and must form a part of any acceptable concept of mind. In contrast, (1), (2), and (6) are debatable, and various positions arise from the fact that they can be judged true or false in various combinations. Others will add

mental → occurs in an experiencing being   [7]

as something else that they believe to be true, but let me first set out the possibilities arising from the debatability of (1), (2), and (6). Initially there are eight (table 11.1), but (ii) through (v) are ruled out, since (3), (4), and (5) are indisputable—(ii) because (1) and (5) entail (6), (iii) because (1) and (4) entail (2), (iv) because (1) and (4) entail (2) and because (1) and (5) entail (6), and (v) because (2) and (6) entail (1).

That leaves (i), (vi), (vii), and (viii). They are by now familiar, but they are worth restatement. Once the options are set out, the air clears

Table 11.1
Possible combinations of entailment relations (1), (2), and (6)

Entailment relation	Combination							
	i	ii	iii	iv	v	vi	vii	viii
(1)	T	T	T	T	F	F	F	F
(2)	T	T	F	F	T	T	F	F
(6)	T	F	T	F	T	F	T	F

T = true, F = false.

a little. One is not obliged to commit oneself to one rather than another. It is, I think, a significant fact about the concept of mind that it is possible for one to see the force of both (i) and (viii), although they contradict each other on all the three points at issue.

Position (i) is strong or all-out naturalized Cartesianism: all mental phenomena are mentally contentful phenomena (and, of course, conversely), and all truly mentally contentful phenomena are experiential phenomena (and, of course, conversely). Hence all truly mental phenomena are experiential phenomena (and, of course, conversely).

Supporters of position (vi) grant that all mental phenomena are mentally contentful but deny that all mental phenomena are experiential. They allow that some nonexperiential phenomena—such as many of the processes that underlie thought or speech—may correctly be called 'mental' even though they are not experiential, and therefore also allow that some nonexperiential processes may be mentally contentful. (This claim was rejected for dispositional phenomena in chapter 6 and treated with slightly more sympathy in the case of occurrent phenomena [pp. 168–170], although it is not clear that there is good reason to be more generous in the case of occurrent phenomena.)

Supporters of position (vii) agree with supporters of position (vi) in denying that 'mental' entails 'experiential'. But they also deny that 'mental' entails 'mentally contentful', and they insist that 'mentally contentful' entails 'experiential'. They hold, that is, that the only acceptable model for mentally contentful states or occurrences is that of experiential states or occurrences: nothing else has mental content, strictly speaking. They do not, however, conclude that all mental states or occurrences are experiential, because they allow that nonexperiential processes can be truly mental processes although they are not mentally contentful. Examples might be the phenomenon of grasping a thought (see pp. 141–142, 173–174) and certain other nonexperiential processes that subserve thought and speech, tennis playing and sculpture; or equally, the processes that subserve dogs' catching balls and frogs' catching flies. A Searlean might include our automatic, nonexperiential exercises of those "background" capacities that are necessary for much of our conscious mental life to be as it is, in the class of mental processes. Searle allows that there is a sense in which processes that have no mental content may be called mental processes (1992, 239–240).

Position (viii) is the most inclusive position. Supporters of position (viii) hold not only that there can be nonexperiential mental phenomena and that mental phenomena need not be mentally contentful, but also that mentally contentful phenomena need not be experiential. They disagree with position (vii) only on this last point and, like the supporters of position (vi), may be motivated by cases like that of the post-hypnotic command (considered on pp. 168–169) to say that there are nonexperiential processes that can nonetheless be thought of as genuinely mentally contentful.

Here, I suggest, we have a diagram of some of the inclinations that govern use of the word 'mental'. To complete the diagram, it may be added that (i) entails (7), and that all three of (vi), (vii), and (viii) can be held in conjunction with (7). In fact, (7) puts a strong and interesting constraint on positions (vi) to (viii), a constraint that may be accepted by many who favor one or the other of them.

To deny (7) is to allow that entirely experienceless entities—constitutionally and permanently experienceless entities—can have genuine mental properties and be in genuine mental states. It is natural to suppose that the word 'mental' won't stretch that far, but one rough argument for the stretch was mentioned in chapter 6, and goes as follows: So far as the natural biological order is concerned, a mind is just a control system of a certain degree of complexity. It may well be that mind is found in nature only in beings that are capable of moving around on their own, but there is no sharp principle that allows us to say where mind begins. It must be conceded that experience is sufficient for mind. It is not obvious that it is necessary.

Here we have a position that denies (7) in a way that does not seem entirely unnatural. There may, however, be a hidden bias in its proponents' apparent willingness to allow that naturally evolved experienceless beings may be said to have minds. For once one has allowed that naturally evolved experienceless beings may have minds, it is not at all clear that one can plausibly deny minds to experienceless chess computers, or to experienceless coleopteroid robots, like "Genghis Khan," that can move around on their own, take evasive action, and so on. And yet quite a number of those who are inclined to ascribe mind to the desert ant *Cataglyphus*—even if they think that *Cataglyphus* is experienceless— will be unwilling to ascribe it to chess computers and robots that they presume to be experienceless. Their bias will be toward naturally evolved organisms that have their place in the great chain of biological being, even when they are explicit in their acceptance of the view that the experienceless may have minds. It will be the picture of the great natural continuum that is swaying them—together, perhaps, with a somewhat abstract use of the word 'mind' that treats particular creatures as individually insignificant manifestations of the great, general, natural phenomenon of Mind. (Perhaps this is "naturalized Hegelianism.")

I think some will find this bias in themselves, but remarks about bias invite immediate denial even when (or perhaps particularly when) they are true, and there are doubtless some who have never been biased in this way. The fact remains that those who are prepared to ascribe mind to naturally evolved creatures that they take to be experienceless have no good reason to deny it to complex experienceless machines like chess computers. They need to assess their attitude to (7) in the light of this. If they persist in rejecting (7), they face the problem of where to draw a line when considering increasingly less complex experienceless machines. This problem has no plausible, nonarbitary solution. Those who have come this far will find it hard to resist some version of Dennettian instrumentalism, according to which we may find it natural or practically indispensable to adopt the "intentional stance" to some machines and not others, that being all that needs to be said, or that can be said (see Dennett 1987).

We are left, then, with seven views. There is (i), which entails (7), and there are the six views that result from coupling (vi), (vii), and (viii) with the acceptance or rejection of (7). The concept of mind is an essentially contestable concept, and it is animated partly by the disputes between these seven views, which interact in various ways with the disputes and partial compatibilities between a number of more familiarly named contestants: functionalism, behaviorism, instrumentalism, eliminativism, intentional realism, cognitivism, materialism, immaterialism, dualism, epiphenomenalism, parallelism, and so on. In philosophical discussion, the concept of mind behaves like a steel-bobbed pendulum suspended above a number of magnets. Perhaps Ryle appreciated this when he said that his book *The Concept of Mind* was "a generation book"—by which he meant a one-generation book. Perhaps his purpose was not simply to dislodge the pendulum from one point of near equilibrium to another (or the other, on one crude view of the dynamics of the system), but rather to set the system in motion by giving the pendulum a strong push in one direction.

Sober naturalism requires us to recover an understanding of the relative conceptual autonomy of the mental. If my position needs to be categorized, it is materialist intentional realism that respects some of the intuitions behind functionalism, rejects all the other positions, accepts (3), (4), (5), and (7), and is agnostic on (1), (2), and (6). This agnosticism allows it to be respectful of—affectionately inclined toward—outright naturalized Cartesianism, which endorses all of (1), (2), and (6), while remaining disposed to accept that there are contexts in which it is natural (within the scope of (7)) to deny all of (1), (2), and (6).

I have little doubt that this view is roughly correct (the doubt attaches only to the commitment to materialism). It seems that we are finally emerging from one of the strangest episodes in the history of philosophy: the widespread subjection of the philosophy of mind in the twentieth century to the magnificently inappropriate principles of public-domain positivism. This subjection took many forms, and some of them were extremely instructive. Those that appealed to facts about language and meaning were in many respects subtle and beautiful. But they contained no truths that are radically incompatible with something close to the commonsense view of mind.

References

Anscombe, G. E. M. 1957. *Intention.* Oxford: Blackwell.

Armstrong, D. M. 1981. "The Nature of Mind." In D. M. Armstrong, *The Nature of Mind.* Brighton: Harvester Press.

Armstrong, D. M. 1981. "The Causal Theory of the Mind." In D. M. Armstrong, *The Nature of Mind.* Brighton: Harvester Press.

Ayers, M. R., 1991. *Locke.* London: Routledge.

Berkeley, G. 1975. *Philosophical Works*, edited by M. R. Ayers. London: Dent.

Block, N. 1978. "Troubles with Functionalism." In *Perception and Cognition Issues in the Foundations of Psychology*, Minnesota Studies in the Philosophy of Science, no. 9.

Block, N. 1986. "Advertisement for a Semantics for Psychology." In *Studies in the Philosophy of Mind*, Midwest Studies in Philosophy, no. 10.

Burge, T. 1979. "Individualism and the Mental." In *Studies in Epistemology*, Midwest Studies in Philosophy, no. 4.

Burge, T. 1989. "Individuation and Causation in Psychology." *Pacific Philosophical Quarterly* 70:303.

Carnap, R. 1956. "Empiricism, Semantics, and Ontology." In R. Carnap, *Meaning and Necessity.* Chicago: University of Chicago Press.

Carroll, L. 1895. "What the Tortoise Said to Achilles." *Mind* 4:278.

Churchland, P. M. 1984. *Matter and Consciousness.* Cambridge: MIT Press.

Churchland, P. M. 1986. "Some Reductive Strategies in Cognitive Neurobiology." *Mind* 95:279.

Cottingham, J. 1988. *The Rationalists.* Oxford: Oxford University Press.

Craig, E. 1982. "Meaning, Use, and Privacy." *Mind* 91:541.

Crane, T., and Mellor, D. H. 1990. "There Is No Question of Physicalism." *Mind* 99:185.

Cussins, A. 1990. "The Connectionist Construction of Concepts." In *The Philosophy of Artificial Intelligence*, edited by Margaret A. Boden. Oxford: Oxford University Press.

Davidson, D. 1984. "Belief and the Basis of Meaning." In D. Davidson, *Truth and Interpretation*. Oxford: Clarendon Press.

Davidson, D. 1987. "Knowing One's Own Mind." *Proceedings and Addresses of the American Philosophical Association*, p. 441.

Dennett, D. 1978a. "Why You Can't Make a Computer That Feels Pain." In D. Dennett, *Brainstorms*. Montgomery, Vt.: Bradford Books.

Dennett, D. 1978b. "Where Am I?" In D. Dennett, *Brainstorms*. Montgomery, Vt.: Bradford Books.

Dennett, D. 1978c. "Intentional Systems." In D. Dennett, *Brainstorms*. Montgomery, Vt.: Bradford Books.

Dennett, D. 1987. "True Believers." In D. Dennett, *The Intentional Stance*. Cambridge: MIT Press.

Dennett, D. 1988. "Quining Qualia." In *Consciousness and Contemporary Science*, edited by E. Bisiach and A. Marcel. Oxford: Oxford University Press.

Dennett, D. 1991a. "Real Patterns." *Journal of Philosophy* 88:27.

Dennett, D. 1991b. *Consciousness Explained*. Boston: Little, Brown and Co.

Descartes, R. 1985. *The Philosophical Writings of Descartes*, vols. 1 and 2, translated by J. Cottingham et al. Cambridge: Cambridge University Press.

Descartes, R. 1991. *The Philosophical Writings of Descartes*, vol. 3, translated by J. Cottingham et al. Cambridge: Cambridge University Press.

Diamond, J. 1991. *The Rise and Fall of the Third Chimpanzee*. London: Radius.

Dretske, F. 1986. "Misrepresentation." In *Belief*, edited by R. Bogdan. Oxford: Clarendon Press.

Dretske, F. 1988. *Explaining Behavior*. Cambridge: MIT Press.

Edelman. G. 1992. *Bright Air, Brilliant Fire: On the Matter of the Mind*. London: Penguin.

Evans, G. 1982. *The Varieties of Reference*. Oxford: Oxford University Press.

Flanagan, O. 1992. *Consciousness Reconsidered*. Cambridge: MIT Press.

Fodor, J. 1981. *Representations*. Brighton: Harvester.

Fodor, J. 1990. *A Theory of Content and Other Essays*. Cambridge: MIT Press.

Fodor, J. 1992. "The Big Idea." *Times Literary Supplement*, July 3, p. 5.

Fodor, J. 1994. *The Elm and the Expert*. Cambridge: MIT Press.

Foster, J. 1981. *The Case for Idealism*. London: Routledge and Kegan Paul.

Frege, G. 1967. "The Thought: A Logical Inquiry." In *Philosophical Logic*, edited by P. F. Strawson. Oxford: Oxford University Press.

Gleitman, H. 1986. *Psychology*, 2nd edition. New York: W. W. Norton.

Gosling, J. 1969. *Pleasure and Desire*. Oxford: Oxford University Press.

Gould, S. J. 1983. "Nonmoral Nature." In S. J. Gould, *Hen's Teeth and Horse's Toes*. London: Penguin.

Greenberg, M. Forthcoming. "Thoughts without Masters."

Gregory, R. 1987. *The Oxford Companion to the Mind*. Oxford: Oxford University Press.

Hacker, P. M. S. 1972. *Insight and Illusion: Witgenstein on Philosophy and the Metaphysics of Experience*. Oxford: Clarendon Press.

Hall, R. 1967. "Monism." In *The Encyclopaedia of Philosophy*. edited by Paul Edwards. New York: Collier Macmillan.

Heil, J. 1992. *The Nature of True Minds*. Cambridge: Cambridge University Press.

Hornsby, J. 1980. *Actions*. London: Routledge and Kegan Paul.

Hornsby, J. 1986. "Physicalist Thinking and Conceptions of Behaviour." In *Subject, Thought, and Context*, edited by P. Pettit and J. McDowell. Oxford: Clarendon Press.

Hume, D. 1947. *Dialogues Concerning Natural Religion*, edited by N. Kemp Smith. Edinburgh: Nelson.

Hume, D. 1975. *Enquiries Concerning Human Understanding*, edited by L. A. Selby-Bigge. Oxford: Oxford University Press.

Hume, D. 1978. *A Treatise of Human Nature*, edited by L. A. Selby-Bigge and P. H. Nidditch. Oxford: Oxford University Press.

Humphrey, N. 1983. *Consciousness Regained*. Oxford: Oxford University Press.

Jackendoff, R. 1987. *Consciousness and the Computational Mind*. Cambridge: MIT Press.

Jackson, F. 1982. "Epiphenomenal Qualia." *Philosophical Quarterly* 32:127.

Jackson, F. 1993. "Block's Challenge." In *Ontology, Causality, and Mind: Essays in Honour of D. M. Armstrong*, edited by John Bacon, Keith Campbell, and Lloyd Reinhardt. Cambridge: Cambridge University Press.

James, W. 1912. "Does Consciousness Exist?" In W. James, *Essays in Radical Empiricism*. London: Longmans, Green and Co.

James, W. 1950. *The Principles of Psychology*, 2 vols. New York: Dover.

Kant, I. 1933. *Critique of Pure Reason*. London: Macmillan.

Kim, J. 1982. "Psychophysical Supervenience." *Philosophical Studies* 41:51.

Kim, J. 1984. "Concepts of Supervenience." *Philosophy and Phenomenological Research* 45:157.

Lashley, K. 1956. "Cerebral Organization and Behavior." In *The Brain and Human Behavior*, edited by H. Solomon, S. Cobb, and W. Penfield. Baltimore: Williams and Wilkins.

Leiber, J. 1991. *An Invitation to Cognitive Science*. Oxford: Blackwell.

Lewis, David. 1983. "Mad Pain and Martian Pain." In D. Lewis, *Philosophical Papers*, vol. 1. Oxford: Oxford University Press.

Libet, B. 1985. "Unconscious Cerebral Initiative and the Role of Conscious Will in Voluntary Action." *Behavioral and Brain Sciences* 8:529.

Libet, B. 1987. "Are the Mental Experiences of Will and Self-control Significant for the Performance of a Voluntary Act?" *Behavioral and Brain Sciences* 10:783.

Libet, B. 1989. "The Timing of a Subjective Experience." *Behavioral and Brain Sciences* 12:183.

Locke, J. 1975. *An Essay Concerning Human Understanding*, edited by P. Nidditch. Oxford: Clarendon Press.

Lockwood, M. 1989. *Mind, Brain, and the Quantum*. Oxford: Blackwell.

Lockwood, M. 1993. "The Grain Problem." In *Objections to Physicalism*, edited by H. Robinson. Oxford: Oxford University Press.

Martin, C. B. 1987. "Proto-language." *Australasian Journal of Philosophy* 65:277.

Martin, C. B. 1994. "Dispositions and Conditionals." *Philosophical Quarterly* 44:1.

Maxwell, J. C. 1877. "The Kinetic Theory of Gases." *Nature* 16:245.

McDowell, J. 1980. "Meaning, Communication, and Knowledge." In *Philosophical Subjects*, edited by Z. van Straaten. Oxford: Clarendon Press.

McGinn C. 1982. *The Character of Mind*. Oxford: Oxford University Press.

McGinn, C. 1989a. *Mental Content*. Oxford: Blackwell.

McGinn, C. 1989b. "Can We Solve the Mind-Body Problem?" *Mind* 98:349.

McGinn, C. 1991. *The Problem of Consciousness*. Oxford: Blackwell.

Millikan, R. 1984. *Language, Thought, and Other Biological Categories*. Cambridge: MIT Press.

Millikan, R. 1993. *White Queen Psychology and Other Essays for Alice*. Cambridge: MIT Press.

Milne, A. A. 1928. *The House at Pooh Corner*. London: Methuen.

Murdoch, I. 1970. *The Sovereignty of Good*. London: Routledge and Kegan Paul.

Murdoch, I. 1992. *Metaphysics as a Guide to Morals*. London: Chatto and Windus.

Nagel, T. 1979. "What Is It Like to Be a Bat?" In T. Nagel, *Mortal Questions*. Cambridge: Cambridge University Press.

Nagel, T. 1986. *The View from Nowhere*. New York: Oxford University Press.

Nelkin, N. 1993. "The Connection between Intentionality and Consciousness." In *Consciousness*, edited by M. Davies and G. Humphreys. Oxford: Blackwell.

Papineau, D. 1987. *Reality and Representation*. Oxford: Blackwell.

Parfit, D., 1984. *Reasons and Persons*. Oxford: Clarendon Press.

Pattison, M. 1988. *Memoirs of an Oxford Don*. London: Cassell.

Peacocke, C. 1992. *A Study of Concepts*. Cambridge: MIT Press.

Pears D. 1988. *The False Prison*, vol. 2. Oxford: Oxford University Press.

Peirce, C. S. 1935. *Collected Papers*, vol. 6, edited by C. Hartshorne and P. Weiss. Cambridge: Harvard University Press.

Pettit, P., 1993. "A definition of physicalism." *Analysis* 53, no. 4: 213.

Pettit, P., and McDowell, J. 1986. "Introduction." In *Subject, Thought, and Context*, edited by P. Pettit and J. McDowell. Oxford: Clarendon Press.

Putnam, H. 1975. "The Meaning of 'meaning'." In H. Putnam, *Mind, Language, and Reality*. Cambridge: Cambridge University Press.

Putnam, H. 1981. *Reason, Truth, and History*. Cambridge: Cambridge University Press.

Putnam, H. 1992. *Renewing Philosophy*. Cambridge: Harvard University Press.

Quine, W. V. 1961. "Two Dogmas of Empiricism." In W. V. Quine, *From a Logical Point of View*. New York: Harper and Row.

Quine, W. V. 1990. *Pursuit of Truth*. Cambridge: Harvard University Press.

Raine, C. 1979. *A Martian Sends a Postcard Home*. Oxford: Oxford University Press.

Ramsey, F. P. 1990. *Philosophical Papers*. Cambridge: Cambridge University Press.

Rey, G. 1993. "Sensational Sentences." In *Consciousness*, edited by M. Davies and G. Humphreys. Oxford: Blackwell.

Rimbaud, A. 1972. *Œuvres complètes*. Paris: Gallimard.

Rorty, R. 1979. *Philosophy and the Mirror of Nature*. Princeton: Princeton University Press.

Rosenthal, D. 1991. "The Independence of Consciousness and Sensory Quality." In *Consciousness*, edited by E. Villanueva. Atascadero, Calif.: Ridgeview.

Russell, B. 1921. *The Analysis of Mind*. London: Allen and Unwin.

Russell, B. 1945. *A History of Western Philosophy*. New York: Simon and Schuster.

Ryle, G. 1949. *The Concept of Mind*. New York: Barnes and Noble.

Schiffer, S. 1987. *Remnants of Meaning*. Cambridge: MIT Press.

Schopenhauer, A. 1969. *The World as Will and Representation*, 2 vols., translated by E. J. F. Payne. New York: Dover.

Searle, J. 1983. *Intentionality*. Cambridge: Cambridge University Press.

Searle, J. 1991. "The Background of Intentionality and Action." In *John Searle and His Critics*, edited by E. Lepore and R. van Gulick. Oxford: Blackwell.

Searle, J. 1992. *The Rediscovery of the Mind*. Cambridge: MIT Press.

Sellars, W. 1965. "The Identity Approach to the Mind-Body Problem." *Review of Metaphysics* 18:430.

Sherrington, C. 1906. *The Integrative Action of the Nervous System*. New York: Scribner.

Shoemaker, S. 1975. "Functionalism and Qualia." *Synthese* 27:291.

Shoemaker, S. 1984. "The Inverted Spectrum." In S. Shoemaker, *Identity, Cause, and Mind.* Cambridge: Cambridge University Press.

Shoemaker, S. 1986. "Introspection and the Self." In *Studies in the Philosophy of Mind*, Midwest Studies in Philosophy, no. 10.

Stich, S. 1983. *From Folk Psychology to Cognitive Science: The Case against Belief.* Cambridge: MIT Press.

Strawson, G. 1981. "Language without Communication Intentions." Unpublished.

Strawson, G. 1989a. "Red and 'Red'." *Synthese* 78, no. 2: 193.

Strawson, G. 1989b. *The Secret Connexion.* Oxford: Clarendon Press.

Strawson, G. 1992. "The Self as Software." *Times Literary Supplement*, August 21, p. 5.

Strawson, P. F. 1985. *Skepticism and Naturalism.* New York: Columbia University Press.

Stroud, B. 1991. "The Background of Thought." In *John Searle and His Critics*, edited by E. Lepore and R. van Gulick. Oxford: Blackwell.

Watson, G., 1982. "Free Agency." In *Free Will*, edited by G. Watson. Oxford: Oxford University Press.

Weiskrantz, L. 1986. *Blindsight: A Case Study and Implications.* Oxford: Clarendon Press.

Wittgenstein L. 1953. *Philosophical Investigations*, translated by G. E. M. Anscombe. Oxford: Blackwell.

Wittgenstein L. 1969. *The Blue and Brown Books.* Oxford: Blackwell.

Wittgenstein L. 1980. *Culture and Value*, translated by Peter Winch. Oxford: Blackwell.

Index

This index does not cite every occurrence of every listed term or topic. Page numbers in italic type indicate the place where a term is introduced, defined, or redefined.